Records Management: Making the Transition from Paper to Electronic

David O. Stephens, CRM

ARMA *INTERNATIONAL®*

ARMA International
Overland Park, Kansas

Editorial Consultant: Mary L. Ginn, Ph.D.
Composition: Rebecca Gray Design
Cover Art: Brett Dietrich

ARMA International
11880 College Blvd., Suite 450
Overland Park, KS 66210
+1 913.341.3808

ISBN-13: 978-1-931786-29-4
ISBN-10: 1-931786-29-1

Contents

Preface   xi
Acknowledgments   xvii

Chapter 1 Introduction: Status and Trends   1

Status of RIM   2
Status of Electronic RIM   3
Inadequate Management Recognition   4
Inadequate Funding   4
Positive Trends   5
Explosive Growth of Electronic Records   5
New Technologies   5
The Growing Role of Information in Organizational Success   6
Large Computer Companies Enter the RIM Business   7
New Regulatory Compliance Mandates   7
Managing Recorded Information: The New Challenges   7
Increasing Litigation Risks   7
RIM at the Desktop   8
RIM and E-mail   8
RIM Standards   8
Paper vs. Electronic Records: Contrasting Capabilities   9
A Professional Discipline in Transition   12
Desired State of RIM   12
International RIM   13

Chapter 2 Building Successful Programs   17

Sustained, Committed Executive Sponsorship   18
Strategic Plan for the Future   19
Commitment to Digital Recordkeeping   19
Governance Structure of Key Stakeholders   20

Optimal Organizational Placement   21

Requisite Funding and Staffing   23

    Define Investment Options   23

    Required Skill Sets   25

    Outsourcing Options   26

Strategic Partnership with IT   27

Development of Requisite Technology Solutions   28

Program Development in Compliance with ISO 15489   29

Proactive Agenda for RIM   30

Chapter 3 Records Retention: Managing the Information Life Cycle 33

The Purpose of Records Retention   33

    Status of Organizational Retention Programs   34

    Managing the Life Cycle of Information Assets   34

    Benefits of Records Retention   34

The Business Case for Records Retention   36

    ISO 15489 and Records Retention   37

    Common Mistakes in Records Retention   37

Retention and Schedule Development   38

    Responsibility for Schedule Development   38

    Database for Schedule Preparation   39

Content, Type, and Format of Retention Schedules   39

    Departmental Retention Schedules   40

    Functional Retention Schedules   41

    Records Series Descriptions   41

    Office of Record Designations   42

    Records Media Specified in Schedules   42

Legally Compliant Schedules   43

    Legal Retention Research Responsibility   43

    Relevant Citations for Retention Requirements   43

    Laws and Regulations Cited in Schedules   44

Legally Valid Retention Periods   48

    Average Distribution of Retention Periods   49

    Expression and Justification of Retention Periods   50

Management Approval of Retention Schedules   50

Chapter 4 Electronic Records Retention: Managing the Data Life Cycle 53

Current Status of Electronic Records Retention   54

Key Trends in Data Storage   55

    Explosive Growth of Electronic Records   55

    Data Storage <u>Mis</u>management   56

Cost-Benefit Considerations   57
Information Life Cycle Management   58
The Desktop and Records Retention   62
   Principles for Desktop Retention   63
   IT-Managed System Applications   64
Sample Policy: Desktop Records Retention   66
Sample Policy: Records Retention Requirements for IT-Managed Applications   67

Chapter 5   Retention Implementation, Auditing, and Compliance   71

Reasonable Retention Goals   71
Retention Training   72
Keys to Success   72
   An Effective Governance Structure   73
   Intranet-Based Schedules, Policies, and Guidelines   74
   Individual Responsibilities for Retention Implementation   74
   Records Purge Days   74
   Compliance Documentation   78
   Penalties for Noncompliance   79
   Retention Audits   79
Retention Implementation in Five Recordkeeping Environments   80
Sample Policy: Corporate Records Retention   75

Chapter 6   Business Recordkeeping and the Law   83

RIM—Legally Discretionary   84
   New Recordkeeping Technologies   84
   Recordkeeping Media   85
   Admissibility into Evidence   86
   Electronic Commerce and Digital Signatures   86
      UN Model Law on Electronic Commerce   87
      UN Model Law on Electronic Signatures   90
      U.S. E-Sign Law   91
      Uniform Electronic Transactions Act   92
New Regulatory Initiatives   92
   Sarbanes-Oxley Act   95
      New Mandate for Internal Control   96
      Sarbanes-Oxley and IT Issues   98
   HIPAA   98
   Gramm-Leach-Bliley   99
   Basel II   99
Authenticity of Records   99
Reliability, Integrity, and Usability   100

Chapter 7   Records Retention and the Law   103

The Government's Role in Records Retention   103
    Compliance with Retention Laws and Regulations   104
    Regulatory Requirements Pertaining to Electronic Records   105
    The Seven-Year Myth   105
Statutes of Limitation   106
Sarbanes-Oxley Act   107
    Retention of Audit Records   107
    Records Retention and Litigation   108
Judicially Imposed Sanctions   110
Litigation and Records   111
    Retention Periods Where Litigation is Likely   111
        Stevenson vs. Union Pacific   112
        Lewy vs. Remington Arms   112
        Rambus vs. Infineon Technologies   113
        U.S. vs. Taber   113
    Retention Obligations in Discovery   113
        Carlucci vs. Piper Aircraft   113
        Prudential Insurance Co. of America   114
        Zubulake vs. UBS Warburg   114
    Retention Obligations Prior to Discovery   115
        U.S. vs. Author Andersen, LLP   115
        Sarbanes-Oxley Removes Ambiguities in the Law   117
Litigation Holds   118
The Andersen Case: The Last Word   119
Summary of Key Legal Principles   119
Sample Policy for All Employees   121
Sample Policy: Legal Hold on Records Destruction   121

Chapter 8   Managing the Message   125

Management Challenges   126
    Legal Issues   127
    E-mail Usage Patterns   128
    IT Issues   129
    Spam   130
    Managing Records as Records   131
E-mail Retention   131
    E-mail Retention Policy   132
    Instant Messaging   133
Voice Messaging   135
Messaging Technology Solutions   136
Sample Policy: E-mail Retention   137

Chapter 9 Improving Recordkeeping System Performance   141

Poor Accessibility: Causes and Consequences   141
Search Queries   143
System Performance Evaluation   145
   Precise Retrieval   146
   Levels of System Performance   146
   Timely Retrieval   147
   Other Measures of System Performance   148
   Qualitative Analysis of System Performance   148
Enterprise Classification and Taxonomy   149
   Systems with No Taxonomy   150
   Unstructured Content   151
   The Enterprise Taxonomy   152
      Standard Categories   153
      Category Selection   153
   Software Solutions for Automatic Categorization   157

Chapter 10 Protecting Information from Disaster   161

Status of Information Protection   162
   Routine Data Losses   163
   RIM's Role   164
   Traditional Data Protection Methodologies   164
   Twelve-Tape Backup Methodology   166
   Data Recovery Speed   167
E-vaulting and Online Backup   167
   Open-File Backup   168
   Storage Area Networks   169
Protection Priorities   169
Application Analysis   170
Degree-of-Criticality Assessments   171
Desktop Records Protection   171
   User Requirements for Desktop Backup   172
   Recovery of Magnetic Media   173
   Retention of Backup Data   174
Lessons of September 11, 2001   174
   Vital Paper Records Protection   175

Chapter 11 Information Access, Privacy, and Security   179

Privacy   179
   Privacy and the Internet   180

International Aspects of Privacy 181
    EU's Data Protection Directive 182
    Privacy in the United States 182
    U.S. Safe Harbor Agreement 183
    Compliance with EU's Privacy Rules 183
    Privacy Laws in California 184
    Canada's New Privacy Law 184
RIM Implications 185
Security 185
    Legal Aspects of Information Security 188
    Uniform Trade Secrets Act 189
ISO Global Information Security Standard 189
Key RIM Actions 190
Sample Policy: Records Access 191

Chapter 12 Software Solutions for Electronic RIM   195

Electronic RIM Issues 196
Categories of Electronic RIM Solutions 197
    RIM Software 198
    Retention Functionality in RIM Software 199
    EDMS Solutions 199
    Retention Functionality in EDMS Solutions 201
    Effecting Destruction Under Retention Rules 202
    Solution Convergence 202
The TR48 Integration Model 203
    Options for Solution Integration 204
    Common Metadata for Solution Integration 205
    Declared Records and ERMS Management 206
    Sample Solutions 206
The DoD 5015.2 Standard 207
    The Standard's Applicability 208
    Compliance Testing 209
    The Standard's Content 209
Europe's MoReq Specification 210
Implementation Issues 211

Chapter 13 Managing Information Content   215

ECM and RIM 216
    ECM—Fad or Long-Term Solution? 217

Knowledge Management	217
KM's Detractors	219
KM and RIM	219
ECM Technology Components	220
Document Imaging / Digitization	220
Imaging Benefits	220
Imaging Media and Applications	221
Assimilating Imaging: Strategic Recommendations	223
Text Retrieval / Content Search	223
Workflow Automation Tools	225
Data Warehousing and Data Mining	226
Enterprise Information Portals	227
EIP Features	228
Building an EIP	229

Chapter 14 Digital Records Preservation   **233**

Archival Data Storage Requirements	235
ISO 15489 and Digital Preservation	236
Media Stability and Technology Obsolescence	236
Digital vs. Paper Preservation	237
Data Preservation Practices	238
Storage Media	238
Data Migration	238
Data Migration Plan	240
Alternatives to Data Migration	240
File Formats	241
Media Recopying	242
Metadata Requirements	243
Systems Documentation	244
Media Storage and Maintenance	245
ANSI Standard for Media Storage	245
Media Inspection	246
Media Refreshing / Rewinding	246
Future Preservation Solutions	247

Glossary	251
Bibliography	265
Index	285
About the Author	291
About the Association	292

Preface

Records and information management (RIM) is a professional field in transition. This book is based on a single key premise: Organizations everywhere are in the midst of a long transition from paper-based to digital recordkeeping. This transition began during the 1960s and '70s, when computer technology was first used for organizational recordkeeping, through the remainder of the twentieth century, when new innovations made possible, for the first time in history, replacement if not complete elimination of paper records from business offices. However, because the process of assimilating new technology solutions for recordkeeping is a relatively slow and lengthy one, the transition to all-digital recordkeeping will not be complete for another few decades at least.

Regardless, the reality is that organizational recordkeeping is not going to be paper-based fifty or even twenty years from now. Thus, the supreme challenge facing records managers everywhere is how to manage this transition from paper to digital recordkeeping effectively and in the best interest of their organizations. The main purpose of *Records Management: Making the Transition from Paper to Electronic* is to give readers the concepts they need in order to make this transition and manage organizational records and information as a professional practice.

Many RIM programs continue to operate under a conceptual definition and set of assumptions that are several decades old: A record is recorded information created or received in the course of an organization's business.[1] That definition is rooted in the notion of records as tangible entities. This definition is inadequate in a world dominated by digital recordkeeping. With the greatest transformation in RIM since the origin of the profession now taking place, the nature and use of both information and records are changing. RIM in the future is likely to bear only a passing resemblance to its past. RIM practitioners need fresh, new insights into the nature of organizational recordkeeping, how they affect RIM programs, and how their professional practices need to change in order to stay responsive and successful.

---

1   Bruce Dearstyne, "Records Management of the Future: Anticipate, Adapt, and Succeed," *The Information Management Journal* 33, no. 4 (October 1999): 4.

The concepts and principles presented in *Records Management: Making the Transition from Paper to Electronic* should enable records managers to evaluate the status and quality of their programs, develop a proactive agenda for the future of RIM within their organizations, and implement that agenda effectively over a period of years. To this end, this book is organized into fourteen chapters, each reflecting a key issue or component of organizational recordkeeping or RIM practice.

Chapter 1 – Introduction: Status and Trends – This chapter addresses the current status of the RIM profession and the major trends that are redefining, even revolutionizing it, in this era in which the methodology for keeping business records has shifted from paper to electronic. The chapter concludes with a discussion of the desired state of RIM and a brief review of some key developments in the international community.

Chapter 2 – Building Successful Programs – This chapter addresses how to incorporate RIM into organizations in a manner that has the best chance of success. This chapter reviews ten key ingredients of success in RIM, which should be regarded as required prerequisites for achieving a high level of professional practice.

Chapter 3 – Records Retention: Managing the Information Life Cycle – Wherever it is practiced, records retention is the cornerstone of RIM, and it continues to dominate professional RIM practice in the U.S., just as it has for decades. Therefore, three chapters are devoted to this key area. This chapter introduces records retention and describes recommended practices for developing retention schedules.

Chapter 4 – Electronic Records Retention: Managing the Data Life Cycle – What happens to computer data as it ages? Does the value of data increase or decrease as time passes? Why are most organizations keeping more data, and keeping it longer, than ever before? What conditions indicate when data should be retired or discarded? Do storage management requirements change as data ages through its life cycle? These fundamental questions form the basis of electronic records retention, sometimes also referred to as information life cycle management. In the world of paper records, these questions are ones that records managers have addressed for decades. However, they are seldom addressed, at least comprehensively for all computer applications, by IT departments. The central thesis of this chapter is that records managers must work cooperatively with IT to apply the principles of records retention to manage the life cycle of computer-based records.

Chapter 5 – Retention Implementation, Auditing, and Compliance – Retention schedules, and the written policies and procedures that accompany them, are nothing more than words on paper. They will not implement themselves. Unless every employee who has custody over records material is required by *mandate* to comply with these requirements, success in retention is likely to remain elusive. This lack of mandate is the single biggest reason that records retention programs fail to achieve their objectives. This matter is not merely of casual importance. In fact, from a legal perspective, to have a retention policy and fail to implement it consistently can be worse than not having one at all. If senior executives have decided that the organization is going to have a records retention program, they should be prepared to demonstrate that the program is being executed systematically and in good faith. This chapter presents recommended practices for implementing an organization-wide RIM retention program.

Chapter 6 – Business Recordkeeping and the Law – Throughout history, business recordkeeping has been a subject of high interest to the legal community. For centuries, governments, or their legislative assemblies, courts, regulatory commissions, and archival agencies, have enacted laws, promulgated regulations, and handed down judicial decisions concerning the manner of recordkeeping in business and government organizations. This chapter discusses these matters in the context of RIM to acquaint records managers with what they need to know to develop and implement RIM programs that can meet the test of legal sufficiency. Although records managers should, indeed must, defer to their organization's attorneys concerning many aspects of the law as it affects recordkeeping, they need to be able to discuss these matters intelligently whenever they work with these lawyers. This chapter is designed to prepare records managers for such conversations.

Chapter 7 – Records Retention and the Law – This chapter addresses some of the most crucial issues facing RIM programs in the context of their role of reducing the organization's exposure to risks posed by lawsuits: How should retention periods be devised for records that have a good probability of being used in litigation? For plaintiffs doing business in litigation-intensive environments, are records favorable or unfavorable in defending liability lawsuits? Under what circumstances do records and information disposal actions become criminal conduct? What are the duties and obligations of organizations and their employees to preserve records and information during the discovery phase of legal proceedings? What are the risks of records and information disposal actions during the prediscovery phase, when proceedings are possible or even probable but have not yet commenced? What are the penalties for unlawful conduct involving records and information preservation and disposal? Finally, how has the law recently been refined in order to eliminate ambiguities concerning the duty to preserve records when litigation is threatened? These key issues are discussed in this chapter, and wherever RIM is practiced, its practitioners must be thoroughly conversant with them.

Chapter 8 – Managing the Message – In this chapter, attention is focused on RIM issues associated with what the American Management Association calls the number one office task: e-mail (and other forms of messaging). During the past ten years, e-mail has become the predominant medium for business communications. Together with other electronic records created at the desktop level, the management of e-mail is one of the biggest RIM challenges today. E-mail is truly a transforming technology; it has revolutionized the way business is conducted, as well as the way in which business records are created, transmitted, stored, and maintained. Thus, the management of the message is, appropriately, at the top of the RIM agenda nearly everywhere. This chapter presents recommended practices for managing the message in accordance with RIM principles.

Chapter 9 – Improving Recordkeeping System Performance – When organizational recordkeeping systems underperform in their role of delivering requested information to their users, records managers are responsible for determining the cause(s) and then prescribing a solution(s) to fix the problem. The goal is to optimize the value of information content throughout the enterprise in order to facilitate the achievement of larger business objectives. Three key issues are addressed in this chapter: An introduction to enterprise accessibility of records and information, methods of evaluating system performance, and applying the principles of classification and taxonomy to enhance enterprise accessibility of information content, particularly unstructured content.

Chapter 10 – Protecting Information from Disaster – Some records managers have put forth a persuasive, even compelling, argument that protecting organizational information from loss due to disaster, whether due to natural, technical, or human causes, is the most important aspect of RIM. The reason is not hard to discern. For most organizations today, their dependence on computer systems is so great that the protection of digital records and information is, literally, a matter of survival. An organization may very well survive the loss of most or even all its paper records, but loss of all electronic records would be truly cataclysmic and perhaps irrecoverable. This chapter provides recommended practices for reducing these risks.

Chapter 11 – Information Access, Privacy, and Security – In managing organizational records, records managers are often involved in questions concerning access and disclosure of records and information. This chapter addresses two key issues concerning this matter: (1) issues related to privacy—the collection, use, and disclosure of information about individuals, and (2) protection of information from unauthorized access, including the theft or misappropriation of proprietary or confidential information. The chapter provides the concepts records managers need to work in conjunction with corporate security and privacy officers to ensure that the organization's confidential or sensitive information, about its trade secrets as well as personal information about its employees and customers, is properly protected from improper use or disclosure.

Chapter 12 – Software Solutions for Electronic RIM – One of the most important occurrences to affect organizational recordkeeping and RIM during the past twenty years has been the introduction of various technology solutions designed to enhance the management of records in both physical and electronic formats. This chapter addresses this key development. The importance of these solutions to RIM can be simply stated: For the first time ever, the goal of enterprise electronic RIM is now within reach for organizations. Records managers must work in close cooperation with IT departments to deploy various types of successful document technology solutions. The major solutions are discussed in this chapter: RIM software, electronic document management software (EDMS), and electronic records management software (ERMS).

Chapter 13 – Managing Information Content – This chapter addresses enterprise accessibility of information. The most important methodologies and technologies of the past five to ten years to help organizations realize the goal of total accessibility of their information content across the enterprise are reviewed, including enterprise content management and its forerunner, knowledge management. Finally, the several technology solutions that organizations are deploying to make enterprise content management a reality are also discussed.

Chapter 14 – Digital Records Preservation – The long-term or permanent preservation of digital data entails challenges unlike any that have ever been encountered in the worlds of RIM and business computing. The only way extended-term data retention requirements can be satisfied is by a series of carefully planned preservation practices that must be implemented by IT departments. The premise of this chapter is that most organizations are now in the embryonic stage of putting into place all that is needed to provide for the long-term retention of the data in applications that require it. Therefore, within the next five years or so, organizations having significant, even modest, requirements to retain computer data for extended periods of time will have to institute more comprehensive and formal data preservation practices. This chapter provides records managers with what they need to know in order to work with IT specialists to preserve electronic data.

Legislation discussed throughout *Records Management: Making the Transition from Paper to Electronic* is current at the time of this writing. However, some laws and regulations may have been updated. Readers are encouraged to keep current with laws and regulations that affect RIM by regularly checking various government web sites.

David O. Stephens, CRM, FAI, CMC
Smithfield, North Carolina

Acknowledgments

My sincere appreciation goes to Kevin Zasio, President of Zasio Enterprises, Inc., for giving me the time and flexibility in my job to enable me to write this book. Bill Saffady, who has been and remains my hero in records and information management, as well as a treasured colleague and friend, also receives my deepest gratitude. Throughout this book, readers will observe his many contributions, which are gratefully acknowledged in the notes. Next, a word of thanks is due to all my consulting clients, too numerous to name here, for providing me the opportunity to apply theory to practice and see what works and what doesn't in "real life" organizational settings where the management of records is concerned. Last, but never least, to Mary, my wife of 31 years, I extend my heartfelt thanks for listening to all my long-winded discussions about the joys and sorrows, the rewards and tribulations, of a career in records and information management.

David O. Stephens, CRM, FAI
Smithfield, North Carolina USA

Chapter 1

Introduction: Status and Trends

Records and information management (RIM) is a professional discipline whose main purpose is to provide better management of organizational records systems and the *information* they contain. As a management discipline, the need for RIM is driven primarily by the volume and complexity of recorded information in organizations, particularly the larger ones, that has risen dramatically in recent decades. This greater complexity is attributable to two primary factors: new technology and increasing regulatory / litigation imperatives. Regardless, organizations everywhere experience persistent problems with their records and information, and they need to address those challenges in a professional way. RIM initiatives are intended to meet this need.

As a specialized business discipline, RIM is primarily concerned with the systematic analysis and control of recorded information, which includes any and all information created, received, maintained, or used by an organization in accordance with its mission, operations, and activities. RIM provides systematic control over all records from the time of their creation or receipt, through their processing, distribution, organization, storage, and *retrieval* to their ultimate disposition.[1]

RIM consists of the leadership, administration, coordination, and other work required to ensure:

- that adequate records are created to document business functions and meet administrative, legal, and other operational needs;
- that *recordkeeping* requirements are analyzed and included when information systems are first developed;
- that professionally sanctioned techniques are applied throughout the records life cycle;
- that records are retained and disposed of based on analysis of their functions and value; and
- that records of continuing value are preserved and accessible.[2]

The central business objective of RIM can be expressed succinctly as follows: to get the right information to the right people where and when they need it and at the lowest possible cost. RIM also endeavors to optimize the value of business information by managing it so that it is timely and accessible, complete, true and accurate, cost-effective, and fully usable for any and all legal and business purposes.

Records Management: Making the Transition from Paper to Electronic is about how to achieve these key objectives for managing **recorded information.** Throughout recorded history, organizations everywhere have created and kept records. Records, for many years, have been created and maintained in physical format; that is, they resided on visible media. They could be seen and touched; their content could be read and comprehended by sight, without the aid of machines. However, with the introduction of computers, organizational records began to be created in nonvisible formats, which have changed RIM.

Today, RIM is a multifaceted field with tens of thousands of practitioners. It incorporates concepts and practices in such related fields as computing and **information technology (IT)**, industrial engineering, **knowledge management (KM)**, library science, and archival administration.[3]

Status of RIM

For many years, one of the RIM profession's greatest unmet needs was the fact that no professional-quality studies had been conducted to determine the current status, the strengths and limitations, and the prevailing practices of the discipline. With the publication of four studies, this situation has been rectified. The results, however, were less than gratifying, as indicated below.

1. **Forrester report** – A survey on the role of **electronic records management** in North American organizations, conducted by Forrester Consulting. The survey was conducted via telephone interviews and online surveys with three groups: **records managers**, IT managers, and general business managers. The sample size was 150 business and IT respondents and 75 records manager respondents.[4]

2. **Cohasset electronic records management study** – This study was cosponsored by AIIM and ARMA International and conducted by Cohasset Associates, a records management consulting firm. Of the four studies, this one had the largest sample size; data was gathered from more than 2,200 respondents, primarily professional specialists in RIM in both the private and public sectors.[5]

3. **Penn, Shoen & Berland study** – A study commissioned by Iron Mountain, currently the largest RIM company in the United States. The study surveyed the RIM practices of 100 U.S.-based Fortune 1000 companies.[6]

4. **Saffady benchmarking study** – Commissioned by ARMA International and conducted by Dr. William Saffady, the study described RIM practices in forty-two large, U.S.-based industrial companies. The sample size, while small, is

nevertheless considered to be authoritative and a valid indication of the current status of RIM practices among large U.S. companies.[7]

The overall findings of these studies are summarized below. Other findings are reported throughout this book.

- **Prevalence of RIM** – A significant number of large organizations do not have a formal RIM program. The Saffady study found that 34 percent of the top 100 U.S. industrial companies have no formal, identifiable RIM program. The Forrester and Cohasset studies reported somewhat smaller, but still significant, figures. However, as RIM is not mandated by statute for most private-sector firms, many have not put a program into place, thereby exposing themselves to significant legal and other business risks, as detailed throughout this book.

- **Quality of RIM programs** – Where formal RIM programs exist, they are often characterized as being of substandard quality with respect to their ability to accomplish their objectives. Both the Forrester and Cohasset studies reported identical results: 41 percent of the responding organizations characterized their program as being of fair or marginal quality. The Cohasset study reported that, for an alarming number of organizations, the job of RIM is simply not getting done. The Penn, Schoen & Berland study reported that, while solid progress is being made, 87 percent of the respondents indicated that they have not implemented the tools needed to ensure efficient and automated RIM; 56 percent fail to regularly evaluate and improve their programs; and 44 percent do not test their programs on a regular basis.

Status of Electronic RIM

All studies were unanimous in finding that the RIM profession has a long way to go before its practitioners can justifiably claim that computer-based records are being managed at a high level of professional practice. The Cohasset study (as well as two prior studies conducted by the firm) concluded that essentially no improvement was made in mitigating, much less meaningfully addressing, the unique demands of electronic RIM during the period 1999–2003. The most recent Cohasset survey found that 41 percent of the respondents indicated that electronic records are not included in their organization's current RIM program. The Forrester study concluded that electronic records are not being managed with the same level of success as records and information stored on paper and microfilm. The Saffady study also found less progress with electronic records than with physical ones, in *records retention* as well as other management initiatives. This study concluded that, despite all the attention given to electronic records in the published literature and at professional meetings and seminars, most records managers are more likely to spend most of their time on some aspect of managing paper records.

RIM practitioners must understand why greater progress has not been made in managing organizational records in a manner closer to top professional quality. Some answers can be seen in the major challenges facing the profession that are discussed in this chapter.

Inadequate Management Recognition

How do senior executives see RIM with respect to its potential to contribute to the overall success of the organization? First, except in rare cases, RIM initiatives do not directly generate revenue. Although these initiatives can and do generate substantial business benefits, they are of the "soft dollar" variety. RIM has often been regarded as a valuable but not essential administrative support function. RIM requires time and effort to do correctly. Moreover, it requires sustained commitment over time; it is not something that can be introduced with fanfare and then forgotten about. Many organizations avoid RIM or relegate it to low priority status because they think it will cost a lot of money, and they do not see its ultimate value.[8] In fact, the Cohasset study characterized the level of management recognition accorded RIM as "benign neglect," something senior executives do not really want to do; they would rather spend their time and money on other priorities.

On the other hand, a number of key trends are now occurring that, taken together, make RIM more imperative than ever. According to Mark Gilbert, the lead analyst for electronic RIM with Gartner Inc., "This is the first time I've seen it [records management] receive this much attention. With the CEO aware of the risks, records management efforts are getting funding. We believe this market will double from close to $100 million today to $200 million in 2007."[9] The effective implementation of RIM is not a simple process. It demands significant business process change and reengineering; it requires a thorough analysis of the way a company does business; and it requires recognition at the most senior level that RIM is pivotal to an organization's entire information management structure.[10] Although RIM programs do not directly contribute positively to the corporate balance sheet, poor recordkeeping and lack of RIM can have significant detrimental effects.

Inadequate Funding

As a corollary to the level of executive recognition accorded RIM, the discipline is frequently underfunded and lacks resources in the context of its mandate. Staffing levels and budgets are inadequate in most organizations. The Saffady benchmarking study reported annual budgets for RIM programs ranging from $147,000 to $2.75 million— a fraction of the estimates required to accomplish mandated missions in an effective manner. If these figures seem sizable, remember that the forty-two companies participating in the study were among the largest in the United States. The study concluded that constrained budgets and staffing levels have forced most RIM programs to adopt a working scope of tasks that can be considered a subset of their overall authority and responsibility.

The situation seems to be improving. In the Penn, Shoen & Berland study, nearly half the companies reported that they planned to spend more on RIM in the next year than they did in the previous year; 21 percent indicated they would spend *substantially* more. The study concluded that new legislation and regulations, as well as the financial burden of litigation-discovery, are the major incentives for companies to increase their investments in improved RIM.

Positive Trends

Despite the significant challenges confronting the discipline, the time for RIM has never been better than it is today. The reason is that business recordkeeping is now in the largest revolution ever, and RIM is in the eye of the storm. The key trends currently driving RIM are reviewed next.

Explosive Growth of Electronic Records

During the last thirty years, paper records have gradually declined in importance, while *electronic records (e-records)* have skyrocketed in importance and growth. In fact, the growth of e-records can only be characterized as explosive. Particularly among larger enterprises, the fundamental problem is that the ability to manage *data* is not keeping up with the growth of data. Perhaps the most substantive analysis of this matter is the "How Much Information" study (see Figure 1.1) conducted by the University of California, Berkeley. The study found that hard drive capacity and server capacity are doubling each year, while PC disk drives are also experiencing a 100 percent annual growth.[11] In short, electronic records are doubling in quantity every one to three years in most organizations.[12] However, the key point is that most organizations need, and do not now have, solutions to address the growth in the number of electronic records that must be stored.

New Technologies

Typically, when new information technologies are introduced, their RIM implications are usually poorly understood, which was the case when office copiers were introduced. The same situation is true for PCs, e-mail, *instant messaging*, and *Voice over Internet Protocol (VoIP)*—a new telecommunications technology that turns a telephone call into a cluster of data similar to data from an instant message or a digital image. When the contents of telephone calls become records, the RIM (and legal)

Electronic Records Growth

Figure 1.1

Worldwide production of original information, if stored digitally, in terabytes circa 2002. Upper estimates assume information is digitally scanned, lower estimates assume digital content has been compressed.

Storage Medium	2002 Terabytes Upper Estimate	2002 Terabytes Lower Estimate	1999-2000 Upper Estimate	1999-2000 Lower Estimate	% Change Upper Estimates
Paper	1,634	327	1,200	240	36%
Film	420,254	7,669	431,690	58,209	-3%
Magnetic	5,187,130	3,416,230	2,779,760	2,073,760	87%
Optical	103	51	81	29	28%
TOTAL	5,609,121	3,416,281	3,212,731	2,132,238	74.5%

SOURCE: Peter Lyman and Hal R. Varian, "How Much Information," 2003. Retrieved from http://www.sims.berkeley.edu/how-much-info-2003 on January 6, 2006.

implications of that change will be wide-ranging. The important point is that these new technologies create significant new opportunities for RIM. Because of new innovations, RIM is needed now more than ever, and it will continue to be needed in the future.

The Growing Role of Information in Organizational Success

In *Managing the Next Society*, Peter Drucker writes, "We are rebuilding organizations around information."[13] During the past half-century, RIM has evolved from a situation in which it played no perceived, significant role in the overall success of organizations, to the point where the management of information is now one of the defining factors in business success. Consider the following examples.

- **The Industrial Age: Information Management Not a Factor in Business Success** – Lee Iacocca, the retired auto executive, recently wrote that when he took a job at Ford Motor Company in 1946, the company's balance sheet was "still being kept on the back of an envelope, and the guys in purchasing had to weigh the invoices to count them." Such was the state of RIM at one of the world's greatest multinational corporations—a company that had invented assembly line mass production, the enabling technology of the Industrial Age, but apparently did not consider the management of business information to play any significant role in the overall success of the business.[14]

- **The Early Information Age: Information Management a Significant Factor in Business Success** – In 1966, when he was running twenty small retail discount stores, mostly in rural Arkansas, Wal-Mart founder Sam Walton attended an IBM school in upstate New York. Based on what he learned there, Walton saw, long before his contemporaries, the value of information for competitive advantage. He hired the best and brightest at IBM and persuaded them to go to Arkansas to computerize his business. Today, Wal-Mart's computer *database* is second only to the Pentagon's in capacity, and it is widely acknowledged that the company's prescient use of information technology has been a major factor in its overall business success. Walton understood that he was really in the information business as much as the retail business. Sam Walton may have been the first true information-age CEO, even though he is rarely remembered that way.[15]

- **Today: Information Management is *the* Crucial Factor in Business Success** – In 1995, a new company called Amazon.com was formed. It became the world's first online retail company, selling books and other products worldwide over the *Internet*. In this company, information technology does not merely support or facilitate the core business, it is the central organizing principle of the entire business. Moreover, this technology was deployed on a global scale from the moment of inception of the business, rather than evolving over time from domestic to international operations as had occurred at more traditional enterprises.

Since the days when Lee Iacocca was a young engineer at Ford, RIM has evolved from a situation in which recordkeeping had no perceived relationship to business success to the point where it is the major factor, at least in many situations. This evolvement underscores the importance of RIM as a key component of the larger information management capabilities of organizations everywhere.

Large Computer Companies Enter the RIM Business

The recent entry of large and influential computer companies into the RIM business with a range of technology solutions, many scaled for enterprise deployment, has raised awareness of the importance of managing electronic records. For example, as this book was going to press, IBM, still the world's largest computer company, announced its planned acquisition of FileNet Corporation, a leading provider of enterprise content management software. According to company announcements, FileNet technology is to be incorporated into IBM solutions for content management, content-centric business processes, and compliance.[16] This acquisition follows IBM's 2002 acquisition of privately held Tarian Software, which IBM said that it was buying so that it could integrate Tarian into its data management software and leverage its RIM capabilities across its entire software portfolio. Other large computer companies, principally in the enterprise content management space (see Chapter 13), have also begun to offer RIM capabilities in their product lines. This encouraging trend has the potential to elevate RIM to a new level of significance.

New Regulatory Compliance Mandates

During the past several years, a number of new regulatory initiatives have occurred in the U.S. that have had a significant impact on RIM. These initiatives have greatly increased the awareness of the need for and benefits of RIM on the part of organizations and their management. The Sarbanes-Oxley Act of 2002 has perhaps greater implications than any single piece of federal legislation in decades. In fact, this law introduced new, compelling reasons for CEOs to view RIM as an essential function, one they must implement and fund to the level of proven success. The main point is that RIM is not simply about the management of paper or other physical objects. It is about applying philosophies and business rules to the management of information as dictated by legislative, regulatory, and corporate requirements to maintain and preserve access to corporate information.[17]

Managing Recorded Information: The New Challenges

As indicated by the results of the studies mentioned previously, members of the RIM profession face serious challenges. These challenges include increasing litigation risks, desktop and e-mail RIM, new standards, and the role of information in organizational success.

Increasing Litigation Risks

In 2002, records managers, and the entire business community, witnessed something that had never happened before. Arthur Andersen, LLP, long one of the leading public accounting companies in the United States, was virtually destroyed by acts related directly to records destruction and retention. Although Andersen's conviction of obstruction of justice by reason of illegal records destruction was later overturned by the U.S. Supreme Court, the reversal in no way lessens the need to operate records retention programs that can withstand legal scrutiny. At the time of this writing, the former CEO of Andersen's client, Enron, has been found guilty of several counts of conspiracy and fraud. Other senior executives of large U.S. companies have faced similar criminal charges. Records have become pivotal in determining the destiny of organizations, as well as the fate of business and government leaders.[18] Concerns about litigation reinforce the perceived value of recorded information as a mission-critical resource rather than a nuisance to be discarded at the earliest opportunity. These concerns also promote the view of RIM as a strategic initiative rather than a prosaic, quasi-clerical administrative function.[19] In the minds of many senior executives, reducing the risks of records in litigation is the single most compelling reason for companies to implement RIM programs.

RIM at the Desktop

Few of the some 100 million desktop users in government and business offices today are furnished with good guidance concerning how to manage and retain the electronic records they create on their PCs and laptops every day. A substantial portion of the work of all organizations is done on these machines. By one account, some 56 percent of all *digital* data resides in single-user systems in the desktop environment.[20] The legal risks of unrestrained desktop retention are greater than for any recordkeeping environment. To bring RIM to the desktop is one of the biggest challenges in RIM today.

RIM and E-mail

According to some estimates, more than 60 percent of all electronic documents are transmitted as *e-mail* attachments.[21] According to studies by the IDC, Ferris Research, and others, up to 60 percent of business-critical information—the greater part of an organization's knowledge base, its intellectual assets, and institutional memory—is stored in its *electronic messaging* systems.[22] In 1999, the figure was just 33 percent.[23] Many e-mail systems were installed, however, without proper RIM and retention methodologies, and significant legal and other risks are associated with its mismanagement. Any organization that wishes to manage its e-records effectively must make better e-mail management a top priority.

RIM Standards

For many years, the RIM profession suffered from lack of technical standards defining best professional practices. Except for textbooks, journal articles, and conference papers, records managers were on their own to decide what practices they should develop and implement in their organizations. In recent years, however, a number of new technical standards have been issued that have been very beneficial to professional practice in RIM. The following standards are the most significant.

- **ISO 9000 Standards for Quality Records (1987)** – The world's first truly international standards related to RIM practices. Although these standards were limited in scope to "quality" records, they have nevertheless been very influential in RIM development among certain types of businesses.[24]

- **AS 4390 Australian National Standard for Records Management (1996)** – Although its scope was limited to a single country, this first national RIM standard was the basis for ISO 15489-1 *Information and Documentation – Records Management – Part I: General*, the international standard for RIM published in 2001.[25]

- **UN Model Law on Electronic Commerce (1996)** – Developed by the United Nations Commission on International Trade Law (UNCITRAL), this law is the world's first global legislative model to prescribe legal standards for recordkeeping in all-digital environments. This model law has been widely adapted, in various forms, by national governments throughout the world, including the United States.[26]

- **DoD 5015.2-STD,** *Design Criteria for Electronic Records Management Software Applications (2002)* – Issued by the U.S. Department of Defense, this standard is the world's first standard prescribing functionality requirements for electronic records in RIM software applications.[27]

- **The MoReq Specification (2001)** – Issued by an agency of the European Commission, the *Model Requirements for the Management of Electronic Records* is a generic specification for systems designed to manage electronic records. It is regarded as the most significant European statement on managing electronic records.[28]

- **UN Model Law on Electronic Signatures (2001)** – Also developed by UNCITRAL, this model law is the world's first global legislative model to prescribe legal standards by which some or all the functions identified as characteristic of handwritten signatures can be performed in an electronic environment.[29]

- **ISO 15489-1:2001,** *International Standard: Information and Documentation – Records Management – Part 1: General (2001)* – This standard is the first global standard for RIM, a true milestone in the history of the field. Since it became effective, it has been influential in enhancing the global legitimacy of the RIM discipline.[30]

Paper vs. Electronic Records: Contrasting Capabilities

Paper records have traditionally been regarded as things that are fixed, tangible, definite, deliberately created, and have a serious purpose and some longevity. Electronic information, by contrast, has inherent *attributes* of fluidity and high capacity for constant change. The technology tools used to create it foster easy, almost casual, and spontaneous information and communication. By its very abundance and omnipresence, it discourages attention to quality, longevity, and value, at least relative to the paper records of the past.[31] Particularly in larger *filing* installations, paper records can be notoriously inefficient. They are labor-intensive to process, and they consume substantial quantities of storage space. Moreover, paper records are frequently hard to control and are easily lost. Relative to electronic recordkeeping systems, access times are slow. In larger, centralized paper filing systems, *access times* can average five to fifteen minutes and sometimes longer. Finally, protecting large collections of paper mission-critical or *vital records* against the risk of loss from disaster or other causes is often difficult, impractical, or inadequate.

Relative to paper, electronic recordkeeping systems provide very rapid retrieval, and they are extremely space effective and easy to update. Further, they can provide random, simultaneous access by multiple users, and when supported by the proper software, they can support full-text and other sophisticated retrieval operations throughout the enterprise. Security storage of backup copies can be handled routinely. Finally, digital recordkeeping provides a host of other opportunities for business improvement: Some electronic document management solutions offer robust functionality for workflow, document version / revision control, and enhanced information sharing in collaborative work environments. Paper records lack these functional capabilities, relative to their electronic counterparts.

Taken as a whole, e-records have high strategic importance to the life of organizations, and their value and criticality increases with every passing year. These assertions have large implications for RIM, as explained next.

- **Higher strategic importance** – The notion that "better records make a better business" has long been true. In the world of paper, however, high-quality filing systems could go only so far in delivering outstanding products or services. With electronic records, their potential for improving the overall management of the business is much greater than paper records. In today's business and technology environment, no organization can hope to deliver top-quality products and services without operating outstanding *recordkeeping systems*.

- **Higher customer expectations** – During the days of paper records, a customer who telephoned a large business with an inquiry could expect to be told, "We'll have to retrieve your record and call you back." This return telephone call might be hours or even days later, and although some customers might have become irritated at this delay, it was entirely consistent with their perceptions of the level of performance that could be expected. In the era of e-records, however, the bar of expectations has risen much higher. At a minimum, customers now expect, even demand, immediate responses with no call back. Beyond that, they expect to visit the Web sites of companies and receive a wide variety of information and interactive services without ever leaving their homes. In many situations, electronic recordkeeping systems can deliver this higher level of performance.

- **Greater accessibility challenges** – Organizations need the capability of knowing where all their records are stored and retrieving them accurately and as quickly as needed. In digital environments, enterprise-wide *accessibility* is more difficult to manage for several reasons. For the structured data residing in databases and typically managed by IT departments, lack of compatibility across hardware and software platforms continues to hamper enterprise-wide accessibility. For e-mail messages and other unstructured data created at the desktop level, lack of file-naming conventions and user training can make accurate, enterprise-wide retrieval of documents residing on PCs and network servers very difficult.

- **Greater risk / consequences of loss** – With electronic records residing in computing environments, the risk and consequences of their loss is even greater than with paper records in file rooms, even though their physical security may be better. With paper records, successful restoration is frequently possible except in cases where they have been destroyed by fire. For electronic records, on the other hand, restoration is frequently much more problematic, if not impossible. The intrinsic uniqueness of the data, the fragility of the media on which they are stored, and other factors prevent restoration. Many organizations could likely survive a loss of most or all their paper records. However, organizations simply cannot take a risk of losing vital computer records. If any such loss is broad-based, it could be cataclysmic and, for all practical purposes, irrecoverable.

- **Much shorter life expectancy** – Most large businesses have used computers for recordkeeping for at least thirty to forty years. However, prior to the use of computers, organizations had never kept them on any media that inherently lacked any real properties of durability or permanent keeping properties. For paper records created on good quality paper stock and stored under good environmental conditions, a *life expectancy* of several hundred years is the norm. For computer-based records, unless preservation measures are instituted, the outer limits of life expectancy ranges between ten to twenty years and sometimes even as few as five years—a period of time consistent with the average service life of the hardware and software required to read and process the records. Although this time period is adequate for some electronic records, for many others it is not.

- **Much more difficult preservation challenges** – In former days, physical records were often preserved by accident rather than by design. They were simply stashed in the basements or attics of organizations and forgotten about until someone discovered them decades later. These records may have experienced some degree of deterioration but nevertheless were still in good and useable condition. No electronic record can long survive without its owner taking a series of defined steps to ensure that it remains in useable condition for long periods of time. The only way extended-term data retention requirements can be satisfied is by a series of carefully planned preservation practices that must be implemented by IT departments.

- **Greater technical expertise required** – Relative to their electronic counterparts, operating high-quality paper recordkeeping systems is not a very technically demanding endeavor. File cabinets, open shelving, file folders, and other supplies must be properly ordered and used; the records must be properly organized and sequenced for efficient retrieval; and the physical security, retention, and *disposition* of the records must be considered. However, to plan, design, and implement a sophisticated computer infrastructure to support high-quality electronic records is another matter. One mistake that many organizations make in attempting to assimilate information technology into their recordkeeping operations is that they fail to employ the requisite expertise.

A Professional Discipline in Transition

Early textbooks, such as William Benedon's classic *Records Management*, which was the first published work to define the scope and content of the then new discipline of records management, emphasized the importance of retention schedules and records center operations as core components of professional practice.[32] (Earlier works had emphasized filing systems and characterized records management as essentially clerical in nature.) More than three decades later, retention schedules and off-site storage of **inactive records** remain RIM's most visible and successful contribution to organizational effectiveness, and they continue to dominate professional practice in the United States today.[33] A neat, clean break between a world dominated by paper-based information and one dominated by electronic / image storage has not yet occurred. For the foreseeable future, both records storage media will continue to demand the attention of records managers everywhere.[34]

Many RIM programs continue to operate under a conceptual definition and set of assumptions that are several decades old: A **record** is recorded information, regardless of physical form or characteristics, created in the course of an organization's business. That definition is rooted in the notion of records as tangible entities. In a digital environment, computer-processable information is fluid, susceptible to constant change, readily transportable, fragile, and transitory. However, with the greatest transformation in RIM since the origin of the profession now taking place, because of the use of digital technology, the nature and use of both information and records are changing. RIM in the future is likely to bear only a passing resemblance to its past. The RIM community needs fresh and broad insights into the nature of these changes, how they affect RIM programs, and how the field needs to change in order to stay responsive and successful.[35]

Desired State of RIM

An organization can consider that it will have achieved state-of-the-art management of its information assets when:

- The organization is managing the transition from a paper-based to a largely digital recordkeeping environment by successfully integrating records in all media into its recordkeeping system; that is, when every record of high strategic value to the enterprise is rapidly and fully accessible for any and all business purposes. The location of all records must be known, and the records must be retrievable accurately and within time frames consistent with the organization's operational requirements which must, in turn, be based on delivering products / services of a high order.

- The organization adopts and implements a standard, enterprise platform for electronic RIM, such that all business-critical documents are easily and instantly sharable with all internal organizational entities and external parties. The standard will include service providers and the public so that the strategic objectives of ***electronic commerce (e-commerce)*** and enterprise-wide collaboration are achieved.

- The organization retains only such records as are necessary to conduct its business, comply with the law, and meet reasonable needs for the archival preservation of historical documentation. All other records, whether paper or electronic, are systematically disposed of under the authority of approved records retention policies and practices.

- The organization fully implements information protection and document security practices so that all mission-critical documents and data are protected against the risk of loss, whether from natural disasters, technical threats, human-caused theft or destruction, or other causes. Moreover, in the event that the organization experiences one of these threats or disasters, its records protection and recovery capabilities are such that it can resume the normal delivery of business services within reasonable periods of time.

International RIM

Because many readers of this book reside in North America, most of what they know about RIM reflects prevailing practices in North America. However, organizational recordkeeping is a global business issue, and bright and talented people throughout the world are dedicated to the task of developing new solutions and practices. If a high level of RIM is to be practiced, it will be based on the best global practices regardless of where they originate.

The United States has long been a leader in developing new RIM methodologies and techniques. In recent years, other countries have made some noteworthy achievements that have the potential to revolutionize RIM practice throughout the world. In Australia, for example, a number of pioneering contributions to RIM theory and practice have been made. These developments include:

- **Australia's Victorian Electronic Records Strategy (VERS)** – VERS is a framework of standards, guidance, and implementation projects centered around the goal of reliably and authentically archiving electronic records created and managed by the Victorian state government.

- **The National Archives of Australia's Designing and Implementing Recordkeeping Systems (DIRKS) strategy** – The DIRKS methodology is an eight-step process that organizations can use to improve recordkeeping and information management practices. The methodology is compliant with, and expands on, the methodological framework of the Australian national standard for RIM, AS ISO 15489-2002.

Australia may have some of the best RIM practices in the world for the following reasons:

- Global leadership in standards development, including the world's first national standard for RIM, as well as a key role in the development of ISO 15489
- Strong identity and recognition of a distinct management discipline
- Strong professional association activity
- An advanced and broad-based vendor community, albeit small in size
- Broad-based integration of RIM activity throughout the IT infrastructure
- A comprehensive educational system in RIM

Records managers throughout the world should endeavor to learn as much as possible about RIM practices in other countries, with a view towards applying their best practices in their own organizations.[36]

In Europe, RIM has traditionally been viewed as an activity for long-term archiving and one of tangential business value. This viewpoint is changing, and Europeans are now aggressively going digital.[37] Electronic RIM is increasingly viewed as a key enabling discipline guiding Europe's transition to a digital society. In 1999, the EU launched *eEurope*, a broad-based initiative for guiding Europe's transition towards an all-digital society. The objective is to bring digital technology, and electronic recordkeeping, to every European citizen, home, business, and government.[38] For example, in the United Kingdom, a directive mandated a comprehensive "e-government." All central government departments were required to produce new records *only in electronic format*. Moreover, public services provided by both the central and local governments also were required to be available online.[39]

The EU's major organization working on electronic RIM issues is the Document Lifecycle Management (DLM) Forum. (The French term *Donnees Lisibles par Machine (DLM)* translates as "machine-readable data.") This group was initially created and funded by the European Commission, but it currently operates as an independent body. The Forum comprises most of the national archives ministries of the EU's twenty-five member states. One key objective is to harmonize the various European electronic archiving initiatives into a common EU-wide set of standards and practices.

During the past thirty or so years, RIM has become increasingly more technology-driven and highly dynamic. The challenges and opportunities associated with electronic recordkeeping are truly historic and unprecedented. *Records Management: Making the Transition from Paper to Electronic* is about these challenges and opportunities and what they portend for RIM. If RIM practitioners can successfully apply the principles discussed in this book, the transition to a higher level of professional RIM practices will have been made.

Notes

1. William Saffady, *Records and Information Management: Fundamentals of Professional Practice* (Lenexa, KS: ARMA International, 2004), 1.

2. Bruce Dearstyne, "Records Management of the Future: Anticipate, Adapt, and Succeed," *The Information Management Journal* 33, no. 4 (October 1999): 10.

3. Saffady, *Fundamentals of Professional Practice*, 3.

4. Connie Moore, Kate Tucker, Susan Wiener, and Stacey Jenkins, *The Role of Electronic Records Management in North American Organizations* (Cambridge, MA: Forrester Consulting, April 2004).

5. Robert Williams, *Electronic Records Management Survey: A Call to Action* (Chicago: Cohasset, Inc., 2004).

6. Penn, Shoen & Berland Associates Study, Commissioned by Iron Mountain, *The Information Management Journal* 38, no. 1 (January / February 2004).

7. William Saffady, *Records and Information Management: A Benchmarking Study of Large U.S. Industrial Companies* (Lenexa, KS: ARMA International, 2002).

8. Alan Pelz-Sharpe, "Records Management Redux: The Nudge Towards Compliance," *KMWorld* (September 2003): 13.

9. Andy Moore, "Pressure Mounts, But RM Immune to Huge Growth," *KMWorld* (October 2003): 3.

10. Gillian Colledge and Michael Cliff, "The Implications of the Sarbanes-Oxley Act: It's Time to Take Records Management Seriously," *KMWorld* (September 2003): S4.

11. School of Information Management and Systems, "How Much Information" (Berkeley, CA: University of California, 2003); see "The Myth of the Paperless Office," *The Information Management Journal* 38, no. 1 (January / February 2004): 10.

12. Jim Lee, "Reduce the Cost of Compliance: Database Archiving and Information Lifecycle Management," *SMS* 8, no. 5.

13. Peter Drucker, *Managing in the Next Society* (New York: Truman Talley Books, 2002).

14. Lee Iacocca, "Henry Ford," *Time*, 7 December 1998.

15. John Huey, "Sam Walton," *Time*, 7 December 1998.

16. www-306.ibm.com/software/data/cm/filenet/faq.html.

17. Colledge and Cliff, "The Implications of the Sarbanes-Oxley Act," S5.

18. Saffady, *A Benchmarking Study*, 68.

19. See, for example, Nikki Swartz, "Acquisitions All Around," *The Information Management Journal* 37, no. 1 (January / February 2003): 6; Bruce Miller, "Implementing Electronic Recordkeeping," *ProfessioNotes*, Institute of Certified Records Managers (Winter 2004): 8.

20. Fred Moore, "Cradle to Grave Storage Management Now a Reality," *Computer Technology Review* (January 2003): 20.

21. Alan Porter, "A Ten-Step Strategy for Defending Your Company's E-Mail System," *Disaster Recovery Journal* (Winter 2004): 26.

22. See, for example, Greg Arnette, "Killer App: New E-mail Requirements are Driving Significant Technology Purchases," *Storage Inc.* (Quarter 4, 2002): 32; Cliff Sink, "E-Mail Management: How to Succeed Step-by-Step, *KMWorld* (March 2004): S16; Michael Osterman, "Records Management Requirements in the Enterprise," in *Proceedings of the 48th Annual Conference, ARMA International, Boston, MA, October 19-22, 2003* (Lenexa, KS: ARMA International, 2003), 200.

23. Bill Tolson, "Controlling the Flood: A Look at E-mail Storage and Management Challenges," *Computer Technology Review* (September 2002):16.

24. See Eugenia Brumm, *Managing Records for ISO 9000 Compliance* (Milwaukee: ASQC Press, 1995).

25. Standards Australia, *Australian Standard 4390: Records Management* (Sydney, New South Wales, Australia, February 1996).

26. United Nations Commission on International Trade Law, UNCITRAL, *Model Law on Electronic Commerce with Guide to Enactment*, 1996.

27. U.S. Department of Defense, DoD 5015.2-STD: *Design Criteria for Electronic Records Management Software Applications* (Washington, DC: Assistant Secretary of Defense for Command, Control, Communications, and Intelligence, 2002).

28. MoReq Specification, *Model Requirements for the Management of Electronic Records*, 2001.

29. United Nations Commission on International Trade Law, *Draft Guide to Enactment of the UNCITRAL Model Law on Electronic Signatures*, 2001.

30. International Organization for Standardization, ISO 15489-1 2001: *Information and Documentation – Records Management – Part 1: General* (Geneva, Switzerland: ISO, 2001).

31. Dearstyne, "Records Management of the Future."

32. William Benedon, *Records Management* (New York: Prentice Hall, 1969).

33. Saffady, *A Benchmarking Study*, 68.

34. Larry Kreger, "Paper and the Information Age," *The Information Management Journal* 33, no. 10 (October 1999): 41.

35. Dearstyne, *Records Management of the Future*, 6-8.

36. See, for example, Laurie Sletten, "Lessons from Down Under: Records Management in Australia," *The Information Management Journal* 33, no. 1 (January 1999).

37. Martin Waldron, "Adopting Electronic Records Management: European Strategic Initiatives," *The Information Management Journal* 38, no. 4 (July / August 2004): 31.

38. See eEurope Action Plan, 2002. Available at: http://europa.eu.int/information_society/ eeurope/2002/action_plan/index_en.htm. (Accessed October 29, 2005).

39. Waldron, "Adopting Electronic Records Management: European Strategic Initiatives," 32.

Chapter 2

Building Successful Programs

Developing a successful RIM program that functions at the highest level of professional practice requires ten key ingredients, as follows:

1. Sustained, committed senior executive sponsorship
2. A strategic plan for the future
3. A commitment to digital recordkeeping
4. A governance structure of key stakeholders
5. Organizational placement to ensure program visibility and impact
6. The requisite funding and staffing
7. A strategic partnership with IT
8. Deployment of the requisite technology solutions
9. Program development in compliance with ISO 15489
10. A proactive agenda for advanced RIM

Traditional RIM programs are organized around paper-based, physical recordkeeping systems and processes. Such programs are often supported by RIM software solutions or otherwise involve the use of *electronic imaging* or other *document* technologies. However, this traditional model is still largely about managing paper. The Saffady *benchmarking* study, in particular, confirms this model with its detailed assessment of prevailing RIM practices among large U.S. industrial companies. These results indicated that the typical RIM program:

- Is headed by a well-qualified records manager
- Reports to a corporate executive who appreciates, but does not fully understand, the objectives of RIM
- Is enabled by a written charter or mission statement that defines the program's purpose, scope, and authority for the benefit of the organization

- Has an effective and long-standing working relationship with the corporate legal department for records retention, *regulatory compliance*, or other matters
- Has an emerging or improving working relationship with the corporate IT department for initiatives involving electronic records, document imaging, and automation of records processes / recordkeeping systems
- Has a formal network of departmental records coordinators who are charged with various duties associated with retention schedule implementation, primarily for paper records
- Promulgates retention policies and guidelines that are reasonably complete, clear, and current for paper records associated with U.S. business operations but are less so for electronic records
- Operates, either directly or through outsourcing companies, facilities for the offsite storage of inactive paper records
- Has nominal responsibility for identifying and protecting vital paper records
- Provides Internet access to RIM policies and retention schedules[1]

The Saffady study also identified the functional components of existing RIM programs among participating companies. These following components were included:

- Records retention – 95%
- Offsite storage – 85%
- Vital records – 65%
- Filing systems – 31%
- Micrographics – 13%
- Electronic imaging – 12%[2]

In order to achieve a high level of professional practice, organizational RIM must reposition itself from the old, paper-based model towards a new model that effectively integrates the management of electronic records.

Sustained, Committed Executive Sponsorship

Apart from the talents of the records manager who runs the program, top-level support is the single most critical issue contributing to the success of any corporate RIM initiative. Wherever it resides, the RIM function must operate in a climate of executive leadership of a positive and proactive nature. The senior executive to whom the program reports must care about the function and act proactively to ensure its success, including allocating the requisite resources. Sustained, committed executive leadership is essential for a successful RIM program.

Frequently, senior executives have superficial views of the recordkeeping function, failing to appreciate its complexity and what is required to enhance its value to the organization. As senior executives rarely come from a RIM background, this perception is understandable. Regardless, these individuals need to have a firm grasp of RIM's potential impact on the organization—the benefits of operating high-quality RIM as compared to the consequences of not doing so. Records managers in such organizations must strive to inform top-level executives of the importance and benefits of having a highly functional RIM program.

Strategic Plan for the Future

More and more, organizations are thinking and operating *strategically*; their very survival depends on it. A good long-range strategic plan is the first thing any organization needs when contemplating major initiatives in RIM. Yet, the traditional RIM model has not contained a strategically oriented skill set.[3] If records managers do not manage information as an asset, their programs will continue to be underresourced, undervalued, underappreciated, and underrespected. Managing information strategically is no different from strategically managing finances, human resources, research and development, or any other business-critical element of the enterprise.[4]

The strategic plan should be the road map to guide the assimilation of a variety of new management initiatives and document technologies over a three to five-year period. First and foremost, the plan should articulate a clear vision for electronic RIM in the context of the larger business goals and objectives of the organization. An analysis must be conducted that assesses past program performance, identifies and evaluates current strategy, assesses future success based on current strategy, determines the need for change, and justifies whatever change is required.[5] Moreover, the plan must contain a clear delineation of short-, medium-, and long-term goals for managing the organization's records and delivering high-quality services to customers or other client groups, as well as high-level strategies for achieving them.

The plan should be considered a dynamic document. It should be updated annually and presented to senior management, particularly during budget-planning cycles and program performance reviews. The plan's overall theme should be the role of RIM in enhancing business performance by facilitating the organization's transition from paper-based to electronic recordkeeping on an enterprise-wide scale and in accordance with well-conceived priorities to be systematically implemented over time.

Commitment to Digital Recordkeeping

Surprising as it may seem, many records managers still cling tenaciously, and irrationally, to the notion that paper will be with us forever; that the long-awaited but hitherto unrealized "paperless office" is and will remain a myth. In one sense, this belief is understandable because paper continues to be created and maintained in abundant quantities decades after the introduction of various technologies intended to replace it.[6] Individuals who doubt the inevitability of the nearly all-digital recordkeeping fail to consider the decisive factor that assures it—not technology, but different skill sets among the younger and future generations of office workers. These people were born digital. They never have and never will use traditional filing cabinets as records storage devices.

Today, no organization can successfully reinvent itself and its business processes if these processes continue to be predominantly paper-based. Thus, in professional RIM environments, records managers must play a key role in accelerating the organization's transition from paper to digital recordkeeping. Organizations everywhere are in the midst of a long transition from paper-based to digital recordkeeping. Inventing and learning how to use the various technologies enabling digital recordkeeping has taken several decades, and perhaps another decade or two will pass before these technologies are fully assimilated. Regardless, the reality is that organizational recordkeeping is not going to be paper-based fifty or even twenty years from now. The question, then, is not *whether* organizations will transition to nearly all-digital recordkeeping but *when* and *how*.

Traditionally, records managers wanting to convert paper-based systems to digital *format* have been required to justify such a conversion project in terms of cost-benefits. A new policy should be adopted stating that, for all recordkeeping systems of strategic importance to the enterprise, digital is the preferred medium. Further, if a department manager wants to continue to maintain paper for business-critical systems, she/he should be required to justify why paper records are in the organization's best interest. Finally, the policy should authorize business units to retain recordkeeping systems of lower value in paper format, so long as the paper format does not adversely impact the organization or its mission. See Chapter 13 for a detailed discussion of the strengths, limitations, and best applications of the various recordkeeping *media* types.

In their long-range strategic plans, records managers should develop detailed plans for document digitization, together with recommendations as to how to implement them over time. An aggressive approach to digital recordkeeping is recommended. The strategic plans should indicate which recordkeeping systems should be converted from paper to digital format and in what order of priority. These plans should be the basis for annual budgeting in which appropriate sums of money are allocated to convert the priority applications to digital format, one or more each year. As a useful if somewhat arbitrary target, organizations should give themselves five to ten years to "de-paper" every recordkeeping system for which the benefits of conversion to digital format are demonstrable.

Governance Structure of Key Stakeholders

As a business discipline, RIM cannot succeed in isolation. Therefore, a governance structure should be put into place to develop and oversee the implementation of enterprise initiatives. The goal is to elevate the status and visibility of RIM, establishing an appropriate leadership structure consisting of the right stakeholders. The establishment of a permanent executive committee on RIM can often be the key to a successful program. This committee should have the authority to oversee all aspects of program development and implementation, and it should be accountable to senior management for the results.

As always, the right leadership and membership composition is crucial to an effective committee. Most such committees are composed of senior representatives of the legal, fiscal, tax, and audit staffs. Sometimes, the organization's records manager serves as the chairperson. At other times, this role is assigned to a senior executive. Where this approach to program governance has been put into place, the committee should exercise aggressive oversight of enterprise RIM initiatives. It should meet regularly, monitor these initiatives, and report the results to senior management.

Optimum Organizational Placement

In any organization, the RIM function should be placed where it has the best chance of succeeding. Many RIM programs fail simply because they lack the status and visibility required to have an appropriate impact in solving recordkeeping problems. If they are to succeed in managing the organization's information assets, RIM programs must be positioned within an organizational setting and at a hierarchical level sufficient to achieve RIM goals and objectives.

Very few RIM programs in the United States are run directly by executives at the vice presidential level. Many programs, however, report directly to vice presidents or to other executives with sufficient seniority to provide the requisite visibility and organizational impact. The Saffady benchmarking study determined the most common organizational placements for RIM programs among the participating companies. Administrative services and legal departments were the most popular placement options, followed by IT.[7] Among U.S. business corporations, seven organizational placement options can be identified as most common. These options are discussed below, beginning with the most common placements, in the context of their advantages, disadvantages, and overall suitability.

1. **RIM as an administrative staff function** – This placement option is the most common among private sector firms. It has been and remains very popular in cases where the RIM function is viewed as a staff function in the larger corporate governance structure. In these cases, the function usually reports to the vice president of administrative services, either directly or to a subordinate executive. In this placement, as a staff rather than an operational or line function, RIM tends to focus on policy planning, compliance monitoring, training, and similar functions. With good executive sponsorship, and if the issue of access to technology resources can be worked out, this placement can work very well. In cases where RIM does not succeed in this environment, it is usually because of the records manager's inadequate skills or inadequate attention by senior management.

2. **RIM as a legal / regulatory function** – This option tends to be popular among businesses subject to heavy government regulation that impacts recordkeeping, and/or those businesses exposed to significant levels of litigation risks. Examples

include pharmaceutical firms, public utility companies, and similar businesses. Because of its high level of organizational influence, this placement option sometimes works very well. On the other hand, many top corporate lawyers who run legal departments are hesitant to assume management responsibility for a program such as RIM, which they see as far removed from their primary mission of providing legal advice and defending the organization in legal disputes. In cases where the organization has a separate regulatory affairs department (e.g., banks and financial institutions, pharmaceutical firms), placing RIM in that department is a particularly popular placement option.

3. **RIM as an IT function** – Few significant RIM problems can be solved without access to appropriate technology resources. These factors suggest that RIM has a viable place in the larger information management arena, which is typically the province of corporate IT departments. In fact, the placement of RIM within IT departments is a trend that has been gathering momentum since the mid-1990s among large U.S. businesses. When placed into IT, RIM is often grouped with other related IT subfunctions such as knowledge management. The obvious advantage is that these placements give RIM a much higher probability of obtaining access to the technology resources they need to solve recordkeeping problems. The major disadvantage is that, today, corporate IT departments have so many priorities on their agenda that they sometimes cannot give RIM the attention it needs to succeed.

4. **RIM as an archival function** – In the U.S., the RIM discipline is an outgrowth of archival practice. As it is known today, RIM was largely "invented" by the U.S. National Archives during and after World War II. The National Archives developed a RIM program for mandatory implementation throughout the U.S. government, which was subsequently emulated by states and local governments, as well as by the private sector. Largely as a result of this history, RIM as an archival function, operated by archival agencies, is still common in government today, particularly at the state level. The major advantage of this placement is that it helps to ensure the preservation of records of enduring value. The major disadvantage is that it often provides inadequate access to the technology resources required for the development and implementation of electronic RIM initiatives.

5. **RIM as an audit / policy compliance function** – The best RIM policies and practices will have very little organizational impact unless they are implemented effectively. In cases where compliance monitoring is deemed critical to program success, placement of the RIM function in an audit services unit can sometimes work successfully. Such placements are relatively rare among U.S. corporations, however.

6. **RIM as a support function to a major operational business unit** – In this option, RIM is placed into the operational business function that experiences the greatest recordkeeping challenges. For example, in some pharmaceutical firms, RIM is placed into the research and development department; in some petroleum firms, it is placed into the exploration and production department. The advantage of these placements is that such departments greatly need what the

RIM program has to offer, and they usually have ample money and power to allocate sufficient resources to implement solutions to whatever RIM problems they face. The disadvantage of such placements is that the enterprise-wide aspects of program development and implementation may not be emphasized under this option.

7. **RIM as a facilities management function** – This placement option is often selected in cases where the RIM function assumes direct responsibility for the management of physical records in file rooms and records storage facilities. Here, RIM is viewed, and largely operated, as a custodial or "housekeeping" function. These placement options tend to be fairly far down on the hierarchical ladder. Prior to the 1990s, placing the RIM function into file rooms was a fairly popular placement option. However, with the transition to digital recordkeeping, having RIM in file rooms is seldom regarded with favor and indeed is not recommended if the organization wishes to achieve any degree of success with electronic records.

Requisite Funding and Staffing

RIM is frequently underfunded in the context of its mandate. With an average of four full-time employees, including the program head plus some combination of RIM analysts, offsite storage coordinators, and administrative support personnel, the Saffady study shows that RIM is often understaffed. A total of 62 percent of the participating companies reported that their current level of staffing is inadequate to accomplish its mandated responsibilities. Only 19 percent reported satisfactory staffing levels.[8] The conclusion is that organizations are often unwilling to allocate to RIM programs sufficient staff and other resources to ensure their successful implementation.

These findings indicate that as long as RIM programs are organized around the traditional model, they are unlikely to receive the staffing and other resources they require. They will just continue to limp along at their current level, be reduced, or eliminated entirely. After all, few executives are eager to invest in a discipline that is organized around an increasingly obsolete business model. Thus, increased levels of investment are contingent upon enhancing the program to a level of practice that senior executives perceive as being of value.

In order to rectify this situation, as a part of the strategic planning process, records managers must define the investment options for their programs to operate at varying levels of quality and then define the skill sets required for each option.

Define Investment Options

Many years ago, the senior executive of a major company was talking about the status of RIM in his company when he said, "Our company is world-class in what we do; we're number one in the world and we intend to stay number one. We're not number one in RIM, however, nor is it our objective to be so. But we don't want to fail in RIM either. So you just tell me what we need to do to put in a decent program, and I'll get the money for it." This vignette demonstrates the attitude of most senior executives concerning the level of RIM they want and for which they are willing to pay. Records managers can dream about world-class RIM, but in most places, funding for their dreams will never materialize. If funding is an issue, the strategic plans and investment proposals of records managers need to reflect this reality. The following recommendations are conceptualized around this notion.

Every organization that wants to implement RIM solutions faces choices of good, better, or best.[9] In other words, are the initiatives going to be basic, state of the art, or something in between? As strategic planners in enterprise RIM solutions, records managers must define these options and present them in a format that decision makers can use in allocating resources. Frequently, the best approach is to present three options for program development or enhancement.

1. **Basic Level of Services** – For organizations that are just getting started with enterprise RIM, this level of services is defined as a high-quality, enterprise-wide RIM program organized around physical (paper) records, utilizing traditional policies and practices. This level would have minimal involvement with, or impact on, electronic records. This level can be recommended only if it is conceptualized as a start-up RIM capability, contingent upon a commitment for systematic enhancement over a three- to five-year period to the intermediate and advanced levels.

2. **Intermediate Level of Services** – This level of services combines basic RIM services with services also directed at managing the organization's electronic records. At this level, the RIM program would be capable of implementing various practices for managing digital records, to include electronic document imaging, data retention and preservation, and various records and document management software solutions. Moreover, the staffing would consist of a cadre of specialists in several areas of document technologies. This level of RIM capabilities thus represents a significant enhancement over the basic level of service.

3. **Advanced Level of Services** – This level of services would introduce Internet, Web-based, enterprise document management initiatives utilizing national and global standards and best practices in the areas of electronic records / document management. This level of services would have the greatest impact on the organization's competitive position or delivery of services based on sophisticated RIM capabilities. For example, at this level of practice, RIM and retention capabilities would be fully integrated at the desktop level throughout the enterprise. Moreover, all computer applications requiring it would be made ***retention-capable.*** The level is thus an augmented implementation of intermediate RIM capabilities. It compares favorably to the most fully developed and effective RIM programs implemented in business and government anywhere. At this level, the organization will have the professional competence it requires to develop and implement a world-class program. The successful attainment of this level of services typically requires a high level of executive support over a five-year period or longer.

To reiterate, the basic level of services reflects the traditional model. The advanced level, on the other hand, should be the goal of every organization, but the reality is that many will not attain it. Consequently, the intermediate level will be the most realistic option for many organizations. In developing long-range strategic plans, records mangers should always define advanced solutions and request funding for them (assuming that they are justified as being in the organization's best interest). Sometimes, when budgets are tight, initiatives can be deferred for a year or two. Other times, intermediate-level funding will have to be accepted. However, enhancement to advanced levels of practice should always be in the strategic plan. To do otherwise would not be in the organization's best interest.

Required Skill Sets

At the mid to high levels of professional competency emphasizing electronic RIM, the organization will require a high order of technical expertise. RIM should never be staffed to the level of an empire in any organization. To "throw bodies at the problem" is seldom the best response to any business problem, including inadequate RIM. Moreover, many tasks associated with RIM can and should be outsourced, thereby minimizing the need for full-time, permanent staff. Finally, at the enterprise level, the role of RIM should be principally one of policy and program development and technology assimilation. To progress towards a high level of professional practice, the organization needs positions for the following skill sets:

- **Executive manager** – has overall responsibility for the RIM program. This key position should be staffed at the vice president, director, or senior manager level. The position should be filled by a person having expertise in all areas of RIM, particularly those areas involving document technologies. Effective relationships with senior IT managers and other executives are requisite for success.

- **Policy planning and compliance monitoring specialists** – plan and monitor the implementation of new policies, procedures, and technical guidelines throughout the organization.

- **Legal records retention research specialists** – perform legal retention research to determine the records retention and other laws and regulations with which the organization must comply. This function is frequently accomplished by *outsourcing* to external parties.

- **Records retention specialists (entry-level positions)** – develop records retention schedules for paper records. As entry-level positions, their duties should be devoted largely to updates and maintenance of the schedules, as well as compliance monitoring. If desired, the development of these schedules can be accomplished via outsourcing.

- **Electronic records retention specialists (mid-level to senior staff positions)** – begin with developing competencies with paper records retention, then graduate to writing retention rules for electronic records. They also work with various units of the IT department to ensure that data purge functionality, consistent with retention periods in the schedules, has been incorporated into all software applications requiring it. Again, the development of these schedules can be accomplished via outsourcing, leaving the proper role of full-time staff for updates, maintenance, and compliance monitoring.

- **Technology solutions analysts** – monitor records and document technologies and determine whether, when, and how they should be implemented. These technologies include, but are not limited to, records / document management software, imaging and workflow applications, full-text retrieval software, and other categories of document and content management solutions.

- **Mergers and acquisitions specialist(s)** – manage the systems integration and other records-related issues associated with mergers, acquisitions, and divestitures or closure of business units.

- **Document classification / taxonomy specialists** – deploy records and document management software and other content-management solutions. Their major task is to custom-design standardized document classification schemes at the workgroup and enterprise levels in order to ensure a higher level of accurate and precise document retrieval.

- **Digital preservation specialists** – develop and implement data migration and other strategies for ensuring the long-term or permanent preservation of all electronic records requiring it. The position requires a combination of archival, records retention, and computer-related skills.

- **Training specialists** – provide training and education in all the technical areas of RIM. This requirement may be satisfied by drawing from other staff positions; that is, the specialists indicated above would be required to conduct training sessions as part of their duties. However, for large organizations, one or more dedicated positions may be justified.

Outsourcing Options

Most, if not all, successful RIM programs augment their own staff resources by utilizing technical skills provided from external sources. As an option for limiting the number of full-time staff required to start-up and operate a RIM program, organizations should consider outsourcing certain functions. Outsourcing is the appropriate business decision in cases where the following conditions apply:

- The tasks require specialized expertise that the organization does not possess and does not need to employ on a full-time basis.
- The tasks are temporary, one-time, rather than ongoing in nature.
- The tasks could be performed better, faster, or cheaper by utilizing external resources.

Based on these criteria, the following RIM functions are frequently outsourced to commercial service providers:

- Strategic planning studies
- Retention schedule development
- Legal retention research
- File plan or classification / taxonomy development
- Technology solution studies

- Staff training
- Offsite storage of paper records
- Offsite protection of vital records

Strategic Partnership with IT

Today, RIM programs cannot succeed unless they can successfully assimilate technology into recordkeeping environments. Access to technology resources and a close working relationship with IT are required. Until the 1980s, business recordkeeping was not predominantly technology-driven. Since then, however, most business-critical recordkeeping systems have migrated from paper to digital environments. Today, significant RIM initiatives require that RIM and IT work closely together. For this reason, IT is, arguably, RIM's most significant stakeholder, even more critical than legal.

The relationship between IT and RIM has never been better, and it continues to improve every year. The Saffady benchmarking study reported that a total of 67 percent of the participating companies reported a satisfactory relationship with their IT departments. On the other hand, the fact that 28 percent of the survey respondents indicated that they have limited interaction with IT departments is not a good sign.[10] Although the relationship has never been better, it still has a long way to go. RIM still needs to solidify its place at the table as a key player in all information management initiatives that fall within the purview of its expertise.

Findings from the Forrester report validate this assertion. Concerning the roles of IT and records managers in developing electronic RIM solutions, the report concluded that, at present, IT—not RIM—plays a dominant role in electronic RIM projects. What is worse, the Forrester study concluded that RIM professionals are *losing* their influence as electronic RIM emerges. Further, the emergence of electronic RIM has significantly changed the reporting relationships for the electronic RIM function, to a greater role for IT and a diminished role for RIM.[11]

The Forrester study recommended that RIM be part of a multidisciplinary team addressing electronic records issues, including IT, legal, compliance, and other stakeholders. The report concluded by stating that, among business and IT executives, a lack of clarity exists about what electronic RIM really is or what its role should be in bringing better management to organizational recordkeeping. Records managers must be proactive in demonstrating the value of RIM to IT or risk being relegated to managing only paper and microforms.[12]

IT needs RIM because it is responsible for managing huge and exploding quantities of electronic records, but it lacks expertise in certain key areas of information management that fall within the purview of RIM. The challenge IT faces is to integrate and be able to access records that cut across different storage technologies, such as paper, film, fiche, and optical media, that have until now been managed under separate RIM methodologies. By some estimates, up to 80 percent of corporate electronic information is in the form of *text files* or *documents*, as opposed to the *structured data* records so common in the number-crunching applications that dominated business computing during its early days. Thus, if 80 percent of what needs to be managed is electronic documents in some form, RIM solutions must be applied in order to manage these information resources effectively—the reason that IT needs RIM.

IT is highly skilled at monitoring and acquiring new technology and deploying various solutions to capture and process the data and other objects in system applications. However, IT has little or no expertise in certain key areas required to manage electronic records effectively. The Forrester report defined the following areas of technical expertise that IT needs from RIM.

- Development of retention schedules for electronic records
- Guidelines for purging electronic records under retention rules
- Identification of mission-critical records for protection planning
- Development of classification and taxonomy schemes
- Guidelines for handling metadata
- Regulatory compliance expertise
- Media selection guidelines (i.e., optical vs. magnetic storage)
- Creating RFPs for acquisition of document technology solutions
- Access and preservation of records
- Development of cost-benefit models[13]

Because of the expertise that IT needs from RIM, the opportunities have never been greater. However, to take advantage of them by building a close, cooperative relationship requires speaking a common language. IT people are unlikely to take the initiative to "speak and do" RIM. Therefore, the onus is on RIM professionals to become conversant with IT terminology, environments, and issues, and to articulate their requirements to them. In fact, RIM professionals have become more knowledgeable about IT since the mid-1990s, but many more years may pass before RIM and IT solidify their relationship and fully assimilate electronic RIM across the enterprise.

Deployment of Requisite Technology Solutions

RIM must work in close cooperation with IT to successfully deploy most if not all the following technology solutions:

- RIM software, for the management of paper-based records in both active and inactive recordkeeping environments
- Electronic document imaging solutions as a replacement for paper-based recordkeeping systems and also to reduce the burden of costly, ***online storage*** of computer data
- Electronic document management software, for the improved management of unstructured electronic documents in networked computing environments, with functionality to manage the ***information life cycle*** under retention rules and policies

- Software and other tools for bringing RIM and retention to desktop computing environments, including e-mail and other forms of messaging and unstructured records residing there

- Document classification and taxonomy solutions, incorporated into environments containing unstructured documents, to facilitate the accurate and timely retrieval of this type of information content

Program Development in Compliance with ISO 15489

The ISO 15489 standard prescribes technical guidelines for recordkeeping in all types of organizational settings, as well as practice guidelines for records managers throughout the world who are responsible for improving the quality of recordkeeping in their organizations.[14] The content of ISO 15489 and its accompanying technical report can best be characterized as consisting of generic requirements or general methodologies for designing, operating, and managing records and recordkeeping systems.

The issuance of this standard was truly a milestone event in the history of RIM, having the effect of legitimizing RIM as a business discipline throughout the world. Moreover, it provides a new benchmarking model, defining best global practices in RIM, something the profession has long needed. Despite these positive aspects, the standard has some possible limitations. For one thing, as a voluntary code of practice, compliance with ISO 15489 is entirely at the discretion of organizations. Therefore, to assume that, with the issuance of this new standard, the budgets of organizations throughout the world will suddenly overflow with money for new RIM initiatives is unrealistic. Nor will senior managers and executives suddenly become convinced that RIM is now the most indispensable new management initiative they must pursue, however long they may have permitted it to languish in their own organizations.

Notwithstanding these realities, for those organizations that want to use it, ISO 15489 provides an ideal model for building and developing a RIM program at a professional level of practice. Records managers should include ISO 15489 compliance as one of their top priorities in their long-range strategic plans. If compliance can be demonstrated, records managers will be able to declare to their senior management that the records of their organizations are being managed in a manner that is world-class, is ISO 15489-compliant, and is based on best global practices.

In order for organizations to build and operate their RIM programs around the standard, and then determine compliance with it, an assessment tool is required. Such a tool has been developed by ARMA International, in collaboration with an organization called *NetDiligence. Risk Profiler Self-Assessment for Records and Information Management* is designed to enable organizations to determine their level of compliance with the best practice standards contained in ISO 15489 and its accompanying technical report. The online tool consists of approximately 100 questions, with additional subquestions, addressing each aspect of RIM practice as specified in the standard. With this tool, records managers have, for the first time, a practical method of evaluating the quality of their RIM program against best global practices as defined by the ISO standard.

Proactive Agenda for RIM

The final key ingredient for success in RIM is the adoption of an aggressive agenda for RIM, designed largely around electronic records. The following agenda is recommended:

- Evaluate the performance of all high-value recordkeeping systems and upgrade those that underperform in delivering precise and timely retrieval to their users.
- Evaluate the protection status of all computer applications and work with IT to ensure the protection of the data against loss.
- Develop and implement an enterprise-wide plan for protecting desktop records against loss.
- Extend the records retention program to provide coverage of computer backup data.
- Work with privacy and security departments to safeguard all proprietary, confidential, or sensitive information from unauthorized access or disclosure.
- Include complete coverage for electronic records in the organization's retention schedules.
- Develop and implement an aggressive strategy for retention implementation—to include *purge days* and compliance *records audits*—for each of the five major recordkeeping environments in the organization: (1) official paper records, (2) personal working papers, (3) boxed and stored paper records, (4) user-controlled electronic records, and (5) IT-managed system *application* data.
- Introduce RIM to the desktop and develop policies and procedures to provide that all desktop records under the control of their creators are retained and disposed in accordance with approved retention rules.
- Extend records retention to IT-managed computer applications; work with IT to make all applications retention-capable; and ensure that expired data eligible for deletion is purged in accordance with approved retention rules.
- Bring RIM and retention to the messaging environment; provide policies and guidelines for the *disposition* of all e-mail under retention rules.
- Work with attorneys to develop and implement policies and procedures to ensure that all records retention and disposal actions are within the law.
- Work with the IT department to assimilate new document technology solutions where required.
- Develop and implement solutions for long-term data retention and preservation.

This agenda is clearly different from the traditional RIM model. Records managers everywhere should give themselves, and propose to their organizations, five years to accomplish this agenda. Those records managers who accomplish it can consider RIM successful in their organizations.

Notes

1. William Saffady, *Records and Information Management: A Benchmarking Study of Large U.S. Industrial Companies* (Lenexa, KS: ARMA International, 2002), 67-68.

2. Ibid., 31.

3. Robert Meagher, "The IM Building Blocks," *The Information Management Journal 37*, no. 1, (January / February 2002): 26.

4. Robert Meagher, "Putting Strategic into Information Management," *The Information Management Journal* (January / February 2003): 51.

5. Ibid., 53.

6. See, for example, Abigail Sellen and Richard Harper, *The Myth of the Paperless Office* (Cambridge, MA: MIT Press, 2002).

7. Saffady, *A Benchmarking Study*, 11-16.

8. Ibid., 19.

9. For application of the Capability Maturity Matrix to the transition from basic to advanced (electronic) RIM, see U.S. General Accounting Office, *Study of Exemplary Practices in Electronic RIM*, May 1, 2003.

10. Saffady, *A Benchmarking Study*, 26.

11. Connie Moore, Kate Tucker, Susan Wiener, and Stacey Jenkins, *The Role of Electronic RIM in North American Organizations* (Cambridge, MA: Forrester Consulting, April 2004), 23.

12. Ibid., 67.

13. Moore, et al., *The Role of Electronic RIM in North American Organizations*, 53-55; 89.

14. International Organization for Standardization, ISO 15489-1:2001: *International Standard: Information and Documentation – Records Management – Part 1: General.* (Geneva, Switzerland: ISO, 2001).

Chapter 3

Records Retention: Managing the Information Life Cycle

What information to keep? How long to keep it? How to effect its systematic disposal upon the expiration of its value? These simple questions pose some of the most vexing dilemmas in RIM circles today. Wherever it is practiced, records retention is the cornerstone of RIM, and it continues to dominate professional practice in the U.S., as it has for decades. Records retention is introduced, and recommended practices for developing retention schedules are described in this chapter.

The Purpose of Records Retention

One principal characteristic of organizational information is that, at some point, it declines in value until it is not needed by anyone for any purpose. Of course, some business information never loses its value and needs to be preserved in perpetuity. However, the great majority of records maintained by businesses and governments should be discarded after they have served their purpose.

Records retention is defined as that component of a RIM program that provides policies and procedures specifying the length of time that an organization's records must be retained. The *records retention program* provides for the systematic destruction of records that no longer serve any useful purpose, as well as the ongoing retention of those of enduring value. It is implemented by effecting the destruction of useless records on a scheduled basis, as specified in the organization's records retention schedule.

Why, then, is records retention needed? In organizational settings, records accumulate in any place that records are stored—internally operated records centers, commercial facilities, network servers, PC hard drives, and a plethora of other computer storage media. Unfortunately, these old records are, all too conveniently, "out of sight, out of mind." The reality is that most employees are too busy during the work week to review older records and effect their proper disposition. Thus, decisions to discard what is unneeded are deferred, often indefinitely. If employees are not compelled by organizational mandate to do otherwise, the stored records may never be reviewed and are simply forgotten. In short, records retention is an extra work task, and storing and retaining inactive records is less trouble (and sometimes even cheaper, at least in the short run) than purging them.

As a result, in organizations in which the retention of records is unrestrained, the records simply languish. This situation happens day after day, year after year, decade after decade, in organizations everywhere. As a practical matter, this unfettered accumulation of records is the reason that records retention is needed.

Status of Organizational Retention Programs

Although records retention dominates professional practice in RIM in the U.S., this emphasis has not resulted in high-quality programs among governmental and business organizations. In fact, anything resembling success in records retention continues to elude many, perhaps most organizations. Success in records retention may be viewed thusly:

The organization is retaining only those records needed for some purpose, while all other records are systematically destroyed as soon as they are no longer needed, immediately upon the expiration of their approved retention periods.

Managing the Life Cycle of Information Assets

As illustrated in Figure 3.1, the concept of records retention is based on the fact that information, as an organizational asset, has a *life cycle*. Although a small percentage of organizational information never loses its value, the value of most information tends to decline over time until it has no further value to anyone for any purpose. The value of nearly all business information is greatest soon after it is created or received, for a few days, weeks, or months. It is highly active during this time, but generally remains active for only a short time—one to three years or so—after which its importance and usage declines. The record then makes its life cycle transition to a semi-active and finally to an inactive state. At this point, many inactive records can be safely discarded at little or no risk to their owners.

Some inactive information, however, requires continuing retention in order to satisfy some legal or business requirement. Deciding when these phases of the information life cycle occur, deciding whether and when destroying the records will be in the organization's best interest, and putting into place all that is required to make the life cycle management program happen is what records retention is all about.

Benefits of Records Retention

Unless organizations have a well-developed and properly implemented records retention program, they will have a greatly impaired capability to accomplish the following key objectives:

- **Comply with laws and regulations** – First and foremost, organizations are obliged to comply with the law. Both business and governmental organizations are legally required to comply with numerous laws and regulations requiring certain of their records to be retained for specified periods of time. U.S. federal

**The Information
Life Cycle and
Data Access**

Figure 3.1

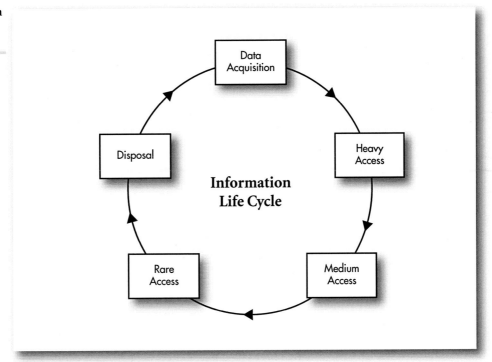

Source: Data from Jim Lee, "Reduce the Cost of Compliance," *SMS* 8, no. 5 (2003).

laws and regulations as well as those promulgated by other jurisdictions in which
the organization conducts business are included. The only way to ensure that the
organization is complying with these requirements is to perform proper legal
research to locate these laws and regulations, incorporate them into the ***retention periods*** for the ***records series*** to which they apply, and faithfully implement
the ***retention periods*** by destroying the records on schedule.

- **Control the growth of records** – Various RIM studies indicate that growth rates
  for paper records typically range between 5 and 10 percent each year, while the
  growth of electronic records generally falls between 20 and 60 percent each year
  and sometimes even higher. Unless organizations have a comprehensive records
  retention program under which useless records are destroyed, they have no
  effective means of controlling the growth of their records. Other studies indicate
  that most organizations retain somewhere between 30 and 60 percent more
  records than are necessary to conduct their business. Most organizations could,
  immediately, discard at least 30 percent of their oldest records and never miss
  them! However, without a good records retention program, organizations simply have no way of addressing the problem of unrestrained retention and the
  resulting uncontrolled growth of records. The ultimate result is higher storage
  and maintenance costs.

- **Reduce records storage costs** – Today, many organizations do not know how
  much they are spending to store and maintain their records. Moreover, many

managers and executives consider these costs to be unmanageable, in the sense that they are simply part of the overall cost of doing business. Finally, many organizations have no plan in place to manage, and reduce, these costs. However, if an organization is, in fact, retaining 30 to 60 percent more records than it needs, proportionate cost reductions can be expected from disposing of the redundant information. Although these costs can be difficult to quantify, they are real and should be taken seriously as a management issue.

- **Facilitate litigation risk avoidance** – Today, every organization that delivers products or services of any kind (or that even hires employees) is faced with threats to its assets as a result of liability lawsuits. Even if an organization has committed no acts that could incriminate it in litigation, the act of complying with document discovery orders can be very burdensome and expensive. In fact, some studies have reported that pretrial discovery, including disclosure of records, accounts for as much as half the cost of civil litigation. Liability lawsuits are often decided on the basis of old records—records that need not exist if they had been properly destroyed under a formal records retention program. From a litigation risk avoidance perspective, an organization's goal should be to retain only those records needed to conduct business, comply with the law, and meet reasonable needs for the preservation of archival documentation. All other records should be systematically destroyed under a records retention program based on retention periods that can be demonstrated to be reasonable—not too long and not too short. Absent any actual or pending litigation or government investigation, such disposal is entirely legal and proper.

The Business Case for Records Retention

The basic premise of records retention is that it is in the best interest of organizations to dispose of records as soon as they are no longer useful or their retention is no longer required by law and that this destruction should occur under authority of a formal records retention program. What, then, is the essence of the business case supporting this premise? The logic behind the business case for records retention can be summarized by the answers to the following questions:

- How much does storing and maintaining all its records, both physical and electronic, cost the organization? When building the business case, the total cost of records storage and maintenance must include the cost of administering the information over its entire life cycle, not just the cost of the storage media or other equipment and facilities in which the records are housed.

- How much of the current volume of stored records is useless? That is, it is inactive and is no longer needed for any purpose.

- What would be the costs and benefits of disposing of all such records? On the other hand, what will be the costs, risks, and benefits of not doing so?

- What has been the rate of growth in stored records in recent years, and what growth rates are forecast in the foreseeable future? How will this growth affect the overall storage situation, including the additional costs that must be borne?

- How could the systematic disposal of useless records contribute to better overall storage management—to the extent that records storage and retention is being currently undermanaged or even mismanaged? What costs and benefits would be quantifiable as a result of this disposal?

The answers to these questions constitute the essence of the business case for records retention. The main point, however, is that these answers are seldom known, as they are not studied and analyzed by most organizations. RIM specialists should work cooperatively with IT specialists to develop answers to these questions and then build the business case for enterprise-wide records retention. Doing so will provide the basis for a records retention program that rises to the level of best practice among organizations in this or any other country.

ISO 15489 and Records Retention

ISO 15489 is the global standard for records management that prominently address-es the issue of records retention. This standard prescribes technical guidelines for recordkeeping in all types of organizational settings, as well as practice guidelines for records managers throughout the world who are responsible for improving the quality of recordkeeping in their organizations. Section 8.3.6 of the standard addresses records retention. The standard states that:[1]

> *Records systems should be capable of facilitating and implementing decisions on the retention and disposition of records. It should be possible for these decisions to be made at any time in the existence of records, including during the design stage of records systems.*[2]

Common Mistakes in Records Retention

The main problems that prevent success in records retention are as follows:

- **Inadequate leadership** – Good leadership is the key to any management initia-tive, and records retention is no exception. Committed, sustained senior-level management support is required for a records retention program to be success-ful. Without such support, the program has inadequate authority, and systemat-ic records disposition never becomes an integrated component of the organiza-tion's business processes.[3]

- **Inadequate policies and procedures** – Frequently, the written policies and pro-cedures that inform employees what to do and how to do it in records retention are not very user friendly. Employees who create and/or retain records should be furnished with clear guidance concerning their responsibilities for records reten-tion and how to comply with them. Moreover, employees should be able to access these policies and procedures via the intranet and read them in 15 min-utes or so. At a minimum, policies are needed in the following areas:

- ◆ Records Retention – General Policy
- ◆ Records Retention at the Desktop Level
- ◆ Management and Retention of E-mail
- ◆ Software Applications: Records Retention Requirements
- ◆ Long-term Data Retention

- **Retention schedules poorly developed** – Although many organizations have *retention schedules,* they are frequently inadequate. Sometimes, the schedules are too general; in other cases, too detailed. More often, the schedules provide inadequate coverage for the organization's electronic records. In any case, where the schedules are poorly developed or out of date, the organization's employees are not provided with clear guidance concerning what to keep and how long to keep it.

- **Inadequate implementation strategy** – Implementation is the single biggest reason that retention programs fail.

Retention Schedule Development

First and foremost, best practice in records retention requires that retention schedules be fully tailored to the organization's own needs and requirements. Some organizations take the "quick and dirty" approach to schedule preparation. They attempt to copy the retention schedules of other organizations whose business is similar to their own. Or, they try to take a retention schedule published in a book and issue it as their own. Such practices are not recommended. Any good retention schedule must reflect the organization's own records, as well as a detailed assessment of the specific legal and business requirements to retain them. No short cut to developing a high-quality, fully customized retention schedule is available.

Responsibility for Schedule Preparation

Who should develop retention schedules? Should retention schedules be developed by the RIM staff (or by outside consultants) for the entire organization, or should schedule preparation be delegated to each major department or business entity?

Common practice among businesses is to take a centralized approach to the development of records retention schedules of enterprise-wide coverage. According to the Saffady benchmarking study, 74 percent of the participating companies assigned the responsibility for schedule preparation to the central RIM staff, while only 7 percent delegated the task to operating departments or business units. The remainder take a team or committee approach to schedule development; but in these situations, the effort is nearly always led by the organization's records manager and staff.[4]

The decentralized approach, in which operating departments are responsible for schedule development, is not popular (nor is it recommended), because of inconsistent quality and the fact that the job is better left for professional specialists. In order to develop retention schedules of organization-wide coverage that contain the type of guidance needed for a successful program, the schedules should be developed by experienced records managers or outside consultants.

A key failure of the Arthur Andersen accounting firm was an inadequate retention schedule. The firm assigned one of its senior partners (an accountant rather than a records manager) to prepare its retention schedule.[5] The end result was retention guidance that was not only vague and ambiguous but also fraught with legal deficiencies. To cite just one example, the policy provided that all documents be retained if a threat of litigation exists. However, the policy apparently did not define "threatened" litigation nor did it explicitly state whether suspension of document destruction would apply in cases involving a government investigation, whether formal or informal. These deficiencies proved to be key factors that led to Andersen's conviction and virtual demise. Therefore, although retention schedule development may not be "rocket science," it is a very specialized area of information management, and solid expertise is required to do it right.

Database for Schedule Preparation

Prior to beginning development of the retention schedules, a database *platform* should be selected for use during the data gathering, analysis, and draft stages of development. Once completed, the approved retention schedules will often be transferred for permanent maintenance to a RIM software system or to some other platform. However, during initial preparation, a suitable database tool should be used. In recent years, Microsoft® Access has been a popular tool for this purpose. This type of database provides excellent capabilities to manipulate fields and run various reports and queries during the drafting of the schedule. Typical database fields include the following:

- Department / subdepartment or function / subfunction
- Name of records series
- Series description
- Media type / format
- Production application
- Office of record (holder of record copy)
- Retention period (total retention)
- Legal citation(s) prescribing minimum retention
- Retention justification
- Notes / comments

Content, Type, and Format of Retention Schedules

If the purpose of a retention schedule is to provide instructions to employees concerning how long to keep the records for which they are responsible, what is the best method of defining and presenting this guidance to them? For appropriate content coverage, the retention schedules need to provide guidance for every separate and discrete type or category of record that is of operational importance or official character, regardless of format or media, and thus needs a specific retention period to provide for its life cycle disposition as a matter of organizational policy. In RIM practice, such categories are referred to as *records series*.

These records series need to be listed and described in separate sections of the schedules for each department or business process. Moreover, great care needs to be taken in the selection of terms identifying the records series, and in describing them clearly so that all readers of the schedules can properly apply the retention periods. With respect to type and format, organizations have two main choices: *departmental* or *functional retention schedules*. Both types are described next.

Departmental Retention Schedules

In traditional practice, records are inventoried at the records series level as they are maintained by each department, subdepartment, or other organizational entities. During the **records inventory**, data describing each records series is collected so that the series can be analyzed to determine its retention value and subsequently added to the schedules. During the inventory, the following data is typically gathered for each records series:

- Name of records series
- Brief description of the series, including its business function and purpose, its document or information content, and the characteristics of its usage over time
- Current retention practices for the series, including events that trigger the transition in its life cycle from active to semi-active and finally to an inactive state

Once these inventory data have been gathered for all records series in all departments, the process of retention analysis and schedule drafting can begin. **Departmental retention schedules** are typically formatted by preparing one schedule for each organizational entity, and one retention period for each records series listed and described within it. The result is a fully customized retention schedule, which provides precise guidance to all types of records maintained by each department.

For larger organizations, conducting a comprehensive records inventory often requires months of dedicated labor. Moreover, departmental schedules tend to be quite detailed and lengthy. Because each recordkeeping entity typically maintains from 5 to 25 or so records series, and because a large organization usually consists of at least 100 and often several hundred organizational units, departmental schedules frequently contain several thousand records series. Consequently, the schedules can be so lengthy that they become cumbersome to use. Moreover, they are more costly to develop and difficult to maintain, as they can quickly become outdated as a result of organizational changes.

For these reasons, the departmental approach to schedule development, based on a comprehensive records inventory, is increasingly viewed as impractical for larger organizations that are looking to simplify their retention practices to the maximum extent possible. For these organizations, **functional retention schedules** are often considered to be the best and most practical methodology.

Functional Retention Schedules

Functional schedules are typically developed at the business process level—one section of the schedule for each major functional area of the organization. The records series listed and described under each function are defined at the highest, most generic level possible. Rather than conduct detailed inventories at the subdepartment level, functional schedules can usually be developed by conducting a limited number of high-level interviews with designated business managers to identify the records categories for each of the major business functions. The end result of this approach is a much shorter retention schedule—one providing retention guidance for perhaps 200 to 500 (nearly always less than a thousand) records series related to a dozen or more major business functions. Thus, functional schedules are less costly to develop and are easier to maintain.

Functional schedules are not without their disadvantages, however. Large organizations are quite complex and they keep many kinds of records. In their zeal to shorten and simplify the schedules, developers often omit critical records series. Such omissions can create significant problems during implementation. To shorten and simplify retention schedules is a worthy goal, but not at the expense of skipping records for which retention policy guidance needs to be provided. In the organization's retention policies, users who are confronted with what to do about retaining records that are not listed on the schedules should be instructed to contact the RIM department to have the records appraised and possibly added to the schedules.

Despite these limitations, the increasing popularity of functional schedules is one of the biggest trends in retention scheduling today. According to the Saffady benchmarking study, functional schedules are clearly the preferred form of retention schedules among large companies. A total of 51 percent of the companies participating in the survey utilize this type of retention schedule, while only 25 percent use the departmental format. (The remaining 25 percent use a combination of both approaches.) With respect to whether the retention schedules are based on an inventory, the study revealed a nearly even split: 52 percent conducted no inventory to build its schedules, while 41 percent conducted a comprehensive inventory.[6]

Increasingly, the time and resources required to collect detailed records inventory data is not perceived to be worth the effort. Although functional schedules may be developed for smaller organizations, departmental schedules remain common practice. For larger ones, however, the functional approach will generally prove to be the most practical approach and is thus endorsed as best / recommended practice.

Records Series Descriptions

Records series appearing in retention schedules need to be listed and described in separate sections of the schedules for each department or business function to which they relate. Great care needs to be taken in the choice of terms identifying the records categories and describing them clearly, so that all readers of the schedules can readily identify the records and properly implement the retention periods. Some retention schedules, however, contain no series descriptions at all. They simply list each series name and show its required retention period. In departmental schedules, this type of schedule can sometimes be an acceptable practice, as the people in each department are knowledgeable about their own records and can readily identify the records series listed for their departments.

In functional schedules, however, series descriptions are generally necessary, as the entire schedule is open for use by all departments and employees. Thus, it is critical that readers of the schedule be able to clearly identify each series and understand its coverage, so that they can properly apply the retention instructions. In short, series descriptions are optional for departmental schedules but required for functional ones.

Office of Record Designations

Traditionally, many retention schedules include a *field* that designates the *office of record* for each records series. In RIM practice, the office of record is defined as the department responsible for maintaining the official or record copy of a particular type of record. The practice of including office of record designations in retention schedules is quite common. In the Saffady benchmarking study, 63 percent of the respondents indicated that these designations are included, while 37 percent indicated that they do not follow this practice.[7]

For departmental schedules, this practice is endorsed as it provides meaningful guidance for the readers who must make judgments concerning how to apply the schedules to their records. In many functional schedules, however, office of record designations are not shown. In these types of schedules, the record copies of designated series are being scheduled. The reader is to assume that the retention guidance applies to the record copy, unless otherwise indicated. Functional schedules are typically accompanied by narrative policies and procedures pertaining to the retention of duplicate records. Such policies typically grant employees the authority to dispose of duplicate copies at their discretion, provided, however, that the retention does not exceed that of the record copy.

Records Media Specified in Schedules

Whether and how to provide guidance in the retention schedules for the retention of records residing on various media types—paper, microfilm and electronic—is an issue that is treated differently in organizations. In the Saffady benchmarking study, 76 percent of the participating companies reported that they do not specify records media in their retention schedules, while the remaining 24 percent do specify records media. The most frequently cited justification for not specifying records media in retention schedules is that the schedules are designed to apply to all records, irrespective of media type.[8] In developing retention schedules, three options are available for providing guidance concerning different records media types:

1. **Multimedia schedules** – These types of schedules list all media types that are used for each records series, with separate retention periods for each media type. This option is most commonly used for traditional, departmental schedules, which typically provide the most detailed retention guidance for their readers.

2. **Media-independent schedules** – These types of schedules list each records series without reference to storage media. This option is most commonly used for functional schedules. This approach is based on the fact that any given series may, in fact, reside on several media formats simultaneously or during various stages of their life cycle, and retention policies should apply irrespective of media type.

3. **Media-specific schedules** – In this option, separate schedules are prepared for electronic records as well as for those on visible media. Under this option, readers know whether they are reading the schedule for electronic records as opposed to the one for physical records. This option is most commonly used when a separate schedule is created for the computer applications managed by IT departments.

Legally Compliant Schedules

Records retention must be about complying with the law—in letter, spirit, and *good faith*. This practice will be critical if the organization's retention practices should ever come under judicial scrutiny during discovery or other legal proceedings. However, developing legally compliant retention schedules can be a challenging undertaking. In at least 20,000 specific citations in U.S. law alone, some statute or regulation imposes a requirement to retain a certain type of record or information for a specified period of time. Sometimes however, no period of retention is specified in the law or regulation. The regulated parties are told that they must retain the information, but the law does not specify for how long. Moreover, locating these requirements can be difficult enough, but applying them is even more so, as someone in the organization must make interpretive judgments as to the meaning of the law and whether it pertains to specific records series.

Legal Retention Research Responsibility

Who should conduct legal retention research? Should it be done by attorneys, paralegals, RIM specialists, or outside consultants who specialize in this type of work? According to the Saffady benchmarking study, 61 percent of the participating companies assign the responsibility for conducting legal retention research to their own RIM staff. For the remaining companies, this task is assigned evenly to the legal department or to outside consultants (22 percent each).[9]

Many legal departments have neither the time nor the inclination to perform this type of research. Further, most research tends to have been performed when the organization's schedules were first developed and frequently no updates have since been done. In order to ensure that the schedules remain legally compliant, annual updates are recommended as best practice.

Relevant Citations for Retention Requirements

Given that some 20,000 retention requirements are in U.S. law alone, the task is to identify only those that impact the retention of one organization's records. A common misconception is that the retention of most business records is driven by government requirements. For the majority of records kept by most businesses, no specific government requirements mandate their retention. For organizations that are lightly regulated by the government, the total number of relevant retention requirements is often less than 100. For more heavily regulated businesses (i.e., pharmaceutical firms, financial institutions, insurance companies, etc.), the figure is higher.

Regardless of the number, locating all applicable requirements can be a difficult task. The best way to accomplish this task is to purchase a special records retention software program that contains them in a searchable database. For U.S. federal and state laws, a number of these software packages are available from commercial sources. Using this type of tool, searches are executed to locate the retention requirements applicable generally to business and governmental organizations, as well as those that apply to the particular lines of business operated by the organization. For samples of U.S. federal and state retention requirements, see Figures 3.2 and 3.3. Retention software databases should be considered as a starting point in conducting the legal research. The research often must be supplemented by consulting online legal databases or jurisdictional Web sites in order to obtain the latest laws and regulations.

These search tools will produce a long list of potentially relevant retention requirements with which regulated parties must comply. The records analyst must then read these laws and regulations and decide whether they apply to the organization as a regulated party and, if so, to which records series. In many cases, these judgments will be anything but straightforward. The reason is that these requirements tend to be written in a manner that satisfies the government's own regulatory objectives, but the language can make linking them to specific records series difficult. When faced with this dilemma, the best guidance is to apply these requirements to a particular records series only when the case is reasonably clear that they do, in fact, apply. Questions should be resolved by consulting with attorneys, business managers, or knowledgeable professional specialists.

The end result of this task is a list of all statutory and regulatory retention requirements with which the organization must comply, linked to the records series to which they apply. For the affected records series, the legally mandated, minimum retention periods have thus been established. The question then becomes whether business needs necessitate that the records be retained longer than the law requires.

Laws and Regulations Cited in Schedules

Some retention software is capable of showing the legal citations that impact the retention of particular records series in the retention schedule by posting them in a dedicated field alongside the series to which they apply. See Figure 3.4 for a sample of this methodology. According to the Saffady study, this practice is not common; 85 percent of the participating companies do not cite such laws and regulations in their schedules, while the remaining 15 percent do follow this practice.[10]

One of the most surprising findings from the Saffady benchmarking study is that most organizations do not cite laws and regulations in their retention schedules. Although some respondents indicated that such citations appear in supporting documentation to the schedules rather than on the schedules themselves, consider

Sample:
Summary of U.S.
Federal Retention
Requirements

Figure 3.2

Citation	Agency Or Jurisdiction	Records Covered And Citation Description	Retention Period/ Defining Action
8 CFR 274a.2(b)(2)(A)	U.S. Department of Justice – Immigration and Naturalization Service	Employers are required to maintain Form I-9, Employment Eligibility Verification Form which are documents that evidence the identity and employment eligibility of the individual	3 Years after the hire date or 1 year after termination, whichever is later
14 CFR 91.417	Federal Aviation Administration – Department of Transportation	Registered owners or operators of aircraft shall retain records of maintenance, preventative maintenance and alteration until superseded or 1 year after work is performed. Records of total time in serve and status of inspections, life-limited parts, overhauls shall be retained and transferred with aircraft when sold	Superseded /Life of Aircraft
26 CFR 1.471-2	U.S. Dept. of Treasury – Internal Revenue Service	Taxpayers are required to retain inventories and records related to disposition of the goods as will enable verification of their values	None Stated
26 CFR 1.6001-1	U.S. Dept. of Treasury – Internal Revenue Service	Corporations subject to income tax are required to keep books of account or records including inventories sufficient enough to establish gross income, deductions, credits, or other matters required to be shown in any return of such tax or information	Expiration of Limitation for Assessment & Extensions
26 CFR 31.6001-1	U.S. Dept. of Treasury – Internal Revenue Service	Retain sufficient to determine whether an employment tax liability is incurred. Records include copies of returns, schedules, statements, records of claimants (person claiming a refund/credit), records of employees (name/address, dates of service)	4 Years After due date of such tax
26 CFR 301.6058-1	U.S. Dept. of Treasury – Internal Revenue Service	Employers or plan administrators of funded deferred compensation plans (pension, annuity, stock bonus, profit-sharing, etc.) must keep available records substantiating all data and information required in the annual report forms, as well as information necessary to determine allowable deductions. Includes records related to qualification of the plan, financial7 condition of the trust, fund, or custodial or fiduciary account, and the operation of the plan	None Stated
Revenue Procedure 98-25	U.S. Dept. of Treasury – Internal Revenue Service	Taxpayer's records that are maintained within an Automatic Data Processing system. Records must provide sufficient information to support and verify entries made on the taxpayer's return and to determine the correct tax liability. Includes records within the meaning of section 1.6001-1	Expiration of Limitation for Assessment & Extensions
29 CFR 30.8	U.S. Dept. of Labor – Office of the Secretary of Labor	Each apprenticeship sponsors (employers or organizations) must keep adequate records of applicant qualifications, application, interviews, basis for selection or rejection; apprentice program including job assignments, compensation, hours of work and hours of training; any other compliance records; statement of affirmative action plan	5 Years
29 CFR 516.5	U.S. Dept. of Labor – Wage and Hour Division	Each employer shall preserve payroll or other records containing employee information, plans, trusts, employment contracts, collective bargaining agreements, total dollar volume of sales or business and total volume of goods purchased or received	3 Years From date of last entry
29 CFR 516.6	U.S. Dept. of Labor – Wage and Hour Division	Retain basic employment and earnings records including timekeeping records, wage rate tables, records of additions to or deductions from wages paid. Also included are customer orders, incoming or outgoing shipping or delivery records, as well as all bills of lading and all billings to customers	2 Years From date of last entry

Sample: Summary of U.S. Federal Retention Requirements—California

Figure 3.3

Citation	Agency Or Jurisdiction	Records Covered And Citation Description	Retention Period/ Defining Action
2 CCR 7287.0	Official California Code of Regulations Administration	Employers shall retain California Employer Information Reports (CEIR) [may also substitute Federal EEO-1 thru 6 reports], applicant identification records (data on race, sex, national origin) or statistical summaries of the collected information; complaints filed under this act shall be retained until final disposition.	2 Years Complaints – Final Disposition
8 CCR 3203	Official California Code of Regulations Industrial Relations	Every employer shall maintain workplace hazard inspection records and safety and health training documentation.	1 Year Medical – Duration of employment +
8 CCR 3204	Official California Code of Regulations Industrial Relations	Employers must retain employee (employees who have worked longer than 1 year) medical records for at least duration of employment plus 30 years (health insurance claims should be maintained separately). Employers must retain employee exposure records for 30 years, except that background to environmental (workplace) monitoring or measuring such as laboratory reports and worksheets, as long as the sampling results, collection methodology, description of analytical and mathematical methods used, and summary of other background data relevant to interpretation of results obtained are retained 30 years. Material safety data sheets are retained for 30 years. Records of chemical identity of substance or agent, where and when used to be retained 30 years (if not retained, then retain material safety data sheets). Analyses using exposure or medical records are maintained for 30 years.	30 Years Employee Exposure – 30 Years Laboratory Reports/Worksheets – 1 Year Material Safety Data Sheets – 30 Years Chemical Identity – 30 Years Analyses – 30 Years
8 CCR 5193	Official California Code of Regulations Industrial Relations	Employers shall maintain a sharps injury log (bloodborne pathogens) for 5 years from the date of the exposure incident; employee occupational exposure records for at least duration of employment plus 30 years; and safety training records for 3 years from date on which the training occurred	Sharps Injury Log – 5 Years from date of exposure incident Occupational Exposure – Duration of Employment + 30 Safety Training – 3 Years from date of training
8 CCR 5208	Official California Code of Regulations Industrial Relations	Building and facility owners shall maintain records of information concerning presence of asbestos for duration of ownership and transferred to successive owners. Employers shall retain records of measurements taken to monitor employee exposure to asbestos for 30 years; objective data for exempted operations for the duration of employer's reliance upon such objective data; employee medical surveillance data for duration of employment plus 30 years; employee asbestos safety training records duration of employment plus 1 year.	Asbestos Facility Information – Duration of Ownership Asbestos Exposure – 30 Years Asbestos Safety Training – 30 Years
8 CCR 11040	Official California Code of Regulations Department of Industrial Relations	Employers in the professional, technical, clerical, mechanical occupations shall keep accurate information on each employee including, name, address, occupation, birth date, time records showing dates and hours worked, total wages paid each payroll period, and incentive plan formula.	3 Years
8 CCR 11070	Official California Code of Regulations Department of Industrial Relations	Employers in the mercantile industry shall keep accurate information on each employee including, name, address, occupation, birth date, time records showing dates and hours worked, total wages paid each payroll period, and incentive plan formula.	3 Years
8 CCR 14300.33	Official California Code of Regulations Industrial Relations	Employers must save Cal / OSHA Form 300, the privacy case list (if one exists), the Cal / OSHA Form 300A, and the Cal / OSHA Form 301 Incident Reports.	5 Years Following the end of calendar year

Sample:
Records Retention
Schedule
(Showing U.S.
Federal, State, and
International
Citations)

Figure 3.4

Environmental / Health and Safety Administration
Safety / Industrial Hygiene / Medical

Business Process / Subprocess Record Series Title / Legal Citations	Record Series Description	Total Retention
Environmental Complaints	Complaints from citizens concerning matters related to environmental health and safety. Records show the company's investigation and/ or response or actions taken	Current Year + 7
Legal Citations: 40 CFR 717.15		
Fire Prevention / Evacuation Plans	Plans and procedures established to protect employees in the event of emergencies	Superseded + 3
Legal Citations: 29 CFR 1910.38; Canada: Canada Labour Code, Occupational Health and Safety Regulations, SOR/86-304 17.8(2), 17.9(2), 17.10(2)		
Material Safety Data Sheets / Hazardous Warning Labels	Material safety data sheets and labels showing the presence and use of substances that may be related to employee health and safety in the plant	Active + 30
Legal Citations: 29 CFR 1910.1020(d); 40 CFR 721.125; MI: MCL 408.1014a; NC: NCGS 95-192; TX: TCA Health 502.005; Canada: Canada Labour Code, Occupational Health and Safety Regulations, SOR/86-304 10.3		
Medical Records – Employee	Records showing the condition / status of employees' health during their tenure with the company. May also show exposure to hazardous substances in the workplace; includes records related to employee audio metric test results and related records	Duration of Employment + 30
Legal Citations: 29 CFR 1910.95; 29 CFR 1910.1020(d); 29 CFR 1910.1030(h); 29 CFR 1910.120(f)(8)(I); 29 CFR 1910.1048; MI: MACR 325.60126; Canada: Canada Labour Code, Occupational Health and Safety Regulations, SOR/86-304 15.11; SOR/86-304 7.3; Alberta: Occupational Health and Safety Act, Chemical Hazards Regulation, AR 393/88; Occupational Health and Safety Act, Noise Regulation, AR 314/81; Mexico: Norma Mexican Official NOM-011-STPS-2001		
Occupational Injuries and Illnesses Records	Includes reports of accidents and illnesses related to employment in the workplace; includes safety and health committee recommendations for safety-related suggestions	Current Year + 5
Legal Citations: 29 CFR 1904.4; 29 CFR 1904.33; MI: MCL 418.805; MCL 408.1061; S. C. Code Regs. 71-304; NC: NCG 95-143; NCGS 97-92 MN: Minn. R. 5208.0050; TX: 28 TAC 120.1; Canada: Canada Labour Code, Occupational Health and Safety Regulations, SOR/86-304 15.11; Alberta: Occupational Health and Safety Act, First Aid Regulation, AR 48/2000		
Safety Plans, Policies and Procedures	Official copies of safety plans, policies, and procedures developed to enhance safety in the workplace and ensure compliance with government safety laws and regulations; includes hazardous communications program	Superseded + 5
Legal Citations: 29 CFR 1910.1200; 40 CFR 721.125		

including them in the schedules, so that all readers can see that the research was performed and that the retention periods are compliant with them.

Legally Valid Retention Periods

Once legally mandated retention requirements have been satisfied, determining how long to keep each records series necessarily involves making choices.[11] Decision makers can choose between long and short retention periods for every records series. In this respect, making records retention decisions is a judgmental, somewhat arbitrary process. How, then, can records managers bring some rational thinking to these judgments? The goal is to develop retention periods that are in the organization's best interest. As recommended practice, these judgments should be based on the following eight principles:

1. **Meet the test of reasonableness** – Assuming that all retention periods are legally compliant, the next most important thing is that they meet the test of reasonableness. That retention periods should always be formulated so that they can be defended as reasonable from both business and legal points of view is the golden rule of retention decision-making. To meet the test of reasonableness, retention periods should be not too long and not too short.

2. **Base retention periods on content value** – The primary determinant of how long any series of records should be retained is the value of its content and how this value changes over time, irrespective of the storage media on which the records reside. Media format issues are indeed important for purposes of satisfying retention requirements. The organization is at liberty to choose whether paper, microfilm, or some digital option would be the optimum storage solution for any given set of records and at any given stage of the life cycle. However, retention decisions should be based primarily on content value rather than media type or format.

3. **Apply the retention options strategy** – When in a quandary about how long to keep a particular records series, start by identifying the shortest and then the longest retention periods that would be feasible. Then, narrow these options until a comfortable and reasonable decision is reached. Often, the optimum retention period will fall somewhere in between the two extremes.

4. **Appraise the records to determine their value** – The *records appraisal* methodology has been regarded as best practice for retention decision-making since it was first articulated by archivists during the 1940s, and it is still valid today. This concept is based on identifying the several uses or values possessed by each records series and then making predictive judgments as to when, over time, these values decline or expire such that disposal can be considered as a wise business decision. Under classic appraisal methodology, a records series may possess one, several, or all the following values: (a) administrative or operational value, (b) legal value, (c) fiscal value, and (4) research or historical value. Each records

series should be appraised to determine whether these values are present, and whether and when they expire. The retention period would thus be based on these judgments.

5. **Consider cost/risk/benefit issues** – The cost/risk/benefit methodology holds that the retention value of any particular records series should be based on an estimate of the costs, risks, and benefits of retaining records for various time periods. This methodology views decisions to retain or discard records as being no different from any other business decision. Although this methodology is valid, quantifying these costs, risks, and benefits for every records series maintained by the organization is simply not practical. Situations do occur, however, when this type of analysis should be performed.

6. **Avoid the every conceivable contingency syndrome** – Retention periods should not be selected in an effort to accommodate every conceivable need for information at any future time, no matter how remote the probability of the need might be. In cases where this approach is the basis for retention decision-making, excessive retention periods are sure to be the result.

7. **Adopt conservative retention policies where warranted** – Information should be retained if a reasonable probability exists that it will be needed at some future time to support some legitimate business or legal requirement and if the consequences of its absence would be substantial. Where warranted, records retention policies should be conservative in the sense that they do not expose the organization to excessive risk. The goal of the retention program should not be total risk avoidance, but if the only gain from short retention is savings in space, exposing the organization to inordinate risk is not justified to attain this reward.

8. **Arrive at a consensus of opinion among responsible persons** – In order to arrive at reasonable and valid retention periods, soliciting the opinions of persons most knowledgeable about the use and value of the information and how they change over time is important. Such persons typically include managers and professional specialists having direct responsibility for the records, as well as attorneys, tax specialists, archivists, and others.

Average Distribution of Retention Periods

Having developed legally compliant and reasonable retention periods for all records series in the draft schedules, performing a quick analysis to determine the average distribution of these periods is a good idea. As Figure 3.5 shows, for the large majority of an organization's records, the average retention period will fall into the four- to seven-year range. Retention periods of this duration are needed if the retention schedules are to be an effective instrument in controlling the growth of the organization's records. Moreover, retention periods of this range are justified by the fact that 90+ percent of all document references are to records that are three years old or less. In other words, older records are sometime needed, but they aren't referenced very often.

Common /
Optimum
Distribution of
Retention Periods

Figure 3.5

Retention Range	Percentage of Records Series
Less than 1 year	10% or less
1 to 3 years	10 to 20%
4 to 5 years	20 to 30%
6 to 7 years	20 to 30%
8 to 10 years	10 to 20%
11 to 30 years	5 to 10%
20 years to permanent	10% or less

Expression and Justification of Retention Periods

A common practice is to include not only the total retention periods for all records series in the schedules, but also retention periods reflecting the storage phases in the life cycle of each series. For example, schedules for paper media typically show a period of active or office retention, as well as a period of storage or records center retention. Similarly, schedules developed for electronic media show an online, near-line, or off-line retention as well as the total retention.

This practice has declined in popularity in recent years and is not generally recommended. The most important reason is that the total retention is properly construed as an expression of mandatory policy, subject to audit compliance, while the active or storage retentions may properly be considered as *optional guidance*, rather than a mandatory requirement. Further, in functional schedules, only the total retention is usually shown.

Some retention schedules are formatted to include fields to designate the justification for the retention period assigned to each records series. Typically, three retention justifications are used:

1. **Legal requirement** – This justification is assigned to records series that must be retained as required by one or more laws or regulations, and the retention is not in excess of the required time.

2. **Business judgment** – This justification is assigned to records series in cases where the determining factor for the retention period was a business judgment made by the organization's management.

3. **Common business practice** – This justification is assigned to records series in cases where the retention period is one that is commonly used by other organizations.

Although these retention justifications can sometimes be useful in facilitating the review of draft schedules, they are not recommended for the final, issued schedules.

Management Approval of Retention Schedules

Once the organization has developed a set of fully customized retention schedules for all departments or business functions, the draft schedules should be submitted for review and approval. Approval should be secured from senior management officials who have a direct, legitimate interest in enterprise records retention matters. These officials include:

- **Departmental managers** – By approving the retention periods for the records for which they have management responsibility, these managers are giving their consent that the retention periods meet the operational requirements of their business units.

- **Legal counsel** – By approving the retention periods for all records listed in the schedules, these attorneys are giving their consent that the retention periods are sufficient to meet the legal needs of the organization. In other words, the retention periods comply with the law, provide the organization with the information it needs to defend itself against lawsuits or to prosecute claims or lawsuits brought against other parties, and meet other legal needs.

- **Chief fiscal officers** – By approving the retention periods for financial records, these managers are giving their consent that the retention periods are sufficient to meet the organization's audit requirements and other fiscal accountability needs.

When retention schedules are developed in accordance with the principles discussed here, they should rise to the level of best practice.

Notes

1. International Organization for Standardization, ISO 15489-1:2001, *International Standard: Information and Documentation – Records Management – Part 1: General* (Geneva, Switzerland: ISO, 2001).

2. Ibid., 10.

3. Robert Williams, *Electronic Records Management Survey: A Call to Action* (Chicago: Cohasset, Inc., 2004), 19.

4. William Saffady, *Records and Information Management: A Benchmarking Study of Large U.S. Industrial Companies* (Lenexa, KS: ARMA International, 2002), 35.

5. See David Stephens, "Lies, Corruption, and Document Destruction," *The Information Management Journal* 36, no. 5 (September / October 2002): 25.

6. Saffady, *A Benchmarking Study*, 37.

7. Ibid., 39.

8. Saffady, *A Benchmarking Study*, 40.

9. Ibid., 34.

10. Saffady, *A Benchmarking Study*, 35.

11. See, for example, David Stephens, "Making Records Retention Decisions: Practical and Theoretical Considerations," *Records Management Quarterly* (January 1988).

Chapter 4

Electronic Records Retention: Managing the Data Life Cycle

What happens to computer data as it ages? Does the value of data increase or decrease as time passes? Why are most organizations keeping more data, and keeping it longer than ever before? What conditions indicate when data should be retired or discarded? Do storage management requirements change as data ages through its life cycle?[1] These fundamental questions form the basis of *electronic records retention*, sometimes also referred to as *information life cycle management*. In the world of paper records, these questions are ones that records managers have addressed for decades. However, they are seldom addressed, at least comprehensively for all computer applications, by IT departments. Records managers must work cooperatively with IT to apply the principles of records retention to manage the life cycle of computer-based records.

Electronic records retention is defined as the act of retaining computer-based records in digital format for specified, predetermined periods of time, commensurate with their value, with subsequent disposal or permanent preservation as a matter of official organizational policy. Like all records, computer data is a highly valued asset to its owners during the early stages of its life cycle. If retained too long, however, the data can become a liability, often a significant one. The management challenge, then, is to manage the information life cycle so that the organization's electronic records remain an asset and never become a liability.[2] As a practical matter, then, electronic records retention is about "getting rid of dead data as soon as it dies." As shown in Figure 4.1, the concept of information life cycle management is required to get rid of dead data, of which electronic records retention is a key component.

This subject is one of the most challenging and important issues in RIM today. If records managers presume to operate enterprise records retention programs at an advanced level, based on best professional practices, they must achieve two main goals:

- Bring records retention to every desktop computer throughout the organization,
- Bring records retention to every IT-managed production application that requires it.

This chapter addresses both of these key RIM issues.

**The Information
Life Cycle and
Data Access**

Figure 4.1

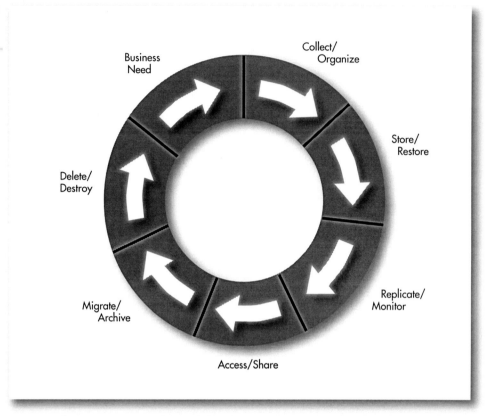

SOURCE: Data from George Symons, in "Take Control of E-mail: Protect the Surging Tide," SMS 8, Issue 4 (2003).

Current Status of Electronic Records Retention

Despite some encouraging recent trends, the current status of electronic records retention is not favorable. The large majority of computer applications now installed were designed without a preconfigured methodology to eliminate data as soon as its retention is no longer required. The situation at the desktop level is no better. To summarize the findings from two recent studies:

- According to a survey of electronic RIM practices conducted by Cohasset Associates, 47 percent of the respondents reported that their organizations have not included electronic records in their retention schedules.[3]

- According to the Saffady benchmarking study, 73 percent of the participating companies indicated that further work was needed to achieve their goals in electronic records retention. In most of the companies surveyed, retention policies for electronic records are less than comprehensive, where they exist at all. Moreover, 81 percent of the respondents indicated that routines for automatic purging of data, under authority of the retention schedules, have not yet been incorporated into their computer applications. Only 17 percent indicated that their companies have modified one or more application programs (other than e-mail) to delete electronic records automatically when their retention periods have elapsed.[4]

Thus, electronic records retention is now in its embryonic stage. It will be, therefore, a new initiative for most organizations and their IT departments, and its success will require close cooperation between RIM and IT specialists. As new initiatives, electronic records retention projects must usually be justified based on a solid business case. In making this case, some key factors will be presented that detail why electronic records retention is an idea whose time has come—one that is in the best interest of most organizations and their IT departments.

Key Trends in Data Storage

Fred Moore, a leading specialist on data storage management, has summarized some key trends in computer data storage that are of direct relevance to why electronic records retention is needed:

- Storage capacity is growing at over 60 percent per year while performance improves at less than 10 percent per year.
- Average annual storage demand rates for all platforms is 50 to 60 percent.
- The value and criticality of data is increasing exponentially while the percentage of data that is actually managed is declining.
- Storage device capacity is growing more than ten times faster than device performance.
- Storage is growing faster than disks are getting cheaper.
- More data is being accumulated for longer periods of time without effective management of its life cycle.[5]

Just these few observations should be enough to lead most observers to conclude that IT departments need to do something about getting rid of dead data as soon as it dies. In a pithy turn of phrase, Moore opines that "accumulating data indefinitely without implementing retirement or retention policies can turn *storage management* into *waste management!*"[6]

Explosive Growth of Electronic Records

Although published accounts vary, the quantity of computer data is exploding, in magnitudes that are unprecedented in organizational history. As indicated in Chapter 1, perhaps the most substantive recent analysis of this matter is the now-famous "How Much Information" study, which was conducted by the University of California, Berkeley. The study found that hard drive capacity and server capacity are doubling each year, while PC disk drives are also experiencing a 100 percent annual growth.[7] Another study by the META Group reported that relational databases are growing at an even greater rate of 125 percent each year.[8]

In the face of this deluge, storage specialists must continually revise their definitions of what constitutes a large volume of data. Just a few years ago, a data warehouse
or transactional database that approached a ***terabyte*** was considered big. Today, "big"
means tens of terabytes. Moreover, the evidence suggests that the explosive growth in
digital storage requirements will continue unabated. According to one estimate, the
explosion in both individual and organizational data that will occur during the next
five years will dwarf all previous estimates of storage growth. The world will need to
store and manage more than 10,000 terabytes of digi-
tized information by 2005. This amount equates to 50
times the amount being managed today.[9]

Major Factors in Growth of Computer Data

- The rapid and accelerating digitization of business processes and the records and information that support them
- The greater capacity of data storage systems (60+ percent annual growth)
- The corresponding declining cost-per-***megabyte*** (declining at 30 to 40 percent annually).[10]

Data Storage *Mis*management

How have IT departments responded to this explosion of
data? By nearly all accounts, the most common response
has been to "buy a bigger electronic warehouse"; that is,
they have purchased additional storage capacity.
However, such a response is counter-productive in that
it may inhibit the implementation of more effective data
management policies. At worst, the unrestrained acquisition of additional storage
resources may set IT on a collision course with the future.[11] Buying a bigger warehouse
merely compounds the problem, because additional storage hardware requires additional staff support (which is the major component of storage costs), as well as other
resources required to administer the storage function. This situation has been characterized as the classic "catch -22" scenario for IT departments, but it has been the all-
too-common practice for decades.[12] In other words, the ever-lower cost to generate digital content and the continually lower costs to store and retrieve data make the growth
of digital content an "event of infinite duration."[13]

In many IT environments, the data storage management function is executed
inefficiently, and these inefficiencies can be very costly, particularly for larger organizations. According to the *InfoWorld* annual storage survey, "at this moment, no
aspect of enterprise computing deserves more attention than storing and maintaining corporate data."[14] The report states that data storage is no longer relegated to the
sidelines of IT; in fact, it has been elevated to top priority status in many IT departments. Consider the notion that the probability of reusing data falls by 50 percent
after the data is three days old. After 30 days since creation, the probability of reuse
normally falls to below a few percentage points.[15] In other words, the electronic storage repositories of many computing environments have been filled to capacity, leaving no room for new incoming data, and a significant percentage of the stored data
is semi-active or inactive.

With the capacity of storage devices increasing at 60 percent or more each year
and storage prices falling at 30 to 40 percent per year, many IT specialists assume,
erroneously, that no valid business case exists for electronic records retention. In fact,
the *reverse* is true! The situation is analogous to closets, basements, and attics where
most people tend to use as much storage space as they have available. Organizations

and their computing environments are, fundamentally, no different. Thus, the large annual increases in media capacity, coupled with decreases in the cost of storage, combine to create a virtually unlimited demand for, and consumption of, data storage. Simply stated, virtually unlimited storage capacity virtually guarantees the unrestrained retention of unused and useless data for indefinite periods of time.

Cost-Benefit Considerations

For IT departments, the fundamental problem is that the total cost of data ownership (TCO) continues to rise, even while media costs continue to decline. According to the Gartner Group, as much as two-thirds of IT budgets are now allocated to data storage management.[16] When asked to rank their top storage priorities in a recent survey, 71 percent of the respondents cited cost reduction. More than 40 percent indicated their top priority to be optimizing the allocation of data storage across the various storage platforms.[17] Electronic records retention can contribute to both goals.

As noted earlier, the cost of management and support staff constitutes the major component of storage costs. In order to arrive at a quick calculation of the total cost of data ownership over its entire life cycle, records managers and data storage specialists can use a simple formula that estimates these costs based on the acquisition costs of storage hardware and software. In published accounts, these cost ratios vary, as follows:

- For every dollar spent on acquiring storage hardware, another $5 to $7 will be required to operate those devices over their useful life.[18]

- For every $1 per megabyte spent on disk storage, the total spent in managing that storage ranges from $3 to $8 per megabyte per year.[19]

- The cost of managing storage hardware ranges from two to ten times the acquisition cost of the storage hardware.[20]

Other formulas employ more detailed multipliers used to calculate the cost of the labor to administer the storage function based on the hardware and software costs in specific storage environments:

- In direct-access storage environments, for every dollar spent on hardware and software, $5.00 is spent on support staff.[21]

- In storage area network (SAN) environments, the ratio is $1 to $1.[22]

Regardless of the specific formula used, records managers and data storage specialists should work together to arrive at valid figures for the following:

- The TCO across the enterprise

- The quantity of inactive data that may be subject to immediate purging during the first and subsequent years of retention implementation

- The cost of retention implementation

- The quantifiable and nonquantifiable costs of failure to address the data life cycle management issue

Ten years ago, the cost-per-megabyte was around $15; today it has declined to less than a dollar.[23] Annual data retention costs typically range from $0.45 to $0.55 per megabyte. Moving data to an appropriate storage platform based on usage and value at various stages of the life cycle can reduce these costs by half.[24] Purging useless data can reduce them even more. Let's consider a couple of common data storage scenarios, in the context of their implications for electronic records retention:

- **Avoidance of storage hardware costs** – Because of growth in data storage requirements, an organization plans to acquire a disk drive at an acquisition cost of $10,000. If the annual cost of operating this device is $5 to $7 for every dollar spent on the hardware, the resulting cost range would be $50,000 to $70,000 per year. However, because this piece of storage hardware would remain in service for approximately five years, the total cost of ownership over its service life would approach a quarter of a million dollars. What if the organization is able to control the growth of its electronic records so that this $10,000 investment is not needed in the first place? *Cost-avoidance* is a management concept whereby funding for a proposed system or project is justified based on the supposition that immediate acceptance will be less costly than a future alternative. Because the organization did not have to spend $10,000 initially, the organization avoided spending $250,000 over five years. In other words, per every $10,000 in storage hardware costs, a good electronic records retention program can return $50,000 to $70,000 annually![25]

- **Cost savings resulting from better allocation of storage resources** – Consider an organization that has 24 terabytes of data residing on its high-end storage arrays, but only 17 terabytes actually require very high performance and availability. Thus, the organization migrates the remaining 7 terabytes of less critical data to *near-line storage* servers, which deliver less performance and availability but cost one-fourth the price of high-end storage. By redeploying the 7 terabytes of less critical storage at a cost of $140,000, the organization frees up $560,000 of high-end storage, for a net immediate payback of $420,000 and an effective return-on-investment (ROI) of 200 percent. Moreover, the newly freed space at the high-end will be needed soon because the organization's total data storage requirements are growing at a rate of 65 percent or more per year.[26]

Thus, the cost-effectiveness of better data life cycle management through a retention methodology is demonstrable, at least in many scenarios. The better electronic records retention can manage the life cycle of data, the greater the returns will be, in both hard and soft dollars.

Information Life Cycle Management

As defined by the Storage Networking Industry Association, *information life cycle management (ILM)* is comprised of the "policies, processes, practices, and tools used to align the business value of information with the most appropriate and cost-effective

IT infrastructure from the time information is conceived through its final disposition."[27] As shown in Figure 4.2, ILM can contribute to a number of data management issues, including better data availability, archiving and backup, recovery, and regulatory compliance.

Joe Tucci, CEO of EMC, one of the world's leading data storage management companies, had this to say about the concept of ILM:

> *There's never been a better time than now for information life cycle management because the growth of information—propelled by business continuity, compliance and the proliferation of unstructured content such as rich media and e-mail—is far outpacing the growth of IT budgets. ILM helps companies around the world deal with this growth in data while lowering costs for sharing, managing and protecting the company's valuable information assets.*[28]

In its public announcements, EMC has embraced the goal of an application-centric data life cycle management solution, coupled with finding the lowest-cost form of media, consistent with the value of the data, for every stage of the life cycle, from creation to deletion.[29] EMC's life cycle management products are targeted at companies that are not managing electronic records in the same way as paper records. Thus, the firm has introduced major enhancements into its ILM software suite.[30]

Electronic records retention is at the core of the ILM concept, and records managers must play a key role in working with IT specialists to make it a reality. However, according to an ***electronic records management*** survey conducted by Cohasset Associates, 67

Top Problems Information Life Cycle Management Can Help*

Figure 4.2

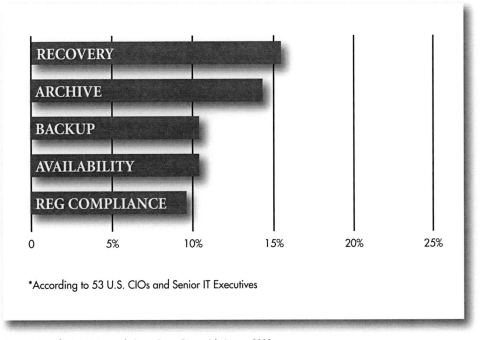

*According to 53 U.S. CIOs and Senior IT Executives

SOURCE: Data from EMC Research Group Focus Groups July-August, 2003.

percent of the respondents reported that they do not believe their organization's IT staff understand the concept of life cycle management of electronic records.[31] Records managers must work with IT specialists to help implement data life cycle management through a retention strategy.

Every life cycle has its stages, and information is no exception. The several stages of the information life cycle have been variously defined by a number of authors, most notably by Fred Moore in a series of articles in *Computer Technology Review*. Moore delineates four stages in the data life cycle, with the probability of reuse *(reference activity)* of stored data decreasing during each stage, as follows:

1. **Active stage** – This stage frequently lasts for 30 days and requires high-performance disk storage. Data access probability: >.5.

2. **Reference stage** – This stage typically lasts for 60 days and usually requires disk and automated tape storage. Data access probability: >.1.

3. **Archival stage** – This stage frequently lasts up to seven years and sometimes longer. Storage solutions range from automated to nonautomated magnetic tape, although the new class of archival disks for fixed-content storage (ATA disks, 160 and 320GB) are gaining in popularity. Data access probability: <.01.

4. **Delete / destroy stage** – The end of the data lifecycle; data access probability: <.001.[32]

For an illustration of data reference patterns over time, see Figure 4.3. Variables in the information life cycle include age, last access, last modification, creation date, and

Data Reference Patterns Over Time

Figure 4.3

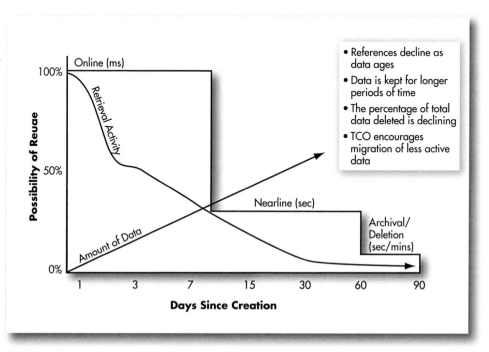

SOURCE: Data from Fred Moore, in "Cradle-to-Grave Storage Managment Now a Reality." *Computer Technology Review* 23, no. 1, January 2003.

other content-based ***attributes***. Effective data life cycle management requires proper classification and allocation of storage resources as follows:

- Data must be allocated and distributed across the storage systems in accordance with life cycle policies.
- The appropriate storage ***repository*** must be matched to the value of the data.
- Data must be on the right storage platform at the right time. For example, some fixed-content data may be relegated to storage that costs about 4 cents per megabyte. Other less active data may then be moved to a penny-per-megabyte repository.
- The entire data life cycle should be automated through the use of enforceable retention rules.[33]

Electronic Records Retention and Data Life Cycle Management Capabilities

- Identification of data aging rates, access requirements, protection levels, and data values and how they change over time
- Development of data retention and storage policies and procedures prescribing where data should be stored based on its changing value over its life cycle
- Automatic migration of aging data onto optimum storage platforms based on its value and life cycle requirements
- Storage of retired data as per the retention policy[34]

Figure 4.4 illustrates data management through the several stages of the information life cycle. Figure 4.5 shows a similar illustration of the allocation of data storage through the several stages of the information life cycle, but in a multi-tier hierarchy of storage resources.

Data life cycle and retention policies and rules should be established to control which data will remain in what storage resource and for how long and where it will be stored in the next stage of the life cycle. The rules should govern the migration of data through the storage hierarchy, with ultimate deletion of expired data.[35]

Data Management Through the Stages of the Information Life Cycle

Figure 4.4

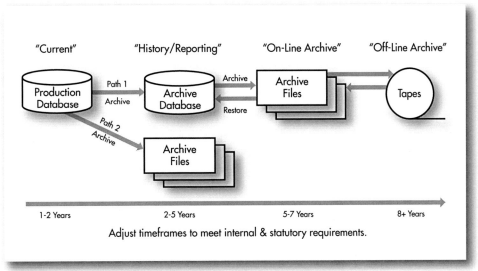

Adjust timeframes to meet internal & statutory requirements.

SOURCE: Data from Jim Lee, "Reduce the Cost of Compliance," *SMS* 8, Issue 5 (May 2003).

ILM Stage Allocation in Multi-tier Hierarchy

Figure 4.5

In an ILM system, enterprise data are moved to different tiers of storage depending on the business value of the information the data contains.

	Classification A Long mission-critical life; long retention	Classification B Short mission-critical life; long retention	Classification C Vital but not mission- critical; short retention
Tier 1 High-performance fiber channel or SCSI, synchronous mirrors, off-site mirroring, "incremental" backups	2 years	1 month	1 week
Tier 2 Mid-performance SCSI, synchronous mirrors, periodic snapshots to ATA, daily backups	2 years	1 month	
Tier 3 ATA for primary storage, weekly backup	3 years	1 year	1 year
Tier 4 Fixed-content disk storage, tape archive	6 years	7 years	
	Disposal	Disposal	Disposal

Source: Data from Leon Erlanger, "Information from Start to Finish," *InfoWorld,* 6 June 2005.

The Desktop and Records Retention

What happens to the countless millions of PC-based electronic records created at the desktops of every office worker in organizations everywhere? Are they systematically destroyed under an established records retention program based on retention times commensurate with their value? Or, are they permitted to languish indefinitely on the hard drives of their host machines or on a network server until they are forgotten about? Regrettably, the latter is the case, at least in many, perhaps most, organizations. In fact, in the U.S. today, saying that the desktop is a "RIM basket case!" is not too strong a statement.

Very few of the untold millions of desktop users in government and business offices today are furnished with good guidance concerning how to manage and retain the electronic records they create on their PCs and laptops every day. A substantial portion of the work of all organizations is done on these machines. By one account, some 56 percent of all digital data resides in single-user systems in the desktop environment.[36] The legal risks of unrestrained desktop retention are greater than for any recordkeeping environment. Bringing professional records retention to the desktop is one of the biggest challenges facing records managers today, and it should be at the top of the RIM agenda for every organization.

The Leahy Award (named for Emmett Leahy, one of the founders of modern records and information management) is one of the highest awards given to practitioners in the RIM field. In his Leahy Award acceptance speech, Bruce Miller offered some prescient observations:

> *[Electronic records management] will be successfully implemented at the desktop level when every desktop user will be routinely declaring records on a daily basis, as a part of their everyday business processes. All declared records will have a correctly assigned classification code, with a 95% or higher accuracy rate. And the disposition of all declared e-records will be governed under approved retention rules that are fully compliant with regulatory requirements. And finally, the volume of stored e-docs will be shrinking rather than growing, because large scale, accountable destruction will be occurring routinely.[37]*

Some RIM professionals, however, believe that desktop records retention is not feasible:

> *Another way to increase storage capacity is for IT administrators to demand that [PC] users themselves clear out their older files (with the added threat that files over a certain age will be automatically deleted from the system if users take no action). This is clearly ludicrous. The cost to a business to (a) spend considerable amounts of time reviewing all their data and then (b) to have to make decisions and act accordingly is inestimable. Users will always believe they use their data more often than they do.[38]*

Although desktop users often do tend to overstate the retention value of the records under their custody and control, experience confirms that desktop users can successfully manage these assets in accordance with sound RIM principles. The principles presented in the next section are recommended as practical measures for bringing records retention to the desktop. They are also incorporated into the sample policies appearing in Figures 4-6 and 4-7 at the end of this chapter.

Principles for Desktop Retention

1. **User responsibility** – Responsibility for desktop retention must of necessity rest with individual desktop users. At the present time, software solutions are not yet available that can review desktop documents and apply retention rules, logically and automatically, without human intervention. As discussed in Chapter 12, even the newer electronic document management solutions require at least some user intervention in document classification and profiling, which are linked to retention rules. Consequently, if desktop retention is going to be done, individual users of PCs must accept the responsibility of making it happen.

2. **Purge days** – Desktop purge days are strongly recommended as best practice for retention implementation in the desktop (or any other) recordkeeping environment. The quotation above stated that the labor requirements to do these purge

days are inestimable, which is not true. Experience indicates that the labor requirements range between four and sixteen hours per user per year (exclusive of e-mail), with one day being the average.

3. **Retention content / value-driven** – Retention of desktop documents should be content-driven and records series related. It can range from one day to forever. However, the only way to apply retention to desktop documents is to require their creators to review their content, match them to the records series appearing in the retention schedules, and apply retention rules accordingly.

4. **Discretionary deletion of duplicate, nonofficial records** – As provided by the organization's policies for desktop retention, users should be at liberty to dispose of all desktop documents of unofficial character at their discretion (provided they do not exceed the retention requirements for official documents). Such disposal may occur daily (at the convenience and discretion of the users) but must occur during desktop purge days.

5. **Two-year default retention** – Most desktop documents are of relatively short-term value—two years or less. PC users can easily review how long they keep the desktop documents they use to do their jobs.

6. **Extended-term retention in a designated ERMS repository** – For desktop documents that require extended-term retention, according to the retention schedule, users should have the option of saving them to a separate repository having fully integrated electronic records retention capabilities. Such functionality is typically designed in fully integrated *electronic records management system (ERMS)* software applications.

IT-Managed System Applications

Apart from the desktop, the other major computing environment in which organizations retain electronic records is the production applications managed by IT departments. Separate strategies are needed to bring records retention practices to records in these areas as well. Organizations need to ensure that these records are properly scheduled for retention and that the retention requirements in the schedules are being properly implemented.

In order to schedule the data residing in production applications for retention, RIM specialists should work cooperatively with IT personnel. They should review these applications, determine the separate bodies of data that need to appear in the retention schedules, and then include them in the schedules, using the decision-making methodologies discussed earlier. The major steps in this process are outlined below.

1. **Collect summary data describing all system applications** – The first step in developing retention schedules for the production applications managed by IT is to obtain a list and description of all the applications, including the names of the business owners of the data and the IT specialists responsible for their man-

agement. Most IT departments already have this information, in an applications portfolio, a systems directory, or similar forms.

2. **Survey system applications** – With the above list of applications in hand, the next step is to collect additional information about these applications. Identify the business function(s) performed by each application, the platform, the hardware and software on which it runs, its size and rate of growth, and other general information describing the application.

3. **Determine current life cycle practices** – For each application, determine whether any provision has been made to identify or segregate inactive data, what data retention practices are in place (if any), whether any inactive data is routinely archived or purged from the application, and when and under what circumstances these actions occur. These questions can usually be answered by the computer specialists who are responsible for managing the application.

4. **Determine retention requirements** – For each application, solicit the opinions of owners of the data concerning how long they believe the data should be retained in order to satisfy the operational needs of organization. The guidance provided in Chapter 3 should be followed in making these decisions.

5. **Integrate data retention requirements into schedules** – When the retention requirements for all applications have been determined, they should be integrated into the retention schedules so that personnel who must implement them will have clear guidance concerning how long the data must be retained.

6. **Incorporate retention functionality into applications** – In order to implement the retention requirements, the software must have the functional capability to recognize expired data and purge it from the system. For many applications, such *retention functionality* will not exist. In these cases, new policy (see the sample policy at the end of this chapter) should be developed requiring that data retention functionality be incorporated either at the time of initial system design or at the time of the next technology upgrade. This new policy should be designed to make all computer applications retention-capable within three to five years.

7. **Satisfy retention requirements in an ERMS repository** – As an alternative to modifying the software code to make existing applications retention-capable, determine whether the applications have the ability to transfer inactive data having continuing retention requirements to a history *file*, which can then be retained in a separate, designated repository having full retention / life cycle management functionality. Such functionality is typically designed in fully integrated ERMS software applications.

8. **Execute data purges in a regular, systematic manner** – Implementing electronic records retention policies in such a way that full compliance with the schedules can be demonstrated is critical. Further, IT departments must delete and purge systematically, in the routine course of system operation, and while preserving adequate documentation of the data deletion and purge processes.

Although electronic records retention has not been widely practiced, it is an idea whose time has come. As mentioned in Chapter 1, one of the most significant trends in electronic records retention today is the entry of large computer companies (i.e., EMC, IBM, Hewlett Packard, Veritas, and others) into the information life cycle management field.[39] Because of the trends in data storage highlighted in this chapter, executives in these companies are coming to the conclusion that information life cycle management can be a viable business opportunity, and they are incorporating retention capabilities into their products with increasing frequency. To cite just one example, one vendor's ILM solution provides a new "audited delete" function, which permits the deletion of stored records, together with the retention of an audit trail providing a history of the document life cycle. The software also permits the management of information by classes as opposed to objects, which permits the application of retention rules to be applied to the classes or categories.[40]

Although no one software solution available today provides fully integrated data retention and information life cycle management for both IT-managed applications as well as the desktop, for the first time ever the technology marketplace is providing viable solutions from which to choose. Also for the first time ever, the goal of enterprise electronic RIM is within reach for organizations. Wherever professional RIM is practiced, these principles and the tools that support them will have been assimilated into electronic recordkeeping environments across the enterprise.

Sample Policy:
Desktop Records
Retention

Figure 4-6

Desktop Records Retention

XYZ Corp. hereby declares that it will manage the life cycle of its PC-based records and information in accordance with its retention schedules and in full compliance with all laws and regulations. All XYZ employees are required to manage the retention of their desktop records on a regular basis, and to retain and dispose of electronic records created on them based on their content, as related to the requirements of the company's records retention schedules. Specific retention requirements appear below.

Although exceptions do occur, PC-based electronic records usually possess relatively short-term retention value. Nearly all such records have business value for less than five years, and most have value for only a year or two. As stated below, PC-based records must be retained and disposed of based on their content, their status as *official records*, and their value to the company.

In making decisions concerning how long to retain PC-based records, employees should first check the records retention schedules to ensure that they are in full compliance with it. PC-based records not explicitly covered by retention schedules are subject to the following policy guidance:

- **Records of official status:** If PC-based records are the only copy of documents of official character, they may not be disposed of except in accordance with the company's records retention schedules. To clarify this principle, if the content of PC-based records relates to an established records category appearing in the records retention schedules and the PC-based record is unique, it must be retained for the period of time specified in said schedules. In such cases, employees have the option of retaining the records in electronic form or they may produce printed copies for retention in the company's paper files. All other PC-based records are of nonofficial character and may be discarded as provided below.

(continued)

Figure 4-6

- **Records of nonofficial status:** If PC-based records consist solely of electronic documents and data used to produce documents of official character are retained elsewhere, then these PC-based versions would not themselves possess status as official records and may thus be deleted at the discretion of the user. They should be destroyed as soon as they are no longer needed to produce updates or revisions to official documents, and in no event should they be retained longer than the official versions of the records. PC users are encouraged to review their electronic documents and files on a regular basis (weekly or more frequently if possible) and to delete all unneeded documents and data from both removable and nonremovable media (i.e., **hard disks**, network servers, and floppy disks). Such actions are required of all employees during Desktop Records Purge Days.

- **PC-based records related to litigation or government investigation:** If the content of a PC-based record is related to actual or pending litigation or a government investigation, it may not be destroyed without the prior written consent of the Legal Department. Employees who violate this policy are subject to disciplinary action by the company, up to and including dismissal, and/or judicial penalties imposed by courts of law.

Desktop Records Purge Days

All departments and business units are responsible for conducting one or more Desktop Records Purge Days each year. During these days, all employees are required to review all PC-based records and files under their custody (including e-mail) and effect the disposal of all records eligible for such action as provided by the company's records retention schedules and this and related policy guidelines. Records eligible for disposal will be deleted / purged from all storage media under user control—hard disks, network servers, and removable diskettes.

All employees using desktop or portable computers are required to accomplish three main tasks on Desktop Records Purge Days:

1. All PC-based records of an official character eligible for disposal will be deleted. The manner of disposal will be sufficient to effect irretrievable erasure, while protecting the security and confidentiality of company information.

2. All personal working files stored on PCs will be reviewed and purged, as provided herein. Employees are encouraged to retain records of this character for the minimum period of time essential to perform their work in an efficient manner, generally one year or less.

3. When PC-based records are deleted from desktop hard drives, all backup copies must be deleted as well.

Compliance Monitoring

At the conclusion of Desktop Records Purge Days, all employees are required to complete a Certificate of **Retention Compliance** (see Figure 5.3), indicating that they are in full compliance with the records retention schedules and with this and related policies and procedures. Any exceptions must be documented and justified. This Certificate of Retention Compliance will be forwarded to the employees' supervisor. Employees are also advised that retention compliance is subject to audit, with possible penalties for noncompliance.

Sample Policy:
Records Retention
Requirements for
IT-Managed
Applications

Figure 4.7

Records Retention Requirements for IT-Managed Applications

This policy specifies requirements and methods for implementing XYZ Corp.'s retention schedules for databases, data files, and other electronic records associated with applications managed by IT departments at corporate headquarters or in individual business units and that operate on network servers, timeshared computers, and other shared or centralized computing resources.

(continued)

Figure 4.7

Implementation

IT departments are responsible for implementing the company's retention schedules for electronic records created and maintained by applications they manage. IT departments must preserve the usability of electronic records in their custody throughout their retention periods and provide effective mechanisms for destroying the records when their retention periods elapse.

Incorporating Retention Functionality into Applications

Applications managed by XYZ's IT departments must incorporate an effective mechanism for identifying and purging electronic records when they are eligible for destruction and for ensuring that electronic records will not be destroyed before that time. At a minimum, this mechanism must be able to:

- Calculate destruction dates for electronic records based on retention periods specified in the company's retention schedules.
- Recompute destruction dates for electronic records when changes are made to the company's retention schedules.
- Generate lists and descriptions of electronic records eligible for destruction for review and approval by business units or other parties.
- Discard electronic records that have been approved for destruction.
- Print certificates of destruction or other evidence indicating that electronic records have been destroyed as provided by the retention schedules.
- Suspend destruction of specific electronic records relevant to litigation, government investigations, or audits when such suspension is authorized by the Legal Department.
- Maintain records documenting the systematic deletion of expired data per the retention policy and schedules.

These records retention capabilities must be incorporated into specifications for new applications developed internally, developed for the company by software contractors, or purchased from software suppliers. Where an existing application lacks the requisite functionality to comply with the company's retention schedules and this policy, the responsible IT department must modify the application to incorporate such functionality. This modification should be done *at the earliest practical opportunity but not later than when each application requiring such functionality is upgraded to a new hardware or software environment.*

Notes

1. Fred Moore, "Cradle-to-Grave Storage Management Now a Reality," *Computer Technology Review* 23, no. 1 (January 2003): 1.

2. Kamel Shaath, "The Present and Future of Policy-based Storage Management," *SMS* 7, No. 5 (2002): 55.

3. Robert Williams, *Electronic Records Management Survey: A Call to Action* (Chicago: Cohasset, Inc., 2004), 5,18.

4. William Saffady, *Records and Information Management: A Benchmarking Study of Large U.S. Industrial Companies* (Lenexa, KS: ARMA International, 2002), 42, 44.

5. Fred Moore, "Data Growth Outruns Ability to Manage It," *Computer Technology Review* 22, no. 2 (February 2002): 20; Moore, "Cradle-to-Grave."

6. Fred Moore, "Digital Data's Future: You Ain't Seen Nothin' Yet," *Computer Technology Review* 20, no. 10 (October 2000): 1.

7. School of Information Management and Systems, Chapter 1: "How Much Information" (Berkeley, CA: University of California, 2003).

8. Jim Lee, "Reduce the Cost of Compliance: Database Archiving and Information Lifecycle Management," *SMS* 8, no. 5 (2003): 18.

9. Bruce Dearstyne, "The View from the Fast Lane: The Future of Information from the Perspective of Fortune's Fastest Growing Companies," *The Information Management Journal* 35, no. 4 (April 2001): 5. See also Rick Whiting, "Bigger & Better." *InformationWeek*, 22 March 2004, 34; and Rick Whiting, "Tower of Power: IT Managers Brace for the Inevitable: Petabyte-Size Databases," *InformationWeek*, 11 February 2002, 40.

10. Moore, "Data Growth Outruns Ability to Manage It," 20.

11. Ibid.

12. Shari Killion, "Effective Storage Resource Management Disciplines and Best Practices," *SMS* 8, no. 2 (2003): 26.

13. Fred Moore, "Sizes of Rich Media Files Are Changing the Rules," *Computer Technology Review* 22, no. 10 (October 2002): 1.

14. Mario Apicella, "Enterprise Storage Part 1: Strategies, *InfoWorld*, 10 February 2003, 31.

15. Moore, "Digital Data's Future," 20.

16. Killion, "Effective Storage Resource Management," 26.

17. Apicella, "Enterprise Storage," 31.

18. Paul Wang, "Understanding Online Archiving," *SMS* 5, no. 11 (2000).

19. David Simpson, "Cut Your Storage Management Costs," *Datamation*, November 1996.

20. Moore, "Data Growth Outruns Ability to Manage It," 20.

21. David Vellante, "In Search of Storage ROI: Part 3 – The TCO Trap," *SMS* 7, no. 4 (2002): 24.

22. Ibid.

23. Whiting, "Tower of Power," 44.

24. Bob Francis, "SNIA Nails Down ILM Definition," *InfoWorld*, 1 November 2004.

25. Wang, "Understanding Online Archiving."

26. Glenn Rhodes, "How to Achieve Significant Savings Through Tiered Storage Implementation," *SMS* 8, no. 2 (2003): 50.

27. Francis, "SNIA Nails Down ILM Definition."

28. "EMC Has High Hopes for ILM," *KMWorld* (July / August 2004), 1, 3.

29. Shaath, "The Present and the Future," 56-57; see also Martin Garvey, "Stoking the Storage Machine," *InformationWeek*, 8 December 2003, 56.

30. Ephraim Schwartz, "EMC Drills Into Compliance," *InfoWorld*, 14 June 2004, 19.

31. Williams, *Electronic Records Management Survey*, 6.

32. Fred Moore, "Archival Data Has a New Mission: Critical," *Computer Technology Review* 37, no. 2 (February 2003): 37.

33. Shaath, "The Present and the Future," 56-57.

34. Ibid.

35. Shaath, "The Present and the Future," 57.

36. Moore, "Cradle-to-Grave," 20.

37. Bruce Miller, "Implementing Electronic Recordkeeping," *ProfessioNotes*, Institute of Certified Records Managers, Winter 2004, 8.

38. Dave Morris, "Migrating Data With HMS," *Document World*, January / February 1999.

39. Christine Chudnow, "No Such Thing as Delete: Information Life Cycle Management," *SMS* 8, no. 5 (2003): 40.

40. Julie Gable, "Innovations in Information Management Technologies," *The Information Management Journal* 38, no. 1 (January / February 2004): 30-31.

Chapter 5

Retention Implementation, Auditing, and Compliance

Retention schedules, and the written policies and procedures that accompany them, are nothing more than words on paper. They won't implement themselves. Unless every employee who has custody over records material is required *by mandate* to comply with these requirements, success in retention is likely to remain elusive. Compliance with retention schedules is the single biggest reason that records retention programs fail to achieve their objectives.

This matter is not merely of casual importance. In fact, from a legal perspective, to have a retention policy and fail to implement it consistently can be worse than not having one at all. Indeed, if the organization's retention program were to come under legal scrutiny, adverse inferences could be attached to sporadic, arbitrary efforts at retention implementation. If senior executives have decided that the organization is going to have a records retention program, they should be prepared to demonstrate that the program is being executed systematically and in good faith.

Reasonable Retention Goals

Records retention is never perfect in any organization. What, then, is a reasonable and attainable goal for an organization in records retention? A goal of 80 to 90 percent perfect is a useful benchmark for defining success in records retention. At any given time, 80 to 90 percent of all records eligible for destruction as provided by the retention schedules have, in fact, been destroyed. On the preservation side, the obverse is true of course—80 to 90 percent of all records supposed to be retained are, in fact, available and ready for immediate use.

Experience reveals that if an organization has a history of a casual, nonaggressive approach to its retention program, it is likely to be operating at a 20 percent success rate. According to one recent survey, 38 percent of the respondents reported that their organizations follow their retention schedules either not regularly or only when time permits.[1] This level of retention schedule compliance is not good enough for a high-level of professional RIM. The goal, then, is to turn a low rate of policy compliance into an 80 to 90 percent rate of compliance. What will be required to achieve this goal? The answer is: Implementation strategies to get all departments and their managers, as well as all employees, to accept their responsibilities for retention implementation and get the job done effectively and consistently.

Retention Training

Many employees are reluctant to undertake records disposal actions unless they are confident that they are acting properly to carry out approved policy mandates. Improving employee confidence requires training. Teaching retention compliance responsibilities may not be effective in every case, but employees have a much better chance of getting it right if they are trained than if they receive no formal guidance whatsoever.[2] Training employees in retention compliance responsibilities is a best practice, and it is also common practice. According to the Saffady benchmarking study, 81 percent of the participating companies conduct employee training, mostly in connection with retention implementation initiatives.[3]

Employee briefings (typically about 30 minutes long) should be conducted at the beginning of every purge day. During these briefings, employees should be apprised of the do's and don'ts of how to execute their responsibilities, as specified in the policies, procedures, and retention schedules. Brief remarks by senior attorneys, chief fiscal officers, and other senior management officials are often very helpful in conveying to employees what they need to know to complete the task effectively. Suggestions for employee retention training sessions are listed in Figure 5.1.

Keys to Success

The biggest single issue in achieving success in records retention is modifying employee behavior to get them to do retention, fully and consistently. Unless an organization has workable strategies for improving employee behavior regarding records retention, it will fail to achieve its retention goals. Most organizations, however, have a poor understanding of what is required to modify the recordkeeping behavior of individual employees so that records retention can be implemented successfully. An aggressive implementation strategy designed to get employees to comply fully with organizational retention requirements is necessary in some situations. Such a strategy contains eight key components:

1. Put an effective governance structure into place.
2. Post schedules, policies, and procedures on the intranet.
3. Define responsibilities for retention implementation.
4. Conduct records purge days.
5. Require compliance documentation for all employees.

Suggested Topics
for Retention
Training

Figure 5.1

Employee Retention Training Sample Topics

- Why records retention at XYZ Corp?
- Legal and business objectives of the retention program
  - Controlling the growth of records
  - Demonstrating regulatory compliance
  - Avoiding litigation risks – lawfully and in good faith
- The XYZ retention schedules and how to use them
  - Schedules by business function: a quick review
  - Requests for schedule revisions
  - Unscheduled records and their proper disposition
- Departmental responsibilities for schedule compliance
  - Personal (individual employee) responsibilities for schedule compliance
  - Purge day do's and don'ts
  - Employee compliance certificates
  - Retention audits
- Applying the retention schedules in XYZ's five recordkeeping environments
  - Active paper records in departmental filing stations
  - Inactive paper records in storage facilities
  - Electronic records in production applications
  - Electronic records at the desktop level
  - Personal working papers
- Questions and answers

---

6. Impose penalties for noncompliance.

7. Conduct retention audits; report results to management.

8. Implement retention in five major recordkeeping environments.

An Effective Governance Structure

Enterprise RIM cannot succeed in isolation, particularly where retention implementation is concerned. Therefore, the first key to success in retention implementation is to put an effective governance structure into place. A mechanism is required to elevate both the authority and responsibility for retention implementation to an appropriate leadership structure consisting of the right stakeholders.

The establishment of a ***permanent records*** retention committee can often be the key to a successful retention program. This committee should have the authority to oversee all aspects of program development and implementation and be accountable to management for the results. As always, the right leadership and membership composition is crucial to an effective committee. Most such committees are composed of senior representatives of the legal, fiscal, tax, and audit staffs. Sometimes, the organization's records manager serves as the chairperson; other times, this role is assigned to a senior administrative officer.

Where this approach to retention governance has been put into place, the committee should exercise aggressive oversight of enterprise retention implementation. The committee should meet regularly and monitor the results of retention implementation of every organizational entity throughout the enterprise.

Intranet-Based Schedules, Policies, and Guidelines

Some organizations post their retention schedules on the intranet, together with all the tools necessary to implement them successfully (policies, practices, litigation and tax hold requirements, employee compliance forms, etc.). This capability for retention implementation should extend to every desktop in the organization.

This implementation strategy has rapidly evolved into common practice, particularly among larger companies. According to the Saffady benchmarking study, 49 percent of the participating companies provide intranet-only access to their retention schedules, while 36 percent provide print-only access. The remaining companies provide a combination of these methods of schedule dissemination.[4]

Individual Responsibilities for Retention Implementation

In many organizations, retention implementation is not successful because the responsibilities for it have not been clearly laid down. In past practice, many retention programs placed this responsibility solely on the shoulders of departmental records coordinators. These persons are typically assigned to each department and are responsible for coordinating retention implementation as a part-time work assignment, to be done as time permits. This method is not endorsed as best practice. Where the retention implementation strategy is based solely on this approach, it is very unlikely to result in anything approximating success. Best practice in retention implementation requires the right combination of contributions from department managers, designated IT personnel, and all employees having custody over records.

Records Purge Days

In order for records retention to be successful, its implementation must be integrated into the required, routine work assignments of departments and their employees. The best method of making this integration is for the organization to conduct regular "purge days." Sometimes referred to as "records retention days," these days are dedicated times when all employees are required to cease other work assignments and implement records retention and disposition actions *as a matter of organizational mandate.* The sample corporate retention policy in Figure 5.2 addresses employee involvement in records retention, including purge days.

To conduct records purge days is not merely best practice—it is required practice! These days are, in fact, the single most effective step in retention implementation. The reason is simple—they work! Although a few recalcitrant employees will always fail to cooperate, the vast majority will give their best efforts to comply with whatever reasonable retention requirements the organization lays down. The fact that these days will not produce perfect results is not a reason not

Corporate Records Retention[5]

Purpose

This policy defines principles and standards for retention of company records. It provides a framework for other company policies, procedures, guidelines, and directives that pertain to specific types of records and recordkeeping practices.

This policy applies to any and all records created, received, or maintained by XYZ departments, business units, and facilities, including any subsidiaries, partnerships, joint ventures, and other business arrangements in which XYZ's ownership exceeds 50 percent.

Policy Statement

The RIM Department, with the approval of the XYZ General Counsel and Chief Financial Officer, is responsible for establishing and implementing a systematic program for retention and disposition of company records. This department will establish a process for issuing and revising records retention schedules, as needed, and coordinate any employee training needed for implementation of this policy.

All company records must be retained and disposed of in accordance with retention periods and guidelines specified in the company's retention schedules and in any related polices, procedures, or directives that XYZ has issued or may issue in the future. The company's retention schedules specify how long records need to be kept for legal reasons and to satisfy business requirements. Compliance with them is mandatory on the part of all company employees. Company records must be retained for the time periods specified in the retention schedules and discarded promptly when their retention periods elapse.

Definition of Company Records

Company records include any and all information created, received, or maintained by any business unit, department, or employee of XYZ in pursuit of the company's legal obligations or in the transaction of company business. This definition of company records encompasses recorded information in all formats and media, including but not necessarily limited to the following:

- Paper documents, including office documents—***original records***, duplicate copies, notes, working papers, and drafts of documents—engineering drawings, architectural plans, and maps
- Photographic films and prints
- Microfilm, microfiche, aperture cards, or other microform media
- Computer files and databases stored on magnetic or optical media
- Audio recordings
- Video recordings

Ownership of Company Records

All records created, received, or maintained by XYZ business units, departments, or employees in relation to the company's mission, goals, objectives, or business operations are the property of XYZ. No XYZ employee has, by virtue of his or her position, any personal or property right to or property interest in such records, even though he or she may be named as the author, recipient, or custodian of them.

Employees may be allowed to remove company records temporarily from company locations for the sole purpose of performing specific duties for the company. They must return such records promptly when that purpose is fulfilled or at any earlier time when instructed to do so. XYZ employees may not take any company records or copies of such records when they retire, resign, or otherwise terminate employment. XYZ employees who have been authorized to remove company records from company offices or facilities must return them when they retire, resign, or otherwise terminate employment.

Retention Standards

All company records must be retained and disposed of in accordance with the following standards:

- The company's retention schedules specify how long company records are to be kept for legal reasons and to satisfy business requirements.

(continued)

Figure 5-2

- The company's records retention policies and practices will comply fully with all applicable laws and regulations. The company will make and keep adequate records to document its compliance with all applicable laws and regulations.
- The company will never alter or destroy company records that must be kept for pending or ongoing litigation, government investigations, tax audits, or internal audits until those matters are resolved. When circumstances warrant, the Legal Department will issue written directives that formally suspend the destruction of specific records until further notice.
- Company records will be destroyed promptly when the time periods specified in the company's retention schedule elapse in order to reduce the cost of storing, indexing, and handling the large quantity of records that would otherwise accumulate.
- Company records must be destroyed in a manner safe and appropriate to the content of the records and to the records media.

Personal Working Papers

Personal working papers consists of documents of quasi- or non-official character that are kept for convenience of reference and are typically maintained in the desks, credenzas, and bookcases of company employees. Employees are permitted to retain this type of records material, but only for one or two years after the date of creation or when the records cease to be active, whichever comes first.

Retention of Duplicate Records

Where the same information exists in multiple copies, the company's retention schedules designate one copy as the official copy to satisfy the company's retention requirements. All other copies are considered duplicate records. Duplicate records must be discarded at the earliest opportunity when they are no longer needed for the purposes for which they were created. In no case are duplicate records to be retained longer than time periods specified for official copies in company retention schedules.

Days Designated for Retention Actions

All XYZ business units and departments must designate one or more days (sometimes referred to as *Records Retention* or *Records Purge Days*) during each year for implementation of retention schedules for company records in their custody. Implementation of the company's retention schedules should be done at a time that will ensure the greatest participation by departmental employees with the least disruption of the department's ongoing operations. At its option, XYZ may designate specific dates, a range of dates, or annual deadline dates for implementation of retention schedules by all business units and departments. Designated retention days are set aside specifically for the disposition of official company records, although nonofficial or duplicate copies may be discarded on these days as well. Employees are, however, authorized to discard duplicate records at the earliest opportunity when they are no longer needed.

Compliance

All XYZ employees must comply fully and consistently with this policy and present evidence of compliance by executing an Employee Retention Compliance Form (see Figure 5.3) at the conclusion of every day designated for retention actions. The managing directors of individual business units are responsible for ensuring compliance with this policy at their facilities. The Internal Audit Department will conduct periodic audits to determine compliance with this policy. Problems of noncompliance will be examined and corrected. Flagrant, willful violations of this policy will result in disciplinary action up to and including dismissal.

Employees who are aware of or suspect any violations of this policy should immediately report such conduct to their supervisors, who will work with the Legal Department to determine whether a problem exists and how it can be corrected.

to have them. They are definitely worth it. If an organization's managers do not want to have purge days, they should not even bother with retention, as it will not be successful.

Sample
Compliance
Certificate

Figure 5-3

Records Retention: Certificate of Employee Compliance

Purpose: XYZ Company hereby declares that it will manage the retention life cycle of its records under approved management policies, to include those listed below. XYZ employees are advised that compliance with the company's records retention policies is mandatory. Further, compliance is subject to audit, and penalties will be imposed for noncompliance, as indicated below.

Penalties for Noncompliance: The specific penalty for retention violations is at the discretion of the supervisor; however, it can include written notices of noncompliance in the official personnel file and related adverse impact in performance evaluations and compensation reviews, to dismissal for repeated and flagrant violations.

Instructions: Every company employee who has custody over any records material, including electronic records created on PCs and portable computers, is responsible for complying fully with these policies. The purpose of this form is to provide a means for all such employees to attest that they are in compliance with these records retention requirements. Please indicate such compliance in the space provided below and return this form to XYZ's RIM Department not later than: [date to be filled in].

1. I have read and understand the following company policies and procedures concerning records retention, including my personal responsibilities as expressed therein:
   a. Records Retention – General Corporate Policy
   b. XYZ's Records Retention Schedules
   b. The Retention of PC-Based Electronic Records
   c. The Management and Retention of E-mail

   Yes ❑   No ❑

   Note: If you do not fully understand your responsibilities under the above policies and procedures, please contact the RIM Department for assistance immediately.

2. I have reviewed all records material under my custody and/or control, including both paper and electronic records, and have properly disposed of or transferred to storage all records material eligible for such actions, as prescribed by the policies and procedures above and the Records Retention Schedule.

   Yes ❑   No ❑

3. I am not in full compliance with XYZ's records retention policies and schedules. The following records are eligible for disposal, and I have not taken this action. My reason(s) is/are as follows:

   _____

   _____

   _____

4. I request the additions, deletions, or other revisions to XYZ's Records Retention Schedules indicated below. NOTE: All such requests must be based on valid business and/or legal considerations. Please explain these below.

   _____

   _____

   _____

   _____

   Name: _____

   Department: _____

   Date: _____

Because they are so effective, records purge days have become common practice in recent years. Although the Saffady benchmarking study did not specifically ask respondents about whether records purge days are a required strategy for retention implementation, many respondents indicated that this method is, in fact, used.[6]

During these days, all employees having custody of records are required to review all records under their custody—both paper and electronic; official and nonofficial—and effect the disposal of all records eligible for such action as authorized by the retention schedules. Typically, employees are required to perform three tasks during purge days:

1. Review all paper-based departmental records and files and assist in making proper disposition of them.
2. Review all electronic documents and data over which they have personal custody and control (i.e., those documents residing on desktop PCs, laptops, common network servers, removable media, etc.) and retain or dispose of them properly.
3. Review all paper-based personal working papers in desks, credenzas, bookcases, etc., and apply proper retention to them.

Because employees are authorized to cease their normal work routines and perform records review and purge activities, these days must be authorized by senior management. Moreover, from a legal point of view, showing that records purge days can be shown to be a mandated and routine work requirement conducted systematically in the normal course of business is critical.

How much time does the average employee need to spend on the tasks associated with purge days? Usually, *somewhere between 8 and 16 hours or one to two days per year for each office employee,* depending on the quantity of records material the employee creates and maintains in the course of his or her work, are required. Owing to the nature of their jobs, some workers create or receive few records, while others create or receive them in large quantities. This average range of hours includes retention implementation for the three categories of records material enumerated above, but it *excludes e-mail.* As discussed in Chapter 8, retention and disposition actions for e-mail should be embedded in daily work routines, although they may occur during records purge days as well.

The organization's records retention policies should require that all departments conduct one or more purge days each year. Some organizations or departments elect to conduct one purge day each year for paper records, and one day or sometimes several partial days for the desktop or other electronic records that are under user custody and control. Every organization should devise a purge day strategy that it thinks will work best.

Compliance Documentation

In this implementation step, employees are required to provide written evidence of their compliance with the retention program. Typically, employees are required to complete a records retention compliance form (see sample policy, Figure 5.2) at the conclusion of each purge day, in which they certify that they have read and understand all retention policies affecting them, that they have reviewed all records material under their custody and control, and that they are in full compliance with all applicable requirements. This form can also be used to request exceptions to the organization's retention policies, or to request schedule revisions.

Although some managers are reluctant to require their employees to sign this type of form, it does serve to reinforce the notion that senior management is serious about records retention and that it expects written evidence of program compliance. Using this type of form is a best practice.

Penalties for Noncompliance

Organizations that are serious about records retention need to decide whether they want to impose any penalties for noncompliance with retention requirements and, if so, how severe they should be. According to the Saffady benchmarking study, the most common penalty for noncompliance levied by the participating companies is an unfavorable report to management.[7] Some organizations choose to adopt a relatively mild and generally stated penalty, to the effect that noncompliance with retention mandates are at the discretion of departmental supervisors. Others go further, indicating that the penalty may include written notices of noncompliance placed in the employee's personnel file, together with adverse implications for performance evaluations and compensation reviews. Some organizations even go so far as to state that retention noncompliance can result in dismissal in cases of repeated, flagrant, and willful violations. Every organization should decide about how stringent its noncompliance penalties should be. Regardless, to reinforce the gravity of the matter and give the program the best chance of success, some form of employee sanctions for noncompliance with retention policies should be considered.

Retention Audits

Should records retention as a business process, be subject to internal audits to determine compliance with its requirements? If so, who should perform the audits? How should the audits be conducted? Experience has shown that the only way a sizable organization can systematically learn about problems with its RIM program is by auditing past acts or monitoring current conduct.[8] Every employee who maintains records needs to know that their compliance with retention rules is subject to scrutiny, that the matter is of some gravity, and that adverse findings and penalties may result from noncompliance.

With respect to prevailing practice, according to the Saffady benchmarking study, in 40 percent of the participating companies, RIM assumes the lead or full responsibility for conducting retention audits. In 31 percent of the companies, this role is assumed by internal audit, while for regulatory affairs, the figure was only 3 percent. The remaining 26 percent did not conduct these audits at all.[9]

Records managers assuming the lead role in conducting retention compliance audits is not a recommended practice, although they can sometimes play a supportive role. These audits are most effective when a senior corporate compliance officer takes the lead role and conducts the audits at random, with little or no prior notice to the department being audited. A less preferred but still effective practice is for the audits to be conducted by the internal audit staff, as a part of regular departmental audits. Finally, outside consultants specializing in RIM are sometimes engaged to conduct the audits. Using consultants is sometimes a good approach, as these specialists generally possess the expertise to know what to look for.

Regardless of who conducts the audit, the purpose is to determine the degree of retention compliance achieved by each department, to report the results to senior management, and to enable departments to take corrective actions to achieve full compliance within designated periods of time. Most importantly, regular audits should be performed for each of the five major recordkeeping environments: (1) official paper records, (2) personal working papers, (3) boxed and stored paper records, (4) user-controlled electronic records, and (5) IT-managed system application data.

Retention Implementation in Five Recordkeeping Environments

In the context of implementing enterprise retention programs, every organization has five major, separate, and distinct recordkeeping environments. If records retention is to be successful, separate implementation strategies are required for each environment. Effective implementation includes establishing special policies, identifying individuals who will have the primary responsibilities for implementation, and acquiring the technology tools to facilitate implementation.

1. **Official Paper Records**
   - **Characteristics:** This recordkeeping environment consists of paper records of official character that are typically maintained in departmental filing stations and sometimes in central filing repositories.
   - **Policy requirements:** Policy requirements are specified in the retention schedules.
   - **Retention responsibility:** Primary responsibility is assigned to department managers (often delegated to departmental records coordinators); secondary responsibility, to all department employees.
   - **Implementation method:** Records purge days dedicated to paper records are observed in each department.
   - **Technology tool:** RIM software to index, track, and monitor the records and manage their retention life cycle.

2. **Personal Working Papers**
   - **Characteristics:** This recordkeeping environment consists of paper records of quasi- or non-official character that are typically maintained in the desks, credenzas, and bookcases of knowledge workers or other office employees.
   - **Policy requirements:** Retention policy should permit employees to retain this type of records material, but only for one or two years after the date of creation or when the records cease to be active, whichever comes first.

- **Retention responsibility:** Each employee is responsible.
- **Implementation method:** Records purge days dedicated to paper records observed in each department. However, as most records of this nature consist of duplicate copies, disposal may occur at the discretion of individual employees, whenever convenient.
- **Technology tool:** None. This type of records material is not customarily managed by any computer tool.

3. **Boxed and Stored Paper Records**
   - **Characteristics:** This recordkeeping environment consists of inactive paper records, boxed, and stored in records centers or other warehouse-type storage facilities that may be operated in-house or by commercial records storage companies.
   - **Policy requirements:** Retention policies are specified in the retention schedules.
   - **Retention responsibility:** Records manager or other administrative or facilities management staff member responsible for operating the organization's inactive records storage program is also responsible for retention.
   - **Implementation method:** RIM policy requiring destruction actions to be effectuated either once each year (most often in January, following the end of the preceding year), sometimes more than once each year, and sometimes continually throughout the year.
   - **Technology tool:** RIM software, which manages the retention life cycle of this type of records material.

4. **User-Controlled Electronic Records**
   - **Characteristics:** This recordkeeping environment consists of electronic records residing at the desktop level, on PCs, laptops or other portable / personal computing devices, and under the direct custody and control of their creators.
   - **Policy requirements:** A desktop RIM and retention policies are utilized.
   - **Retention responsibility:** Individual employees.
   - **Implementation method:** Desktop purge days that are conducted in each department, once, twice, or sometimes four times each year.
   - **Technology tool:** Electronic document / RIM software, having the functionality to incorporate retention and life cycle management into the desktop computing environment.

5. **IT-Managed System Application Data**
   - **Characteristics:** This recordkeeping environment consists of electronic records residing in the production applications managed by IT departments but owned by the various departments throughout the organization.
   - **Policy requirements:** A policy that requires the integration of purge functionality sufficient to implement the retention requirements contained in

the schedules established for all system applications requiring it at the time of the next technology upgrade.

- **Retention responsibility:** The chief information officer or other IT manager to whom responsibility for electronic records retention has been delegated.

- **Implementation method:** Running data purge routines in conformance with the retention requirements as specified in the schedules. The data retention may be effectuated in the native application or in a separate repository.

- **Technology tool:** Data retention functionality integrated into the software used in managing the computer applications, or in a separate repository established for the purpose of archival retention.

Notes

1. Robert Williams, *Electronic Records Management Survey: A Call to Action* (Chicago: Cohasset, Inc., 2004), 5.

2. Randolph Kahn, "Records Management & Compliance: Making the Connection," *The Information Management Journal* 38, no. 3 (May / June 2004): 34.

3. William Saffady, *Records and Information Management: A Benchmarking Study of Large U.S. Industrial Companies* (Lenexa, KS: ARMA International, 2002), 46.

4. Ibid., 45.

5. William Saffady, Unpublished manuscript, n.d.

6. Saffady, *A Benchmarking Study*, 47.

7. Ibid., 48.

8. Kahn, "Records Management & Compliance," 34.

9. Saffady, *A Benchmarking Study*, 47.

Chapter 6

Business Recordkeeping and the Law

Throughout history, business recordkeeping has been a subject of high interest to the legal community. For centuries, governments—their legislative assemblies, courts, regulatory commissions, and archival agencies—have enacted laws, promulgated regulations, and handed down judicial decisions concerning the manner of record-keeping in business and government organizations. Although records managers should, indeed must, defer to their organization's attorneys concerning many aspects of the law as it affects recordkeeping, they need to be able to discuss these matters intelligently whenever they work with these lawyers.

Although the laws affecting organizational recordkeeping can be bewilderingly complex, they are based on a few simple principles. The primary interest is that organizations keep and maintain records such that the ends of justice may be served. Specifically, organizations must manage their records in a manner that enables them to demonstrate:

- That the organization is conducting its business with honesty and integrity, and in a manner consistent with the public interest as well as its own

- That the organization's records are properly maintained and preserved, in case they may be needed as evidence in government investigations, litigation, audits or other legal proceedings

- That the organization is in full compliance with all applicable laws and regulations, in letter, spirit, and good faith

In the U.S. and elsewhere, government officials want organizations to manage their records in such a manner that they are *complete, true and accurate, accessible, legible, retained as required, and fully usable for any and all legal purposes should the need arise.* Some new and significant regulatory initiatives have underscored the need for organizations to apply best practices in RIM in order to demonstrate compliance with their requirements. Perhaps the most significant of these new laws is the

Sarbanes-Oxley Act, which is, from a RIM perspective, one of the single most important pieces of federal legislation in decades.

RIM—Legally Discretionary

Records managers need an understanding as to the basic legal underpinnings for their professional discipline, as it is practiced in the U.S. Many people commonly assume that, in the U.S., RIM programs are mandated by statutes and regulations. Many people in government and business are under the impression that, somewhere, an existing law requires their organization to establish and implement a RIM program. This statement is largely true for government, but it is largely untrue for business firms in the private sector. Although RIM programs are mandated by statute and regulations for agencies of the U.S. government, and for many if not most state and local agencies of government, RIM is largely a discretionary undertaking in the private sector.

However, some notable exceptions exist: nuclear power plants are required to implement RIM programs. Other heavily regulated firms are not specifically required to have RIM; but if they don't, they have no real way to comply with government-mandated recordkeeping regulations. Most business corporations are under no legal obligation to establish any formal program for the management of their records. Thus, for most businesses, RIM, as a formal management discipline, is legally discretionary but nevertheless highly advisable. Without RIM, organizations have no practical way of implementing initiatives to assure the trustworthiness and authenticity of their recordkeeping systems, achieving compliance with numerous regulatory requirements, or achieving other key legal objectives.

New Recordkeeping Technologies

One of the most common legal issues centers around new recordkeeping technologies and their legal status. Whether new recordkeeping technologies must receive formal endorsement by the government before they are legally proven and thus safe to implement is the primary focus. The legal system in the U.S. is based on English common law. One of the chief tenets of English common law is that citizens enjoy maximum freedom from government intrusion; that is, before the law, citizens may presume that they are free to do a thing unless that act is expressly prohibited by law. In this case, the "acts" are the use of any particular type of records media or recordkeeping technology. Absent formal government endorsement, organizational officials need not feel constrained from either experimenting with new recordkeeping technologies or moving more aggressively toward widespread adoption of them, if they perceive clear and substantial business / competitive advantages from doing so.

As used here, the term *legally proven* means that a body of law—in the form of specific statues, regulations, and judicial precedents—expressly approves of a particular information technology and prescribes the conditions of its use. If organizations waited to receive formal government endorsement before assimilating new technology solutions, based on the legally proven standard, they would wait for years if not decades before concluding that such assimilation poses little if any legal risk. The legal community, which consists broadly of legislative bodies, regulatory agencies, and the courts, is simply not equipped to position itself on the leading edge of technology development, even if it would be in the public interest to do so.

The assimilation of any new recordkeeping technology is no different from any other business decision. It should be based on a careful analysis of costs, risks, and benefits, a determination of what the priorities for the assimilation should be, and whether the organization's best interest would be served in being an early adopter, a late adopter, or perhaps a mid-term adopter. Consequently, whether and to what extent any recordkeeping technology is legally acceptable or proven based on formal government endorsement would be one factor in the assimilation decision, but not the sole or even the major, determining factor.

Recordkeeping Media

Another much-debated issue is the question: In the eyes of the law, are some records media appropriate for use while others are not? The answer is that, although laws or regulations do sometimes specify what recordkeeping media may or must satisfy the government's requirements in particular situations, no blanket provision specifying any particular information recording technology or media type is available in U.S. law.

In RIM circles, this issue surfaced most recently during the 1980s, when electronic document imaging technology, then a new and revolutionary approach to recordkeeping, was introduced to the U.S. market. Many observers approached this new technology with extreme caution, advising against its widespread adoption unless and until it received formal endorsement from the legal community in a form roughly equivalent to the body of law surrounding the use of microfilm technology. Most of the concern related to whether imaged records would be acceptable as legal evidence in courts of law, whether revenue authorities would be willing to audit imaged records, or whether such records would be acceptable for other legal purposes.

Generally, the law does not favor any of the media types or document recording technologies commonly used by government and business over others. Readers of the law may, perhaps, infer a preference for paper records, but that is only because paper was the predominate recordkeeping medium when most older laws were enacted. In general, the attitude of the government towards records media or recordkeeping technologies is, appropriately, one of neutrality.

Legal acceptance of business records does not depend on media type per se. The key question is what are the characteristics that government and the law require business records to possess? The answer is that the law requires these records to be legible, accessible, complete, true and accurate, capable of reproduction, and retained for appropriate periods of time. These factors apply irrespective of the particular form or format on which business records have been recorded. The issue, then, is not media type, but whether the records can be read, whether they can be demonstrated to be trustworthy (i.e., they have not been falsified in pursuit of some nefarious purpose), and whether they are fully usable for any regulatory or other legal purpose.

Admissibility into Evidence

Organizations maintain large quantities of records, and many of them could conceivably be deemed relevant to some type of legal proceeding or otherwise be subject to scrutiny by the government at some future time. In fact, some of these records will, almost certainly, be requested as legal evidence. How should an organization operate its recordkeeping systems so that they will be considered legally sufficient in the eyes of the law? What role should RIM specialists play in this responsibility?

Legal evidence is defined as oral testimony of witnesses or facts or opinions imputed from physical objects, such as records, that are submitted for introduction in legal proceedings. When thus submitted, the litigants or the court itself may call into question the authenticity of the items. The rules of evidence govern whether and how the court will find that the items are authentic and thus eligible for admittance into evidence. On the other hand, the records may engender the opposite finding and be deemed untrustworthy and thus admissibility will be denied.

Evidence that a judge or jury can consider on merit is termed admissible. To meet the requirements of *admissibility* as evidence, a record must satisfy two requirements: (1) Its content must be relevant to the issue at hand, and (2) its authenticity must be firmly established. To meet the authenticity requirement, the record must satisfy three key tests:

1. The record must have been created at or near the time of the event that is at issue in the proceedings;

2. The record must have been created by a person with knowledge of the event;

3. The record must have been maintained in the regular course of an organization's business.[1]

The main role of records managers concerning evidence admissibility is to establish policies, procedures, and other guidelines to ensure that the organization's recordkeeping systems are maintained in a manner that will not compromise the possible future admissibility of information as evidence in legal proceedings. Measures must be instituted to ensure that these three questions can be answered to the court's satisfaction. The measure must also ensure the information content of the recordkeeping systems is complete, true and accurate, accessible, legible, and reproducible as required.

Electronic Commerce and Digital Signatures

Another legal issue that records managers need a solid understanding about relates to the legality of commercial transactions in highly technology-oriented environments. Many persons erroneously assume that, in order to be legally acceptable, commercial transactions must be supported by original records and/or authenticated signatures. This assumption is based on the fact that many current laws were enacted in a pretechnology era, when pen, ink, and original paper were the basic raw materials of business recordkeeping as well as the documentation reflecting commercial transactions between buyers and sellers of goods and services. However, in the Age of the Internet, such old fashioned recordkeeping practices are no longer sustainable. New methods of recordkeeping, and the legal basis for them, must be adopted in this new era.

The law grants parties engaged in commercial business transactions the right to reach mutual agreement as to what form of documentation (including those bearing signatures) is acceptable to them. The law may be characterized as *technology-neutral* in that it does not impose any recordkeeping type or media on these parties. On the other hand, new laws do encourage new technologies as the basis for recordkeeping in commercial transactions.

UN Model Law on Electronic Commerce

In 1996, the United Nations Commission on International Trade Law (UNCITRAL) developed the world's first global legislative model that prescribed legal standards for recordkeeping in all-digital environments. This legislation was the Model Law on Electronic Commerce, and it has revolutionized the laws of electronic recordkeeping throughout the world. This new "supernational" model legislation was designed for adoption or consideration by the UN's member states worldwide. The basic purpose of the model law is to offer national legislative bodies a set of internationally accepted rules as to how existing legal obstacles may be removed, and how a more secure legal environment may be created for conducting business electronically. This model law has been widely adopted, in various forms, by national governments throughout the world, including the U.S.

Many older laws, enacted in a pretechnology era but still on the books, contain provisions that require original records or documents bearing authenticated signatures in order for business transactions to be legally binding or enforceable. The UN model law is designed to overcome such impediments so long as the electronic recordkeeping systems and the documents they contain can be demonstrated to possess the requisite integrity and trustworthiness—they must be accessible, legible, true, and accurate, and retained for appropriate periods of time.

With respect to the notions of written, signed, and original documents, the model law was based on what was termed the *functional equivalence* approach. This approach is based on an analysis of the purposes and functions of the traditional paper-based requirement, with a view to determining how those purposes or functions can be fulfilled through electronic commerce techniques. For example, among the functions served by a paper document are the following:

- To provide a medium such that a document will remain unaltered over time
- To allow for the reproduction of a document so that each party in a business transaction will hold a copy of the document(s) agreed to
- To allow for the attestation of the ***integrity*** of the content of the document by means of a signature
- To provide that a document will be in a form acceptable to the courts and other public authorities

The premise of the model law is that electronic records can, if managed correctly, provide the same level of functionality as their paper counterparts. On the other hand, UNCITRAL observes that a digital record, in and of itself, cannot be regarded as an equivalent of a paper document in that it is of a different nature and does not necessarily perform all conceivable functions of a paper document. Thus, the model law does not attempt to define a computer-based equivalent to any kind of paper document. Instead, it singles out basic functions of paper-based requirements, with a view to providing criteria which, once they are met by electronic records, enable such records to enjoy the same level of legal recognition as corresponding paper documents performing the same function. The framework of the model law, then, is intended to provide equivalent levels of reliability, traceability, and unalterability as would be found in properly managed paper-based systems.

The model law applies to any kind of electronic records in the form of data messages used in the context of commercial activities. The term data messages is defined in the law to refer to "information generated, sent, received, or stored by electronic, optical, or analogous means including, but not limited to, electronic data interchange, electronic mail, telegram, telex or telecopy." In other words, data messages are, to all intents and purposes, synonymous with the generic term *electronic records*. The notion of "data message" as used in the model law is not limited to communication but is also intended to encompass computer-generated records that are used for any business purpose. The aim of the definition of "data message," UNCITRAL notes, is to encompass all types of messages generated, stored, or communicated in essentially paperless form. Thus, the notion of "message" as used in the model law is analogous to that of "record." The model law includes a broad definition of the term "commercial activities"; "matters arising from all relationships of a commercial nature, whether contractual or not."

For the U.S. and other countries that have elected to adopt this model law or some version of it, its provisions will be of special significance to anyone engaged in the management of electronic records. The main provisions of this model law that are of direct relevance to the management of electronic records are contained in Chapter II, "Application of Legal Requirements to Data Messages," and are summarized as follows:

- **Legal recognition of electronic records** – Chapter II, Article 5 provides that "Information shall not be denied legal effectiveness, validity, or enforceability solely on the grounds that it is in the form of a data message." In 1998, UNCITRAL revised this language to read "Information shall not be denied legal effect, validity or enforceability solely on the grounds that it is not contained in the data message purporting to give rise to such legal effect, but is merely referred to in that data message." Article 9 of the same chapter elucidates this principle further. "In any legal proceedings, nothing in the application of the rules of evidence shall apply so as to deny the admissibility of a data message in evidence: (a) on the sole grounds that it is a data message, or, (b) if it is the best evidence that a person adducing it could reasonably be expected to obtain, on the grounds that it is not in its original form." Thus, the model law confers legal status on data messages as business records and further provides for their admissibility as evidence in courts of law, unless some reason for not doing so arises.

- **Legal requirements that information be in writing** – Chapter II, Article 6, provides that "Where the law requires that information be in writing, that requirement is met by a data message if the information contained therein is accessible so as to be usable for subsequent reference." This provision can be construed to provide a general endorsement of new technologies for business recordkeeping, provided that organizations assimilating such technologies adhere to the basic provisions indicated in Article 8.

- **Legal requirements pertaining to electronic signatures** – Chapter II, Article 7, provides that "Where the law requires a signature of a person, that requirement is met in relation to a data message if (a) a method is used to identify that person and to indicate that person's approval of the information contained in the data message; and (b) that method is reliable as was appropriate for the purpose for which the data message was generated or communicated . . ." In 2001, UNCITRAL published requirements pertaining to electronic signatures in a separate model law.

- **Legal requirements for original records** – Chapter II, Article 8, states that "Where the law requires information to be presented or retained in its original form, that requirement is met by a data message if (a) there exists a reliable assurance as to the integrity of the information from the time when it was first generated in its final from, as a data message or otherwise; and (b) where it is required that information be presented, that information is capable of being displayed to the person to whom it is to be presented."

- **Criteria for assessing the integrity of electronic records** – Under Chapter II, Article 8, the criteria for assessing the integrity (trustworthiness) of electronic records "shall be whether the information has remained complete and unaltered, apart the addition of any endorsement and any change which arises in the normal course of communication, storage, and display . . ." Article 9 clarifies that principle still further: "In assessing the evidential weight of a data message, regard shall be had to the reliability of the manner in which the data message was generated, stored or communicated, to the reliability of the manner in which the integrity of the information was maintained, to the manner in which its originator was identified, and to any other relevant factor."

- **Electronic records as a retention medium** – Provisions relating to the retention of electronic records are contained in Article 10 of Chapter II. The important ones are:

  - (1) "Where the law requires that certain documents, records or information be retained, that requirement is met by retaining data messages, provided that the following conditions are satisfied:
    - (a) the information contained therein is accessible so as to be usable for subsequent reference; and
    - (b) the data message is retained in the format in which it was generated, transmitted or received, or in a format which can be demonstrated to represent accurately the information generated, sent or received; and

- ▪ (c) such information, if any, is retained as enables the identification of the origin and destination of a data message and the date and time when it was sent or received."

- ◆ (2) "An obligation to retain documents, records or information in accordance with paragraph (1) does not extend to any information the sole purpose of which is to enable to be sent or received;

- ◆ (3) "A person may satisfy the requirement referred to in paragraph (1) by using the services of any other person, provided that the conditions set forth [in this paragraph] are met."[2]

UN Model Law on Electronic Signatures

In May 2001, UNCITRAL issued its second major pronouncement concerning electronic recordkeeping—the Model Law on Electronic Signatures. This law provides much more comprehensive guidance for the legislative framework of *digital signatures* than the brief treatment appearing in the earlier e-commerce law, and it is certain to be of equal global significance in the development of international law relative to its subject.

Electronic signatures are defined in the model law to mean "data in electronic form in, affixed to, or logically associated with, a data message, which may be used to identify the signatory in relation to the data message and indicate the signatory's approval of the information contained in the data message." To reiterate the need for this legislation, existing country laws impose or imply restrictions on the use of modern means of communication, for example, by prescribing the use of "written," "signed" or "original" documents. In an electronic environment, however, the "original" of a message is indistinguishable from a copy, bears no handwritten signature, and is not on paper. The potential for fraud is considerable, due to the ease of intercepting and altering information in electronic form without detection, and the speed of processing multiple transactions. Thus, the objective of this and other digital signature laws and the various technology tools associated with them is to offer the means by which some or all the functions identified as characteristic of handwritten signatures can be performed in an electronic environment. These functions are:

- To identify a person;
- To provide certainty as to the personal involvement of that person in the act of signing;
- To associate that person with the content of a document;
- To indicate the intent of a person to be legally bound by the content of a signed document;
- To provide an indication of a person to attest ownership of or otherwise endorse the authorship of the text and content of a signed document.

Based on these principles, Article 6 of the model law states that: "Where the law requires the signature of a person, that requirement is met in relation to a data message if an electronic signature is used which is as reliable as was appropriate for the purpose for which the data message was generated or communicated . . ."

With respect to the reliability of an electronic signature, the model law enumerates four tests:

1. "The signature creation data are, within the context in which they are used, linked to the signatory and to no other person;

2. The signature creation data were, at the time of signing, under the control of the signatory and of no other person;

3. Any alteration to the electronic signature, made after the time of signing, is detectable; and

4. Where a purpose of the legal requirement for a signature is to provide assurance as to the integrity of the information to which it relates, any alteration made to that information after the time of signing is detectable."[3]

UNCITRAL states that the model law is intended to apply where electronic signatures are used in the context of commercial activities. It is not intended to override any existing rule of law for the protection of consumers.

The U.S. E-Sign Law

In June 2000, President Clinton signed into law the *Electronic Signatures in Global and National Commerce Act*, commonly referred to as the "E-Sign Act." According to many observers, this new law totally changes the landscape pertaining to the use of electronic information in commercial transactions in the United States. The law does not, however, grant any special status to electronic records. It merely removes the impediments in existing law to conducting business electronically. In this sense, the law may be characterized as "media-neutral." Electronic records are subject to the same legal scrutiny as physical ones. The law does not provide any broad authority or mandate for businesses to convert all types of records from paper to electronic format. The law implicitly recognizes that paper records will be utilized as a medium for business recordkeeping for some time to come.

The new E-Sign Act contains provisions that pertain directly to electronic records retention in e-commerce environments and thus are of high interest to records managers. These provisions are as follows:

"(d) Retention of Contracts and Records.

(1) Accuracy and accessibility. If a statute, regulation, or other rule of law requires that a contract or other record relating to a transaction in or affecting interstate or foreign commerce be retained, that requirement is met by retaining an electronic record of the information in the contract or other record that:

a. Accurately reflects the information set forth in the contract or other record; and

b. Remains accessible to all persons who are entitled to access by statute, regulation, or rule of law, for the period required by such statute, regulation, or rule of law, in a form that is capable of being accurately reproduced for later reference, whether by transmission, printing, or otherwise."

Based on these provisions, the law provides three key tests for the legal acceptability of electronic records as a retention medium in e-commerce transactions:

1. The record must accurately reflect the information contained in the original contract or transaction; and

2. The record must remain accessible to those entitled by law to access it, for the period required by law; and

3. The record must be capable of being accurately reproduced, whether by printing or otherwise.

If these criteria are not satisfied, the record cannot be used to enforce the organization's legal rights. For records managers, the central issue is whether the organization's e-commerce applications, and the electronic records that comprise them, can be demonstrated to comply with these requirements.

Uniform Electronic Transactions Act

The Uniform Electronic Transactions Act (UETA) is a model law adopted by the National Conference of Commissioners on Uniform State Laws in July 1999. The purpose of the UETA is to provide states with a model law that would promote uniformity among state laws addressing electronic records in technology-neutral e-commerce business environments. UETA indicates that the requirement to retain records "does not apply to any information the sole purpose of which is to enable the record to be sent, communicated, or received." However, failure to maintain such metadata may severely limit one's ability to prove the integrity of the transactions. Section 12 of the UETA addresses the issue of electronic records retention. It states:

"(a) If a law requires that a record be retained, that requirement is satisfied by retaining an electronic record of the information in the record which:

(1) accurately reflects the information set forth in the record after it was first generated in its final form as an electronic record or otherwise; and

(2) remains accessible for later reference."

Section 12 further provides:

"(f) A record retained as an electronic record in accordance with subsection (a) satisfies a law requiring a person to retain a record for evidentiary, audit, or like purposes, unless a law enacted after the effective date of this [Act] specifically prohibits the use of an electronic record for the specified purpose."

These retention provisions largely mirror those contained in the E-Sign Act. Again, the overall effect will be to promote the widespread adoption of e-commerce technologies and the records that will document the transactions occurring in these types of computing environments.

New Regulatory Initiatives

During the past several years, a number of new regulatory initiatives have occurred in the U.S. that are having a significant impact on RIM (see Figure 6.1). As illustrated in Figure 6.2, these initiatives pose significant compliance challenges for organi-

**Laws Affecting
Business
Recordkeeping**

Figure 6.1

	U.S. Laws Affecting Business Recordkeeping								
Regulation by Technology	**SOX IAS**	**HIPAA**	**Gramm- Leach- Bliley**	**Basel II**	**21 CFR Part II**	**Sec 17A-4**	**Patriot Act**	**CA SB 1386**
Financial compliance/BPM/ analytical application	X			X				
ERP	X			X				
Business intelligence & data warehousing	X			X				
Data/application integration	X			X	X			
Document/content management & access	X	X	X	X	X	X	X	X
Records and information management	X	X		X	X	X		
Archiving	X	X	X	X	X	X	X	X
Security	X	X	X	X	X	X	X	X
Storage SW/HW	X	X		X	X	X	X	

Source: Data from IDC as reported by Julie Rahal in "What Role Will Content Technologies Play in this Era of Regulatory Compliance?" *KMWorld*, June 2004.

**Regulatory
Compliance
Infrastructure**

Figure 6.2

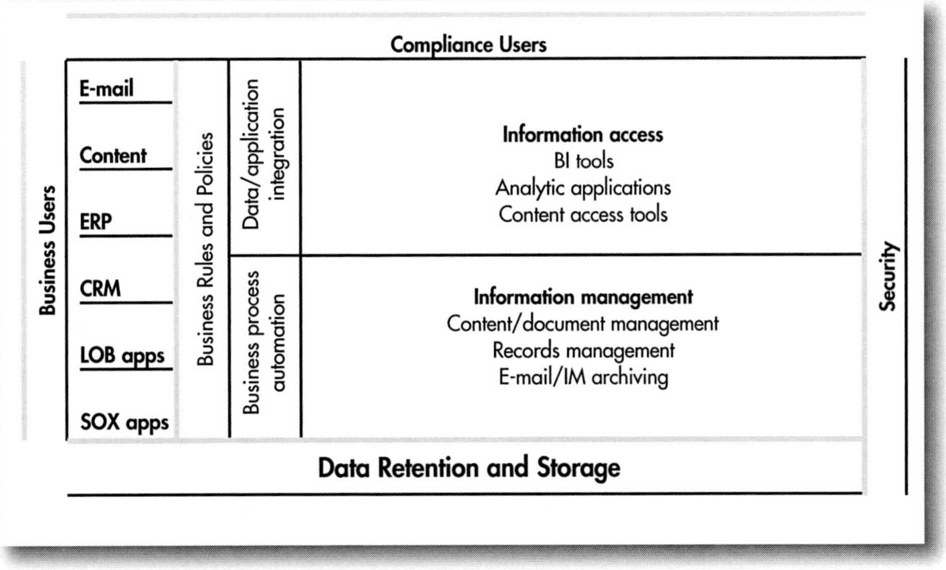

Source: Data from IDC, 2004.

zations, and they have greatly increased the awareness of the need for and benefits of RIM. According to one commentator, when scrutinized by a court, regulator, or the wary investing public, anything that is perceived as good and reasonable corporate policy and behavior can transform a potentially bad situation into a nonevent and one that is more likely to be overlooked as a one-time occurrence."[4]

RIM's goal in regulatory compliance should be to ensure that the organization's recordkeeping systems are being managed such that the integrity of their information content can meet the tests of authenticity, integrity, and reliability. The ISO 15489 standard addresses RIM's requirements in the face of regulatory requirements. The standard states, "All organizations need to identify the regulatory environment that effects their activities . . . An organization should provide adequate evidence of its compliance with the regulatory environment in the records of its activities." ISO further states that an organization's regulatory environment consists of statutory and case laws and regulations relating specifically to records, archives, access, privacy, evidence, electronic commerce, data protection, and information.[5]

As illustrated in Figures 6.3 and 6.4, the new regulatory compliance mandates have common features in at least three areas: (1) ensuring the integrity of relevant information and the business processes in which it is created and managed; (2) man-

Regulatory Compliance Challenges

Figure 6.3

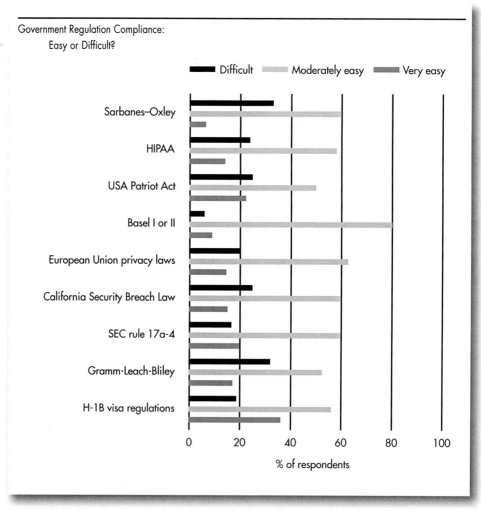

Government Regulation Compliance:
Easy or Difficult?

Difficult   Moderately easy   Very easy

(chart categories, top to bottom: Sarbanes–Oxley, HIPAA, USA Patriot Act, Basel I or II, European Union privacy laws, California Security Breach Law, SEC rule 17a-4, Gramm-Leach-Bliley, H-1B visa regulations)

x-axis: 0   20   40   60   80   100

% of respondents

Source: Data from *InformationWeek* Media Network Compliance study of 200 business-technology professionals.

**Information
Access and
Compliance**

Figure 6.4

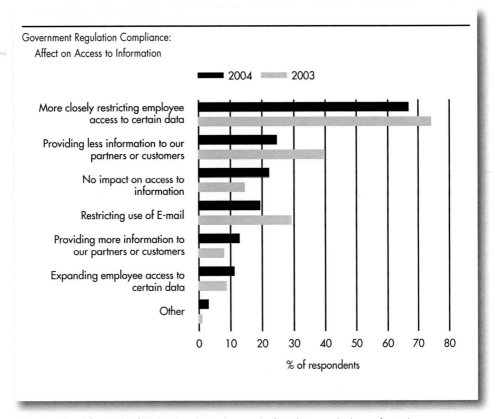

Government Regulation Compliance:
Affect on Access to Information

Source: Data from *InformationWeek* Media Network Compliance study of 200 business-technology professionals.

dated records retention requirements; and (3) restricting the access to and privacy of information. The most significant of the new regulatory initiatives are:

- Sarbanes-Oxley
- Gramm-Leach-Bliley
- HIPAA
- Basel II
- EU and California privacy requirements

From a RIM perspective, Sarbanes-Oxley is the most far-reaching of the new regulatory initiatives, so it is discussed first. The RIM implications of the EU and California privacy requirements are discussed in Chapter 11.

Sarbanes-Oxley Act

During the past several years, the U.S. has been beset by a number of business scandals that brought to light the need for greater corporate accountability, particularly in matters relating to shareholder accountability and the integrity of the financial and accounting systems of publicly held companies. Perhaps the most infamous of these scandals was the Enron-Arthur Andersen affair. In the wake of these scandals, the

United States Congress enacted the Public Company Accounting Reform and Investor Protection Act of 2002 (popularly referred to as the Sarbanes-Oxley Act, in recognition of its two main Congressional sponsors, Senator Paul Sarbanes and Congressman Michael Oxley), which was signed into law by President Bush on July 30, 2002.[6]

This new law was designed to improve the quality of financial reporting and restore public confidence in the integrity of financial statements of public companies. William Donaldson, chairman of the U.S. Securities and Exchange Commission, referred to the Act as "the most important securities legislation since the [enactment of the] original securities laws of the 1930s."[7] A key provision of the act requires CEOs and CFOs to personally attest to the accuracy of their company's financial statements and reports. This requirement exposes these executives to significantly greater liability than in the past, and it has significant implications for both IT and RIM.

The Sarbanes-Oxley Act introduces compelling reasons for CEOs to implement corporate RIM. Prior to the enactment of this legislation, many corporate executives were inclined to regard RIM as a discretionary endeavor, one unrelated to the overall success of the business and thus not worthy of serious management attention. However, with Sarbanes-Oxley on the books, these executives are much more likely to regard RIM as an essential function, one that they must initiate, fund, and manage to the level of proven success. Noncompliance is now a federal crime and can result in punishment of up to twenty years in prison for some violations.[8]

Notwithstanding the gravity of these matters, many RIM professionals apparently have yet to appreciate the full ramifications of the Act on their profession. According to one recent survey, only 12 percent of the respondents reported that Sarbanes-Oxley had had a meaningful impact on their organization's RIM program.[9] A sharply differing view was expressed by Senator Patrick Leahy (D-Vermont), one of the Act's chief sponsors in the U.S. Senate. He observed that information management specialists will play a key role in implementing the Sarbanes-Oxley Act. He wrote that, "As gatekeepers of corporate recordkeeping, it will be they who ensure that a corporation's policy and culture matches its legal requirements . . ."[10]

The recordkeeping provisions of Sarbanes-Oxley that affect auditors' copies of accounting work papers apply to all U.S. public companies and public accounting firms regardless of size. However, the Act's records retention provisions apply only to public accounting firms who audit publicly traded companies. The Act also applies to foreign accounting firms, including those that perform audit work for foreign subsidiaries of U.S. companies.

A central focus of the Act is to improve the integrity of the audit process for publicly traded companies and the reliability of audit reports on corporate financial statements. Therefore, corporate accounting and related records must be accurate, complete, and fully accessible. A significant corporate compliance initiative in which IT and RIM should work in close concert, together with finance, accounting, and other key stakeholders is required.

New Mandate for Internal Controls

A central focus of Sarbanes-Oxley is to improve the integrity of the audit process for publicly traded companies and the reliability of audit reports on corporate financial statements. For many companies, a significant new corporate compliance initiative, of which adequate *internal controls*, including RIM, is the key element will be required. Reliable recordkeeping systems are, in fact, a precondition for compliance with Section 302(a) and 404(a) of Sarbanes-Oxley, as follows:

- **Section 302(a)** – Under this section, the company's signing officers must certify that quarterly and annual reports filed with the SEC fairly present the company's financial condition and results of operations for the indicated period. Further, signing officers must establish and maintain internal controls to ensure that they are aware of "material information" relating to the company and its subsidiaries during the periods covered by the reports. Signing officers must also disclose to the company's auditors and audit committee all significant deficiencies "which could adversely affect the issuer's ability to record, process, summarize and report financial data."

- **Section 404(a) (2)** – This section requires that the company's annual report include management's assessment of the effectiveness of the company's internal control structure. Section 404(b) requires the company's public accountants to attest to and report on the assessment.

Although the rules and regulations of the SEC do not define standards for the effectiveness of a company's internal controls as provided by the Act, they do suggest that the internal control framework defined in 1992 by the Committee of Sponsoring Organizations (COSO) of the Treadway Commission are acceptable. According to the COSO framework, internal controls consist of five interrelated components:

1. A control environment that sets the tone for an organization
2. Risk assessment to identify and evaluate risks from external and internal sources
3. Policies and procedures to ensure that management directives are carried out
4. Systems to capture and communicate information, and
5. Ongoing monitoring for compliance

A systematic RIM program is fully compatible with and supportive of this internal controls framework. By ensuring that recorded information will be controlled by directives rather than discretion, a systematic RIM program supports the internal controls of COSO. For example, a systematic RIM program is driven by policies and procedures that specify how long information must be kept to satisfy the company's legal and operational requirements. Further, a RIM program includes procedures for the retrieval and distribution of information needed for specific purposes. Finally, a RIM program includes provisions for compliance auditing.[11]

To ensure proper compliance with the internal controls requirements of Sarbanes-Oxley, records managers should work closely with corporate finance, IT, legal, and other key stakeholders. Special attention should be devoted to the proper management and integrity of the data residing in financial and other relevant recordkeeping systems. Information residing in these systems must be managed such that a high degree of integrity can be demonstrated. In brief, the law requires that a company's financial records must be complete, true and accurate, accessible, retained in accordance with the law and good faith, and fully usable in support of any audits, investigations, or other regulatory requirements.

Sarbanes-Oxley and IT Issues

The heart of Sarbanes-Oxley is about the integrity of corporate financial data. From an IT perspective, the reporting of financial results that can be demonstrated to possess a high degree of integrity and thus be considered compliant with Sarbanes-Oxley presents special challenges because financial data frequently resides in multiple applications and storage repositories, including PCs, where the final consolidation of the data is often done.

If the records (not only the formal certified reports but also e-mails, voicemails, databases, data warehouses, or any other form of corporate records), in whatever form or location, show that the certified financial reports are not accurate, the executives could be liable for sanctions.[12] Where once financial reporting was limited to data residing on the general ledger and other financial systems, now every aspect of a company's business that materially impacts its financial performance must be reported on as well. Such data, of course, is maintained on many disparate systems throughout the enterprise. Many observers believe that a single enterprise system, or one that can retrieve data from multiple applications, may be required in order to fully satisfy the compliance requirements of Sarbanes-Oxley.[13]

Whether Sarbanes-Oxley will prove to be a force that significantly alters the landscape of RIM remains to be seen. As always, enforcement is the key to the "teeth" in any law. However, for the first time ever, corporate executives are confronted with a statutory imperative for RIM that cannot be ignored. Sarbanes-Oxley clearly has the potential to elevate the RIM function to a new and higher level than it has ever enjoyed in the life of U.S. business corporations. Future developments will determine whether this elevation proves to be the case.

HIPAA

The Health Insurance Portability and Accountability Act (HIPAA) (Public Law 104-191), was enacted in 1996 to combat fraud and abuse in heath care, as well as to improve healthcare systems by encouraging the electronic transfer of medical information. Under this law, the U.S. Department of Health and Human Services (HHS) has promulgated health information privacy regulations (the Privacy Rule), which require regulated parties—health plans, healthcare clearinghouses, and certain healthcare providers—to implement a variety of privacy protections for patients, insured parties, or other individuals subject to the rules. These rules govern access to patient medical records, requirements for patient consent to permit the sharing or disclosure of health information for treatment or payment purposes, patient recourse for privacy violations, and other requirements. Anyone in an organization involved in an insurance-related transaction in any way is subject to HIPAA's privacy requirements. The RIM professional in an organization may therefore have considerable involvement with those requirements; for example, workers' compensation claims, various health insurance information, dispensary and first-aid records, and many other records typically found in businesses. Managers of medical record-keeping systems must ensure that patient-specific records are stored, maintained, transmitted, and accessed in a secure fashion, so as to protect the privacy of the individuals to which they relate.

Gramm-Leach-Bliley

This law is formally known as the Financial Modernization Act of 1999 (Public Law 106-102), but it is commonly referred to by the names of its principal legislative sponsors. The law addresses the privacy of customer-specific financial records and information, and applies to banks and financial institutions that are subject to the regulatory authority of the U.S. Department of the Treasury, the Federal Deposit Insurance Corporation, and the Federal Reserve.

In recognition that banks and financial institutions collect many forms of customer-specific personal information (i.e., names, addresses, credit card data, telephone and social security numbers, etc.), Title V of the Act requires these companies to alert customers, in writing or electronically, of their policies and practices in disclosing customer information. These alerts must provide a procedure to "opt out" of the disclosure of nonpublic personal information. The act puts the onus on the financial institutions to protect the security and confidentiality of the "personally identifiable" financial information pertaining to their customers.[14]

Records managers of financial institutions subject to Gramm-Leach-Bliley should work with managers of recordkeeping systems containing customer-specific financial information to ensure that the systems are managed in a way in which compliance with the Act can be demonstrated.

Basel II

Developed by the European Committee on Banking Supervision, Basel II is a revised code on risk management for global financial institutions that went into effect in 2006. The goal of the regulation is to make banks' assessments of their loans and investments more sensitive to risk, such as loan defaults or volatile global financial markets. This regulation has significant implications for information management, particularly among multinational financial companies. To comply with Basel II, financial institutions will need to establish linkages of databases and risk management systems around the world, many of which are based on different technical standards. The data residing within those systems will also need to be verified.[15]

Authenticity of Records

Authenticity, in a RIM context, refers to the fact that a record is what it purports to be and has not been tampered with or otherwise corrupted since its creation; that is, it possesses proven reliability over time. The record must be genuine and determined to have been managed by specific records custodians through all phases of its life cycle. RIM has a key role to play in the authenticity and integrity of business records. Indeed, the entire discipline of RIM has been characterized as "the process of managing the corporate memory in a way that makes trustworthy records readily accessible any time they are required."[16] However, in U.S. practice, the integrity and authenticity of recordkeeping systems and the information content residing in them has not been a top RIM priority. According to a recent study, 62 percent of the respondents reported that they are "not at all confident" that their organization could demonstrate that its electronic records are accurate, reliable, and trustworthy over time, many years after they are created.[17]

The most recent authoritative statements concerning the authenticity of business records and the role of records managers in supporting it were issued by the International Organization for Standardization, in its international standard for RIM (ISO 15489, 2001). According to the standard, an authentic record is one that "can be proven to be what it purports to be, to have been created or sent by the person purported to have sent it, and to have been created or sent at the time purported."

To ensure the authenticity of records, the ISO standard requires that organizations implement and document policies and procedures designed to control the creation, receipt, transmission, maintenance, and disposition of records. Moreover, the information content of records must be "protected against unauthorized addition, deletion, alteration, use, and concealment."

Reliability, Integrity, and Usability

The ISO standard contains further details for supporting the authenticity of records, including requirements for ensuring their reliability, integrity, and usability. These requirements are summarized as follows:

- **Reliability** – The ISO standard defines a reliable record as one whose contents can be trusted as a full and accurate representation of the transactions, activities, or facts to which they attest and can be depended upon in the course of subsequent transactions or activities. To be demonstrated as reliable, the standard specifies that records be created at the time of the transaction or incident to which they relate, or soon afterwards, by individuals who have direct knowledge of the facts or instruments routinely used within the business to conduct the transaction.

- **Integrity** – The ISO standard defines the integrity of a record as one that is complete and unaltered. Moreover, the standard specifies that a record be protected against unauthorized alteration. RIM policies and procedures should specify what additions or annotations may be made to a record after it is created, under what circumstances additions or annotations may be authorized, and who is authorized to make them. Finally, any authorized annotation, addition, or deletion to a record should be explicitly indicated and traceable.

- **Usability** – The ISO standard defines a usable record as one that can be located, retrieved, presented, and interpreted. Further, a usable record should be capable of subsequent presentation as directly connected to the business activity or transaction that produced it. The contextual linkages of records should carry the information needed for an understanding of the transactions that created and used them. It should be possible to identify a record within the context of broader business activities and functions. Finally, the standard specifies that the links between records that document a sequence of activities should be maintained.

To accomplish the above requirements, the ISO 15489 standard specifies that management of recordkeeping systems be supported by adequately documented policies, assigned responsibilities, and formal methodologies. The standard requires that organizations implement various control measures (i.e., access monitoring, user verification, authorized destruction, and security) for every compliant recordkeeping system, so that the integrity of the information content can be demonstrated. These controls may reside within the recordkeeping system or external to it. Finally, for electronic recordkeeping systems, the standard indicates that organizations may need to prove that any system malfunction, upgrade, or regular maintenance does not compromise the integrity of the data.[18]

RIM specialists have a key role to play in the authenticity and integrity of business records. Indeed, the entire discipline of RIM has been characterized as the process of managing the corporate memory in a way that makes trustworthy records readily accessible any time they are required. RIM specialists need to work closely with attorneys, IT specialists, and the business managers having responsibility for recordkeeping systems to achieve these objectives, based on the principles discussed in this chapter.

Notes

1. William Saffady, *Records and Information Management: Fundamentals of Professional Practice* (Lenexa, KS: ARMA International, 2004), 60.

2. United Nations Commission on International Trade Law, UNCITRAL, *Model Law on Electronic Commerce with Guide to Enactment*, 1996.

3. _____, *Guide to Enactment of the UNCITRAL Model Law on Electronic Signatures*, 2001. Draft.

4. Randolph Kahn, "Records Management & Compliance: Making the Connection," *The Information Management Journal* 38, no. 3 (May / June 2004): 32.

5. International Organization for Standardization, ISO 15489-1:2001, *International Standard: Information and Documentation – Records Management – Part 1: General* (Geneva, Switzerland: ISO, 2001), 4-5.

6. Sarbanes-Oxley Act, Public Law 107-2004, 116 Stat. 745, (2002).

7. Frank Moore and Nikki Swartz, "Keeping an Eye on Sarbanes-Oxley," *The Information Management Journal* 37, no. 6 (November / December 2003): 20.

8. Gillian Colledge and Michael Cliff, "The Implications of the Sarbanes-Oxley Act: It's Time to Take Records Management Seriously," *KMWorld*, September 2003, S-4.

9. Robert Williams, *Electronic Records Management Survey: A Call to Action* (Chicago: Cohasset, Inc., 2004), 38.

10. Patrick Leahy, "Preserving the Paper (and Electronic) Trail," *The Information Management Journal* 37, no. 1 (January / February 2003): 17.

11. William Saffady, *Compliance with Recordkeeping Provisions of Sarbanes-Oxley Act of 2002.* Unpublished manuscript, August 31, 2004.

12. J. Edwin Dietel, "Recordkeeping Integrity: Assessing Records' Content After Enron," *The Information Management Journal* 37, no. 3 (May / June 2003): 48.

13. Cathleen Moore and Ephraim Schwartz, "Sorting Through SarbOx," *InfoWorld*, 14 July 2003, 54.

14. Susan Haller, "Privacy: What Every Manager Should Know," *The Information Management Journal* 36, no. 3 (May / June 2002): 38.

15. Julie Rahal Marobella, "The World Is Watching," *The Information Management Journal* 39, no. 2 (March / April 2005): 18-19.

16. Kahn, "Records Management & Compliance," 30.

17. Williams, *Electronic Records Management Survey*, 6.

18. International Organization for Standards, ISO 15489-1:2001, 7.

Chapter 7

Records Retention and the Law

Although reductions in storage costs are indeed an important reason that organizations are motivated to utilize records retention as the means of managing the life cycle of their records, legal reasons are often considered to be far more compelling. In fact, organization executives are often motivated to institute records retention initiatives for two main reasons: They want to be able to demonstrate compliance with regulatory requirements, and they want to reduce the risks associated with the possible use of records and information in litigation actions or government investigations.

Both these reasons are entirely justified and indeed legally permissible. However, if they are to achieve the level of legal sufficiency, records retention programs must be developed and implemented with care and caution. Records and information management specialists need to work in close concert with attorneys to ensure that their retention programs are within the law and can withstand legal scrutiny. Records retention policies were precisely the issue that lead to the virtual demise of Arthur Andersen, LLP. In a case unprecedented in U.S. history, senior executives of this well-known public accounting firm were convicted in federal court of obstruction of justice by reason of illegal records destruction. Although the conviction was later overturned by the U.S. Supreme Court, the reversal was hardly a declaration of innocence. Rather, the reversal was based on the Court's finding that the jury instructions were too vague and broad for jurors to determine correctly whether Andersen's executives obstructed justice.

The Government's Role in Records Retention

Many persons, including many senior executives, are wedded to the notion that, in the U.S., the retention of business records is largely driven by the government. On the contrary, records retention in the U.S. is largely driven by business needs. The perception that the retention of business records is largely driven by government requirements is predicated on two assumptions, both of which are false.

1. **The retention of most business records is driven by government requirements** – The answer to this assumption depends on how stringently a particular organization is regulated, both generally and more particularly with respect to the retention of its records. To clarify the matter in terms of a specific question: If an organization maintains, say, 1,000 separate types of records, for how many of these can any specific law or regulation be found that directly / specifically mandates how long they must be retained? The reality is that, for organizations that are lightly regulated by the government, no more than 20 to 25 percent of its records will be subject to a law or regulation that directly and specifically requires them to be retained for any specified period of time. Even for heavily regulated businesses (i.e., public utility companies, pharmaceutical firms, etc.), this figure seldom exceeds 40 to 50 percent. These percentages would be substantially higher if *indirect* retention issues were considered; that is, if the question is rephrased to state: What percentage of an organization's records need to be retained for certain periods of time because of significant legal issues that imply how long it may be in the organization's best interest to retain records? The answer to this question will definitely be higher—say, 50 percent or more of the records of many organizations.

2. **Retention laws and regulations are the determining factor in most retention decisions** – In cases where laws or regulations can be found that directly mandate the retention of certain records for specific periods of time, the question is: Are these periods of time the *determining factor* in the retention decision, or do other factors necessitate the retention of the records for longer periods of time? In the majority of cases, actual or perceived business needs will exceed the retention requirements imposed by the government. Of the thousands of government-imposed retention requirements, the majority are of relatively short duration—less than five years. More often than not, business people will articulate retention needs that exceed these requirements. Thus, in these instances, although these laws and regulations are one factor, they are not the determining factor in the retention decision.

Compliance with Retention Laws and Regulations

As stated previously, most organization executives are motivated to institute records retention initiatives for two main reasons: (1) to be able to demonstrate compliance with regulatory requirements, and (2) to reduce the risks associated with the possible use of records and information in litigation actions or government investigations. Of these two reasons, litigation risk avoidance is, by far, the more compelling, as perceived by an organization's senior attorneys and executives. The reason is simple: The risks are so much greater. People have indeed gone to jail for obstruction of justice by reason of illegal records destruction; but rarely, if ever, is this penalty meted out for failure to comply with retention regulations promulgated by regulatory authorities.

Many executives tend to take a somewhat casual attitude toward retention laws and regulations. Many have never performed comprehensive legal research to determine the laws and regulations with which they are required to comply. Even where this research has been performed, it often has not been recently updated. Although full compliance with the law is expected of all regulated parties, the risk of noncompliance with retention requirements is rarely great. A lackadaisical attitude towards compliance with the government's retention requirements is not recommended, however. As corporate citizens, regulated parties are obligated to comply with the law fully—in letter, spirit, and good faith. The reality is that litigation risks are much greater.

Regulatory Requirements Pertaining to Electronic Records

With respect to government-imposed retention requirements that apply to electronic records, the most important thing to understand is that government-mandated records retention requirements may apply to but do not usually specify an *electronic* record as an authorized or required retention medium. The majority of federal and state laws and regulations that require records to be retained are silent on the issue of which recordkeeping medium may or must be used to satisfy the government's requirements. Therefore, unless a particular storage medium is specified in the law or regulation, regulated parties may feel at liberty to retain the required records on any medium they desire, as long as the authenticity and integrity of the records have been preserved, and they may be reliably produced.[1]

During the past several years, a number of new laws and regulations specifically addressing electronic records media have been enacted. This flurry of legislative activity is expected to continue for at least another ten or so years as lawmakers grapple with vexing questions such as how to protect consumers and the public where recordkeeping occurs in the most advanced technology environments.

The Seven-Year Myth

The myth in records retention that most business records should or even must be retained for seven years predominates all other myths. Indeed, in the minds of many persons, keeping business records for seven years is an article of faith if not law. How this myth became so pervasive among managers and other office staff in the U.S. is unclear. Until the recent enactment of the Sarbanes-Oxley Act, no real basis in U.S. law supporting the seven-year rule existed. Except for the seven-year retention requirement in Sarbanes-Oxley, of the thousands of records retention requirements in U.S. law, very few expressly require any records to be retained for seven years. Moreover, the few seven-year requirements contained in U.S. law have narrow applicability; they do not apply to any broad segment of business records.

Nevertheless, over the years countless people have been heard to state, with near moral certainty, that, "we have to keep such-and-such records for seven years." This sentence is usually followed by the qualifying assertion that "that's what the IRS requires, right?" The reality is that the U.S. Internal Revenue Service has no such requirement. The most credible explanation for the seven-year myth stems from the fact that, in matters of federal corporate taxation, the IRS has three years to conduct audits of taxpayers' accounts (a period of time referred to as a *limitation on assessment*), after which it forfeits its right to do so. However, extensions for an additional three years are often sought and granted, which makes six years. Finally, an additional year must be added because tax adjudications do not occur until the year after filing; thus, six plus one additional year equals the "magic seven."

Finally, for a given tax year, the tax documentation of corporate taxpayers can remain open to scrutiny by revenue authorities for still longer periods of time—sometimes ten years or longer. "Open" tax years do not become "closed" until all audit exceptions—disputes between the IRS and taxpayers as to the legitimacy of deductions or other issues in dispute—have been resolved. Sometimes these disputes cannot be resolved administratively and evolve into litigation, which can take many years to be adjudicated by the tax courts. Again, nothing in the Internal Revenue Code limits taxpayer liability to seven years. Although for many types of business records, seven years is indeed a good retention period, but a seven-year requirement is not enshrined in the tax codes of the U.S. Internal Revenue Service.

Statutes of Limitation

In the U.S., statutes of limitation have been and remain a major factor in organizational records retention. The role of these laws in records retention is often misunderstood, however. For example, many persons assume that:

- Statutes of limitation are, in fact, records retention requirements; adherence to them is mandated by law in establishing retention schedules;
- In cases where multiple jurisdictions are involved, the **statute of limitation** for the "longest" jurisdiction mandates the operative retention requirement.

Both assumptions are false. Statutes of limitation do not impose any records retention mandates on regulated parties. These laws merely specify the length of time that the parties in some type of legal relationship may institute legal proceedings against each other. Thus, they are of high, but *indirect*, importance to records retention because they indicate the length of time that relevant records may possess legal value and may be needed in the resolution of disputes concerning matters to which they relate.[2]

Various individual state statutes of limitation on written contracts are illustrative of these points. These laws give parties in contractual relationships the right to sue for breach—to seek relief from the courts in cases where they believe their rights under the contract have been violated. The period of time during which such suits may be brought varies from three to twenty years, generally beginning from the date of the breach, with six years being the average. During these periods of time, retaining whatever records the parties believe would be useful to either prosecute a suit against another party or defend one against themselves, keeping in mind that the presence or absence of any such records may be either helpful or harmful to the case of either party, is advisable, *but not legally required*. Because most legal actions will probably be instituted either during the active life of the contract or soon thereafter, most organizations have elected to go with the average, rather than the longest statute of limitation, in cases where multiple jurisdictions are involved.

Other statutes of limitation often considered to be relevant to records retention include those concerning wage administration, personal injury, professional malpractice, improvements to real property, assessments for taxation, and product liability.

A complicating factor in statutes of limitation in making retention decisions is identifying the exact time period in the law at which the number of years becomes operative. For example, statutes of limitation begin when an event, such as a personal injury or breach of contract, occurs, not when records related to that event are created. Thus, care should be exercised in making interpretive judgments concerning retention periods that reflect the length of time that relevant records should be retained in light of their possible future use in resolving legal disputes. Records and information managers should consult with legal counsel concerning these matters.

Sarbanes-Oxley Act

The impact of the Sarbanes-Oxley Act[3] on RIM is among the highest of any federal statutes, particularly among pubic companies. The Act does not address the requirements of a records retention program that can be demonstrated to be in compliance with its provisions. The Act does, however, contain several important provisions pertaining to records retention and document destruction. In particular, public companies must have in place policies, procedures, and practices to ensure that information related to their financial condition is retained for as long as necessary and protected from inadvertent damage or destruction during that time.

More broadly, however, the most important aspect of the impact of Sarbanes-Oxley on corporate records retention is the need to be able to clearly demonstrate that these programs are designed and operated solely to serve legitimate business purposes such as reduction of storage requirements and associated costs. In their development and implementation, corporate records retention programs must avoid any possible inference of motivation to dispose of information that may be needed in government investigations or for other legal purposes. To do otherwise would constitute **bad faith**. The Act appears to make illegal any policy, including records retention, designed to avoid exposure to pending government investigations.[4]

Retention of Audit Records

The most important provision of Sarbanes-Oxley that directly affects records retention is one of very narrow impact—the retention of audit records of public accounting firms. The Act requires registered public accounting firms to "prepare, and maintain for a period of not less than seven years, audit work papers, and other information related to any audit report, in sufficient detail to support the conclusions reached in [the audit report]." Title VIII, Section 802(A) and its associated rules and regulations specify a retention period of seven years for work papers and certain other documents maintained by public accountants who audit issuers of securities. This provision of Sarbanes-Oxley has been codified into a new section of the U.S.

Code (Section 1520 of Title 18) that requires accounting firms subject to its provisions to retain all audit and review work papers for five years.[5]

This seven-year retention requirement in Sarbanes-Oxley does not apply to records and information maintained by audited companies. Rather, it is limited to records and information maintained by public accounting firms. The U.S. Securities and Exchange Commission (SEC) rules and regulations for Section 802(A) state that audited companies are not required to retain copies of records that public accountants have examined during their audits and reviews; they may do so at their discretion, however. Consequently, a "default" retention period of seven years is often recommended for many corporate finance and accounting records, unless other laws, regulations, or business requirements necessitate a longer period. The SEC has issued rules under Sarbanes-Oxley that specify a seven-year retention requirement (17 CFR 210.2-06).

Many records specialists wonder why a difference exists between the retention requirements for audit work papers—seven years in the Act but five years in the federal criminal laws in Title 18 of the United States Code. According to U.S. Senator Patrick Leahy (D-Vermont), who was one of the leading Congressional sponsors of Sarbanes-Oxley, the five-year period was based on the time period considered reasonable and necessary for the enforcement of the criminal and securities laws, most of which have five-year statutes of limitations. However, following enactment of Sarbanes-Oxley, the SEC issued rules under the Act that further define this retention requirement. In 17 CFR 210.2-06, the SEC lengthened the five-year period to seven years. The SEC was apparently concerned that having two different retention times would cause needless confusion for public companies, so it decided to standardize the seven years.[6]

The retention requirements in Section 103 apply to registered public accounting firms that conduct audits of publicly traded companies. The Act itself does not specifically impose such requirements on records and information maintained by the audited companies themselves. Some analysts, however, assert that Sarbanes-Oxley creates an implied though not expressed requirement for seven-year retention of most if not all financial, accounting, or other records and information that would be needed to demonstrate compliance with the Act. Consequently, a minimum default retention of seven years is often recommended for records needed to demonstrate compliance with Sarbanes-Oxley, unless other laws, regulations, or business requirements necessitate a longer period.

Sarbanes-Oxley also contains some important provisions relating to the obligations of organizations that may be the target of federal investigations to preserve relevant evidence prior to the onset of such investigations or proceedings. These provisions are reviewed later in this chapter.

Records Retention and Litigation

One of the most important issues related to records retention—one with which every records manager should be conversant—is the role of records in litigation. Examples of questions regarding the treatment of records in litigation are listed in Figure 7.1.

Records in Litigation

Figure 7.1

Questions to Raise Regarding Records in Lawsuits

- How should retention periods be devised for records that have a good probability of being used in litigation?
- Are records favorable or unfavorable in defending liability lawsuits?
- Under what circumstances do records disposal acts become criminal conduct?
- What are the duties and obligations of organizations and their employees to preserve records during the discovery phase of legal proceedings?
- What are the risks of records disposal actions during the prediscovery phase, when proceedings are possible or even probable but have not yet commenced?
- What are the penalties for unlawful conduct involving records preservation and disposal?
- How has the law recently been refined to eliminate ambiguities concerning the duty to preserve records when litigation is threatened?
- Should retention periods for records that may encounter use in litigation be longer or shorter?
- Is retaining the records for longer periods of time advisable, in situations where they may be favorable or exculpatory to the organization in legal actions?
- Would a shorter retention period be in the organization's best interest if the records may be harmful or even incriminating to the organization?

The main U.S. federal statute that requires the preservation of documentary evidence that is or may be relevant to legal investigations is Title 18 of the United States Code (USC). It states that:

> "Whoever withhold[s] testimony, or withhold[s] a record, document, or other object, from an official proceeding [or] cause[s] or induce[s] any person to ... alter, destroy, mutilate, or conceal an object with intent to impair the object's integrity or availability for use in an official proceeding ... shall be fined under this title or imprisoned not more than ten years, or both."

In other words, if criminal conduct has or may have occurred, every person or organization connected with the event is legally required, on pain of imprisonment, to preserve any and all evidence that may be related to it, including documentary evidence in the form of business records. If the ends of justice are to be served, the court needs access to *all* relevant evidence, so that the matter can be judged fairly on its merits. The importance of such evidence in legal proceedings may be seen in the following observations of Senator Patrick Leahy. Commenting on the Andersen case, Senator Leahy wrote that:

> "As a former prosecutor, I know that no matter how egregious the crime, you can't prove a case without the evidence. Unfortunately, the Arthur Andersen case demonstrated that corporations are well aware of this simple lesson. The most striking aspect of Andersen's Enron document shredding binge [highlighted below] was that is was not the work of one or two rogue employees. The company itself was convicted. In fact, the Arthur Andersen document destruction policy was devised after another embarrassing case for the express purpose of hiding damaging documents from regulators and victims. Something is wrong with our corporate culture when

the lesson learned from a previous case of corporate misconduct is *not to change business practices but to destroy the evidence better next time.*[7] [Emphasis added]

Senator Leahy's comments have large implications for records retention. In devising retention policies, organizations have a right to construct retention periods with a view towards mitigating their risks in litigation. However, they must do so within the law and without any inference of bad faith. In the opinion of many observers, the opportunity to reduce the risks resulting from liability lawsuits constitutes the most compelling reason to implement records retention initiatives. In many business environments, these risks are so onerous that a records retention program will be justified based on this benefit alone. Today, organizations must conduct business in a highly litigious environment; one in which lawsuits are frequently the means of resolving business disputes. This issue is greatest among businesses that manufacture products that are subject to failure in performance and/or may be harmful to the health of consumers or the general public. These types of organizations frequently face significant levels of exposure to liability lawsuits. Such litigation actions are often decided on the basis of documentary evidence; evidence that comes to the attention of the litigants or the courts during a pretrial procedure known as **discovery**.

However, every organization that produces products or services of any kind (or that even hires employees) is faced with threats to its assets as a result of liability lawsuits. These lawsuits are often decided on the basis of old records—records that need not have existed if they had been properly destroyed under an established records retention policy immediately upon expiration of their value for legal and business purposes. Even if the organization has committed no acts that would render it liable under the law, the act of responding to document discovery orders can be very burdensome and expensive. In fact, some studies have reported that pretrial discovery, including disclosure of records, accounts for as much as half the cost of civil litigation. These risks and burdens can, however, be greatly mitigated by a well-developed and carefully implemented records retention program.

Judicially Imposed Sanctions

Typically, the courts will impose sanctions when defendants destroy information in violation of court orders that compel its production, in a manner that is willful or in bad faith, or causes prejudice to the opposing party.[8] The **adverse inference** sanction is a judicially imposed penalty whereby the jury is instructed that it is at liberty to infer that the defendant destroyed potentially relevant evidence because it feared that the evidence would be unfavorable or incriminating. Typically, in order to impose this sanction, the court must conclude that a party has attempted to suppress unfavorable evidence by means of the disposal of records, whether carried out under authority of its records retention program or not.[9]

In imposing adverse inference sanctions for **spoliation** of evidence, the courts typically weigh the following criteria:

- The party having control over the evidence had an obligation to preserve it at the time it was destroyed.

- The records were destroyed with a culpable state of mind.

- The destroyed evidence was relevant to the party's claim or defense such that a reasonable trier of fact could find that it would support that claim or defense.[10]

Further, in cases where the destruction of documentary evidence occurred in accordance with a routine records retention policy, the courts typically arrive at adverse inference sanctions based on three tests:

1. Whether the records retention policy is reasonable considering the facts and circumstances surrounding those documents

2. Whether lawsuits or complaints have been filed frequently concerning the type of records at issue

3. Whether the document retention policy was instituted in bad faith[11]

Litigation and Records

As every lawyer knows, depending on how things work out, records in litigation can be a blessing or a curse. That is, any particular record can be favorable or unfavorable to the organization's case.

An organization's attorneys can more easily defend the absence of documents that have been systematically destroyed under an established retention policy than they can defend the destruction of records not in accordance with an established policy or retention schedule. From a litigation risk avoidance perspective, the goal should be to retain only those records needed to conduct business and comply with the law. All other records should be systematically destroyed under a formal RIM program based on records retention periods that are as short as possible. Retention periods are as short as possible if they reflect the minimum (but still reasonable) time periods required to operate the business and comply with the law. If retention periods are constructed based on these principles, they can go a long way toward mitigating the legal risks that can be associated with the use of document-based evidence in liability lawsuits.

Retention Periods Where Litigation is Likely

As stated previously, the "golden rule" of retention decision-making is that retention periods must meet the test of reasonableness. Assuming that all retention periods are fully compliant with all applicable statutes and regulations, the next most important thing is that they be formulated in such a way that they can be defended as reasonable from both business and legal points of view. To meet the test of reasonableness, retention periods should be *not too long and not too short*. They must also satisfy one other key test: They must avoid any inference of bad faith. When the retention periods were devised, the executives *knew or should have known* that a particular type of record has a high probability of being used in litigation. Consequently, setting the retention period too short can infer that the organization's executives acted in bad faith and were motivated to rid the organization of evidence that may, in future litigation, be unfavorable to its defense. For those types of records that have a history of being required in litigation cases to which the organization is party, the retention period may need to be quite lengthy—until the organization's decision-makers consider that it has no further liability for the business matters reflected in the records. Records managers should, of course, consult with counsel on these matters.

The objective of a records retention program must never be to exercise file scrubbing or file cleansing, the purpose of which is to rid the organization of unfavorable evidence. The law typically characterizes such conduct as evidence spoliation. *Evidence spoliation* is defined as the intentional or unintentional destruction or disappearance of documents or other forms of evidence that are or may be relevant to legal proceedings.[12] An adversary in legal proceedings can make a strong case of bad faith in the spoilage of evidence by convincing a jury that a records retention schedule is nothing but a sham for destroying potentially incriminating evidence of negligence or other wrongdoing. The following court cases illustrate these points.

Stevenson vs. Union Pacific

This case arose out of a train-car grade crossing accident in which the plaintiff, one Frank Stevenson, was injured and his wife was killed. The plaintiff filed a motion for sanctions on the ground that Union Pacific had destroyed evidence in the form of a voice tape of conversations between the train crew and dispatch at the time of the accident. The company's policy was to retain voice recordings for a period of 90 days, after which they were overwritten by new recordings. Union Pacific's attorneys argued that sanctions were not justified because it destroyed the documents in good faith pursuant to its routine document retention policies.[13]

> The court disagreed. It held that "a voice tape is the only contemporaneous recording of conversations [between the train's dispatcher and engineer] at the time of the accident and will always be highly relevant to potential litigation . . ." and that Union Pacific had general knowledge that such tapes would be important to any litigation involving accidents at grade crossings. Therefore, the court affirmed a finding of adverse inference because the destroyed evidence was prejudicial to the plaintiffs.[14]

Lewy vs. Remington Arms

The defendant (Remington Arms) in this case maintained records of previous complaints concerning the safety latch of a gun that discharged by accident in the Lewy household, injuring the plaintiff, Mrs. Lewy. The appeals court considered the issue of the reasonableness of Remington's customer complaints and gun examination reports. Under the company's records retention policy, the records were required to be retained for a period of three years, with subsequent destruction if no action regarding a particular record was taken during that period. However, Remington had failed to produce the records under court order, and the company justified its failure on the fact that the records had been properly destroyed under its retention policy. The appeals court did not rule on the issue of the reasonableness of the retention policy. Rather, it remanded the case to the trial court for retrial, with the following instructions for the trial court to consider:

...the court should determine whether Remington's record retention policy is reasonable considering the facts and circumstances surrounding the relevant documents. For example, the court should determine whether a three-year retention policy is reasonable ... A three-year retention policy may be sufficient for documents such as appointment books and telephone messages, but inadequate for documents such as customer complaints.[15]

The court went on to state that ". . .if the corporation knew or should have known that the documents would become material at some point in the future then such documents should have been preserved."[16]

Rambus vs. Infineon Technologies

In this case, the court criticized the adoption of a records management program intended to prevent information from being available to people the organization planned to sue.[17] The defendant filed a motion to compel the production of documents and testimony relating to the plaintiff's document retention policy because the plaintiff allegedly destroyed documents when it knew or should have known of an impending patent infringement action. The plaintiff admitted that its document retention system was adopted due to discovery-related concerns but denied that it was trying to keep unfavorable information from its adversaries. The court held that even if the plaintiff had not instituted its document retention policy in bad faith, it would be guilty of spoliation if it reasonably anticipated litigation when it implemented the policy.[18]

U.S. vs. Taber

The defendants in this case sought discovery sanctions because the U.S. government destroyed certain of its files pertaining to a 1988 Navy contract in which Taber served as a vendor or subcontractor. The court held that "even if the court finds the policy to be reasonable given the nature of the documents subject to the policy, the court may find that under the particular circumstances certain documents should have been retained notwithstanding the policy. For example, if the corporation knew or should have known that the documents would become material at some point in the future, then such documents should have been preserved."[19]

Retention Obligations in Discovery

When a legal investigation evolves to the point where relevant records are requested in discovery, they must of course be produced on pain of a charge of obstruction. Unfortunately, however, some organizations have attempted to circumvent their obligations to produce documents even in the face of a subpoena.

Carlucci vs. Piper Aircraft

One of the most famous cases where obstructive conduct occurred during the discovery process was *Carlucci vs. Piper Aircraft*, which was adjudicated in South Florida in 1984. Having found that the defendant consistently ignored requests for production of documents by the plaintiff, the court sanctioned Piper for showing an "obstructionist attitude" toward production of requested records. Further, the court reviewed Piper's document retention policy and found that the policy authorized the disposal of only those records deemed detrimental to the company—a fact that the court construed as blatant bad faith.

According to testimony by Piper's employees, "the stated purpose of the destruction of records was the elimination of documents that might be detrimental to Piper in a law suit." Any such assertion is blatantly bad faith. Piper's executives further admitted that employees had selectively destroyed documents despite the fact that their production was required under court order. In the face of these admissions and evidence, the court held that:

- "Piper has utterly failed to demonstrate that its document retention policy is actually implemented in any consistent manner . . . Piper's absolute failure to provide any evidence on this issue must be construed that the policy is a sham."

- "The policy of resolving lawsuits on their merits must yield when a party has intentionally prevented the fair adjudication of the case. By deliberately destroying documents, the defendant has eliminated the plaintiffs' right to have their cases decided on the merits. Accordingly, the entry of a default is the only means of effectively sanctioning the defendant and remedying the wrong."[20]

The plaintiff moved for a default judgment against Piper, which was granted. The judgment was reported to be $10 million, a significant penalty for failure to turn over relevant records in discovery as required.[21]

Prudential Insurance Co. of America

In the case of *In re Prudential Ins. Co. of Amer. Sales Practices Litig.*, the court imposed sanctions against the company based in part on the failure of senior management in properly managing the discovery process, to include the prevention of document destruction. The court held that "It [Prudential] has no comprehensive document retention policy with informative guidelines and lacks a protocol that promptly notifies senior management of document destruction. These systematic failures impede the litigation process and merit the imposition of sanctions . . . The obligation to preserve documents that are potentially discoverable materials is an affirmative one that rests squarely on the shoulders of senior corporate officers."[22]

Under these sanctions, Prudential was fined $1.0 million, and the court mandated that the company establish a records management program after concluding that the "haphazard and uncoordinated" treatment of records in various sales offices threatened the litigation process. This penalty reinforces the importance of full compliance with the demands of the discovery process.

Zubulake vs. UBS Warburg

The plaintiff in this case, Laura Zubulake, an equities trader specializing in Asian securities, brought suit against her former employer for gender discrimination. Since the filing of the case in 2002, federal judge Shira Scheindlin of the Southern District of New York has issued five opinions and orders, some of RIM significance.[23] Ms. Zubulake, through her counsel, moved to sanction UBS Warburg for its failure to produce relevant information and for its tardy production of such material during discovery. In order to determine whether sanctions were warranted, the court was obliged to answer the following question: Did the defendant fail to preserve and timely produce relevant information and if so, did it act negligently, recklessly, or willfully? The judge's final determination that UBS Warburg should be sanctioned with an adverse inference for spoliation of evidence was predicated on a finding of it or its agents having a culpable state of mind.[24]

Judge Scheindlin concluded that the defendant acted willfully in destroying potentially relevant information, in the form of e-mails, and considered sanctions designed to restore the plaintiff (Zubulake) to the position that she would have been in had UBS Warburg faithfully discharged its discovery obligations. Sanctions took the form of an adverse inference finding, plus compensation to pay the costs of any depositions required by the tardy production.[25]

Retention Obligations Prior to Discovery

Once an organization has received a subpoena for document production and the discovery process has begun, the duty to preserve relevant evidence is clear and unambiguous. However, what are the obligations to preserve such evidence prior to this period, when litigation or a government audit or investigation has not yet commenced but may be predicted with some degree of certainty? Here the law is not quite as clear, and it is open to some degree of interpretation. In the wake of the Enron-Arthur Andersen affair, some ambiguities in the law had to be clarified by means of new legislation, which were contained in the Sarbanes-Oxley Act of 2002.

U.S. vs. Arthur Andersen, LLP

The Andersen case concerned whether the document disposal activities that occurred prior to receipt of the first subpoena constituted obstruction of justice.[26] It was about Andersen's top executives' obstructive conduct in attempting to conceal their role in misleading the investing public concerning Enron's (one of its clients) financial position by colluding with Enron in overstating its revenues and understating its losses. In a records context, this case was about illegal records disposal actions that occurred during the weeks prior to November 8, 2001, when Andersen received the first subpoena for document production. By August 2001, Andersen was apprised of significant financial irregularities at Enron and by early October, the auditing company was aware that it would be the target of an investigation by the SEC. Despite this knowledge, during the second week in October the company launched a massive, worldwide document destruction effort that continued until receipt of the subpoena.

On the morning of October 12, 2001, Nancy Temple, an attorney for Arthur Andersen, LLP, arrived early at her office in Chicago. At the top of her agenda that morning was the situation concerning document retention in the firm's offices in Houston, Texas. Andersen had a document retention policy, Ms. Temple knew, but enforcement was lax. This lack of retention policy enforcement was particularly troublesome, in view of the fact that Andersen's representation of Enron Corporation, also based in Houston, would likely come under regulatory scrutiny. Ms. Temple sent an e-mail to Michael Odom, a partner and head of risk management for the Houston office, at 8:53 A.M. "Mike," she wrote, "it might be useful to consider reminding the engagement team of our documentation and retention policy. It will be helpful to make sure that we have complied with the policy." Ms. Temple then included a link to the policy, contained on Andersen's internal Web site.[27]

Any reasonable person would fairly conclude that this simple e-mail message was the most routine of office administration tasks. However, Ms. Temple's e-mail set into motion a chain of events that led to her firm's conviction on criminal charges and subsequent virtual demise. When this e-mail came to light several months later and doubts about its legality entered the public debate, Andersen's CEO Joseph Berardino, was at pains to characterize it as innocuous. "Nancy just told people to use their judgment . . . accountants are pack rats . . . we save a lot of stuff that's not relevant." Unfortunately for Andersen, the U.S. Department of Justice did not see it that way. Rather, they were inclined towards the view that Andersen's records destruction activities in the wake of Ms. Temple's e-mail were not innocent housekeeping but incriminating evidence of criminal intent.[28]

The problem with Ms. Temple's advice, nearly all legal commentators agreed, was that, at the time her e-mail was written, an investigation into Enron's financial affairs by the SEC was highly likely. If this was indeed the case, Ms. Temple's e-mail was not just bad legal advice; it constituted a *prima facie* case of obstruction of justice. If, when she wrote the October 12th e-mail, Ms. Temple's state of mind was that an SEC investigation was likely, the proper advice to have given Mr. Duncan was:

> "In view of the fact that it is likely that we will be investigated by the SEC, effective immediately, all employees must cease any and all disposal of records related in any way to our representation of Enron. This applies to all audit work papers as well as official audit reports, all electronic records (including e-mail) as well as physical ones, and continues until further notice."

Had Ms. Temple given this advice, Andersen would likely never have been prosecuted, let alone convicted. In all fairness, a reasonable person might well give Ms. Temple the benefit of the doubt. After all, who has not dashed off a quick e-mail on some substantive matter, without stopping to consider its possible consequences? Unfortunately, just such ill-considered e-mails are the basis on which juries often return guilty verdicts, as they did in the Andersen case.

Commenting on Andersen's contention that its efforts to apply its retention policy in the weeks following Ms. Temple's e-mail were nothing more than routine housekeeping, Mr. Buell went on to state that "There's nothing criminal about having a document retention policy." Characterizing the retention policy as one that had "gathered dust on the shelf," he said, "What is a crime is to take it out and blow it off in the middle of an SEC investigation because you want to be able to control what documents the government gets to see and what documents it doesn't." The lesson here is simple: At the *first sign of potential trouble*, an organization must not suddenly press compliance with records retention rules it had failed to follow, even if the rules would have otherwise allowed the organization to clean house.

The legal question, then, is: When litigation or a government investigation is possible to the point where it is reasonably foreseeable, exactly when or under what circumstances is an organization legally required to suspend the disposal of any and all records and information that may be deemed relevant? When proceedings have been *formally instituted,* or earlier, when they are merely at an "informal" stage? Throughout the trial, Andersen's lead defense attorney, Rusty Hardin, argued strongly that his client was fully entitled to purge its files of unwanted material at its own discretion, so long as it had not received concrete notice from the authorities of a possible investigation in which the company may be a party. He stated, "There's got to be something that puts [Andersen] on notice about it. They just can't sit around and guess about it."[29]

Sarbanes-Oxley Removes Ambiguities in the Law

Despite the fact that Hardin's argument was of dubious legal merit, it did serve to highlight a loophole in the law that needed closing—lack of clarity about the duty to preserve evidence in the face of possible or probable government investigations. Thus, in the wake of the Andersen case, the U.S. Congress clarified this key question in the Sarbanes-Oxley Act of 2002. One of the Act's key provisions was a new felony offense, codified in Section 1519, Title 18 of the U.S. Code, for destroying, altering, or falsifying a record with the intent to obstruct an investigation. Resulting from the Andersen case, records destruction activity that is intended to obstruct *informal* as well as *formal* investigations is now defined as criminal conduct. The new law abolishes the requirement that prosecutors must establish a close link between document destruction and a pending government investigation. This new criminal prohibition on records destruction applies not only when a government investigation starts, but also to obstructive conduct in contemplation of a potential investigation—a considerably more stringent legal standard than had existed in prior law.[30]

Some commentators have raised questions concerning whether prohibitions against evidence tampering in Title XI, Section 1102, require procedures to prevent the accidental destruction or overwriting of electronic records. However, such accidental events do not seem to constitute criminal intent as defined in the Sarbanes-Oxley Act. Rather, Sarbanes-Oxley is designed to punish records destruction actions that are motivated by the intent to suppress or conceal unfavorable or incriminating information—destruction motivated to control what evidence the authorities do and do not get to see.

Finally, Title VIII, Section 802(a), and Title XI, Section 1102, deal with the preservation of financial and audit records and the destruction or fabrication of evidence relevant to government investigations. They amend Title 18, Chapter 73, Sections 1512 and 1519 of the U.S. Code to establish criminal penalties for destroying, mutilating, altering, concealing, or falsifying documents "with the intent to impede, obstruct, or influence" a federal government investigation, any official proceeding, or any case filed under Title 11 of the U.S. Code. These provisions also criminalize the act of persuading another person to engage in illegal document destruction but not to do it oneself.[31]

When litigation or an investigation seems reasonably foreseeable and has reached an informal state, disposal actions involving information that may be deemed relevant must cease immediately. If they do not, the organization and/or those involved in the destruction could be liable for criminal prosecution and, if convicted, suffer fines or even imprisonment. Suspension of records destruction at the first sign of trouble is recommended as the prudent course of action to avoid getting into trouble with the law. This principle should be incorporated into the legal retention holds policies of companies, and records managers should work closely with corporate attorneys to ensure its proper implementation fully—in letter, spirit, and good faith.

Sarbanes-Oxley reinforced the legal principle that organizations must be prepared to demonstrate that the design and operation of retention programs is solely to serve legitimate business purposes such as reduction of storage requirements and associated costs. More specifically, in their development and implementation, these programs must avoid any possible inference of motivation to dispose of information that may be needed in government investigations or for other legal purposes. To do otherwise would constitute bad faith. In short, the Act appears to make illegal any policy designed to avoid exposure to future government oversight or investigation.[32]

Litigation Holds

Best practice in records retention requires that organizations have a plan to notify employees when litigation or a government investigation requires a temporary suspension of destruction for specified records. Despite this fact, many organizations have no such procedure in effect. According to one survey, 59 percent of the respondents reported that their organizations do not have a formal system for records hold orders in place.[33] These suspensions of records disposal actions are often referred to as *litigation holds*, and they are typically issued by the organization's legal department. In these notices, the legal department identifies the affected records, and where they are kept. Moreover, subsequent notifications must be issued to employees (as well as to RIM personnel) advising them when the holds are released and that records destruction may resume.

The case of *Zubulake vs. UBS Warburg* has large implications with respect to the obligations of counsel in the administration of a litigation holds policy, particularly where evidence preservation is concerned. From this case, the following conclusions may be drawn:

- Counsel must be familiar with the client's document retention policies and their implementation.

- Counsel must take proactive steps to ensure the preservation of relevant evidence in discharging its obligations to direct the document discovery process. Merely issuing a written notice to suspend the disposal of records may not be sufficient.

- Counsel must issue a litigation hold at the outset of litigation or whenever litigation is reasonably anticipated. The "at the first sign of trouble" standard is recommended as the most prudent time to institute the hold. The litigation hold should be periodically reissued so that new employees are aware of it, and so that it is fresh in the minds of all employees.

- Counsel should communicate directly and meet with the key players in the litigation; that is, the employees most likely to possess or maintain relevant information, and take steps to ensure that they understand their role in and duty to preserve relevant evidence. These key players should be periodically reminded that the preservation duty is still in place.

- Counsel should instruct all employees to preserve electronic versions of relevant records and information (including e-mails) under their custody and control as well as physical records.

- Counsel must ensure that all backup media that the organization has a duty to preserve is identified and stored in a safe and secure manner.[34]

The Andersen Case: The Last Word

On May 31, 2005, the last word on the Andersen case belonged to the highest court in the land, the U.S. Supreme Count. In a unanimous decision, the Court overturned Andersen's conviction. The Court's decision was written by its chief justice, William Rehnquist. The chief justice wrote that, in her instructions to the jury, Judge Melinda Harmon "failed to convey the requisite consciousness of wrongdoing." Many legal observers interpreted this statement to mean that a jury cannot properly convict without first being required to conclude that a defendant had intended to engage in criminal conduct. Traditionally, in the adjudication of white-collar litigation, a potential fraud or obstruction of justice is only illegal if the defendant acted with the knowledge and intent to commit a crime. In its decision to overturn the Andersen conviction, the Supreme Court found that the judge's instructions resulted in a jury being able to convict simply by making a finding that Andersen impeded the government's ability to find facts in the Enron investigation, without any requirement of concluding that there was a dishonest motive.[35]

Summary of Key Legal Principles

Notwithstanding the Supreme Court's ruling that the requisite knowledge of wrongdoing and intent to commit criminal acts are required to sustain convictions in obstruction of justice actions, records managers should exercise the utmost caution in document destruction activities where litigation or government audits or investigations are likely. The following seven principles should form the basis of records retention conduct:

1. **Comply with the law** – First and foremost, RIM specialists must never put themselves in legal jeopardy in exchange for a paycheck from their employers. If any

employees have questions concerning the legality of any records disposal action, they should contact their Legal Department. If they are still not satisfied, they should contact the authorities. If the choice is between the company and the law, comply with the law and cooperate with the authorities, even if resigning is necessary.

2. **Dispose of unneeded business records** – Under most circumstances in the life of an organization, destroying unneeded records is a perfectly legal act, regardless of whether such disposal occurs under an established records retention program or as just a casual, somewhat arbitrary act of hitting the Delete key, overwriting data, or simply discarding records as office waste. In short, business people routinely and lawfully discard unneeded records every business day. The only circumstances under which the disposal of records is an illegal act is when their retention is required by law or regulation or if they are relevant to an actual, pending, or potential litigation action or government audit, or other official investigation.

3. **Suspend disposal of records relevant to a lawsuit or investigation** – Under the law, destroying documents relevant to an actual or potential lawsuit or government investigation is a crime, punishable by fines and possible imprisonment. This legal prohibition on document destruction begins from the moment at which a person or organization learns of a possible lawsuit or government investigation, even though proceedings have not yet officially commenced. The "at the first sign of trouble" standard is recommended as the prudent course of action. Consequently, at the point in time at which litigation or a government investigation is contemplated as a reasonably foreseeable event, the destruction of relevant evidence becomes potentially criminal activity and the destruction of any and all relevant records must cease immediately.

4. **Retain documents based on their content** – With respect to the legality of document destruction, the law makes no distinction as to whether documents happen to reside on paper, computer media, or any other format, or whether they are official records or are merely work papers or duplicate copies rather than original records, according to an organization's RIM definitions of these terms. If the *content* of any document is or may be deemed relevant to the subject of the lawsuit or investigation, that document may not legally be destroyed, and it must be turned over to authorities if requested.

5. **Dispose of records for the right reasons** – If records relevant to litigation or a government investigation are requested and cannot be produced, the investigating authorities will demand an explanation. If the records were disposed of, the circumstances surrounding that disposal will be investigated. The investigators will want to know specifically *what records were destroyed, what they contained, who destroyed them, when, and why.* If investigators can show that the motivation behind the disposal was to suppress or conceal incriminating or even unfavorable evidence, those individuals who authorized and/or carried out the disposal could be held liable.

6. **Set retention periods for records of possible legal value** – In devising retention policies, organizations have a right to construct retention periods with a view towards mitigating the risks associated with the use of records in litigation. Assuming that all statutory or regulatory requirements have been satisfied, organization executives may consider that they have some freedom to make the retention periods relatively short. However, in view of the fact that they may come under judicial scrutiny, the retention periods must meet the test of reasonableness and avoid any inference of bad faith. If an organization's managers *knew or should have known* that the documents will or may become material evidence at some point in the future, the retention period should reflect the legal value of the records.

7. **Use records retention schedules lawfully** – The foregoing requirements of the law supersede any and all organizational policies authorizing document destruction, including the authority granted in records retention schedules. In other words, executives or any employee of the organization cannot attempt to use the authority granted them in records retention policies as justification for destroying information relevant to actual or pending litigation or government investigation. Records retention cannot be a shield to justify the unlawful disposal of records.

Sample Policy for all Employees

The policy in Figure 7.2 should be made available to any and all employees throughout the organization who create, maintain, or otherwise have access to records material. It should be incorporated into the organization's RIM and retention policies, procedures and guidelines, and it should be emphasized during employee training sessions pertaining to RIM and retention.

Sample Policy: Legal Hold on Records Destruction

Figure 7.2

Records Related to Litigation or Government Investigation

If the content of a record is related to actual or pending litigation or a government investigation, it may not be destroyed without the expressed written approval of the Legal Department. This restriction begins from the moment at which any employee gains knowledge that litigation or a government investigation is reasonably foreseeable (even though the lawsuit or investigation has not yet officially commenced) and continues until removed by the Legal Department. Employees who violate this policy are subject to disciplinary action by the company, up to and including dismissal, and or judicial penalties imposed by courts of law.

Notes

1. David Stephens and Roderick Wallace, *Electronic Records Retention: New Strategies for Data Life Cycle Management* (Lenexa, KS: ARMA International, 2003), 15-16.

2. See, for example, Donald Skupsky, *Recordkeeping Requirements* (Greenwood Village, CO: Information Requirements Clearinghouse, 1994).

3. Sarbanes-Oxley Act, Public Law 107-2004, 116 Stat. 745, (2002).

4. LeBoeuf, Lamb, Greene & MacRae, LLP, "Effect of Sarbanes-Oxley on Document Retention Policies," May 30, 2003, 1.

5. Patrick Leahy, "Preserving the Paper (and Electronic) Trail," *The Information Management Journal* 37, no. 1 (January / February 2003): 17.

6. Ibid.

7. Ibid., 16.

8. Shira Scheindlin and Kanchana Wangkeo, "Electronic Discovery in the Twenty-First Century," 11 Mich. Telecomm, *Tech. L. Rev* 71, (2004): 80.

9. *Stevenson v. Union Pacific.* 354 F.3d739 (8th Cir. 2004), 3.

10. John Montaña, "The End of the Ostrich Defense," *The Information Management Journal* 39, no. 1 (January / February 2005); 28.

11. *Stevenson v. Union Pacific*, 2.

12. John Isaza, "Know When to Hold 'Em, When to Destroy 'Em," *The Information Management Journal* 39, no. 2 (March / April 2005): 39.

13. *Stevenson v. Union Pacific*, 8.

14. Scheindlin and Wangkeo, "Electronic Discovery in the Twenty-First Century," 81.

15. *Lewy v. Remington Arms Co., Inc.*, 836 F.2d 1104 (8th Circuit, 1988).

16. Ibid.

17. Thomas Allman, "Fostering a Compliance Culture: The Role of *The Sedona Guidelines*," *The Information Management Journal* 39, no. 2 (March / April 2005): 36.

18. *Rambus Inc. v. Infineon Technologies,* 220 F.R.D. 264, 282 (E.D. Va. 2004); see also Scheindlin and Wangkeo, "Electronic Discovery in the Twenty-First Century."

19. Isaza, "Know When to Hold 'Em, When to Destroy 'Em," 43.

20. *Carlucci v. Piper Aircraft Corp.*, 102 F.R.D. 472 (S.D. Florida. 1984).

21. Robert Austin, "Ten-thousand Reasons for Records Management," *Records Management Quarterly* 19, no. 3 (July 1985): 3.

22. *Prudential Ins. Co. of America Sales Litig.*, 169 F.R.D. (D.N.J., 1997)

23. *Zubulake v. UBS Warburg, LLC.* 220 F.R.D. 212, 217 (S.D.N.Y.2003), ("Zubulake IV"); *Zubulake v. UBS Warburg, LLC.* No. 02 Civ. 1243 (SAS), 2004 WL 1620866, *12 (S.D.N.Y. July 20, 2004), ("Zubulake V").

24. Montaña, "The End of the Ostrich Defense," 27.

25. Zubulake V, 27.

26. *U.S. v. Arthur Andersen, LLP.* 374 F.3d281 (5th Cir. 2004).

27. For the definitive account of Enron's bankruptcy and its aftermath, including the Andersen case, see Kurt Eichenwald, *Conspiracy of Fools* (New York: Broadway Books, 2005).

28. For an excellent summary of the Andersen case and its records retention implications, see Christopher Chase, "To Shred or Not to Shred: Document Retention Policies and Federal Obstruction of Justice Statutes, *Fordham Journal of Corporate and Financial Law,* 2005. See also David Stephens, "Lies, Corruption, and Document Destruction," *The Information Management Journal* 36, no. 5 (September / October 2002).

29. Randolph Kahn, "Records Management & Compliance: Making the Connection," *The Information Management Journal* 38, no. 3 (May / June 2004): 28; Stephens, Ibid.

30. Leahy, "Preserving the Paper (and Electronic) Trail," 17.

31. Ibid.

32. LeBoeuf, et al., "Effect of Sarbanes-Oxley on Document Retention Policies," 1.

33. Robert Williams, *Electronic Records Management Survey: A Call to Action.* (Chicago: Cohasset, Inc., 2004), 5, 21.

34. Zubulake V; Montaña, "The End of the Ostrich Defense," 31-32.

35. Kurt Eichenwald, "Reversal of Andersen Conviction Not a Declaration of Innocence," *New York Times,* 1 June 2005.

Chapter 8

Managing the Message

The American Management Association considers *e-mail* (and other forms of messaging) to be the *number-one office task*. Together with other electronic records created at the desktop level, e-mail management is one of the biggest records management challenges today. Some experts believe that e-mail is the most significant new technology for business communication since the advent of the telephone. Because e-mail results in the creation of recorded information, its business significance exceeds that of the telephone. For this reason, the RIM implications of e-mail are equally significant.

By some estimates, more than 90 percent of all business documents are created electronically, and 60 percent of those are transmitted as e-mail attachments; but as few as 30 percent are ever stored or printed for offline storage in paper files.[1] E-mail is a transforming technology that has revolutionized the way business is conducted, as well as the way in which business records are created, transmitted, stored, and maintained. Managing e-mail messages is, appropriately, at the top of the RIM agenda nearly everywhere.

E-mail has been the predominant form of written business communication for nearly ten years. The first time that more e-mail was sent than postal mail occurred in 1996. Since that time, both the usage and importance of e-mail have skyrocketed to the point where e-mail has become one of the most business-critical of all computing applications. According to various studies, as much as 75 percent of business-critical information—the greater part of the organization's knowledge base, its intellectual assets, and institutional memory—is stored in electronic messaging systems.[2] In 1999, the figure was just 33 percent.[3] This situation alone makes managing e-mail and other electronic messages among the most important RIM issues today.

When e-mail is viewed from the perspective of individual users, its importance is no less compelling than it is for the organizations for which they work. According to a survey conducted by Osterman Research, most users would rather do without the telephone than give up their e-mail. Reliance on e-mail has become virtually obsessive, particularly among higher-level managers and executives.[4] In most organizations, the e-mail inbox, as well as private and shared folders, has become the primary de facto repository for recording electronic conversations, agreements, customer interactions, and other business-related activities and transactions.[5] In short, the messaging environment is the primary business platform for many, perhaps most, organizations.

Despite its importance, most organizations do not have a strategy to capture, organize, or leverage the information content within the messaging environment.[6] Consequently, records managers must work to develop and implement, across the enterprise, appropriate management controls (including retention rules) for these records as one of their top priorities.

Management Challenges

E-mail poses significant management challenges for organizations, and it has been called the worst-managed form of records. Management problems associated with e-mail have become so severe, at least in some environments, that some commentators wonder aloud about the future viability of this communications technology. In an article entitled, "Can E-Mail Be Saved?," Eric Allman, author of the Sendmail™ program that has served as the Internet's primary mail transfer agent for more than two decades, stated, "I know several people who've just given up on e-mail."[7] Spam, discussed later in this chapter, is the worst problem. E-mail can, and often does, get out of control, to the point where it is intrusive, even detrimental to other work assignments. Ray Ozzie, creator of Lotus Notes®, observes that e-mail has been pushed to the breaking point, past the limits of its original, intended purpose, thereby resulting in lower and lower productivity gains.[8]

E-mail is frequently left unmanaged in user mailboxes and is subject to random retention and disposition by users.[9] In many organizations, e-mail management works as follows: Automatic messages are sent to all e-mail users telling them to reduce the number of messages in their mailboxes, that their mailboxes have exceeded size limitations set by the administrator, and that they may not be able to send or receive new mail until they reduce the size and quantity of messages in their mailboxes. These notices also suggest that users delete items they are no longer using. When such methods are used, no effective RIM process is in place.[10] Users' e-mail *archives* can easily become massive and unwieldy. Users resist classification schemes, ignore structured searches, and frustrate policy-managed archiving and retention. Another problem is backup. The Osterman Research study found that 82 percent of e-mail users use personal archives, but only 61 percent of these archives are backed up.[11] Managing e-mail archives is vital to protecting organizations from data storage burdens, litigation and regulatory liabilities, and other management problems.[12]

StorageTek conducted a study in 2002 to quantify the cost of e-mail management in the absence of formal policies or management tools and estimated losses in user productivity of $2,013 per employee per year.[13] In many environments, e-mail overload is an issue requiring immediate management attention. According to one study, employees spend approximately one hour each day on the 36 percent of irrelevant e-mail messages or those that require no response.[14]

Legal Issues

Consider the vast differences in behavior patterns in creating the traditional business letter as compared to creating an e-mail message. The very act of writing a letter forces the creator to be thoughtful, contemplative, and careful in wording and construction. Business letters and office memoranda frequently evolve through multiple drafts, with supervisory reviews at intervals and sign-off approvals prior to dispatch. The end result of this process is highly formal and meticulously constructed documents, which often elicit equally formal replies. Most e-mail and other electronic messages lack these attributes. Such messages tend to be casual, spontaneous, and informal. These characteristics create the basis for the legal issues surrounding e-mail and other electronic messages.

If a smoking gun is to be found among the records of an organization, it is likely to be found in the messaging environment. According to a recent survey conducted by the American Management Association and the ePolicy Institute, 21 percent of employers have had e-mail subpoenaed by courts and regulatory authorities, and 13 percent of lawsuits are triggered by employee e-mail.[15] Commenting on the high value of e-mail as legal evidence, Irwin Schwartz, president of the National Association of Criminal Defense Lawyers, states, "e-mail has become the place where everybody loves to look [in discovery]." *Fortune* magazine has referred to e-mail as the most legally risky form of business communication and that e-mail "was supposed to make life easier. Now e-mail has become a prosecutor's No. 1 weapon and the surest way for companies to get sued." The article recounts how e-mail has morphed into "evidence mail," and why the solution is often worse than the problem. "Think of e-mail as the corporate equivalent of DNA evidence—the single hair left at the crime scene that turns the entire case. In theory, you can explain it away, but good luck trying."

The Microsoft antitrust case with Netscape illustrates these points. During the trial, an e-mail surfaced in which Microsoft Chairman, Bill Gates wrote to executives of AOL, "How much do we need to pay you to screw Netscape." Verbiage of this kind is indeed hard to explain away, as it tends to have high jury impact. The underlying problem is that people tend to be more candid in expressing their thoughts in an e-mail, often to the point where many messages are written in a very casual, conversational style, using informal, even "chatty" modes of expression. However, e-mail message writers should ask themselves how they would feel if they saw one of their e-mails on the front page of a newspaper or saw it introduced as evidence in court. They should maintain a constant awareness that these disquieting events are by no means beyond the realm of possibility.

However, even in cases in which executives have instituted aggressive purging strategies, e-mail purges do not delete those messages stored on desktop hard drives; they do not eliminate messages that have been printed out and filed in folders and cabinets; nor do they eradicate messages that have been sent or forwarded to external parties. Even if messages have been purged from e-mail servers, they may survive on backup media. Aggressive purge strategies can reduce only the legal risks associated with e-mail, not eliminate it.

The courts have ruled that failure to produce e-mails can result in sanctions, even in cases where such failure results from negligence rather than bad faith. In a recent case involving Residential Funding Corp. (RFC), a subsidiary of General Motors Acceptance Corp., RFC was unable to produce e-mails residing on backup media, even after it hired a leading discovery firm to recover them. No evidence existed that RFC had improperly or illegally suppressed the e-mails. However, an appellate court found that lack of such evidence was still no excuse for failure to produce them. The court remanded the case to the trial court, and an unspecified settlement was paid. The following quick summaries of other recent, significant cases illustrate problems caused by e-mail messages:

- Five large Wall Street brokerages paid $8.5 million in fines for failure to preserve electronic messages, as securities regulations require. In October 2003, the SEC began requiring public accounting firms to retain all electronic communications associated with company audits. The regulations were tightened when government investigators examining Enron found that certain Wall Street energy traders were using cell phones and instant messaging in order to circumvent surveillance of their client communications via e-mails and desk telephones.[16]

- In Linnen v. A.H. Robbins Co., the defendant was forced to bear expenditures of more than $1.1 million to search backup tapes for *only 15 mailboxes.*[17]

Some executives often argue that electronic messages rarely represent the official position of an organization; rather, they represent the personal opinions of those who wrote them. Yet the courts and regulatory bodies can, and often do, construe message content as reflecting the official company position on a matter, regardless of whether this opinion is justified or not. When words have been memorialized in an e-mail, they tend to be seen as somehow "cast in stone."[18]

E-mail Usage Patterns

Most office employees report that, unless they are on the telephone or out of the office, they are spending most of their time doing e-mail related tasks. According to some studies, the average employee now spends at least 25 percent of the workday on e-mail. With respect to the quantity of messages sent and received per employee per day, the most common figures range between 30 and 60 (exclusive of spam), but many managers report much higher numbers. In addition to the time spent in reading incoming mail and sending replies, e-mail users spend, on average, from one to three hours per week managing their mailboxes, including tasks such as cleaning out old messages, deleting spam, and otherwise complying with e-mail deletion and retention requirements.[19]

Nearly all e-mail usage studies report strong growth in the volume of message traffic. According to one study, the number of e-mails sent and received by individual users is growing at the rate of 29 percent per year. With the proliferation of attachments of increasingly greater length, the size of messages is growing at 92 percent each year. A typical 3,000-user system will handle more than one terabyte of message traffic each year.[20] Another study put growth rates for e-mails and attachments at 35 percent each year.[21] A recent article in *Computer Technology Review* cited the following figures:

- Average growth of e-mail message size – 90%
- Average size of e-mail messages and attachments in 2002 – 50KB
- Average size of e-mail messages and attachments in 2007 – 650KB[22]

Additional e-mail growth metrics are shown in Figure 8.1. The rise of e-mail usage has been the single most important factor driving the growth of electronic content across the enterprise.[23] According to AMR Research, on average, e-mail users generate approximately 10 megabytes of message storage requirements each business day, and strong growth is projected for the future.[24] These and other reports affirm the significance of e-mail as an IT issue.

IT Issues

Managing the message has become a major issue for IT departments—in terms of staff time as well as data storage requirements. According to one study, e-mail administration tasks, including backups and restores, can consume up to 43 percent of IT support costs.[25] Moreover, a similar percentage of IT administrators called managing mailbox storage and other requirements "their biggest server management challenge."[26] Other studies report that the average IT administrator spends up to six hours per week recovering old messages. Recovering messages over a year old may require up to 11 hours. Further, IT administrators spend as much as 20 percent of their time backing up e-mail systems.[27] E-mail is one of the more significant resource issues confronting IT departments today.

Finally, messaging systems pose one of the most significant threats to the integrity of computing infrastructures. E-mail systems are more prone to outages than other mission-critical systems. A recent e-mail survey revealed that 56 percent of responding organizations reported disruptions in e-mail service, while disruptions for other business-critical applications were in the 21 to 25 percent range.[28] Viruses in e-mail attachments can easily overload an e-mail system and bring it down.

Growth of E-Mail

Figure 8.1

	Year				
	2002	**2003**	**2004**	**2005**	**2006**
Average size of e-mails (KB)	50,000	96,000	184,320	353,894	679,477
Average # of e-mails per employee per day	60	77	100	129	166
Average storage per day per employee (KB)	3,000,000	7,392,000	18,432,000	45,652,326	112,793,182
Average mailbox limit (KB)	40,000,000	40,000,000	40,000,000	40,000,000	40,000,000
# of days before mailbox limit is reached	13.33	5.41	2.17	0.88	0.35

SOURCE: Data from Bill Tolson, "Controlling the Flood: A Look at E-mail Storage and Management Challenges," *Computer Technology Review*, September 2002.

Spam

As shown in Figure 8.2, by some estimates, unsolicited and unwanted messages, commonly known as *spam,* now comprise more than half of all e-mail traffic.[29] In some environments, the figure can be as high as 90 percent. One company estimates that spam and obscenity filtering software intercepts some 7,000 of the 20,000 e-mails that arrive at its e-mail servers each day.[30] Some commentators believe that spam is now so pervasive that it has the potential to stop the use of e-mail altogether.

According to Microsoft founder Bill Gates, however, spam will have been virtually eradicated in the near future. In a recent speech to the World Economic Forum in Switzerland, he stated that his company is currently working on solutions to greatly mitigate if not eliminate the spam problem.[31] The best that can be said about this remark is that anything resembling the elimination of spam has yet to occur. In most environments, the spam menace keeps getting worse.

Apart from their virus threats and repugnant content, spam messages are a costly proposition for IT departments that have the misfortune to receive them in great quantities on their servers. One estimate puts the cost at anywhere from 3 to 8 cents per item, which includes lost revenue and decreased user productivity.[32] Nucleus Research estimates that companies lose $874 per employee annually in lost productivity due to spam.

Attempts to control if not eradicate spam found legislative expression in the new "CAN SPAM" law (formally known as the Controlling the Assault of Non-Solicited Pornography and Marketing Act of 2003). The law is designed to reduce the incidence of deceptive and unsolicited e-mails. Among other things, the new law prohibits spam perpetrators from disguising their identities by using false return addresses. However, as with many pieces of legislation, enforcement is expected to be a problem in achieving the goals of the law.[33]

Spam Management

Figure 8.2

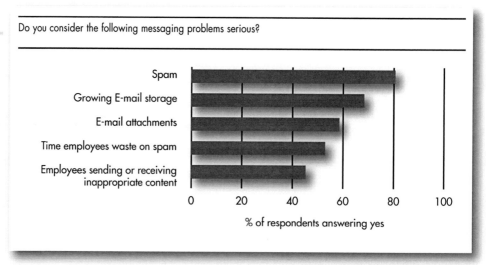

Do you consider the following messaging problems serious?

% of respondents answering yes

SOURCE: Data from Osterman Research survey of 108 IT managers.

Managing Messages as Records

From a RIM perspective, e-mail and other electronic messages should be regarded as methods of delivering information, rather than record types. As information content, e-mails should be subject to the same RIM rules as other documents. In this sense, they are just another form of business record. Because messages are considered information-based property, they must be subject to RIM policies. In order to manage e-mail properly in accordance with RIM objectives, the following actions are recommended:

- Capture and securely store all messages and their associated attachments and metadata on their initial entry into the system.
- Provide basic message indexing capabilities based on an enterprise classification/taxonomy scheme.
- Provide basic retrieval capabilities based on content descriptors such as unique message ID, subject, date, name of sender and recipient, and other basic attributes.
- Provide enhanced retrieval capabilities, including full-text searches against message text as well as attachments.
- Institute effective backup and restore methodologies, verifiable as to accuracy and quality, to safeguard messages against loss or corruption.
- Institute policy-based life cycle management under retention schedule methodologies in which messages are retained and discarded based on the legal and business values of message content.
- Provide for the preservation of message content such that applicable government requirements pertaining to their authenticity and accessibility in immutable form are respected.

E-mail Retention

From a RIM perspective, e-mail content must be subjected to enforceable retention rules and policies. Unrestrained retention of e-mail messages is simply not an acceptable option for most organizations today. The inevitable result will be massive volumes of messages that are costly to retain and even more expensive to search through in response to discovery requests. According to some studies, 14 percent of e-mail users use their inbox as a repository for old messages, attachments, and other information.[34] Some e-mail users retain hundreds, even thousands, of e-mails in their messaging environment. An e-mail system is not, and was never intended to be, an archive; rather, it is a platform for current business communications. As a matter of policy, e-mail use should be restricted to current communications only. A top RIM priority is to ensure that the messaging system is not morphed from an e-post office into an unmanaged archive. The recommended practices discussed in this section are designed to keep such an evolution from happening.

Why do users retain e-mails? According to an e-mail retention survey conducted by the IDC in 2002 (see Figure 8.3), the main reasons for retaining e-mail messages

Primary Reasons
for Retaining
E-mail

Figure 8.3

Reasons	Percentage of Respondents n = 557
Personal Reference	51%
Corporate Reference	35%
Legal Compliance	25%
Disaster Recovery	22%
Industry Practice	6%

Note: "No policy" and "don't know" responses are excluded.

SOURCE: Data from IDC's E-mail Retention Survey, 2002, reported by Mark Levitt and Robert Mahowald, "E-mail Retention Trends and Challenges," *KMWorld*, January 2003.

are personal preference (51 percent) and corporate reference (35 percent). However, the retention value of most messages is short-term. As a general rule-of-thumb, 70 to 80 percent of e-mail can be archived immediately or destroyed under proper RIM practices.[35]

According to the IDC e-mail retention survey, nearly half the respondents indicated that message retention is handled in a decentralized manner in their organizations. Consequently, little reliability and predictability are related to what message content is retained and for how long, or how the content can be accessed.[36] In these decentralized messaging environments, e-mail retention is in the hands of the user. The reasoning is that because users are closest to the e-mail's content, they are in the best position to decide whether the messages should be retained or deleted.[37] However, these retention decisions are often accomplished without formal tools or processes.

Many organizations have adopted an "all or nothing" approach to e-mail retention. They either attempt to save everything indefinitely in case it might be needed in the future, or they quickly delete messages that are not absolutely critical to minimize storage and reduce the risk of unfavorable information in lawsuits. The best approach, however, is a middle path between these two extremes—intelligent, selective retention, based on content and value, for appropriate periods of time as provided by approved retention rules, coupled with an archiving technology to automate the process and minimize reliance on human compliance.[38]

E-mail archiving should be part of a coordinated, systematic records retention initiative. Generally, best practice is that e-mail retention must be content-driven; that e-mail messages related to an established records series appearing in the retention schedules must be retained as per that policy; and that such retention must be outside the messaging environment. These principles have been incorporated into the recommended policy on message management summarized in this section and appearing in Figure 8.5 at the end of the chapter.

E-mail Retention Policy

Every organization that relies on electronic messaging to conduct its business needs an e-mail retention policy. Many, however, do not have one. Various studies report that over 50 percent of organizations have no such policy.[39] The main features and attributes of an e-mail retention policy are as follows:

- User requirements for managing and retaining e-mail embedded into employees' daily work routines. In order to carry out their responsibilities for managing and retaining e-mail, most users will need to dedicate at least 15 minutes each workday.

- E-mail should not be saved unless a legitimate business reason for doing so exists. All such retention should be outside the messaging system.

- Based on message content, users are required to follow the organization's retention schedule when deciding what messages to retain and for how long.

- Users should be given menu options to specify the retention of specific e-mail messages at the time the message is created or received. The options could provide default retention periods linked to the organization's retention schedule.

- In cases where e-mail messages (and/or attachments) are deemed to be of official character and require continuing retention as provided by the organization's retention policies, they must be migrated from the messaging environment to another software program providing managed storage in accordance with those retention rules.

- Nonrecords may be deleted immediately, or they may be left in the messaging system (Inbox and Sent and Deleted folders) and automatically deleted in accordance with an approved "default retention" applicable to items in the mailbox.

- Default retention should be short—30, 60, or 90 days, and it should be enforced by incorporating "auto-delete" functionality in the messaging system to purge all opened items that have aged to the 30, 60, or 90-day period.

- Backup of e-mail from the servers should be for business continuity purposes only, not long-term retention. The backup retention period should be equivalent to that of the messaging system itself—30, 60, or 90 days.

Instant Messaging

Paul Saffo of the Institute for the Future states, "By the time we get all four corners of e-mail turned down, the important communications are going to be instant messaging. And no one knows what to do with that."[40] Instant messaging (IM) is an immediate issue for many companies. It is ubiquitous, generally unmonitored, and it provides an easy way to circumvent restrictive corporate e-mail policies.[41] ICQ ("I seek you") software on the Internet was the first mass-market IM software available. As freeware, it spread rapidly. IM technology allows users to communicate in real time between computers without a record of the conversation. The messages can be captured in record form and retained on the IM server only if special software is installed on the organization's computer networks. In these respects, IM technology is more akin to telephony rather than e-mail.[42]

In the case of both the telephone and e-mail, widespread assimilation by businesses did not occur until many years after initial introduction of those technologies. By contrast, IM is reportedly the fastest-growing communication medium ever and might soon overtake e-mail—IM is faster and is not flooded with spam—among other reasons. IM can potentially result in significant savings in telecommunications and network costs, including storage space, as the technology would reduce telephone, e-mail, and network traffic.[43]

Initially considered a toy for teens, nearly half of all U.S. and Canadian companies are now using some form of IM.[44] Many applications are of the "bootleg" variety; that is, they have not been formally sanctioned by management, nor are they subject to controls by IT departments, which can pose significant management issues.

In business situations where one employee needs to reach another employee or outside vendor who is constantly on the telephone, IM is a particularly valuable tool. IM is faster than e-mail, delivering messages that pop up on the users' computer screen instantaneously, regardless of what task the user is working on. IM software typically displays a "buddy list" of persons with whom the user frequently communicates and who are online at any given moment. By clicking on a small box on the computer screen, the user can type a message that appears on the recipient's screen within a second or two after it is sent. The replies are dispatched in similar fashion just as quickly.[45]

IM users can conduct multiple sessions at one time and perform other tasks (i.e., talk on the telephone, attend a meeting, compose an e-mail message) simultaneously, in a stream of free-flowing, continuous communications between two parties or larger collaborative workgroups. Because of its free-flowing nature, users will often start a conversation, and, seemingly in mid-sentence, change the subject and then return to the original subject minutes or hours later. IM does not lend itself to traditional document creation, *classification*, or cataloging systems. It is much more like an electronic version of a telephone call.[46]

Major issues associated with the use of IM among large organizations include:

- **Legal risks** – User behavior patterns and modes of expression are typically even more casual than with e-mail and are very similar to those used in face-to-face or telephone conversations.

- **Security risks** – IM service providers send unencrypted messages through public networks. Moreover, threats from viruses can be even greater than with e-mail, which generally requires the user to open an attachment to trigger the corruption.

- **Interoperability issues** – The major IM providers—AOL, Microsoft, IBM, and Yahoo—all offer proprietary solutions. At the time of this writing, however, a collaborative agreement was announced by the three companies, thereby providing intersystem message communication.[47]

Some organizations have elected to treat IM like most telephone conversations and voice mail—unrecorded and undocumented and therefore not subject to formal retention as organizational records. The "recordworthiness" of instant messages can be called into question when IM retention and archiving are not centrally managed. For example, in recognition that IM is being used among securities trading firms to process client transactions, the National Association of Securities Dealers went on record in opposition to using this technology to circumvent proper recordkeeping: " . . . [the] lack of formality of instant messaging does not exempt it from the general standards applicable to all forms of communication with the public." In other words, when used to buy and sell securities, IMs must be subject to applicable government retention requirements for the protection of the investing public.[48]

Even in unregulated industries, "it is critical to have auditing, logging, and security with IM, as well as requirements for what content needs to be preserved and for how long," states Michael Osterman president of Osterman Research.[49] Management options include limiting IM only for selected types of intracompany communications, as well as requiring the retention of written records of the exchanges. Finally, special IM software is available to enable the creation and management of a central archive of messages and conversations, providing auditing capabilities necessary to comply with applicable regulations or other business requirements.

Voice Messaging

Voice-mail, while not a new technology, is potentially the next messaging technology to receive the kind of management attention that e-mail gets today. Traditional voice-mail products are proprietary systems that cannot easily be integrated within an organization's larger computing infrastructure. However, the days of standalone voice-mail systems are coming to an end. More sophisticated messaging platforms are beginning to integrate voice-mail into more comprehensive, enterprise deployments. Soon, voice-mail will become just another digital object—a computer file just like e-mail or a word processed text document.[50] Consider a scenario in which all the organization's e-mail and voice calls would sit together in a single inbox accessible from a PC, notebook, or PDA. The next wave of business communications to be made available through a technology is called *VoIP*.

Voice over Internet protocol (VoIP) describes a variety of approaches for running call control and ***digitized*** voice traffic over enterprise IP data networks. The technology represents the convergence between voice and data communication systems. Instead of being in a separate "silo," voice content is on the verge of becoming simply another network application that can integrate with other real-time applications to enhance collaboration among geographically dispersed workgroups or partnering organizations. VoIP turns a telephone call into just another digital packet on the IP network—a cluster of data no different from an instant message or a digital image. VoIP can merge with e-mail, instant messaging, and other applications in a multimedia customer service center that can greatly improve customer service in situations where a high degree of collaboration is required. It can also facilitate communications among frequent business travelers and telecommuters.

The director of IT at Milliman, an actuarial and consulting firm, states, "We gave our telecommuters VoIP telephones in their homes. Now we can give them a direct dial number here at the main office and all their calls ring on their remote IP telephone in their homes."[51] For business travelers, a softphone installed on a notebook can provide an office telephone in any location with Wi-Fi capabilities—a hotel room, airport, etc.

The challenges of managing the message have just begun. During the coming years, records managers will be called upon to manage as records the information content residing in these advanced technology environments.

Messaging Technology Solutions

The world's largest messaging systems—Microsoft Office Outlook, IBM's Lotus Notes, and Novell's Groupwise®—provide some resources for retention operations or other RIM capabilities.[52] For example, the more recent versions of Microsoft Outlook permit users to set up retention settings for e-mail, using the AutoArchive feature, which can automatically delete expired items and archive older items from users' mailboxes. These retention settings can help users comply with organizational retention policies that specify the length of time that specified categories of documents must be retained. Users can specify an expiration date on items in Outlook at the time they create or send the item, or do it at a later date. When the retention periods for such items have lapsed, the item is irretrievable and is shown on a folder list with a strike-out mark through it.[53]

Apart from the capabilities provided in native messaging software, e-mail archiving solutions fall into two broad categories: (1) Software that auto-categorizes *all* messages based on header information such as the names of senders and recipients, dates, and subjects. (2) Software that selectively auto-categorizes only *relevant* messages based on the content of the message body and attachments. These solutions use techniques such as content filtering that apply rules to content to categorize and organize messages by subject or topic.

Filtering and collaboration tools scan e-mail content and then automatically route messages to the indicated recipients based on subject matter or other criteria. These solutions are often used in collaboration or workflow applications, such as customer service call centers. They focus on indexing, search and retrieval, routing, and storage. E-mail security tools, on the other hand, typically scan e-mails for malignant code, quarantine suspicious e-mails, or encrypt outgoing messages. Some of these tools purge or encrypt sent e-mails after designated periods of time.[54]

Sophisticated e-mail archiving solutions typically include other retention management capabilities. These solutions, shown in Figure 8.4, allow e-mail administrators and records managers to define retention policies for various classes of e-mail.[55]

Some software solutions permit users to archive and delete e-mail based on message content and the organization's rules and policies for records retention. The most advanced systems index the content of messages and attachments, and provide granular search and retrieval capabilities to end users.[56] A more ideal approach for managing e-mail and capturing what is valuable is to apply intelligent classification technology to messages. This technology requires the application of content-aware classification tools that are just now beginning to be introduced for e-mail. The objective is to be able to assess e-mail content automatically by looking for certain content markers so that the software can apply retention rules and other predefined RIM requirements.[57]

**E-mail Archiving
and Retention**

Figure 8.4

E-mail Archiving/Retention Solution
Should Provide:

---

1. A convenient, effective method of storing and organizing e-mail and attachments
2. An effective method of providing access to messages by authorized persons
3. The ability to retrieve messages by words or phrases in all or part of a message
4. The ability to create and maintain an indexed repository of e-mails that warrant retention
5. Support for multiple archival repositories having differing retention periods
6. The ability to define archiving policies for different types of e-mail
7. The ability to specify multiple archiving criteria
8. The ability to specify archiving criteria and methods for messages and/or attachments
9. The ability to implement retention policies for e-mail on servers or other dedicated, specified repositories
10. The ability to enforce retention policies for e-mail[58]

**Sample Policy:
E-mail Retention**

Figure 8.5

The Retention of E-mail

All XYZ employees are required to manage retention of their e-mail daily, and to retain and dispose of messages based on their content, as related to the requirements of the company's records retention schedules. Specific retention requirements appear below.

As a matter of policy, XYZ Corp. regards its e-mail system as a tool to facilitate communication among its employees and other external parties relative to current business matters. The company's e-mail system is not a suitable platform for retention of official records and files. Therefore, this policy forbids the extended-term retention of e-mail messages within the messaging environment.

When the content of an e-mail message possesses long-term retention as required by the company's retention schedules, such retention must occur in a storage repository outside the messaging environment. The company's requirements for e-mail retention are as follows:

- **E-mail of short-term value** – A significant portion of e-mail messages are of transitory value and do not require extended-term retention. Under this policy, e-mail users are authorized to delete all such messages daily, immediately after reading, replying, or taking other action concerning them.
- **Default retention in messaging system** – Within the messaging environment, the maximum retention period for e-mail shall be 30 days [alternatively 60 or 90 days] after the message is opened/read by its recipient. This policy applies to documents attached to e-mail messages, as well as to the messages themselves. All opened e-mail older than 30 days remaining in employees' mailboxes will be automatically purged by the IT department. One week prior to executing this purge, all employees will be notified, in order to provide sufficient time to review their e-mail and comply with this policy.
- **E-mail required for longer retention** – If the content of an e-mail message, or a document(s) attached to that message, possesses business value for longer than 30 days, as specified by XYZ's retention schedules, it should be made a part of an established file and retained appropriately as per the retention period in the schedules. In such cases, employees are required to:
  - Generate a hard-copy printout and place it into the proper paper file for further retention in accordance with the retention schedules; or
  - Migrate the message (and/or attached documents) from the e-mail system to another software application providing managed storage under retention rules so that it may be saved for the retention period specified in the retention schedules.

(continued)

Figure 8.5

- **Retention of e-mail backups** – The retention of e-mail data on backup media will not exceed 30 days [alternatively 60 or 90 days].
- **E-mail related to litigation or government investigation** – If the content of an e-mail message is related to actual or pending litigation or a government investigation, it may *not* be destroyed without the expressed written approval of the Legal Department. This restriction begins from the moment at which any XYZ employee gains knowledge that litigation or a government investigation is reasonably foreseeable (even though the lawsuit or investigation has not yet officially commenced) and continues until removed by the Legal Department. Employees who violate this policy are subject to disciplinary action by the company, up to and including dismissal, and/or judicial penalties imposed by courts of law.

Notes

1. Alan Porter, "A Ten-Step Strategy for Defending Your Company's E-Mail System," *Disaster Recovery Journal* (Winter 2004): 26.

2. See, for example, Cliff Sink, "E-Mail Management: How to Succeed Step-by-Step," *KMWorld*, March 2004, S16; Greg Arnette, "Killer App: New E-mail Requirements are Driving Significant Technology Purchases," *Storage Inc.* Quarter 4, 2002, 32; Michael Osterman, "Records Management Requirements in the Enterprise," in *Proceedings of the 48th Annual Conference, ARMA International, Boston, MA, October 19-22, 2003* (Lenexa, KS: ARMA International, 2003), 200; and Ben Worthen, "Message Therapy," CIO, 15 January 2005, 51.

3. Bill Tolson, "Controlling the Flood: A Look at E-mail Storage and Management Challenges," *Computer Technology Review*, September 2002, 16.

4. Michael Rosenfelt, "Never a Good Time to be Without E-Mail," *Disaster Recovery Journal* (Spring 2004): 44.

5. Mark Levitt and Robert Mahowald, "E-mail Retention Trends and Challenges," *KMWorld*, January 2003, 44.

6. Ibid., Arnette, "Killer App," 32.

7. Paul Boutin, "Can E-Mail Be Saved?" *InfoWorld*, 19 April 2004, 46.

8. Ibid., 49.

9. Bassam Zarkout, "Next-Generation Records Management," *KMWorld*, June 2002, S7.

10. Alan Pelz-Sharpe, "Records Management Redux: The Nudge Towards Compliance," *KMWorld*, September 2003, 13.

11. Osterman, "Records Management Requirements," 200.

12. Christine Chudnow, "Business Dilemma: Email Retention Policy," *Computer Technology Review*, January 2003, 1.

13. Tolson, "Controlling the Flood," 16.

14. Diane, Carlisle, "Managing E-mail Overload," *The Information Management Journal* 38, no. 2 (March / April 2004): 70.

15. Peter Mojica, "Simply Speaking: Messaging as a Corporate Record," *KMWorld*, March 2005, S8.

16. Nicholas Varchaver, "The Perils of E-mail," *Fortune*, 17 February 2003, 96-100.

17. Arnette, "Killer App," 32.

18. Susan Cisco and Bob Guz, "Managing Electronic Messages: Policies and Technologies," in *Proceedings of the 48th Annual Conference, ARMA International, Boston, MA, October 19-22, 2003* (Lenexa, KS: ARMA International, 2003), 173-174.

19. Tolson, "Controlling the Flood," 16; Osterman, "Records Management Requirements," 200.

20. Tolson, "Controlling the Flood," 16.

21. Chudnow, "Business Dilemma," 1.

22. Fred Moore, "Cradle-to-Grave Storage Management Now a Reality," *Computer Technology Review*, January 2003, 20.

23. Levitt and Mahowald, "E-mail Retention Trends and Challenges," 24.

24. Ephraim Schwartz, "Rethinking Message Storage," *InfoWorld*, 14 June 2004, 14.

25. Chudnow, "Business Dilemma," 10.

26. George Symons, "Take Control of E-mail: Protect the Surging Tide," *SMS* 8, Issue 4 (2003), 16.

27. Tolson, "Controlling the Flood," 16.

28. Porter, "A Ten-Step Strategy," 26.

29. Moore, "Cradle-to-Grave," 20.

30. Varchaver, "The Perils of E-mail," 100.

31. ARMA International, "Worldwide War on Spam Continues," *The Information Management Journal* 38, no. 2 (March / April 2004): 16.

32. Arnette, "Killer App," 32.

33. ARMA International, "President Bush Signs Law to Can Spam," *The Information Management Journal* 38, no. 1 (January / February 2004): 17.

34. Osterman, "Records Management Requirements," 200.

35. Fred Moore, "Archival Data Has a New Mission: Critical," *Computer Technology Review*, February 2003, 36.

36. Levitt and Mahowald, "E-mail Retention Trends and Challenges," 24.

37. Tracy Caughell, "The Corporate Records Conundrum," *The Information Management Journal* 37, no. 3 (May / June 2003): 59.

38. Levitt and Mahowald, "E-mail Retention Trends and Challenges," 24.

39. Robert Williams, *Electronic Records Management Survey: A Call to Action* (Chicago: Cohasset, Inc., 2004), 5, 36.

40. Varchaver, "The Perils of E-mail," 102.

41. Deborah, Juhnke, "Electronic Discovery in 2010," *The Information Management Journal* 37, no. 6 (November / December 2003): 39.

42. Patrick Cunningham, "IM: Invaluable New Business Tool or Records Management Nightmare?" *The Information Management Journal* 37, no. 3 (November / December 2003): 28-29.

43. ARMA International, "IM the Focus of Investigations," *The Information Management Journal* 38, no. 1 (January / February 2004): 8.

44. ARMA International, "Instant Messaging Goes Corporate," *The Information Management Journal* 37, no. 4 (July / August 2003): 8.

45. Ibid.

46. Cunningham, "IM: Invaluable New Business Tool," 30.

47. ARMA International, "IM Interoperability – At Least for Business," *The Information Management Journal* 38, no. 5 (September / October 2004): 16.

48. Cunningham, "IM: Invaluable New Business Tool," 32; Franklin Curtis, Brian Chee, and Mike Hack, "Getting Serious About IM," *InfoWorld*, 23 February 2004, 38.

49. Curtis, Chee, and Hack, "Getting Serious About IM," 38.

50. Caughell, "The Corporate Records Conundrum," 60.

51. Leon Erlanger, "The 411 on VoIP," *InfoWorld*, 7 June 2004, 45. See also Leon Erlanger, "Calling All VoIP Apps," *InfoWorld*, 16 August 2004.

52. Cisco and Guz, "Managing Electronic Messages," 175.

53. Ibid., 175-177.

54. John Harney, "Managing the Message," *KMWorld*, April 2003, 12.

55. Symons, "Take Control of E-mail," 18.

56. Ibid., 16.

57. Caughell, "The Corporate Records Conundrum," 59.

58. William Saffady, Unpublished manuscript, n.d.; see also Chudnow, "Business Dilemma," 10-11.

Chapter 9

Improving Recordkeeping System Performance

The value of information is directly proportionate to its accessibility. This statement is one of the most time-honored and important dictums in RIM. An organization may possess a single kernel of information upon which its entire future rests, but if it cannot be found, it is worthless. Every employee in every organization has, at one time or other, searched in frustration for what is desperately needed, but it could not immediately (or ever) be found.

When organizational recordkeeping systems underperform in their role of delivering requested information to their users, records managers must determine the cause(s) and prescribe a solution(s) to fix the problem. The goal is to optimize the value of information content throughout the enterprise in order to facilitate the achievement of larger business objectives. Optimizing the value of information is, in fact, a key component of professional RIM practice. Achieving this objective depends on three main components: (1) enterprise accessibility of records and information, (2) system performance, and (3) the application of the principles of classification and taxonomy to enhance enterprise accessibility of information content, particularly unstructured content.

Poor Accessibility: Causes and Consequences

Today, many business recordkeeping systems, both paper and electronic, are not well designed and operated. Until the 1980s, prior to the advent of PCs, office filing systems tended to be relatively well operated. Responsibility for filing was typically placed with file clerks and departmental secretaries, many of whom had received formal training in filing systems and techniques in business and secretarial schools. However, with widespread adoption of desktop computers during the 1980s and '90s, coupled with reductions in office support staffs due to business restructuring and downsizing, professionally trained filing personnel became a vanishing breed. At the same time, however, PC users everywhere began to create and maintain substantial quantities of electronic records, often with little or no guidance as to how to maintain them in accordance with professional RIM principles.

The problem, as it has evolved over the last twenty or so years, is that employee's ability to create information has substantially outpaced their ability to retrieve it effectively. During the days of paper, the average office worker would typically create a limited number of letters, memos, or other documents requiring filing per day or week. PCs, with e-mail and other advanced communications capabilities, have greatly increased personal productivity and the filing requirements that flow from them. The result is greater challenges with information accessibility across the enterprise.

The most substantive recent study to quantify the business consequences of not being able to find needed information was conducted by the IDC in 2002.[1] The study analyzed the "search and retrieve" activities and behavior patterns of "knowledge workers," defined broadly as any organizational employee whose job requires frequent access to and usage of stored information. The major findings were:

- Knowledge workers spend from 15 to 35 percent of their time searching for information (see Figure 9.1).

- Searches are fully successful only 50 percent of the time or less.

- Only 21 percent of searchers find what they seek 85 to 100 percent of the time.

- Knowledge workers spend more time recreating existing information than they do creating new information.

- Approximately 50 percent of Web searches are abandoned without having achieved a successful result.[2]

Using these metrics, the study leaders made some extrapolations concerning the enterprise-wide consequences of inadequate accessibility of information (see Figure 9.2). The following estimates were based on a "typical" enterprise having 1,000 knowledge workers earning an average salary of $80,000 per year:

Hours Dedicated to Information Seeking

Figure 9.1

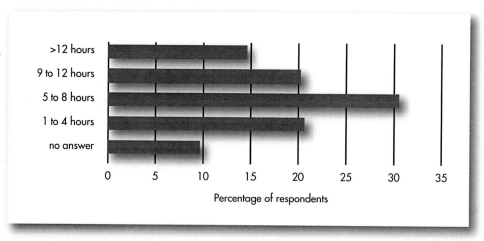

SOURCE: Data from IDC 2002.

Estimated Revenue Lost Due to Inadequate Searches

Figure 9.2

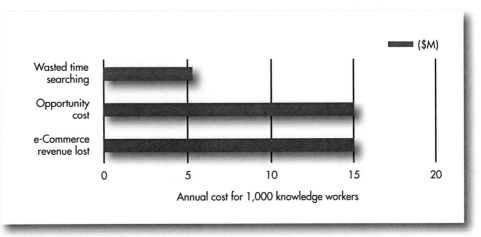

SOURCE: Data from IDC 2002.

- The time spent looking for and not finding information costs a total of $6 million per year, exclusive of opportunity costs (the value of additional work that could have been done if information searched for had been readily found) or the costs of reworking information that exists but cannot be located.

- The cost of reworking information; that is, recreating existing information because it has not been found is estimated at an additional $12 million per year.

- The opportunity cost resulting from the nonproductive time spent in searching for information is estimated at $15 million per year.[3]

- Poor classification of information results in some $1,000 in lost opportunity costs per knowledge worker each year.[4]

The negative impact of poor information accessibility cannot be denied. It can only be characterized as nonproductive—a waste of time. The business benefits of operating high-performing recordkeeping systems are demonstrable and considerable, and the consequences of limping along with underperforming systems equally so. If these estimates are at all reflective of the norm, the conclusion is inescapable: Information accessibility is a strategic business issue and needs to be managed as such.

Search Queries

Any request for information can be simple and straightforward, or it may be frightfully complex. For example:

- Find all the documents and data on all customers whose aggregate annual purchases exceeded $5,000 and who sent letters or e-mails during the past five fiscal years complaining about inadequate services or deficiencies with purchased products.

- Locate and assemble a complete history of all information on file throughout the organization on a specific customer or organization.

Both search queries are complex; have enterprise-wide scope; and encompass the various media types, storage platforms, and life cycles. What, then, is needed to satisfy such queries? In organizations where best practices for enterprise search and retrieval have not been implemented, the following situations are probable:

- **Disparate, incompatible computer systems** – Here, the searcher is likely to confront a bewildering variety of software programs and operating systems maintained throughout the computing environment. Some records will reside in applications run by IT departments, many of which are proprietary and thus do not "talk" to other systems. Other records are likely to have been created at the desktop level on a variety of software programs, including e-mail. Such records are typically saved on hard drives and network servers under filenames that were arbitrarily selected by their creators. Consequently, no one but the creator is likely to know of the existence or location of such records, or to be able to find them with any semblance of efficiency.

- **Undermanaged paper recordkeeping systems** – Here, the searcher is likely to confront a plethora of systems, maintained in any number of central file rooms, departmental filing stations, and records centers or other storage facilities. Assembling the requested records, however, is no minor matter. The existence and location of all relevant documents and data must be known. Unless an enterprise-wide RIM software system has been deployed, computer-based capability does not exist. In these cases, accurate and timely retrieval of all relevant documents and information is largely if not solely dependent on the knowledge of filing personnel about these recordkeeping systems and how to access them. When these persons retire or otherwise leave employment, the institutional memory of the organization is diminished. Just knowing what records exist becomes difficult; retrieving them efficiently is often very problematic.

Despite over thirty years of heavy investments in computers and related technologies, the above retrieval scenarios remain common practice in many, perhaps most organizations today. Wherever professional RIM is practiced, its goal is to ameliorate these problems.

Retrieving documents and information is simple and straightforward when the following three situations occur:

1. The person requesting the records articulates the search query intelligently and specifically, using language comprehensible by the system. What is sought necessitates single-item look-up only, and the records are identified by only one or two descriptors.

2. The address / location of the requested records match the instructions in the search query.

3. The existence and location of the records are known, they are accessible from a single location, and they are, in fact, present and available for immediate use.

In these scenarios, precise and timely retrieval and full user satisfaction are the probable result of the search. Conversely, document retrieval is complex, difficult, and frequently problematic when the following situations occur:

1. The person requesting the record really does not know exactly what he/she is looking for. What is sought is subject-based documentation—unstructured content—that may conceivably be found under any number of descriptors.

2. The person requesting the records expresses his/her search query in a general way or in language that is not readily comprehensible to the system; therefore, restatement or refinement of the query is required.

3. All requested records are stored in multiple locations and/or multiple recordkeeping systems and media types.

4. The existence and precise location of the records are not known; search tools are nonexistent, rudimentary, or have not been intelligently deployed.

In these scenarios, precise retrieval and full user satisfaction are frequently very difficult to achieve. In summary, most organizations experience some or all the following problems related to the accessibility of information from their recordkeeping systems:

- The systems are often poorly designed and implemented with the absence of technical expertise and professionalism.

- The systems are not centrally managed; no formal, uniform policies or procedures on content organization, indexing, classification, or other aspects of system management exist.

- Personnel maintaining and using the systems receive no training in system operation or usage.

- Classification decisions are arbitrarily made; indexing or classification schemes are nonexistent or poorly developed.

- System content is poorly organized / structured; highly fragmented; search and retrieval is slow and imprecise.

- Inadequate or no technology solutions have been applied to improve system performance.

In cases where underperforming recordkeeping systems display some or all these symptoms, further analysis of their operation and management is required. The following guidance is recommended as best practice.

System Performance Evaluation

As stated previously, when organizational recordkeeping systems underperform in their role of delivering requested information to their users, records managers are responsible for determining the cause(s) and prescribing a solution(s) to fix the problem. A physician observes the condition of the patient, asks questions and runs tests, and then arrives at a diagnosis, together with a prescribed course of treatment to effect the cure. Records managers must do likewise with underperforming recordkeeping systems.

What criteria need to be used in evaluating system performance? The performance characteristics of every recordkeeping system, regardless of media type, can be evaluated on the basis of the following seven criteria:

1. Precise retrieval
2. Timely retrieval
3. Accuracy ratio
4. Activity ratio
5. Reference analysis
6. Reference time
7. Turnaround ratio[5]

The first two criteria—precise and timely retrieval—are by far the most important.

Precise Retrieval

Precise retrieval is the most important measure of recordkeeping system perform-ance. It is defined as the ability of a recordkeeping system to consistently deliver to its users *exactly* the information they request—no more and no less. How, then, is precise retrieval measured? Consider the following scenario: In response to any search query formulated by any person seeking information from the enterprise doc-ument storage, one, and only one, of five things can happen:

1. The system delivers all documents specified in the query and no others.
2. The system delivers all documents desired as well as others deemed not relevant.
3. The system delivers some specified documents but not all.
4. The system delivers some documents, none of which are deemed relevant.
5. The system delivers no documents, and some documents relevant to the query are known to exist.

The above scenario is based on the presupposition that the search query is properly formulated and that relevant records do, in fact, exist to satisfy the request. These five possible search results are discussed further in this section in order to arrive at a deeper evaluation of system performance.

Levels of System Performance

System performance results are evaluated on five levels, as presented in the previous section.

1. **Top performance (precise retrieval)** – The system delivers *all* the document(s) desired by the user in response to any given search query *and no others*, and the system can perform at this level *consistently*—in response to, say, 95 percent+ of all search queries. Wherever advanced technology solutions are deployed, they should deliver this level of performance. Although performance expectations for paper-based systems tend to be lower, they too, should be managed to this level of quality.

2. **Good performance (semi-precise retrieval)** – The system can consistently deliv-er to its users *all* documents specified in a search query as well as others deemed

not relevant. In these cases, users' needs are being consistently satisfied, but they must spend some amount of time browsing through nonrelevant documents. A burden is placed on the shoulders of the user. This burden may be moderate if it occurs infrequently and the browsing requirements are not too onerous. In certain situations, however, delivery of nonrelevant records along with the requested ones can be a very significant problem. For example, some search engines may produce lengthy lists of potentially relevant documents, lists containing so many items that the searcher gives up in frustration and abandons the effort.

3. **Marginal performance (imprecise retrieval)** – The system delivers *some* of the documents desired by the user, *but not all*. Its performance would be considered marginal if only a portion of the requested documents is delivered with any frequency. The user has not been fully satisfied and must conduct another search. The system is experiencing a degree of failure, and some form of remedial action is required. At this level of performance, the users' confidence in the system begins to erode, and complaints can be expected. For example, in cases where users are expected to forward documents they create to a central repository for archival maintenance, they will have a strong disincentive to do so if the system performs at this level. If these users retain their own records in their personal archives, no one repository will have complete documentation and enterprise searches cannot be accomplished.

4. **Poor performance (failure in retrieval)** – The system delivers some documents, but none are deemed relevant to the user's query statement. The search has failed and another one must be attempted. This event may not be evidence of total system failure, as its cause may be that the user did not formulate the search query statement with sufficient precision or specificity or in the language of the system. Therefore, the system could not produce a satisfactory result. However, if such poor retrieval occurs with any frequency, something is significantly wrong with the system's design and/or its implementation, and remedial action will definitely be required.

5. **Total system failure (no documents delivered)** – The system delivers no documents in response to a search query *and some are known to exist*, but they are missing and no one knows where they are. The system has failed. Virtually every solution in the entire practice of RIM is designed to prevent this eventuality, including those discussed in this chapter and in Chapters 12 and 13.

The standard of precise retrieval is often very difficult to achieve with any consistency, particularly in large paper-based recordkeeping systems. Too many factors intervene that create the likelihood of suboptimal performance. The main point, however, is that in professional RIM environments, this standard of performance must be adopted and pursued with diligence.

Timely Retrieval

Timely retrieval is defined as a measure of the interval of time between the time documents are requested by a user and the time the information is delivered to the user.

Next to precise retrieval, timely retrieval (also referred to as *access time*) is the most important measure of system performance.

Depending on business needs, optimum access time can range from one to several seconds but seldom longer that a minute or two in well-designed electronic recordkeeping systems. This level of access time depends on the storage media utilized, the quality of the indexing and search engine, the skill with which users formulate search queries, and other factors. Generally, the greater the value and strategic importance of the records, the faster the access requirements, and the higher the level of technology that must be deployed to achieve them.

When confronted with underperforming recordkeeping systems, records managers should use these two main criteria to diagnose the problems. This diagnosis should be done by testing the system in order to analyze the results of, say, 100 search queries, to determine the number that fall into each of the five performance categories defined above.

Other Measures of System Performance

Records managers will often need to utilize the following criteria for evaluating the performance of recordkeeping systems. They are just different ways of analyzing precise and timely retrieval.

- **Accuracy ratio** – A measure of the number of requested documents found, as compared to the number sought.

- **Activity ratio** – A measure of the degree of reference activity in a recordkeeping system, calculated by dividing the number of records requested during a given period of time by the total number of records in the system.

- **Reference analysis** – A statistical breakdown of requests for records during a specific period of time to determine the usage characteristics of individual types of records of varying ages. Also referred to as *query analysis.*

- **Reference time** – A measure of the average time consumed to consult a record while it is in possession of the user; also referred to as *viewing time.*

- **Turnaround ratio** – A measure of access time, expressed in ratio format; the average time required to retrieve a record and deliver it to a user, divided by the total number of requests.[6]

Qualitative Analysis of System Performance

Results of a quantitative analysis of system performance should be supplemented by performing a *qualitative* analysis. This analysis requires the records manager to conduct interviews with a representative sample of personnel who have some role in the system (i.e., users, operators, managers and other persons). During these qualitative assessments, the records manager will need to collect facts and opinions concerning the following:

- The information content of the records
- The business function, use, and purpose of the records

- The quantity of both active and archived records
- The storage media on which the records reside at the several stages of the information life cycle
- The usage characteristics that include a description of the community of users and the manner in which they interact with the documents or information content. A detailed assessment of all primary and secondary uses of the information is required.
- The current methods of document indexing, to include the limitations of the current situation as well as the several pathways by which the users require access into the records collection and the descriptors required to support such access.
- The average access times from the time information is requested until the time it is delivered to the users.
- The frequency of reference or number of retrievals
- The point in time at which the records transition from a dynamic to a static state; that is, when and under what circumstances they transition from active to semi-active and finally to inactive status.
- An assessment of any problems associated with the records collection, to include the current and optimum performance levels, as well as the perceived business benefits of attaining optimum performance

Of course, user assessments of system performance in response to open-ended questions necessarily elicit perceptive judgments and opinions. Some opinions will be valid and insightful, others less so.

Enterprise Classification and Taxonomy

What will enable an organization to find exactly the records it wants and needs, every time, all the time, in response to any user query, as quickly as needed? Or, to put it another way, given that large organizations have literally millions of documents and records in all media forms and formats, how, exactly, can a user locate any one of them on demand?

The answer is that these millions of documents must be organized and identified into recordkeeping systems in a manner that supports accurate and timely retrieval, on the part of any user, across the enterprise. Appropriate technology tools also must be in place to support these requirements. Computer systems alone are not enough, however. Documents can be electronically lost or misfiled just as easily as paper ones. The only way to assure accurate and timely retrieval of all stored records is to combine a standard records structure—an enterprise document classification and taxonomy—with appropriate hardware and software resources. This combination is a key component of professional RIM practice, and creating it requires specialized expertise. In an era in which unstructured content dominates the recordkeeping systems of organizations everywhere, this combination of standard recordkeeping practices and hardware and software is one of the most important, and neglected, issues in information retrieval today.

The word ***taxonomy*** comes from the Greek words "taxis," meaning arrangement or division and "nomos" meaning law. Taxonomy is defined as the science of classification according to a predetermined system.[7] Enterprise classification and taxonomy systems are based on the concept of organizing and retrieving information whereby documents and records are organized and indexed in a hierarchical structure of major and subordinate categories (sometimes referred to as "nodes"), from the most general to the most specific. The modern term is "enterprise taxonomy," but other terms such as "document classification schema," "controlled vocabulary," "thesaurus," "file plan," "uniform filing system," or even "master index" have also been used in RIM over the decades.[8] Newer software solutions designed to automate classification and taxonomies are usually known as "categorization" software.

The development of these types of document filing and retrieval systems was common practice in RIM during the 1960s and '70s. However, during the '80s and '90s, they declined in popularity, primarily because of the advent of desktop computers. With the computer's ability to support Boolean logic and keyword search capabilities, many records managers came to the erroneous conclusion that these schemes were no longer needed—the computer could find anything (or so they thought)! During the 1990s, however, the fallacy of this logic became readily apparent. Many organizations invested large sums of money in various document technology solutions, only to see them fail to perform as expected. These systems failed because they did not include a methodology under which records could be entered into the system according to a scheme designed to ensure that they could be found if sought.

Software applications portals, content management systems, knowledge management systems, search and retrieval software, and data warehousing / mining (discussed in Chapter 13) can all benefit from taxonomy.[9] By the late 1990s, document classification and taxonomy were again recognized as key components of organizational recordkeeping systems.

Systems with No Taxonomy

The essence of organizational recordkeeping systems is that, if no standard records structure or enterprise document classification scheme is present, the system users will typically make an arbitrary decision to assign a filename or other identifying descriptor to newly created documents when they need to be saved in the recordkeeping system for future reference. They may need to save any number of files each day, and they may also assign similar or different filenames to them, again in an arbitrary manner. Every other person in the entire organization may do the same. However, as time goes by, numerous documents bear filenames that were arbitrarily assigned by whoever entered them into the system. The result is a poorly organized and structured enterprise recordkeeping system that is highly fragmented and very difficult to use. In such cases, like records maintained by different workgroups and departments are very difficult to retrieve, especially in cases where an enterprise-wide search must be conducted and the documents are of any age.

In order to obtain a better understanding of the importance of classification and taxonomy, consider the analogy of shopping for products at a supermarket. In these types of facilities, products are organized in logical categories and subcategories by aisles and shelves, and then by sections and subsections of the aisles and shelves. The index to major product categories appears on signs suspended over each aisle in a manner that is easily visible to customers. The supermarket may stock hundreds of thousands of individual products in hundreds of major and thousands of subordinate categories in thousands of square feet of floor space, but any single item can be located within two to five minutes or so, with no special customer training required. Only a general familiarity with the basic concept of product organization is needed.

In theory, document retrieval should be no more difficult; at least in all but the most complex and specialized recordkeeping situations. In practice, however, organizational recordkeeping systems must be operated based on the principles of structure and discipline that are employed by any supermarket that expects to maintain a large base of satisfied customers.

Unstructured Content

Since the advent of the relational database, organizations have been able to manage structured information effectively. Unstructured information—the 80 percent (or even greater) of organizational information content that does not neatly fit into the rows and columns of a database—is far more difficult to manage, as it is scattered throughout documents, e-mails, and Web pages. Unstructured information, by definition, is not created within a predetermined framework, such as a database schema. *Classification*, whether manual or automatic, is the process of applying a common filing language to unstructured documents and data. This filing language appears in a topic-based hierarchy or taxonomy.[10]

Taxonomies classify information into logical categories that allow users to readily browse through content. They are often used in tandem with search and retrieval tools (keyword or concept-based) to help locate target information. However, unlike search technology alone, taxonomies reveal the overall structure of a knowledge base in a hierarchy that is visible to the user. The user navigates through subcategories to narrow the search, a process that helps avoid false hits of information outside the area of interest. Therefore, when used with search and retrieval tools, taxonomies aid in efficiency by limiting the volume of material that must be searched.[11]

Enterprise document classification schemes are typically designed for installation in single or multiple workgroups / departments or throughout the organization. Their most important characteristic is that they provide a standardized filing structure and a uniform filing language or vocabulary to guide system users in making files classification decisions. The major benefit is a significant reduction in the arbitrary judgments made thousands of times each business day concerning how to identify documents for filing and where in the system they should reside. The inevitable result of arbitrary files classification decisions is highly fragmented filing systems and imprecise / untimely document retrieval. Without consistent files classification based on a standard record structure, high-quality recordkeeping systems are not possible, particularly for larger organizations that create and maintain large, complex, and diverse collections of unstructured content.

The Enterprise Taxonomy

Unlike libraries, which have predeveloped classification systems such as the Dewey Decimal Classification System or the Library of Congress classification system, no universal standard taxonomies are available for businesses. Consequently, each enterprise taxonomy must be custom-developed based on the organization's unique business requirements. Taxonomies are challenging to build for three main reasons:

1. Taxonomy development is a complicated, time-consuming, and highly subjective exercise requiring specialized expertise. Moreover, once developed, effective usage requires training so that classification decisions are made accurately and consistently, based on system rules.

2. Taxonomies need to be fully customized to the organization's business processes and the records within those processes so that the retrieval needs of all users are adequately reflected.

3. Taxonomies need to be developed at an appropriate level of detail in order to be useful. When developed to the third and fourth levels, hundreds of categories and subcategories are often required. On the other hand, anything beyond four levels may inhibit users' ability to navigate easily within the structure, which impedes retrieval.

The two most common types of taxonomies are functional and organizational. Functional taxonomies are organized by the major and subordinate business functions or processes of the enterprise. This approach is recommended as best practice in the ISO 15489 standard.[12] The major advantage of functional taxonomies is that they are less affected by reorganizations. Perhaps the major disadvantage is that they are often very difficult to develop as they invariably encounter resistance by individual department managers, who want their information organized under their own proprietary categories. As a result, approval of the schema is often difficult to obtain. In the organizational taxonomy, the major and subordinate categories are arranged by department and subdepartment. The major advantages are that this type of taxonomy is relatively easy to build and, once built, it is easy to understand and use, as the categories are familiar to all. On the other hand, this type of taxonomy typically requires frequent updating due to organizational changes. Moreover, organizational taxonomies encourage proprietary ways of thinking about the enterprise document store.

In practice, however, most enterprise taxonomies represent a hybrid approach between functional and organizational characteristics. In the functional schemes, many terms used to identify and describe the categories will be the same or very similar to those describing various departmental entities. Terms describing functions and subfunctional business processes will be instantly recognizable to users. In functional schemes, however, terms that are too organizationally specific and thus subject to change should be avoided.

Building the enterprise taxonomy involves careful study of the organization and its business processes, coupled with interviewing staff at the departmental level, in order to customize the category schema for maximum effectiveness.

Standard Categories

As previously discussed, the enterprise taxonomy consists of predefined subject or category terms that constitute the basis for document classification. These standard categories are designed to impose logic and order upon record content. Taken as a whole, they should be mutually exclusive, unambiguous, and inclusive of all information content used throughout the enterprise. The main headings must be inclusive of all subheadings below them. For example, everything below "eye diseases" is and must be an eye disease. Taxonomies are media independent; they represent the intellectual content of any format of information-bearing objects, irrespective of storage media. They may be used successfully in paper-based or electronic environments—wherever unstructured information content resides.[13]

The hierarchy of categories in enterprise document classification schemes is developed in a manner that reflects the major and subordinate functions reflecting the organization's business processes, typically at the following levels:

- Enterprise
- Business process
- Sector / region
- Staff or department
- Subdepartment / workgroup
- Workstation / desktop

Then, the standard categories reflecting the information maintained by these groups are organized in a multitier tree or "parent-child" hierarchical arrangement, as follows:

- First level – primary categories
- Second level – secondary categories
- Third level – tertiary categories
- Fourth level – quaternary categories
- Fifth level – quintenary categories

Should the taxonomy be built from the top down or the bottom up? In practice, a marriage of the two approaches is usually followed. The primary and even the secondary categories can often be developed by analyzing the organizational structure and its business processes, functions, and subfunctions. Categories in the lower levels of the hierarchy will, however, have to be developed in close consultation with departmental staff. When interviewing these staff members, developing a detailed understanding as to what functions and business processes are performed, what types or categories of records are maintained in support of each function and subfunction, what document types comprise each category, and how each category is accessed on a routine and exceptional basis is essential. From this information, the category schema can be completed as discussed below.

Category Selection

The methodology for selecting the document categories in an enterprise classification scheme is based on the following basic principles:

- Standard categories should be selected to serve the specific needs of the users. All categories should be fully customized to reflect the document retrieval requirements of each business process. Although a document may be classified in more than one place within the taxonomy, the document itself should be stored in only one location.

- Categories should be based on probable secondary as well as primary usage of information content. Secondary uses are defined as potential uses of content other than the reason the records were created (their primary business purpose). If these possible or probable future uses of content are not carefully considered in designing the taxonomy, its utility in delivering precise and timely retrieval will suffer. Taxonomy designers must work in close collaboration with users to hazard predictive judgments or educated guesses concerning the kinds of queries that will or may arise and then devise categories that will be responsive to them.

- Categories should be based on a comprehensive identification of the set order of records in logical groupings. Certain records belong with other records, and their meaning and context would be compromised or destroyed if the relationships inherent in their set order are not reflected in the taxonomy.

- Primary and subordinate categories should be selected in a manner that achieves the right degree of fragmentation with respect to how information will be segmented. If categories are too broad, too specific, overlap, or fail to cover a subject / functional area, users will experience retrieval difficulties.

- The scheme should be designed to provide a place for every document. The more general the document, the higher its place in the hierarchy. The more specific the document, the lower its place in the hierarchy. Ideally, any given document should be filed in only one place. The goal is to develop categories that are mutually exclusive with respect to their contents. However, depending on context, many documents can and indeed should be classified under multiple categories.

Frequently, enterprise document classification schemes need not be developed below the secondary or, at most, tertiary levels. The depth to which these schemes need to be developed depends, chiefly, on the nature of the business process and the complexity of the recordkeeping systems that support them. In many instances, a two-level structure is adequate to facilitate proper document classification and accurate retrieval. If the structure is developed at levels deeper than is required, it can be cumbersome to implement and may hamper retrieval operations. When developed in this manner, the system rules sometimes permit individual users to develop subordinate subcategories below the secondary level to suit their own needs.

All categories in the taxonomy are open and available for use by all employees in paper and electronic recordkeeping systems. However, the categories are used only as needed. Therefore, individual users can personalize their own filing schemes to fit their unique filing requirements, so long as the basic rules of the system are respected.

Hierarchical content classification schemes are designed to be flexible and readily expandable as the organization and its recordkeeping needs change over time. New categories can be introduced at any level of the hierarchy without affecting other categories, and existing categories can be subdivided as necessary. A sample of a multilevel taxonomy / document classification scheme appears in Figure 9.3.

Taxonomy/ Content Classification Scheme Developed to Third Level of Hierarchy

Figure 9.3

Levels of Classification Scheme Hierarchy

Primary Categories

- Corporate Administration
- Energy and Environmental

Primary categories are frequently accompanied by what are called *scope notes*. These notes are brief narrative descriptions of each category that inform the reader of the inclusive and exclusive contents of the category, as well as other information that may facilitate its proper usage.

Secondary Categories

- Corporate Administration
  - Corporate Documents
  - Policies and Procedures
  - Facilities Management
  - Communications and Public Relations
- Energy and Environmental
  - Development Projects
- Operations and Maintenance
  - Contracts and Agreements

Tertiary Categories

- Corporate Administration
  - Corporate Documents
    - Articles of Incorporation
    - Corporate Chargers and Bylaws
    - Board Meetings
    - Board Minutes – Corporate
    - Board Minutes – Subsidiaries / Committees
  - Policies and Procedures
    - Parent Company
    - Subsidiaries
  - Communications and Public Relations
  - News Releases
  - Speeches
- Energy and Environmental
  - Development Projects
    - Alternative Energy Projects
    - Contracts and Agreements
  - Project Management Documents
    - Environmental Planning
    - Environmental Assessments
    - Environmental Remediation
  - Production Projects
    - Environmental Planning
    - Environmental Assessments
    - Environmental Remediation

Once the standard taxonomy categories have been developed, a coding scheme is frequently added. This coding scheme consists of alphabetic, numeric, or alphanumeric codes assigned to all primary and subordinate categories to aid in identifying documents classified within them. Alphanumeric coding schemes frequently utilize two- or three-letter alpha codes, constructed as mnemonic devices for ease of recognition and recall by system users. For example, the category for administrative records may bear the ADM alpha code, while the category for legal documents may be coded by the LEG alpha indicator. A sample of this type of coding scheme appears in Figure 9.4.

The taxonomy provides a scheme and set of rules for content organization, classification and indexing, while the retention schedule provides policies and rules prescribing how long information content must be preserved. In many best practice environments, these two RIM methodologies are combined so that recordkeeping systems are designed with functionality for disposition and life cycle management as well as content organization and classification. In such cases, each level of the taxonomy must be directly linked to a retention schedule item. In most such situations, this linkage occurs at the secondary level of the scheme; that is, the secondary categories in the taxonomy are linked directly with their equivalent records series in the retention schedule. The end result is a recordkeeping system that provides optimum

Taxonomy/ Content Classification Scheme with Alphanumeric Coding

Figure 9.4

Alphanumeric Coded Classification Scheme

- COR 1.0 Corporate Administration
    - COR 1.1 Corporate Documents
        - COR 1.1.1 Articles of Incorporation
        - COR 1.1.2 Corporate Chargers and Bylaws
        - COR 1.1.3 Board Meetings
        - COR 1.1.4 Board Minutes – Corporate
        - COR 1.1.5 Board Minutes – Subsidiaries / Committees
    - COR 1.2 Policies and Procedures
        - COR 1.2.1 Parent Company
        - COR 1.2.2 Subsidiaries
    - COR 1.3 Communications and Public Relations
        - COR 1.3.1 News Releases
        - COR 1.3.2 Speeches
- E&E 1.0 Energy and Environmental
    - E&E 1.1 Development Projects
        - E&E 1.1.1 Alternative Energy Projects
        - E&E 1.1.2 Contracts and Agreements
    - E&E 1.2 Project Management Documents
        - E&E 1.2.1 Environmental Planning
        - E&E 1.2.2 Environmental Assessments
        - E&E 1.2.3 Environmental Remediation
    - E&E 1.3 Production Projects
        - E&E 1.3.1 Environmental Planning
        - E&E 1.3.2 Environmental Assessments
        - E&E 1.3.3 Environmental Remediation

retrieval capabilities together with systematic, policy-based retention and life cycle management of content.

Software Solutions for Automatic Categorization

In recent years, a new type of document management software—***automatic categorization***—has made its way into the marketplace. In these types of software solutions, categorization is defined as the assigning of an object to a preexisting subject category within a taxonomy structure, also called *classification*. Manual classification, performed by humans, is slow, expensive, and does not scale effectively when applied to the millions of unstructured documents created by large organizations. Moreover, search operations that depend exclusively on keywords suffer because the context and meaning inherent in unstructured content is ignored. According to Hadley Reynolds, director of research at Delphi Group, "The problem has always been that traditional keyword search doesn't provide a very rich core of meaning, because all it knows about is the occurrence of words."[14] Automatic categorization software systems, supported by enterprise taxonomy tools, are designed to overcome these limitations.

The primary objective of this type of software is to understand and be able to recognize the concepts and ideas that group like documents together, while at the same time excluding unlike documents that are not relevant to search queries. The definition of context is that which surrounds, and gives meaning to, something else. The relevancy of any information content presented to users during search operations is entirely subjective to the searcher. Only each individual can judge how relevant a particular bit of information is to what he or she is attempting to discover. The document may be too general or too technical or out of date. Context, then, is the determining factor in the relevancy of search results. Taxonomy or categorization software is designed to facilitate contextual searching by delineating the conceptual relationships that exist within and between various topics contained in the multitude of unstructured content across the enterprise.

Automatic categorization systems support placing or classifying existing electronic documents within their proper categories in a taxonomy. In a typical deployment, the system administrator points the software at the body of documents to be classified on hard disks, servers, intranet sites, portals, and Web sites. The taxonomy engine residing on servers then performs the categorization process and usually populates a database of metadata to support subsequent retrieval and maintenance operations.[15] These types of tools are designed to identify and extract patterns and concepts in unstructured content, thereby increasing the accuracy and results of search-and-retrieve operations. Automatic categorization or taxonomy software provides the potential means to automatically (i.e., without human intervention) file documents into either a predefined taxonomy, or into user-defined categories. Most automatic categorization systems, however, still require human intervention in some aspect of their deployment. Humans develop custom taxonomy schemes, define the rules under which the system must operate, or monitor its results.

Automatic categorization software products are generally designed to classify information in real time and within multiple contexts. This ability to dynamically classify information and to highlight relationships between and among the various categories of a taxonomy can greatly enhance the accuracy of the search process. However, at the technology's current state of sophistication, these software solutions often perform with a limited level of accuracy. They tend not to work very well on short documents having limited content, very long documents having diverse content, or documents without uniform content.[16]

Automatic categorization systems employ two principal approaches: pattern matching and rule-based methodologies:

- *Pattern-based systems* use word patterns and concepts within the electronic records to associate the records with predefined file categories in the taxonomy.

- *Rule-based systems* depend on user-defined sets of rules to associate the occurrence (or exclusion) of names, phrases, or concepts contained in documents with the categories in the taxonomy. These systems can precisely define the criteria by which a document is classified. The rule measures how well a particular document meets the criteria for membership in that topic. The computer parses the documents, identifies the user-specified entities, and assigns the documents to the appropriate categories based on the rule set.

The accuracy of all automatic categorization systems is highly dependent upon the effort and care in defining the rules under which the system performs its document classification. In systems using pattern matching, the selection of rules that accurately represents the content of each subject heading in the taxonomy is critical to accuracy in performance.[17] Of course, no single taxonomy methodology or software system is superior to another for every application. The trend is to combine multiple methods to categorize the corpus of documents to increase the accuracy and relevancy of grouping similar documents. Some taxonomy providers are developing and marketing systems targeted towards specific vertical markets such as pharmaceuticals, legal / law firms, healthcare firms, etc. Even so, most vendors supplying prebuilt taxonomies allow user-defined customization of the classification scheme to suit specific business requirements.[18]

With so much emphasis on records retention, improving recordkeeping system performance is often neglected in RIM practice, particularly in the U.S. However, if RIM is to be practiced at a professional level, the existence and location of all information content must be known, and precise and timely retrieval must be the rule rather than the exception so that the organization's recordkeeping systems effectively support its larger business objectives.

Notes

1. Susan Feldman, "The High Cost of Not Finding Information," *KMWorld*, March 2004, 9.

2. Ibid.; Delphi Group, *Taxonomy & Content Classification: Market Milestone Report*, 2002.

3. Feldman, "The High Cost of Not Finding Information," 10.

4. Delphi Group, *Taxonomy & Content Classification*, 7.

5. Mary Robek, Gerald Brown, and David Stephens, *Information and Records Management*, 4th ed. (New York: Glencoe / McGraw-Hill, 1995), 164-165.

6. Ibid.

7. Denise Bruno and Heather Richmond, "The Truth About Taxonomies," *The Information Management Journal* 37, no. 2 (March / April 2003): 45. See also Eric Woods, "The Corporate Taxonomy: Creating a New Order," KMWorld, July / August 2004.

8. Susan Cisco and Karen V. Strong, "The Value Added Information Chain," *The Information Management Journal* 33, no. 1 (January 1999), 6.

9. Delphi Group, *Taxonomy & Content Classification*, 7.

10. Ramana Venkata, "The Importance of Hierarchy Building in Managing Unstructured Data," *KMWorld*, March 2002, S4.

11. Judith Lamont, "Dynamic Taxonomies: Keeping Up With Changing Content," *KMWorld*, May 2003, 8.

12. International Organization for Standardization, ISO 15489-1:2001: *International Standard: Information and Documentation – Records Management – Part 1: General.* (Geneva, Switzerland: ISO, 2001), 13-14.

13. Bruno and Richmond, "The Truth About Taxonomies," 50.

14. Cathleen Moore, "Bringing Structure to Data," *InfoWorld*, 20 September 2004. See also Susan Feldman, "Why Categorize? *KMWorld*, October 2004; and J. Meyers, "Automatic Categorization, Taxonomies, and the World of Information: Can't Live With Them, Can't Live Without Them," *E-docs*, Nov. / Dec. 2002, 15.

15. Delphi Group, *Taxonomy & Content Classification*, 20.

16. Kirk Lubbes, "Automatic Classification: How It Works, Related Issues, and Impacts on Records Management," *The Information Management Journal* 35, no. 10 (October 2001): 42; Kirk Lubbes, "So You Want to Implement Automatic Categorization," *The Information Management Journal* 37, no. 2 (March / April 2003), 66.

17. Lubbes, "So You Want to Implement Automatic Categorization," 66.

18. Delphi Group, *Taxonomy & Content Classification*, 54.

Chapter 10

Protecting Information from Disaster

Many RIM specialists engage in a persuasive, even compelling, argument that protecting organizational information from loss due to disaster—whether due to natural, technical, or human causes—is the most important aspect of RIM. Although enhancing accessibility, managing the record life cycle, and other common RIM assignments are indeed important, the protection of business-critical records and information from disaster is transcendent. The reason is not hard to discern. For most organizations, their dependence on computer systems is so great that the protection of digital records and information is a matter of survival. One of the many lessons learned from the September 11, 2001, tragedy is that an organization may very well survive the loss of most or even all its paper records, but loss of all electronic ones would be truly cataclysmic and perhaps irrecoverable. Although the findings reported in published studies vary, lost or damaged records are a consequence of most *information security* threats experienced by organizations (see Figure 10.1).

According to statistics kept by the National Fire Protection Association, 47 percent of all businesses that suffer a catastrophic fire cease operations within one year.[1] A U.S. Bureau of Labor study revealed that 93 percent of companies that experience a significant data loss go out of business within five years.[2] However, organizational survival in the face of complete or near-complete loss of vital computer records may not be a matter of years or even months. It is more likely to be weeks or even days. According to one survey, when asked how soon after a major computer-related disaster the survival of their organization would be at risk:

Information Security: Records Threats

Figure 10.1

Trends in Corporate Records Security	2003	2004
Information security budget as a percentage of overall IT budget	10.93%	11.27%
Records lost or damaged	58%	37%
No downtime experienced due to lost or damaged records	26%	32%

SOURCE: Data from *CIO, CSO,* and PricewaterhouseCoopers as reported in "Businesses Improve Cyber Security," *The Information Management Journal* 38, no. 6 (November/December 2004): 18.

- 40 percent said within 72 hours
- 21 percent said within 48 hours
- 15 percent said within 24 hours
- 9 percent said within 4 hours
- 3 percent said in about one hour
- 4 percent said within the hour[3]

Many organizations that suffer significant losses of vital computer data have a very small window of time in which to recover before facing disastrous consequences. Even if organizational survival is not at risk, the cost of business interruption due to disaster is often unacceptably high. In a recent survey, respondents were asked to estimate the cost to their organization of each hour of downtime resulting from a system interruption. The results were:

- 46 percent said up to $50,000
- 28 percent said between $51,000 and $250,000
- 18 percent said between $251,000 and $1 million
- 8 percent said more than $1 million[4]

For a summary of a survey estimating the cost of downtime by industry sector, see Figure 10.2.

Status of Information Protection

Being able to say that the status of information protection has reached an acceptable level after the terrorist attacks of September 11, 2001 (which was the largest RIM-

Downtime Cost by Industry Sector

Figure 10.2

	Downtime Cost	
Industry Sector	Revenue per Hour	Revenue per Employee Hour
Energy	$2,817,846	$589
Telecommunications	2,066,245	186
Manufacturing	1,610,654	134
Financial Institutions	1,495,134	1,079
Insurance	1,202,444	371
Retail	1,107,274	244
Pharmaceuticals	1,082,252	168
Banking	996,802	131
Utilities	643,250	381
Health Care	636,030	143
Average – All Sectors	1,010,536	205

SOURCE: Data from Fred Moore, "Backup is Important, Recovery is Everything," *Computer Technology Review*, March 2002. META Group.

related disaster in U.S. history), would be comforting. Regrettably, such is not the case, as indicated by the following study results:

- Although some surveys indicate that most organizations have at least some type of disaster recovery plan in place (see Figure 10.3), other studies report that fewer than 25 percent of surveyed organizations have comprehensive, adequately documented, and regularly / rigorously tested business continuity capabilities in place.[5]

- Across all computing environments, from local area networks to distributed computing platforms, and now to Internet and intranet environments, the level of vulnerability has increased while the level of protection has decreased.[6]

- In mid-range computing environments, some IT specialists have estimated that only 15 percent of data centers would be able to recover more than 30 percent of their applications within any time frame, while less than 4 percent could recover their applications within the same day.[7]

Routine Data Losses

Executives must consider the inevitability and consequences of routine data losses, regardless of whether a disaster of any magnitude occurs. An old saying among computer people is that only two kinds of data owners exist—those who *have* lost data and those who *will* lose data. Even if the large losses that may never befall an organization are ignored, the smaller but significant ones still occur. In fact, most losses of data are not attributable to headline-grabbing events such as fires, floods, earthquakes, or similar catastrophic events. One study indicates that 44 percent of data loss is caused by hardware or systems failure, 32 percent by human error, and 14 percent by software or program error.[8] Cables become unplugged or are accidentally severed, electronics fail, disks stop spinning, batteries run down, viruses propagate and, regardless of defined policies or procedures, electronic records continue to be accidentally or inadvertently discarded and overwritten. Even with the introduction of specialized hardware and fault-tolerant solutions, data can and will continue to be lost.[9] Organizations must increase their vigilance against such losses, which requires the application of certain RIM principles and techniques.

Disaster Recovery Plan Status

Figure 10.3

Percentage of Employees Who Know the Status of Their Company's Disaster Recovery Plan	
Responses	% Answering
Do not know	3%
No plan to implement a disaster recovery plan	10%
Plan to implement a disaster recovery plan	19%
Disaster recovery plan in place	68%

SOURCE: Data from Mario Apicella, "Fail-Safe Continuity." *InfoWorld*, 17 February 2003.

RIM's Role

The importance of this matter—in terms of loss of revenue if not organizational survival—can hardly be overstated. What is the proper role of RIM in mitigating these risks? In the past, the protection of computer data from disaster has largely been the province of IT specialists. However, unless records managers work in close concert with these specialists, a comprehensive *data protection* program is not likely to be realized. In best practice environments, records managers provide the following assistance:

- Assess the degrees of criticality of electronic records and assign protection priorities commensurate with the consequences of loss.
- Develop and apply retention rules to backup copies of vital computer data.
- Assist business units in retrieving all offsite backup records in the event of a system interruption or disaster.
- Develop and implement protection strategies for protecting vital computer data residing in desktop environments.
- Assume the lead role in media reclamation efforts; develop and oversee the implementation of recovery procedures for the data residing on storage media that have been damaged by exposure to disaster conditions.
- Work with IT specialists to ensure the recovery of the RIM system.
- Apply digital preservation methodologies to ensure the integrity of data of long-term retention value residing on backup media.

Traditional Data Protection Methodologies

In order to work with IT specialists on applying RIM principles to data protection tasks, a basic understanding of these tasks is required. Methodologies include traditional, off-line tape-based data protection, as well as more advanced online methodologies.[10] Two commonly misunderstood terms—data backup and data archiving—refer to two completely different data storage management tasks. When used properly, the term *data archiving* refers to the migration of data from online processing environments to near-line or *off-line storage* systems for purposes of providing for its long-term retention on storage media suitable for that purpose. *Data backup* refers to making a copy, at regular, scheduled intervals, of data residing on primary, online storage devices. The data is copied or backed up to secondary media for purposes of off-line, offsite security storage. The intent of data backup routines is to provide the capability of recovering data when online processing is interrupted or when a data loss of any cause occurs. Typical backup routines are as follows:

- **Full backup** – Under this methodology, all data files and directories selected for backup are copied. A full-system backup produces a duplicate security copy of all disk-based files, including all data files and software resident on the system each time the backup is performed. In the event of a system interruption, IT specialists can restore all data files and software to get the system back online. Entire disk volumes may be selected for backup, or administrators may choose specific files and directories. Limitations of this methodology are that full backups are time-intensive, and many files may be backed up unnecessarily as they have not changed since the last backup.

- **Incremental backup** – This type of data backup copies only those files that have been changed or modified since the last incremental (but not full) backup. This methodology greatly reduces the time and media requirements. Full system restoration thus requires restoring the most recent full system backup copy, and then successively restoring each incremental backup copy containing the changed records. Despite the obvious time and cost advantages, the limitation is that this method requires the administrator to first restore from the first full backup and then apply all incremental backups to the required date of restore, which can be a cumbersome and tedious process.

- **Delta backup** – This type of data backup is an enhancement to the incremental backup method. Under this methodology, only the changes that have occurred since the previous backup are transferred across a network. This method is designed to overcome the bandwidth limitations that frequently make transfer-ring full, incremental, or differential backups across networks impractical. This methodology utilizes an algorithm that compares the images of each data file with the image of the same file from the last backup. This comparison generates a list of blocks within the data file that have changed. These blocks of data are then compressed and encrypted and then transmitted across the network.

- **Differential backup** – Under this methodology, all files that have been changed or modified since the last full backup are copied. This routine is applied to the last full backup and the latest incremental. The advantage is that differential backups are simpler and quicker than incremental routines; e.g., every day of the week. The differential backup can be used to restore the entire system, using only the full system backup plus the differential backup. Both old and updated files would be contained on the resulting two sets of backup media.

The traditional method for protecting computer data is to transfer a copy of the data from disk storage to removable media at scheduled intervals using full, incremental, and differential backup methodologies. *Magnetic tape* has long been the medium of choice in these routines. Until recently, the low cost of tape-based storage relative to the cost of online disk storage made magnetic tape the most practical medium for data backup. For the majority of organizations, magnetic tape remains the storage medium of choice for backing up vital data.[11] The tape medium, however, is not with-out its disadvantages, which include slow backup speed, infrequent verification to determine the integrity of backup data, and delays in accessing and recovering backed up data from offsite tapes. Traditional tape backup strategies require significant band-width to meet short backup and recovery time frames. Despite these limitations, tape is likely to remain the medium of choice for those applications requiring infrequent access, as well as those applications that can afford to wait a longer period of time for completion of recovery operations.[12]

In many data protection situations, off-line / offsite tape backup provides a three-tiered level of backup:

First Tier: Active data resides on primary storage arrays.

Second Tier: IT backs up less active data to secondary online or near-line disks or tape systems with disk front-ends.

Third Tier: IT migrates inactive data from the near-line system to tape for offsite storage.[13]

Twelve-Tape Backup Methodology

To reduce the time and cost for resumption of mission-critical business operations, organizations should strive for 100-percent recoverability of its vital computer data following a disaster or other adverse event. Recoverability is best achieved through full backup of hard drives at frequent intervals. Compared with incremental and differential backup methods, full backup permits faster resumption of computer operations following a disaster. The 12-tape cycle methodology is the recommended approach for preparation and offsite storage of backup copies.[14] This type of protection strategy is usually applied to vital computer data stored on network servers and timeshared computers. It is generally implemented as follows:

- For each network server or timeshared computer, twelve magnetic tape cartridges are labeled with the following designations:

◆ Monday	◆ Friday 1	◆ Month 1
◆ Tuesday	◆ Friday 2	◆ Month 2
◆ Wednesday	◆ Friday 3	◆ Month 3
◆ Thursday	◆ Friday 4	◆ Month 4

- Each label should also indicate the date the tape was first used, the computer being backed up, and the backup software employed.

- A full backup of all computers is performed Monday through Thursday, using the tape cartridges labeled for those days. The resulting backup tapes are sent to the offsite storage location at the close of each business day.

- A full backup of all computers is performed on the first, second, and third Friday of each month, using the appropriately labeled tape. For months that have five Fridays, an additional backup tape is prepared on the fourth Friday of the month. These backup tapes are sent to or deposited in the offsite storage location.

- On the last Friday of each month, a full backup is performed on one of the monthly tapes, beginning with the tape labeled "Month 1."

Backup tapes for Monday through Thursday are removed from offsite storage and discarded or reused throughout the week. The Friday tapes are discarded or reused at the end of each month. The monthly tapes are discarded or reused at the end of four months. New tapes are preferred for reliable backup operations. If they are not discarded, previously used tapes should be reserved for purposes other than backup. If tapes will be reused to create additional backup copies, they should be discarded after four uses.

Applying this procedure, the following backup tapes will be in offsite storage on any given day:

- Tapes produced on the three previous business days
- Tapes produced at the end of the three (occasionally four) previous weeks
- Tapes produced on the last Friday of the three previous months

Data Recovery Speed

Until a few years ago, simple data backup routines were enough. Typically, IT backup specialists take down applications at night, back up the data to tape, and send the tapes offsite for secure storage. More recently, however (and particularly after September 11, 2001), the speed of data recovery is clearly what is really important. If IT backs up the data but cannot restore it within acceptable time limits, the backed up data is useless.[15] This problem stems from the fact that most data protection plans emphasize backup processes but give inadequate attention to the critical role of data recovery and the speed with which it can be effected. Recovery is, all too often, an afterthought. Time-to-recovery and ease-of-recovery are frequently overlooked in planning and testing activities. Although backup processes are regularly tested during scheduled backups, recovery time is often untested until a disaster strikes.[16]

Recovery is the process of recovering data from a corrupted source—whether that source is experiencing a software malfunction or has suffered a severe physical trauma—by locating files on the disk drives and recreating the file structure so that normal operations can be resumed. In contrast to rebuilding from scratch, data recovery retrieves the most recent files—a significant distinction when the typical backup window for many organizations is eight hours.[17]

New rapid database recovery solutions are available that can fully recover and restart any database within minutes rather than hours, regardless of the size of the database. These rapid recovery solutions rewind rather than rebuild the databases following a system interruption. These tools are designed to roll back in time and restart the database at any point before the loss or corruption occurred. Operations then resume from that point in time. These solutions may be analogized to a rolling movie of the data, as opposed to a time-specific snapshot, thus eliminating the risk of data loss that may occur between snapshots. Further, because this undo process eliminates the need to apply transaction logs for data reconstruction or to restore full volumes of data, recovery time can be reduced from hours or days to minutes.[18]

E-vaulting and Online Backup

Electronic vaulting is designed to overcome the limitations associated with tape backup. For organizations with highly critical data, the issue is whether to add additional data protection capabilities on top of traditional off-line / offsite backup systems. *E-vaulting*, an increasingly popular solution, is commonly defined as the movement of data over private or public communications lines from a local (primary) computer storage device to a remote (secondary) storage device for the purpose of restoring the data in the event the primary copy is lost or otherwise unavailable. The process thus avoids the time-consuming and cumbersome requirements associated with the physical handling of tape media.

This type of data backup can be executed either by in-house computer specialists, or it can be outsourced to commercial data protection companies. The transition to e-vaulting from traditional tape backup has greatly accelerated in recent years, due to high bandwidth network connections, highly scalable redundant array of independent disk (RAID) storage systems, and better backup software.[19]

Online backup refers to the use of high-performance disk drives rather than off-line media to accomplish data protection methodologies. Data *disk mirroring,* snapshots, and replication are all forms of online backup. Their primary purpose is to enhance the speed of recovery over what off-line methodologies can deliver.[20] According to the InfoWorld 2003 Storage Survey, these forms of data protection are also growing in popularity. The survey reported that 37 percent of the respondents have already deployed some form of disk-based online backup and that an additional 24 percent plan to deploy this type of backup solution in the near future.[21] Replication routines are used to backup incremental changes to disk while mirroring keeps an identical copy of the data residing on the primary server on a secondary system. Both replication and mirroring can operate locally or remotely, and often do both for highly sensitive data.

Replication and mirroring are useful backup methodologies, but if errors are in the data when these routines are run, the errors will be replicated in the backed up data. In other words, anything that happens to the primary data also happens to the secondary (mirrored) data.[22] Data snapshots are a useful way of addressing this problem. These protection routines are used to record and store changes to data at set intervals.[23] Although data mirroring, especially remote mirroring, is an important tool in data protection, it is not a substitute for conventional backups. It offers no protection against several important causes of data loss such as accidental deletion or virus infection.

Open-File Backup

In many business-critical environments, IT can no longer schedule data backups in so called "after-hours." With global networks operating across all time zones, after-hours do not exist—business operations and the data processing that supports them occurs 24/7. In these situations, a major issue is how to prevent open-file data losses to files that remain open and in-use during scheduled backups. Open files have historically been a data backup specialist's worst nightmare. Traditionally, during a backup, files that are open or in use get skipped during the backup routines.[24] Most backup systems will attempt to access the open files again at the end of the backup; but if the files are still open, they may again be skipped and remain unprotected.

Organizations with *open-file backup* issues need the ability to ensure a full-system backup without skipped, corrupt, or unsynchronized files. A backup solution that consistently captures open and in-use files without interrupting applications or continuous system operations is needed. Open-file backup software is designed to fill this need. These solutions are designed to monitor the file system for read requests that originate from the backup program. When the backup application accesses the first file, the open-file software determines when no partial transactions are pending. When this state is discovered, the software performs its backup routines for all open files on the system.

Storage Area Networks

In the aftermath of the September 11, 2001, terrorist attacks, many organizations have begun to consider new strategies for the centralized management of backup data that can be stored decentrally on servers in widely dispersed locations. The objective is to prevent a single point of failure from bringing down the entire organization. One such approach is the use of *storage area networks (SANs)*. SANs are dedicated storage networks in which servers and storage devices are connected by hubs and switches. The network's software permits the centralized management of data regardless of platforms or media. The data itself can be easily and quickly dispersed to secure, offsite locations. In a SAN data storage environment, if one site is taken out of commission, the whole enterprise is not affected by the event. The SAN architecture simplifies the process of creating mirror data images at remote locations, thus ensuring that remote, up-to-date copies of databases are available in case of disaster at the main location.[25]

Protection Priorities

Records managers should play a role in assessing the degrees of criticality of electronic records and assigning protection priorities commensurate with the consequences of loss. In the context of an organization's data protection and recovery requirements, *all data are not created equal*, but many IT departments tend to treat data that way. Data that has lost its criticality gets backed up over and over again, while business-critical data that does not reside on central servers is sometimes ignored. Some applications can tolerate a delayed recovery time, while others require near instantaneous recovery in the event of an outage.[26]

IT departments should prioritize their data protection investments based on the criticality of the data to the life of the business, as well as the speed-of-recovery requirements. The most critical data—the applications that must be restored to full availability the fastest—should be allocated the highest levels of protection. Consequently, instituting online backup, together with multilevel protection, will be required. Data protection specialists should assign storage devices and backup schemes accordingly, reserving the highest-performance data protection solutions for the most critical data.[27] However, many IT departments do an inadequate job of assessing the criticality of data and prioritizing protection and recovery strategies based on these assessments. Often, IT departments simply lack the analytical talent or time to conduct them. Because of their exposure to owners of computer data throughout the organization as well as their skills in analyzing the value of information, RIM specialists are often in the best positions to make judgments concerning these issues—solely or in collaboration with other data protection specialists. In best practice environments, records managers interview data owners to determine the most critical applications based on the value of the information and the consequences of its loss. Then, protection and backup priorities can be recommended.

Application Analysis

For each computer application managed by IT, data protection and RIM specialists should work collaboratively to determine the following:

- Application name
- Application description (business function, history)
- Application type (batch, online, client-server, Web)
- Application size (storage requirements, lines of code)
- Business units supported
- Approximate number of users supported
- Application complexity (high, medium, low)
- Prior data interruptions or losses and actual consequences
- Possible or probable consequences of potential data losses, interruption or outages of varying degrees of severity and length
- Degree of criticality (high, medium, low)
- Recovery time requirements (minutes, hours, days)
- Recommended backup methodology
- Frequency of backup
- Backup retention requirements

For all applications having data criticality ratings of *high* or *medium*, a detailed assessment should be conducted to determine the following:

- **Business impact analysis** – An estimate of the consequences of the loss or unavailability of the application data, resulting from various risks or disaster scenarios, on the operations of specific business units as well as the organization as a whole, including all quantifiable and intangible consequences.
- **Recovery time objective** – An estimate of the maximum allowable recovery time between the time of the application outage and the resumption of normal business operations, as determined by the business impact analysis.
- **Recovery point objective** – An estimate of the maximum amount of lost data between when the application outage occurs and the condition of the data when restoration is complete, as determined by the business impact analysis.

- **Return-on-investment** – For the recommended method of protection of the application, an estimate of the time required before the investment in data protection and recovery will pay for itself.[28]

Degree-of-Criticality Assessments

In making the all-important degree-of-criticality assessments during the business impact analysis, the following guidelines are recommended:

- **High criticality** – These applications contain data of the highest strategic importance; data without which the organization could not operate, or it would suffer grave business consequences such as loss of customer base, confidence of investment community and customers, etc. Generally, the data in these applications are unique and irreplaceable, the recovery time is short, and the consequences of loss are unacceptable. These applications should be protected by the most advanced backup solutions.

- **Medium criticality** – These applications contain data that are still critical for business operations, but the consequences of loss are less, the recovery time is longer, and the possibility for regenerating the data exists. Frequently, however, the cost of recreation will exceed the cost of protection, and if the consequences of loss are severe enough, some applications will be worthy of high-performance backup solutions.

- **Low criticality** – These applications contain data that would be inconvenient to lose and that would be useful, but not essential, to the organization in resuming normal business operations. These applications can be protected by low-end, off-line / offsite backup methodologies.

Desktop Records Protection

Today, the desktop is where much of the most current work of business is done, including documentation related to active and open projects, transactions, and other immediate matters. According to a recent study by Pepperdine University, 60 percent of corporate information resides on PCs (including portable as well as fixed-location devices).[29] This statistic alone suggests that the desktop environment is business-critical for purposes of data protection planning. Therefore, data protection should not be limited to servers. It must also provide protection to desktop and workgroup environments. Some of the most critical data in most organizations likely does not reside on a file or application server. Rather, it is distributed across the hard drives of the desktop and laptop computers used daily by managers, executives, and other professional specialists.[30]

The desktop environment, with the deluge of incoming spam e-mails, is exposed to significant virus issues which, in turn, results in significant threats to the integrity of electronic records. In a recent virus prevalence survey, more than 64 percent of all servers experienced a virus-related outage, up from only 9 percent in the previous survey. The same survey reported that the incidence of viruses in e-mails has also sharply increased, as has the percentage of organizations that have experienced a virus-caused data loss.[31]

Elsewhere in this book, the desktop is characterized as a "RIM basket-case," in reference to the quality of management of the records residing in this environment. With respect to data protection, the situation is not a great deal better. Although desktop documents receive adequate backup protection if they have been saved to a common network server, many current documents remain unprotected. An estimated less than 5 percent of single-user desktop PCs have adequate protection for the data residing on their hard drives. In other words, distributed computing, through the desktop infrastructure, has exposed organizations to a much greater degree of vulnerability.[32]

Expecting individual employees to back up the data on their PCs regularly is unrealistic at best and dangerous at worst. Therefore, backup routines that are not user-dependent are required. In some implementations, data residing on servers and PCs at all locations can be automatically backed up. The data can be backed up over the Internet to a secure offsite vault, and the backup routines can be designed to run in a manner that is transparent to users. Recovery can be done using a Web-based user interface. In other implementations, data residing on mobile computing devices can be backed up automatically in background mode whenever the users log on to their systems.

Desktop users should not be completely absolved from responsibility for the protection of the mission-critical electronic records under their custody. Guidelines outlining individual responsibilities for protecting the valuable documents residing in their desktop environments are provided in the next section.

User Requirements for Desktop Backup

In most cases, electronic records created by desktop software applications are stored on hard drives for convenient access. These records require backup protection to ensure recovery of important information if a system malfunction or other adverse event occurs. Backup protection is obtained by making a copy of electronic records on removable media for off-line storage. Electronic records stored on common network hard drives are backed up by network administrators without involvement by desktop computer users. Use of network drives to store electronic records with significant information content or continuing operational value is recommended for minimizing backup requirements at the desktop level.

Desktop users should be held individually responsible for backup of electronic records they create or receive. Such employees should be required to store important electronic records on network servers, rather than local hard drives, whenever possible. Where using network servers is not practical, desktop users should be required to make backup copies of word processing documents, spreadsheet files, databases, digital images, or other electronic records stored on personal computers whenever those records are changed. Such backup copies may be produced on *floppy disks*, recordable compact disks (CDs), recordable DVDs, or other removable media. The backup media should be sent to the same offsite repository used for backup tapes. The following guidelines for backing up desktop files are recommended:

- Backup copies should be produced for all work in progress, for electronic records that need to be retained for possible future reuse, and for electronic records with unique information content that have continuing operational value.

- Backup copies should be produced at the earliest available opportunity and replaced with updated versions as appropriate.

- Depending on the personal computer configuration, electronic records stored on local hard drives should be copied onto magnetic tapes, floppy disks, CDs, or DVDs for backup protection.

- Backup copies should be labeled to identify the department or computer user that produced them and the electronic records they contain.

- Backup copies should be stored in a safe place until needed for recovery of information.

- When electronic records are deleted from local hard drives in conformity with the organization's retention schedules, all backup copies must be deleted as well.

Recovery of Magnetic Media

In most disasters, all is not lost to complete destruction. Some records media will have just been damaged, and in many cases, restoration to business use is possible. Records managers should assume the lead role in media reclamation efforts. They should develop and oversee the implementation of recovery procedures for data residing on storage media exposed to disaster conditions. Removable *magnetic media* can be successfully salvaged if they are water-soaked but have not been exposed to high temperatures. In some instances, magnetic tapes have been fully recovered and returned to service after having been fully immersed in unclean river water for a period of two weeks. The integrity of data on magnetic tapes is imperiled at temperatures in excess of 150 degrees Fahrenheit, and diskettes (the most vulnerable of all records media) are threatened with loss of data at 125 degrees Fahrenheit or a relative humidity exceeding 80 percent. The recovery of fixed magnetic disks is, however, much more problematic if they have been exposed to either water or high temperatures. Such media often cannot be restored, and the data cannot be recovered.[33]

In cases where no backup media are available, the restoration of water-damaged magnetic tapes becomes critical. The tapes may be hand-dried with lint free cloths; then put through a tape cleaner or winder (but not on a regular tape drive), followed by running cleaning tissues over them. When the tapes are reasonably dry, they should again be processed in this manner, and then read to determine the condition of the data. If the integrity of the data has been irreparably compromised, the tapes may then be copied onto new media and returned to normal use. Water-soaked diskettes should be kept in cool distilled water, dried with lint-free towels, and then copied onto new diskettes, if they have not been warped or magnetically damaged.[34]

Retention of Backup Data

Like all organizational information, data residing on backup media need to be retained under approved retention rules. Kevin Rodin, CIO of Iron Mountain, states, "Data protection has moved beyond the traditional scope of backing up and securing information to encompass the notion of data life cycle management."[35] Under their responsibilities for developing organization-wide retention policies, records managers should develop retention periods for all backed up and protected data.

Generally, retention periods for backup data should reflect the length of time the data is required for purposes of recovery from loss or interruption. As backed-up data consists of duplicate copies of data retained elsewhere for the full duration of its value for legal and other business purposes, the retention requirements for recovery from loss are typically quite short. Typical retention periods for backup data are as follows:

- Daily backups are retained for one cycle (one week – 7 days)
- Weekly backups are retained for one cycle (one month – 4 to 5 weeks)
- Monthly backups are retained for one cycle (one year – 12 months)[36]

Records managers should work closely with IT data protection specialists as well as with business owners of the data to develop retention periods for backup data that are adequate to meet the organization's needs for the restoration and recovery of lost data.

Lessons of September 11, 2001

The impact of the events of September 11, 2001, will be felt for decades—in many areas of national and international affairs. These events were, by far, the largest disaster in American history where RIM was concerned.[37] The September 11 terrorist attacks on the World Trade Center have changed the face of disaster preparedness for businesses and governments in the U.S., which must now prepare for the kinds of threats and a scale of damage never before imagined. Lessons learned as a result of these terrorist attacks include:

- Disaster recovery planning works for those who do it right—the biggest lesson.[38] For the most part, the critical systems of major financial institutions and other large businesses seem to have recovered quickly and according to plan. "In the most high-risk, high-exposure environments, we had great success," said Joseph Walton of EMC Corp.
- The ability to respond to a disaster successfully is not an optional management initiative but an essential component of the cost of doing business.
- Even organizations that do not think of themselves as prime terrorist targets do not have the luxury of considering themselves exempt from terrorism where dis-

aster planning is concerned. Terrorism and threats of war should be taken seriously in most if not all disaster planning scenarios.

- After the September 11 attacks, only a few companies required help with mainframe recovery; the biggest challenges were restoring mid-range systems and servers and restoring connectivity to computer networks and the desktops, as well as obtaining access to the stored backup information.

- One company in the World Trade Center had its IT operations located on one tower and its relocation facility in the other. Backup facilities supporting mission-critical business functions should not be located where they may be subject to the same disaster that affects the primary site.

- Disaster recovery plans should be based on the assumption that telephone service and Internet connections may not be restored for up to several weeks following a cataclysmic disaster.

- Organizations should base their information protection strategies on the concept of reducing their dependence on a single data infrastructure or location.[39]

Vital Paper Records Protection

Although this chapter is largely about the protection of electronic records, September 11, 2001, also obviously resulted in major consequences, and lessons learned, concerning paper records. One commentator wrote, "The sight of all that paper scattered among the ash is stark proof of the need for good records management that integrates paper with electronic records in a total solution."[40] Concerning paper records, the major lessons to be learned include the following:

- Because paper records have been declining in importance relative to computer-based records for many years, organizations that have aggressively applied new technologies to automate their business processes are much less vulnerable than organizations that have not.

- For most organizations today, to lose all paper records would be extremely inconvenient, but it would not put the organization out of business. To cite just one example, the Port Authority of New York and New Jersey had its headquarters' offices in the World Trade Center until September 11, 2001. Nearly all paper records were destroyed, but the Port Authority recovered from this loss and continues its regular operations. On the other hand, if an organization lost all its computer records, it would be truly cataclysmic and would very likely result in the demise of the organization.

- Offsite protection has always been a better and more reliable means of protecting vital data than onsite protection, but the September 11 tragedy highlighted the futility of onsite protection strategies. For many years, RIM specialists have relied on fire-resistive filing cabinets and fireproof vaults as the primary methods for protecting paper records onsite, in cases where protecting them by means of sending either the originals or duplicate copies to a secure offsite location is not feasible. The lesson from September 11 is that organizations should not keep valuable records—records they cannot afford to lose—in paper form with no backup. Protecting records by storing them offsite through the data backup methodologies discussed here is an excellent strategy for protecting vital records.

- Organizations should adopt the long-term goal of converting to digital format every paper-based recordkeeping system of mission-critical importance, as soon as resources and priorities allow. Records managers should survey all such applications, and develop a plan for conversion from paper to digital format that can be implemented over a period of several years.[41]

Notes

1. Steve Aronson, "The Crucial Role of Vital Records in Business Continuity / Disaster Recovery," *SMS* 8, Issue 1 (2003): 16.

2. "Survey Reveals Disaster Recovery Expectations and Reality," *The Information Management Journal* 37, no. 6 (November / December 2003): 8.

3. Jim Reinert, "Data Recovery Completes Disaster Recovery," *Disaster Recovery Journal* (Spring 2004): 67.

4. Ibid.

5. Aronson, "The Crucial Role of Vital Records," 14.

6. Fred Moore, "Backup is Important, Recovery is Everything," *Computer Technology Review* 22, no. 3 (March 2002): 18.

7. Ibid., 20.

8. Moore, "Backup is Important, Recovery is Everything," 18.

9. Eric Harless, "Dissecting Disaster Recovery Solutions," *SMS* 8, Issue 3 (2003).

10. Ray Ganong, "The Emergence of E-Vaulting," *The Information Management Journal* 37, no. 1 (January/February 2003): 21. See also Mary Robek, Gerald Brown, and David Stephens, *Information and Records Management*, 4th ed. (New York: Glencoe / McGraw-Hill, 1995), 21, 28.

11. Aronson, "The Crucial Role of Vital Records," 17.

12. Ganong, "The Emergence of E-Vaulting," 22.

13. Christine Chudnow, "Issues in Online Backup," *SMS* 8, Issue 2 (2003): 9.

14. William Saffady, unpublished manuscript, n.d.

15. Chudnow, "Issues in Online Backup," 8.

16. Ron Levine, "Rapid Database Recovery," *SMS* 8, Issue 3 (2003): 23.

17. Reinert, "Data Recovery Completes Disaster Recovery," 66.

18. Levine, "Rapid Database Recovery," 24.

19. Ganong, "The Emergence of E-Vaulting," 24.

20. Chudnow, "Issues in Online Backup," 9-10.

21. Mario Apicella, "Enterprise Storage Part II – Fail-safe Continuity," *InfoWorld,* 17 February 2003, 37.

22. Ganong, "The Emergence of E-Vaulting," 25.

23. Chudnow, "Issues in Online Backup," 10.

24. Jeanne Blair, "Re-centralizing Backup Management, *SMS* 7, Issue 4 (2002): 24.

25. David Stephens, "Protecting Records in the Face of Chaos, Calamity, and Cataclysm," *The Information Management Journal* 37, no. 1 (January/February 2003): 38.

26. Moore, "Backup is Important, Recovery is Everything," 18.

27. Chudnow, "Issues in Online Backup," 8.

28. Jason Buffington, "New Acronyms for Disaster Recovery," *SMS* 8, Issue 3 (2003): 13-14.

29. "The Data Protection Agenda," *CIO*, n.d., S2.

30. Harless, "Dissecting Disaster Recovery Solutions," 19.

31. Moore, "Backup is Important, Recovery is Everything," 20.

32. Ibid., 18.

33. Robek, Brown, and Stephens, *Information and Records Management*, 88.

34. Ibid.

35. "Data Protection Agenda," S1.

36. Ganong, "The Emergence of E-Vaulting," 25-26.

37. Stephens, "Protecting Records in the Face of Chaos," 33.

38. Mark Ferelli, "What Has the IT Industry Really Learned from 9/11?" *SMS* 7, Issue 4 (2002): 8.

39. Stephens, "Protecting Records in the Face of Chaos," 38.

40. Ted O'Leary, "Paper Amid the Rubble," *E-doc*, November/December 2001, 20.

41. Stephens, "Protecting Records in the Face of Chaos," 39.

Chapter 11

Information Access, Privacy, and Security

In managing organizational records, records managers are often involved in questions concerning *access* and disclosure of records and information. This chapter addresses two key issues concerning this matter: (1) issues related to privacy—the collection, use, and disclosure of information about individuals, and (2) protection of information from unauthorized access, including the theft or misappropriation of proprietary or confidential information. Organizational executives need to work in conjunction with corporate security and privacy officers to ensure that the organization's confidential or sensitive information about its trade secrets, as well as personal information about its employees and customers, is properly protected from improper use or disclosure.

Privacy

Among the many kinds of records and information kept by organizations are records of individuals—employees, customers, clients, and citizens. However, special issues are associated with records of individual persons, issues that have relevance for how they should be managed. Chief among these is the issue of privacy. For example, under what circumstances should collecting, using, and disclosing information about individual persons be permissible?

Privacy has been defined as "the claims of individuals, groups or institutions to determine for themselves when, how and to what extent information about themselves is communicated to others." Simply stated, privacy is the "right to be left alone." Conversely, the loss of privacy is "the extent to which individuals are known to others." In an organizational context, privacy encompasses how personal information is collected, used, and disseminated, in both paper-based and electronic formats.[1]

Privacy is one of the most important information-related issues facing businesses today. Because records of individual customers or potential customers often have high market value, personally identifiable information has been described as the world's new currency. For many businesses, privacy has become an issue of strategic importance. In these situations, the principles of RIM need to be applied to ensure that reasonable privacy rights are respected while business goals are achieved.[2] Several major developments have dominated the privacy issue during recent years—innovations in information technology, new legislation, the global leadership role of the European Union (EU) as well as the State of California, the rise of identity theft, and other factors.

These issues could not be more timely and compelling. For many organizations, cybercrime, perpetrated by sophisticated computer hackers, has eclipsed traditional means of thievery as the greatest threat to information privacy and security. A case from the newspapers illustrates this reality with graphic clarity. Reed Elsevier PLC, a London-based company that maintains personal records on most citizens in the U.S. reported that personal data on some 32,000 people were fraudulently accessed from LexisNexis, one of its subsidiary companies. The security breach occurred at a data warehouse facility that stores and lawfully sells personal data to a wide variety of customers, including law enforcement agencies, as well as other businesses. Spokespersons for Reed Elsevier stated that the alleged data theft included names, addresses, Social Security and drivers' license numbers, but not medical records, credit history, or other financial information. The breach was discovered after a customer complained of a billing discrepancy, whereupon LexisNexis immediately informed U.S. law enforcement and notified the persons whose records were compromised, requesting them to check their credit card bills for any suspicious charges. A preliminary investigation revealed the method by which the crime was committed—the thieves had obtained access to passwords from legitimate customers.[3]

Privacy and the Internet

More that any other development, the Internet has revolutionized the privacy issue. Just a few years ago, neither homes nor businesses had computers connected to the Internet. Now Internet connections are common among businesses and in homes. In the Age of the Internet, concerns about privacy have skyrocketed. Identity theft is of particular concern. As U.S. Senator Charles Schumer put it in recent Congressional hearings concerning information privacy and security, "What bank robbery was to the Depression era, identify theft is to the information age."[4]

According to a survey conducted by the Gallup organization, 82 percent of Internet users reported that they are concerned about the privacy of personal information that they give out on the Internet, as well as the privacy of what they do on the Internet. An even greater percentage of respondents reported that they do not trust online companies to keep their personal information confidential, and most of these respondents indicated that laws should hold companies and their executives accountable, on pain of imprisonment, for violations of privacy laws or even their own stated policies. When data and documents are transferred across poorly controlled networks and repositories of personal data are accumulated in hidden databases, the potential for corrupted information or compromised personal privacy increases.[5]

Among the key Internet technologies that pose great concern for privacy is the use of *cookies*—tiny files hidden inside virtually every desktop Internet browser that can disclose to others what PC-users are doing on their computers. Cookies are blocks of text characters that a Web server places onto a user's desktop by using HTTP protocol when Web pages or images are transmitted. Their main purpose is to enable a complex application to work better by preserving a history of the pages a user had visited previously. Although this functionality is useful in executing Internet functions, cookie files also permit users' net surfing activities to be tracked and monitored, including online purchases and other activities that may be considered personal in nature. Whether and under what circumstances these files should be made available for scrutiny is one of the major Internet related privacy issues today.[6]

International Aspects of Privacy

Because of the global reach of the Internet, which makes sending personal data from one continent to another nearly instantaneous, privacy is an issue of high international concern. Via the Internet, a company located in one country with one set of privacy rules can send personal data about an individual, or a database containing millions of individual records, to another country with a different set of privacy rules.[7] This situation is particularly worrisome because of the globalization of business operations. When companies export their business operations abroad, they may also send sensitive customer data overseas. Once sent abroad, the company may be at liberty to market or otherwise disseminate the personal data with impunity. In countries where no laws to protect personal data exist, sensitive data relating to individuals can be sold to other parties without their consent, or it may be exposed to the risks of identity theft.[8]

The EU has adopted strict rules, with mechanisms for global enforcement, to mitigate these risks. Europe has the world's most stringent set of rules governing how companies and governments must manage personal data such as age, marital status, buying patterns, and similar information. In Europe, privacy is generally viewed as a basic human right, enforceable by stringent legal protections, and the Europeans have become global leaders in setting the standards for privacy and attempting to promote them throughout the world. In the United States (with the singular exception of California), such protections are considerably less stringent, as business interests have generally opposed any legislation or regulations that restricts their ability to collect and use or even sell or exchange personal information at their discretion, without government interference.

The EU's privacy laws require retailers to obtain permission to collect data, trade it to partners, sell it, or even use it for their own marketing—all common practices in the U.S. European companies are required to grant individuals open access to records and data about them and correct any inaccuracies. The EU restricts how much information companies can collect on customers and employees and how long they are permitted to retain it. Video surveillance tapes, for example, must be erased after a short period of retention. With its high global standard of tight restrictions on personal data, the EU has been quite successful in influencing the adoption of privacy laws throughout the world. EU-inspired privacy laws are now the norm in Canada, Australia, New Zealand, and parts of Asia and Latin America.[9] The EU influence is also being felt in the U.S. as indicated by the laws discussed in this section.

EU's Data Protection Directive

In 1998, the EU issued its *Directive on Data Protection* (95/46/EC). The directive was devised because some EU member states did not have privacy protection for individual citizens, while other countries had incompatible laws. To address this problem, the EU's parliament issued its directive on data protection, which was intended to harmonize European privacy laws and afford a continent-wide standard of protection for all European citizens.

The directive's most significant feature is that data subjects—persons from or about whom data is collected—must unambiguously grant their consent before such data is collected, after having been informed about the purpose(s) for which the data will be used. The directive applies to the collection, transmission, and processing of personal data, which is defined as "any information relating to an identified or identifiable natural person" residing within a member state of the EU. The directive applies to data that directly or indirectly identifies an individual, which includes a person's name, as well as other personal data about the person, such as address, telephone number, or other information of a personal nature. However, the directive expressly forbids the collection of personal information that could be characterized as sensitive, which is defined as a person's racial or ethnic origin, political opinions, religious beliefs, or sexual preferences.[10]

The directive consists of regulations relating to the collecting, processing, and handling of personal data maintained within the EU, as well as personal data transferred from the EU to other countries. The directive requires that personal data be managed such that it is:

- Collected for specified and legitimate purposes and not processed further
- Relevant and not excessive for the purpose collected
- Accurate and updated as necessary
- Kept in a form that permits identification of data subjects for no longer than necessary

Privacy in the United States

In sharp contrast to the situation in Europe, the United States does not have a comprehensive privacy law and, generally, has promoted industry self-regulation rather than legislation as the best means of balancing privacy interests against the demands of electronic commerce. The Privacy Act of 1974 protects personal information about U.S. citizens captured in records maintained by agencies of the federal government, but the law has no applicability outside the federal sector. However, specific laws and regulations do apply to personal records and information, such as credit history and other financial records, telephone records, educational records, and patient medical records, maintained by certain types of businesses. For example:

- **Health Information** – The Health Insurance Portability and Accountability Act of 1996 (HIPAA) and the Privacy Rule of 2001, impose privacy restrictions applicable to health information, typically in the form of patient-specific medical records. Regulations promulgated under the Act and Privacy Rule require regulated parties (i.e., health plans, healthcare clearinghouses, and certain healthcare providers) to implement a variety of privacy measures for patients, insured parties or other individuals subject to protection under the rules. These include rules governing access to patient medical records, requirements for patient consent to permit the sharing or disclosure of such records, patient recourse for privacy violations, and other restrictions.

- **Financial Information** – The Gramm-Leach-Bliley Act of 1999 requires financial services companies to establish privacy policies and governs how customer financial data can be shared within and between institutions. Title V of the Act contains provisions pertaining to the privacy of customer-specific financial records by banks and other financial institutions. As of July 2001, financial institutions are required to provide notice and an opportunity for customers to opt out of disclosures of nonpublic personal information to nonaffiliated third parties.[11]

U.S. Safe Harbor Agreement

One of the main features of the EU privacy directive is that it is designed to ensure that corporations, including U.S. multinational companies doing business in Europe, do not circumvent the EU's data protection requirements by exporting personal data to countries that are not subject to the EU's privacy rules.[12] The directive prohibits data transfers to non-EU countries, including the United States, unless those countries provide adequate protection for the data. Through this mechanism, Europe is attempting to make its data protection rules the enforceable global standard for privacy. At the time of this writing, the U.S. has not been deemed to provide adequate protection of personal data. During the past several years, negotiations have been continuous, often contentious, between Europe and the U.S. to seek an acceptable compromise. To date, this has taken the form of "safe harbor" data protections.

The U.S. Department of Commerce, in consultation with the European Commission, developed the Safe Harbor Agreement by which U.S. companies can avoid sanctions imposed by the EU if they voluntarily embrace a somewhat less stringent version of the EU privacy directive. Under the agreement, before personal data about European citizens may be transferred to the U.S., American companies must promise to handle data about EU citizens in accordance with the EU's standards while the data is maintained in the U.S.[13] However, detailed provisions, including enforcement, have yet to be worked out between the U.S. and the EU.[14]

Compliance with EU's Privacy Rules

An incident that occurred with General Motors Corporation (GM), the world's largest industrial company, which is based in the U.S. and has offices, production plants, and other facilities worldwide illustrates the practical application, and sometimes burdensome nature, of the EU privacy rules to U.S.-based multinational businesses. This company undertook a seemingly innocuous administrative task of updating its company telephone book / directory, which exists in electronic format and contains the names and telephone numbers of its employees in Europe and throughout the world. The EU data protection authorities, however, asserted that the act of transmitting names and telephone numbers of GM staff members in Europe to other countries constituted an act subject to EU data protection rules. Failure to comply with these rules could invoke sanctions by the EU, or even worse, GM would be exposing itself to the risk of a criminal offense by some European countries. As a result, the company's chief privacy officer and its staff in both the U.S. and Europe spent six months preparing the required documentation to demonstrate compliance with the EU's privacy rules so that it could complete the update of its global telephone directory.[15]

Privacy Laws in California

In the United States, the State of California has positioned itself at the forefront of the privacy movement. On July 1, 2004, the first online privacy law ever enacted in the U.S.—California's Online Privacy and Disclosure Act of 2003—went into effect. The new law requires all commercial entities operating in the state that collect personal information online to clearly post a privacy policy to inform citizens concerning the collection and use of data about them. In recent years, the State of California has enacted a plethora of new privacy laws. In brief, these laws:

- Require businesses to inform customers when personal data is shared with other parties.
- Require businesses to notify customers when their personal data has been exposed to a security breach.
- Restrict the use of Social Security numbers as a means of identification.
- Prohibit unsolicited advertising by means of fax and e-mail.
- Prohibit the sending of test messaging advertising to cell phones and pagers.
- Require financial institutions to obtain permission before sharing personal information with nonaffiliated companies or parties.
- Prohibit businesses from obtaining medical information about individuals for marketing purposes without their consent.[16]

These California legislative initiatives are expected to be the benchmark for consideration of privacy initiatives by other U.S. states in the coming years.

Canada's New Privacy Law

Elsewhere in North America, privacy in Canada is much more in line with the European model than is the case in the U.S. According to a recent study, Canadian businesses tend to view privacy practices positively—as an opportunity to improve relations with customers—while U.S. firms see privacy measures more in the context of burdensome government compliance.[17]

Canada has a new privacy law that is much more similar to the EU data protection model than anything in the U.S. Canada's new federal privacy law (the Personal

Information Protection and Electronic Documents Act), which became fully effective in 2004, extends privacy protection to all personal data collected by companies on Canadian citizens, regardless of when the data was collected. Companies doing business in Canada must now review how they handle personal data previously collected. The law applies to all commercial activities in Canada, as defined in the trade and commerce section of the Canadian constitution. The law requires that personal information be used only for identified purposes, that disclosure be limited except where prior consent is obtained, and that data must be properly destroyed when no longer needed.[18]

RIM Implications

RIM professionals can and should play a key role in organizational privacy initiatives because privacy protection requires that organizations adopt recordkeeping practices consistent with information protection and disclosure policies, as well as relevant national and international statutes, regulations, and directives.[19] Organizations subject to privacy or data protection issues will have to implement carefully considered RIM initiatives to comply with global standards and to minimize their legal liabilities at the same time. Records managers should work with their organization's chief privacy officer, or with other managers having responsibility for information protection and security, to ascertain the privacy status of the organization and how to comply with whatever requirements are applicable to it. Recommendations for RIM compliance with privacy laws are presented in Figure 11.1.

The role of records managers in the protection of personal information is affirmed by ARMA International in its *Code of Professional Responsibility:*

> [We] affirm that the collection, maintenance, distribution, and use of information about individuals is a privilege in trust: the right to privacy of all individuals must be both promoted and upheld . . . Information and records managers strive to protect the individual's privacy while, at the same time, having to reconcile that right with the right of access to information by others. The information and records manager must ensure that effective policies, systems and technologies are in place to protect information about individuals from unauthorized disclosure.[20]

These principles are recommended for inclusion into the privacy and RIM policies and practices of every organization that maintains personal information and records.

Security

Although personal data about individuals should be subjected to careful management controls as specified under privacy policies, these records are by no means the only type of records that require special protection against the risk of loss or misuse. Private business corporations typically maintain significant quantities of other records requiring protection by special security measures. These records include

Guidelines for
RIM Privacy
Compliance

Figure 11.1

Guidelines for RIM Compliance with Privacy Requirements

- Organizations should prepare a privacy policy of enterprise-wide coverage that places appropriate restrictions on the collection, use, dissemination and disclosure, and retention of personal information.
  - Such policies should state categorically that no unauthorized use will be made of the information that conflicts with the policy in any way.
  - Breach of the organization's privacy policies should be a disciplinary offense.
  - Deliberate breaches should be considered gross misconduct, with appropriate remedies.
- Organizations maintaining personal data should consider encryption as one means of enhancing the security of the data.
  - Encrypt records containing names, Social Security numbers, credit card numbers, and other personal data whenever possible to reduce the risk of breaches.
- All recordkeeping systems containing personal information should be systematically audited to determine the adequacy of the management controls.
  - All records eligible for disposal should be properly destroyed.
- RIM staff should determine exactly how many recordkeeping systems that contain personal data on individuals are maintained, where those files are kept, what they contain, and how the information is used, distributed, and disclosed.
  - Conduct a comprehensive and detailed inventory of all records and files containing information concerning individual employees, customers, or other persons.
- Records managers should carefully reexamine their records retention practices.
  - Retain only *factual* data concerning individuals and retain all such records for the minimum periods of time required to meet business needs and comply with the law.
  - Destroy all other records—particularly those containing *opinions* about individuals—under an approved records retention policy.

---

trade secrets, marketing data, intellectual property, and other information of a proprietary, confidential, or sensitive nature. Information of this nature frequently resides in storage repositories for which records managers have direct management responsibility. What do records managers need to know about the legal aspects of information security? Are proper security measures in place? Nearly every business day, executives and other employees leave their jobs—often on favorable terms, but sometimes under duress. Regardless of the nature of their departure, what happens to the records under their custody? Again, are proper security measures in place? What, if anything, can records managers do to prevent the theft or other unauthorized disclosure of sensitive company documents or information? What are the potential consequences if records managers fail to take reasonable measures to prevent the unauthorized disclosure of information containing company secrets? These issues are addressed next.

As used here, the term *information security* is defined as any measures instituted to prevent the unauthorized disclosure of confidential, proprietary, or otherwise sensitive business information. In this era of intense business competitiveness, the risks associated with the loss of sensitive information from theft or industrial espionage have never been greater. These risks exist at virtually every location in which organizational records are maintained, including homes, airports, hotels, and wherever computing devices are kept.

In the Age of the Internet, these risks are far greater now than ever before. According to a recent survey of some 600 IT professionals, nearly 30 percent of the respondents indicated that malicious code, including Trojan horse programs, worms, viruses, and other Internet-borne threats constitute the greatest single risk to their computer networks. Less than half the respondents expressed strong confidence in the security of their enterprise networks. Indeed, the growth rates of viruses, worms, spam, spyware, and similar threats have raised serious concerns about the future viability of the Internet itself.[21] Somewhat surprisingly, the greatest needs were not new technology tools but increased security staffing and better employee training.[22]

Threats to information security are by no means limited to external sources such as the Internet. According to a global information survey conducted by Ernst & Young, organizations worldwide are failing to safeguard their data against risks posed by people within their own organizations. The survey revealed that companies remain focused on external threats, such as viruses, while internal threats—including those posed by their own employees—are consistently underemphasized. These realities are illustrated with graphic clarity in the case study highlighted in Figure 11.2. The survey concluded that, as companies move towards more decentralized business models through globalization, outsourcing, and other external partnerships, they have increasing difficultly retaining control over the security of their information.[23]

A Famous Case

Figure 11.2

General Motors Corporation vs. Volkswagen Group

In the spring of 1992, Mr. John F. Smith, then CEO of General Motors Corporation (GM), made an appointment that would prove to be historic in the legal history of this company. Mr. Smith promoted José Ignacio López de Arriortúa, head of purchasing for GM in Europe, to the position of head of worldwide purchasing at GM headquarters in Detroit.

After a short but stunningly successful tenure, Mr. López resigned his position at GM to accept an executive appointment at Volkswagen Group (VW), Europe's largest automaker. Upon his departure, he cleaned out his office, packed his personal effects in boxes, and left. Soon thereafter, however, rumors began to circulate that secret GM documents were missing and that Mr. López was the party who had purloined them. Smith declared that the missing records described vital manufacturing processes that "we plan to use through the rest of the 1990s." The quantity: fourteen cartons, a figure that was later revised to twenty.

Three months after Mr. López left GM, police in Wiesbaden, Germany, seized four cartons of the missing documents in an apartment occupied by two of Mr. López's assistants who had followed him from GM to Volkswagen. The most damaging documents were strategic plans for new GM models, considered by many legal observers to be incriminating evidence of industrial espionage. German authorities learned that, at Mr. López's direction, the assistants had engaged in what was characterized as a massive copy-and-shred operation that required several days of effort. Later, the evidence mounted when police discovered other GM documents in Germany, including some on VW property.

Based on this evidence, GM filed suit against Volkswagen, alleging "conspiracy, fraud, breach of fiduciary duty, and misappropriation of trade secrets." Events were going GM's way when, in December 1996, German prosecutors indicted Mr. López, charging him and three of his colleagues with industrial espionage. Volkswagen's liability was considered to run in the billions of dollars if GM were awarded treble damages under the U.S. Racketeer Influenced and Corrupt Organizations law—the RICO statute. Finally, on January 9, 1997, the dispute ended when the two sides signed settlement papers, and VW agreed to compensate GM to the tune of $100 million, hardly a trifling sum, but a far cry from the billions that GM had long sought.[24]

Governments, too, face significant information security challenges. According to one survey, many federal agencies are consistently failing to secure their IT systems. Rated on a scale of A to F, the average grade was a D+, and several agencies (including the U.S. Department of Homeland Security) received the failing grade of F.[25]

In 1997, the U.S. Federal Bureau of Investigation estimated that American businesses were sustaining measurable financial losses resulting from the theft of trade secrets or other intellectual property at the rate of some $2.0 billion per month.[26] Since that time, the magnitude of the information security problem has continued to grow.

Legal Aspects of Information Security

In the aftermath of the López affair, American business interests prevailed upon the U.S. Congress to enact stricter laws concerning information security. The result was the passage of the U.S. Economic Espionage Act of 1996 (EEA). This law made the theft of trade secrets a federal offense for the first time. In the context of information or document security, the EEA defines theft as the knowing misappropriation of a trade secret without its owner's consent. Trade secrets are defined in the law as follows:

> ". . . all forms and types of financial, business, scientific, technical, economic, or engineering information, including patterns, plans, compilations, program devices, formulas, designs, prototypes, methods, techniques, processes, procedures, programs, or codes, whether tangible or intangible, and whether or how stored, compiled or memorialized physically, electronically, graphically, photographically, or in writing if (a) *the owner has taken reasonable measures to keep such information secret,* and (b) *the information derives independent economic value,* actual or potential, from not being generally known to, and not being readily ascertainable through proper means by, the public." [emphasis added]

The EEA defines economic espionage as "Whoever . . . steals, or without authorization appropriates, takes, carries away, or conceals, or by fraud, artifice, or deception obtains a trade secret [or] without authorization copies, duplicates, sketches, draws, photographs, downloads, uploads . . . transmits . . . mails, communicates, or conveys a trade secret" for the purpose of benefiting any foreign government, foreign instrumentality, or foreign agent . . ." The law imposes stringent penalties for violations.

The EEA's reasonable measures clause in the trade secrets definition is relevant to an organization's ability to ensure that its confidential information will be found to be protectable under the law. Consider the case of Gordon Employment, Inc. v. Jewell et al. In this case, the court held that Gordon's customer lists, which it had always considered to be a proprietary and valuable company asset, could not be considered a trade secret protectable under the law, because the company *had not taken reasonable measures to protect this asset.* The court noted that the customer lists were kept in unlocked filing cabinets in a public reception area; further, Gordon had no written policy designating these or any other records as "proprietary," nor were they marked "confidential."[27]

If organizations want the courts to accord protective status to their records and information, they must manage them in a manner commensurate with their value. *Reasonable measures* is "the sum total of all acts to identify and safeguard the information that an organization wishes to protect from unauthorized access." These measures must be appropriate for the degree of sensitivity of the information.

Conceivably, unless records managers take appropriate measures to protect sensitive information, they may themselves be obliged to shoulder the blame for their organization's loss of its legal rights to protect its trade secrets.

Most organizations have a long way to go before they properly secure all records media containing confidential information. Not so long ago, a large records collection occupied an entire file room and was thus not transportable in its entirety. These days, removable media containing the records of an entire file room can be secreted away in briefcases if the records have been converted to digital format. These days, removable media containing the records of an entire file room can be secreted away in briefcases if the records have been converted to digital format. For example, a multinational pharmaceutical firm stored its product formulas—the "crown jewels" of its business—on unsecured optical media, along with other proprietary and highly sensitive R&D data on new products under development. Although the firm suffered no loss, it exposed itself, unnecessarily, to high risk.

Uniform Trade Secrets Act

In the U.S., individual states have enacted laws governing the protection of trade secrets. During the past several years, at least forty states have adopted some form of the Uniform Trade Secrets Act (UTSA), a model law that provides protection of intellectual property classified as trade secrets. The UTSA defines trade secrets as "Information of value that is not generally known or knowable by others and that has been reasonably protected to maintain its secrecy." If a company's legally protectable trade secrets have been stolen or otherwise misappropriated, the UTSA provides relief to the owners, in the form of court-ordered injunctions prohibiting further use of the trade secrets. The Act also provides penalties for the recovery of damages in the amount of the actual losses resulting from the misuse, plus any unjust profits made by unauthorized users.

ISO Global Information Security Standard

The International Organization for Standardization (ISO) has published a global standard (ISO 17799) for information security that provides a template for the development of a comprehensive program. Among its other uses, this global standard is widely relied upon by insurance companies in their underwriting assessments of the risks associated with the loss of sensitive information. In many cases, insurance companies require their clients to demonstrate compliance with ISO 17799 in order to achieve favorable treatment as to coverage and premiums. The standard includes the following ten security control recommendations:

1. **Information security policy** – This document contains the mission statement and defines the requirements for information security in the organization.[28]

2. **System access control** – Control measures for detection and prevention of unauthorized access to information among all employees.

3. **System development and maintenance** – Measures designed to ensure that appropriate controls are in place for all stages in the information life cycle of all information subject to special security protection.

4. **Personnel security** – Measures to reduce exposure to human error as well as fraud, theft, or other misuse of information.

5. **Physical and environmental security** – Measures for controlling physical access to areas where sensitive information is maintained.

6. **Security organization** – The roles and responsibilities of the organization's security staff as well as of committees or stakeholders.

7. **Asset classification and control** – Requirements for assigning levels of protection to information, based on the nature of its content, the degree of its criticality, and the consequences of threats to its integrity.

8. **Communications and operations management** – Measures related to operational procedures of the information security staff.

9. **Business continuity management** – Measures associated with development of the information security aspects of the organization's business continuity plan and its testing and maintenance.

10. **Compliance** – Measures to ensure that the organization meets its legal and regulatory responsibilities for information security, and follows its internal policies.[29]

Organizations will, of course, need to customize their information security programs to meet their specific needs, but the framework and methodology provided by the ISO 17799 standard should provide the basic structure for the information security programs.

Key RIM Actions

What, then, should records managers do to help their organizations reduce the risks of loss of vital information due to misappropriation, theft, or other unauthorized access? The following steps are recommended:

- *Step 1:* Attain knowledge of current information security situation. Does the organization's security program address documents and records specifically? Does the program extend to the organization's overseas locations? What records and information are most susceptible to theft or misappropriation? Where is it? What is its protection status from a RIM point of view?

- *Step 2:* Define an appropriate RIM role. Many records managers have never communicated with corporate security personnel about information access and security, let alone defined a proper role for themselves and taken steps to carry it out. Records managers should meet with them, offer their services, and define an appropriate role for their involvement in the organization's overall information security program. At a minimum, records managers should ensure that all records for which they have direct management responsibility (i.e., records centers and other storage repositories) are properly secured.

- *Step 3:* Develop written policies and procedures. Although most businesses have written policies and procedures concerning their intellectual property, very few of these address RIM issues related to information security. A sample policy appears in Figure 11.3.

- *Step 4:* Develop an information security classification system. For many years, agencies of national governments (particularly those in the defense or intelligence communities) have implemented systems for classifying documents and information with respect to degree of sensitivity and the level of protection that must be accorded them. Except for defense contractors, this practice is rarely followed in the private sector. Because records managers typically possess the only enterprise-wide inventory of categories of records maintained by the organization, they are ideally suited to work with the corporate security staff to develop information security classification schemes. Such a scheme is provided in the sample policy in Figure 11.3.

- *Step 5:* Implement **RIM software.** This type of software is seldom implemented with the goal of information security in mind, and yet it can serve a critical security role. Without RIM software, the records in most recordkeeping systems are not indexed. Therefore, if any records are unlawfully removed, no record of their existence is available. When evidence of the existence of the removed records exists, the organization will be in a better position to press its claims for recovery of its lost property. If all records are indexed on RIM software, a record exists to document the existence of folders containing the missing records.

Sample Policy:
Records Access

Figure 11.3

Access to Company Records[30]

This policy specifies conditions and circumstances under which XYZ Corp.'s employees and others can retrieve, consult, read, review, or otherwise obtain access to company records or the information such records contain. This policy also indicates restrictions that limit such access.

Basic Principle

Access to company records and the information they contain is determined by the categories described below. Persons requesting access to company records must provide convincing proof that they are authorized to retrieve, consult, review, read, or otherwise access the records. However, the final responsibility for determining whether a person is authorized to access a company record or the information it contains rests with the business unit or department that has custody or control of the record rather than with the intended recipient.

Nothing in this policy prevents those who are authorized to access records from doing so or from using the records or the information they contain in the regular course of company business. Nothing in this policy prevents XYZ Corp. from producing records in response to a subpoena.

Public Information

Company records in this category are available to the general public. Examples of such records include published descriptions of company products and services, annual reports, financial statements, press releases, information submitted to government agencies, and information available at the company's Web site. Records in this category are not subject to restrictions on distribution or use, except for restrictions associated with copyrights, trademarks, or other intellectual property considerations.

Internal Use Only

Company records in this category are available to XYZ employees on a need-to-know basis only. Employees must have a demonstrable, verifiable requirement to retrieve, consult, review, read, or otherwise access such

(continued)

Figure 11.3

records or the information they contain in order to do their jobs. For example, an employee who requests copies of technical specifications for the company's products must be working on a project or other activity for which the specifications are required. Similarly, an employee who requests a copy of a contract must be involved in evaluation, execution, renewal, or auditing of the contract. Employees who obtain access to company records in this category must not share those records with or disclose their contents to the public or to other employees unless those employees have a demonstrable, verifiable business need to consult the records or know their contents. Specific records in this category may be made available to contractors, external auditors, or other nonemployees on a need-to-know basis related to company business.

Confidential

This category is reserved for records that must be protected from wide distribution or unauthorized access in order to avoid harm to the company or its employees, customers, or suppliers. Records in this category are available only to predetermined XYZ employees identified by names and/or job titles. Such employees must have a demonstrable business need to access the records to do their jobs. XYZ employees who obtain access to company records in this category must not share those records with or disclose their contents to other employees unless those employees are specifically identified as authorized to access the records. Records in this category are not available to contractors, external auditors, or other nonemployees unless need-to-know is firmly established and a confidentiality agreement has been executed. Examples of recorded information that merits a confidential designation include:

- Business plans and proposals
- Proprietary information about the company's products, services, and facilities
- Trade secrets and other intellectual property
- Marketing and pricing strategies
- Competitive intelligence
- Information about past, present, or prospective customers and suppliers
- Personal, performance, or salary information about the company's employees
- Any information given to the company in confidence

Responsibilities of the Legal Department

The Legal Department will:

- Establish company-wide procedures for clearly identifying records in the internal use and confidential categories as defined in this policy.
- Advise business units and departments regarding approved methods of identifying records subject to limitations on access as defined in this policy.
- Provide training to company employees regarding this policy and any related procedures and directives that limit access to company records.
- Authorize and/or conduct periodic, comprehensive, or selective audits of business units and departments to determine compliance with this policy and any related policies, directives or guidelines.

Departmental Responsibilities

All business units and departments of XYZ Corp. are responsible for implementing procedures developed by the Legal Department under the authority of this policy. Specifically, business units and departments will:

- Designate accurately and clearly identify access categories for company records in their custody.
- Identify employees who are authorized to access **confidential records** in departmental custody.
- Advise departmental employees about restrictions on access to company records.
- Ensure that access to company records is limited as specified in this policy and in any related policies, directives, or guidelines.
- Confer with the Legal Department regarding reported violations of this policy.

(continued)

Figure 11.3

Employee Responsibilities

All XYZ employees are obligated to protect the company's information assets from improper disclosure. Specifically, employees must:

- Understand the limitations on access associated with each category of records defined in this policy.
- Observe all restrictions on access to and use of company records and information.
- Request access only to records and information needed to do their jobs.
- Limit sharing of company records, including verbal discussion of the contents of records, to persons who are authorized to access such records.
- Handle all records with care to prevent unauthorized access to company information.
- Discard confidential records promptly and in a secure manner as soon as they are no longer needed.
- Report all violations of this policy promptly to their supervisors.

Notes

1. Wendy Duff, Wally Smieliauskas, and Holly Yoos, "Protecting Privacy," *The Information Management Journal* 35, no. 4 (April 2001): 14.
2. Gary Clayton, "Safeguarding the World's New Currency," *The Information Management Journal* 36, no. 3 (May / June 2002): 18.
3. Yasmine El-Rashidi, "LexisNexis Owner Reports Breach of Customer Data," *The Wall Street Journal*, 10 March 2005, A3.
4. Christopher Conkey and Emily Nelson, "Senate Spotlight Turns to Data Brokers," *The Wall Street Journal*, 11 March 2005.
5. John Phillips, "Privacy vs. Cybersecurity," *The Information Management Journal* 36, no. 3 (May / June 2002): 46.
6. Phillips, "Privacy vs. Cybersecurity," and Patrick Cunningham, "Are Cookies Hazardous to Your Privacy?" *The Information Management Journal* 36, no. 3 (May / June 2002): 52, 54.
7. Michael Fjetland, "Global Commerce and the Privacy Clash," *The Information Management Journal* 36, no. 1 (January / February 2002): 54.
8. Nikki Swartz, "Offshoring Privacy," *The Information Management Journal* 38, no. 5 (September / October 2004): 24.
9. David Scheer, "Europe's New High-Tech Role: Playing Privacy Cop to the World," *The Wall Street Journal*, 10 October 2003, A1.
10. Fjetland, "Global Commerce and the Privacy Clash," 54, 55.
11. Susan Haller, "Privacy: What Every Manager Should Know," *The Information Management Journal* 36, no. 3 (May / June 2002): 36.
12. Amy Worlton, "Overview of the EU Privacy Directive," Wiley Rein & Fielding LLP, 2002, 1.
13. Scheer, "Europe's New High-Tech Role," A16.
14. Fjetland, "Global Commerce and the Privacy Clash," 57.
15. Scheer, "Europe's New High-Tech Role," A1.
16. Allan Holmes, "Riding the California Privacy Wave," *CIO*, 15 January 2005, 48.

17. ARMA International, "U.S., Canadian Firms Have Different Views of Privacy," *The Information Management Journal* 38, no. 5 (September / October 2004): 14.

18. Clayton, "Safeguarding the World's New Currency," 20, 23.

19. Duff, Smieliauskas, and Yoos, "Protecting Privacy," 14.

20. Michael Pemberton, "Chief Privacy Officer: Your Next Career Move?" *The Information Management Journal* 36, no. 3 (May / June 2002): 58.

21. Scott Berinato, "How to Save the Internet," *CIO*, 15 March 2005, 71.

22. Paul Roberts, "The Shaky State of Security," *InfoWorld*, 26 July 2004, 34.

23. Arthur McAdams, "Security and Risk Management: A Fundamental Business Issue," *The Information Management Journal* 38, no. 4 (July / August 2004): 38; and ARMA International, "Businesses Improve Cyber Security," *The Information Management Journal* 38, no. 6 (November / December 2004): 18.

24. Peter Elkind, "Blood Feud: The GM – VW Battle," *Fortune*, 14 April 1997, 90-102.

25. Eric Chabrow, "Federal Group Formed to Boost Poor Security," *InformationWeek*, 21 February 2005, 26.

26. Alan Farnham, "Spy vs. Spy: Are Your Company's Secrets Safe?" *Fortune*, 17 February 1997; and Alan Farnham, "How Safe are Your Secrets," *Fortune*, 8 September 1997.

27. Michael Budden, "Safeguarding Trade Secrets," *Security Management*, March 1997, 87.

28. Mark Ungerman, "Sign Up For a Corporate Information Security Policy," *SMS* 9, Issue 1 (2005): 21.

29. McAdams, "Security and Risk Management," 40.

30. William Saffady, Unpublished manuscript, n.d.

Chapter 12

Software Solutions for Electronic RIM

One of the most important occurrences to affect organizational recordkeeping and RIM during the past twenty years has been the introduction of various technology solutions designed to enhance the management of records in both physical and electronic formats. As discussed previously, in order to achieve an advanced level of professional practice, records managers must work in close cooperation with IT departments to deploy various types of document technology solutions successfully. The major solutions are: records management software, electronic document imaging solutions (discussed in Chapter 13), and *electronic document management system (EDMS)* software. When functionality for the management of electronic records is added to RIM software, these types of solutions are referred to as electronic records management systems (ERMS).

The importance of these solutions to professional practice in RIM can be simply stated: For the first time ever, the goal of enterprise electronic records management is within reach for organizations. The business benefits of ERMS solutions are many and significant. They include:

- Centralized, computer-based management and control over organizational records, under approved RIM policies and practices. ERMS solutions are targeted particularly towards unstructured information content, which constitutes some 80 percent of the total information resources of most organizations.

- A single system for managing records. It provides support for applying consistent business rules and RIM policies across a wide variety of records types and information content.

- Enhanced enterprise accessibility of information, particularly business-critical records, including those required for enhanced levels of customer / client services. ERMS solutions enable the organization to come closer to the goal of precise and timely retrieval of unstructured content across the enterprise.

- Enhanced, enterprise-wide capabilities for compliance with government regulations, including new and more stringent corporate governance requirements (i.e., Sarbanes-Oxley) as well as RIM / retention requirements and auditability of records throughout their authorized period of retention. These systems also provide greatly enhanced capabilities for responding to discovery requests and other aspects of litigation management.

- Assurance of secure, long-term management and control over information content declared as records in immutable (i.e., nonerasable, nonrewritable) form, thereby addressing requirements for record integrity and authenticity.

- Operational efficiency improvements, including reduction of manual processing and routing, as well as reduction of paper storage. Transmitting electronic documents around computer networks is better than shuffling pieces of paper around offices; storing them in digital repositories is better than in boxes on the shelves of records centers.

- Various IT benefits, including scalability to accommodate increasing volumes of information over time in a cost-effective manner; a single, integrated platform to maintain and administer; and the ability to manage information at both the application software and storage levels.[1]

These and other significant business benefits are what organizations seek when they consider new, enterprise ERMS solutions.

Electronic RIM Issues

Several studies have reported unfavorably on the status of electronic records management as currently practiced in the U.S. One study reported that 41 percent of the respondents indicated that electronic records are not included in their organization's current RIM program. Another study reported that some three-quarters of RIM programs of large U.S. businesses had no involvement in electronic document management software, while 38 percent reported no involvement in electronic document imaging.[2]

These findings are indeed disheartening; electronic document imaging is the major technology that serves as a replacement for paper-based recordkeeping systems; document management software is the major technology for enhanced management of electronic records in desktop / network computing environments. The fact that high percentages of the surveyed companies report limited or no RIM involvement with these technologies confirms that records managers need to embrace the management of electronic records as perhaps their highest professional priority. The Forrester report, in particular, contains some additional findings that are significant to the role of the RIM discipline in the management of electronic records. The study reported that:

- As perceived by IT and other business managers, the two biggest challenges associated with implementing ERMS solutions are budget limitations and the fact that organizations have other technology priorities that take precedence.

- Other reported problems with ERMS deployment among the surveyed organizations: lack of executive sponsorship, lack of ERMS technology and RIM skills, and lack of clearly established responsibility for assimilating ERMS solutions.

- IT managers tend to underestimate the complexity of ERMS assimilation; a lack of clarity about what electronic RIM really is prevails.

- RIM professionals perceive significant challenges with executive support, resistance to change, lack of mandate for managing electronic records, poor vendor support, and high costs.[3]

Despite these rather gloomy assessments, some positive trends in electronic RIM are emerging. In recent years, large computer companies, principally those offering solutions in the enterprise content management space, have begun to offer RIM capabilities in their product lines. For example:

- In late 2002, IBM, still the world's largest computer company, acquired the assets of privately-held Tarian Software. In company announcements, IBM stated that it planned to integrate Tarian into its data management software, leverage Tarian's records management capabilities across its entire software portfolio, including IBM Content Manager, DB2 Database, and Lotus software, and offer its ERMS solution worldwide.[4]

- Similarly, in 2003, EMC, one of the world's leading computer data storage companies, acquired Documentum, which had earlier acquired TrueArc, companies that offered strong capabilities in the document and RIM spaces respectively. Soon thereafter, EMC opened an information life cycle management (ILM) business that featured retention and regulatory compliance as core components. Many observers saw this new business as particularly significant. With its advanced offerings in enterprise storage and content management as well as records and document management, ILM customers can acquire all components from a single source, rather than assembling multiple technologies and solutions from disparate sources.[5]

These and similar initiatives are some of the most encouraging trends in RIM today. When large computer companies enter the RIM business and incorporate electronic RIM functionality, scaled to the enterprise level, throughout their product lines, the RIM discipline has a real opportunity to significantly impact the management of electronic records throughout the organization.

Categories of Electronic RIM Solutions

Two categories of electronic RIM solutions are presented in this chapter. These two categories are:

1. *RIM software evolved during the early to mid-1980s to bring better management to paper-based recordkeeping systems.* When functionality for managing electronic

records is added, these software applications are referred to as electronic records management system (ERMS) software. They are defined as software for the management of both physical and electronic records created by and residing in a computer system or application according to accepted principles and practices of RIM. As its core objective, an ERMS provides a method for tracking the life cycle functions of electronic records from the point at which work-in-process documents are declared as records until their final disposition, under approved retention rules and policies.[6]

2. *EDMS software evolved during the late 1980s and early '90s to bring better management to electronic documents created in desktop computing environments.* EDMS solutions provide electronic management of electronic documents, in many forms and formats, contained in an IT system, using computer equipment and software to manage, control, locate, and retrieve information in the electronic system. The primary focus of an EDMS is to support the processes of creating, editing, and reviewing work-in-process documents in daily use.[7]

Although these solutions evolved as separate and distinct families of products serving their own markets, a considerable amount of convergence has occurred among them during the past five or more years. This convergence provides the capability of delivering more comprehensive and robust solutions to the general problems associated with managing records and documents in multimedia formats throughout the enterprise.

RIM Software

This type of software was initially developed for the purpose of indexing, tracking, and monitoring the location and retention status of physical records (i.e., paper and microfilm). The development of the ERMS and EDMS software products has been one of the most significant occurrences in RIM during the past twenty years. Prior to the development of RIM software, most organizations had little or no computer capability to track and monitor the existence and location of their physical records. Nor did they have any computer capability to manage the retention of those records during the several stages of their life cycle. RIM software was developed to provide a solution to these needs.

These software products were initially developed to operate on PC computer platforms and were designed to provide various types and levels of computer control over various RIM functions. Most early implementations tended to be application-specific and scaled to the workgroup level. The newest generation of software is developed for enterprise deployments. RIM software can be applied to facilitate the management of active records maintained in single filing stations, throughout a department or division, or throughout the entire enterprise. These solutions can be applied to inactive records maintained in storage facilities. Finally, if the software combines active and inactive RIM functionality into a single, integrated solution, the system is capable of providing the organization with something it has never had before: a computer capability to establish total life cycle control over all its records, regardless of location or retention status.

RIM software can also significantly enhance the performance of recordkeeping systems by improving the accessibility of the information contained in the records. When paper-based records and files are not indexed, the information in them can only be accessed by a *single pathway*—a pathway reflecting the manner in which the records are organized and sequenced. On the other hand, when the records are indexed on the database of a RIM software system, information in the records is accessible by any number of keywords or other record identifiers. Most applications support a multilevel classification scheme, provide circulation control over records withdrawn from and returned to the system, and provide a variety of reports showing system activity.

Retention Functionality in RIM Software

Almost all RIM software is designed around records retention as one of its core objectives. For physical records, the basic retention functionality in RIM software products generally includes the following capabilities:

- Provides support for the development of records retention schedules, including the entry of records inventory data, the inclusion of citations for statutory and regulatory retention requirements, and the maintenance of approved retention schedules in the database.

- Stores and maintains the retention schedules in a database; supports the implementation of the schedule's disposition and retention requirements by linkage of records series to stored records, with subsequent assignment of retention periods and destruction dates to all records managed by the system.

- Calculates the dates on which records are eligible for destruction, based on the retention periods contained in the retention schedules, and prints reports listing records whose retention periods have expired, in order to secure management approval of the destruction.

- Places holds on records in cases where authority to dispose of them has been suspended as a result of litigation, audit, or other requirements issued by legal authority.

- Provides documentation for records that have been destroyed under the authority of the retention schedules.

EDMS Solutions

EDMS software solutions provide for the management of unstructured documents typically created by desktop software applications. EDMS software evolved during the 1980s and early '90s in response to the PC revolution that brought computers to the desktops of office workers everywhere. During the early days of PCs, when the DOS operating system served as the predominant tool for managing electronic records created on PCs, the management of these records tended to be very primitive and rudimentary. Throughout the 1980s, whenever most PC users would save a document, they would assign a filename consisting of eight characters followed by a three-character extension. In many PC computing environments, this brief and cryptic filename (known only to those who assigned it) tended to be the only management device applied to the mass of desktop documents throughout the organization. This situation obviously cried out for better management, and EDMS solutions were developed in response.

EDMS software is designed to help organize the production of electronic documents, and provide for their access and distribution over networks, at both the workgroup and enterprise levels. Typical EDMS functions include the following:

- Check-in / check-out control from the electronic repository
- Integration with electronic document editing or capture applications
- Search and retrieval capabilities
- Access and security controls
- Document version / revision control
- Document review and approval capabilities[8]

An EDMS is designed to capture, route, and organize electronic documents in workgroups and on an enterprise-wide scale. Many of these systems also provide document collaboration, distribution, revision / version control, secure access, and many other features. In addition to standard text documents, the more sophisticated systems support other object types such as voice and video clips and Web documents. EDMS solutions are frequently integrated with other classes of document technologies in the content management space, including full-text retrieval, imaging, workflow, and others.

EDMS solutions are based on the concept of a central document repository into which documents that are declared as records are saved, stored, and managed. Most products store records in their original or native formats as binary objects, together with descriptive metadata, in a relational database. The database management system is used to store and access information associated with the documents saved in and managed by the system. The database contains index or document profile data, as well as and other metadata about the record objects. In most EDMS implementations, document creators are required to fill out document profiles, which are abstracts or descriptions that must be completed for each indexable document to be managed by the system. These profiles contain index data describing the document in terms of subject keywords and other key descriptive elements. Typical profile fields include:

- Filename
- Title
- Author(s)
- Recipients; audience
- Subject(s) or keywords
- Date created
- Version / date modified

- Access restrictions / authorized viewers
- Retention / life cycle management data

Seeing how EDMS solutions can enhance the management of electronic records far beyond what can be accomplished with a simple user-assigned filename is easy with these basic profile metadata.

Retention Functionality in EDMS Solutions

For the most part, EDMS solutions were developed without significant input from the RIM community. As a result, the early products included little if any functionality for records retention or document life cycle management. Part of the problem is that RIM specialists and document management software vendors often apply very different meanings to the term *document life cycle*. Records managers typically apply this term to mean the transition of records from an active to a semi-active and finally to an inactive state. In document management parlance, on the other hand, the document life cycle often refers to the controls applied to a document through multiple editing, revisions, and versions prior to its issuance or publication.

Thus, through the mid to late 1990s, most document management software packages provided little or no retention functionality. A few products provided a field for retention periods in the document profile. With respect to life cycle management, the "date of last access" has traditionally been considered the prime factor determining whether a document should be kept online, near-line, or off-line. This date, however, does not govern whether or when the document is eligible for destruction under approved retention rules. The majority of the early EDMS solutions tended to address the retention issue by simple metadata fields, without an integrated methodology for implementing a formal records retention strategy.[9]

The situation has improved substantially with today's EDMS products that frequently include a life cycle / retention component. However, some of these products are not as robust as RIM applications which are designed with life cycle management as one of their core objectives. Retention functionality in EDMS environments require the software to be capable of classifying documents in accordance with the organization's records retention schedule, automatically attaching a retention period to documents based on the classification chosen, recognizing that retention may have to be calculated from a trigger event (for example, the expiration of a contract or permit). The following discussion details these matters. The principles apply equally to ERMS as well as EDMS solutions.

Retention policy issues in EDMS / ERMS environments include:

- What rights and privileges should end-users have in retention matters? Should all users have equal privileges in adding documents, editing them, and deleting or assigning retention periods to them?
- How should users distinguish between draft documents and final documents for purposes of applying retention rules? What retention rules should govern drafts and final documents?

- Should documents receive a retention period at the time of creation? Should document creators be responsible for classifying documents for retention and for assigning retention periods? Can retention periods be assigned automatically?

- What procedures will govern the disposition process when documents reach their full retention?

In integrating retention functionality into the EDMS, one of several approaches may be adopted in the assignment of retention periods:

- They may be assigned from the database.

- They may be user assignable.

- They may be assigned based on rules associated with records series prefixes or document types.[10]

RIM specialists should work with IT specialists to address these issues during the pre-acquisition stage of solution assimilation. No EDMS / ERMS solution should be acquired or deployed unless the retention and life cycle management issues have been worked out.

Effecting Destruction Under Retention Rules

Once retention functionality has been incorporated into an EDMS / ERMS solution, it must be properly implemented. The scheduled destruction of electronic records in EDMS / ERMS applications is just as important as in other recordkeeping environments. Although individual documents can be deleted even by desktop applications, an EDMS / ERMS solution should provide tools and safeguards to assure that this activity occurs responsibly and efficiently. Document management methods and practices can be applied only to documents created within or managed by the system itself.

An EDMS / ERMS system should enable deleting documents singly by users or in bulk mode by system administrators. Some volume deletions will need to be initiated automatically based on retention periods or other available guidance or existing document metadata such as automatic last accessed date, index value, or document type. A period of undeletion should be available subsequent to which the documents are completely ablated in order to assure that they cannot be reconstructed. Finally, document deletion should be auditable with appropriate notices generated when necessary and in compliance with overall enterprise records retention schedules.

Solution Convergence

The development of EDMS / ERMS software solutions over the past ten or so years has been characterized by vendors taking different approaches to incorporating ERMS into EDMS and other enterprise applications. Some software developers created paper-based RIM products to which functionality for managing electronic records was added. Other developers specialized in the EDMS space and later added RIM capabilities to their solutions. Still other software vendors provided software and toolkits for integrating RIM functionality into other applications. Finally and more recently, other vendors have developed fully integrated EDMS / ERMS by migrating software code from one of these solutions into their original application. Examples of these various approaches are discussed in the next section.

For the most part, an ERMS does not generate records. Rather, records are imported from other applications for archival management and retention. Thus, a key element of ERMS deployment is to integrate the system with other applications in which the organization's records are created. As used here, integration is defined as the combination of two or more software applications such that data can be transferred from one application to others through a common interface. The basic purpose of deploying an integrated EDMS / ERMS is to ensure that documents residing in the EDMS that qualify as records will be designated as such and that they will retain their integrity for the full duration of their retention period. Both EDMS and ERMS have functional and technical elements that are often similar and sometimes identical (i.e., repository management, database support). However, the sharing or co-ownership of data, potentially both application and object metadata, as well as actual data objects, is typically required in order for two separate systems to operate in an integrated manner.

Computer applications in which documents are created may or may not have EDMS and ERMS functionality, but as best practice such systems should be capable of exporting their documents and other content into an EDMS and ERMS. Prior to declaration as records, electronic documents in the EDMS may be created, altered, deleted, or saved. Saved documents may be declared records, and copies of such documents may be exported to the ERMS for subsequent management in accordance with RIM rules. However, declared records may not be edited or altered in an ERMS environment. An ERMS permits export of records to an EDMS for repurposing of those records, as well as the creation of new documents, which may themselves be declared records and then exported to the ERMS.

Any discussion of EDMS / ERMS integration needs to make mention of ODMA, the open document management API (application programming interface). The ODMA API is a broad purpose tool that simplifies the integration and interoperability of common desktop applications with EDMS solutions. ODMA is an open, voluntary de facto industry standard that provides an interface between the application software and the application platform, across which services are provided. The API supports application portability. Using ODMA, desktop applications can access and manipulate electronic documents managed by the EDMS as easily as if they were residing in the locally accessible file system.[11]

The TR48 Integration Model

The most substantive effort to date in defining the integration of EDMS and ERMS solutions has been performed by AIIM International's C30 Standards Committee on Integrated EDMS / ERMS. The committee is comprised of representatives from ARMA International, federal agencies (including NARA), software vendors, systems integration companies, and other interested parties. In 2004, the Committee issued its report—*ANSI/AIIM/ARMA TR48-2004: Framework for Integration of Electronic Document Systems and Electronic Records Management Systems.*[12] As defined by the TR48 model, integration of EDMS / ERMS is achieved when both solutions share common functionality and metadata.

The TR48 integration model identifies thirteen components for which common functionality and metadata must be considered in achieving full EDMS / ERMS integration. These components are:

1. Content creation and capture
2. Content management
3. Records and asset management
4. Content organization
5. Content use management
6. Metadata management
7. Content repurposing and publishing
8. User management
9. Search and browse
10. System configuration
11. System administration
12. Workflow management
13. Management reporting[13]

Options for Solution Integration

The TR48 integration model defines three general approaches to EDMS / ERMS solution integration:

- **Option 1: Integrate Two Standalone EDMS / ERMS Products** – In this scenario, the organization already has an installed EDMS in place and wants to add ERMS capability to that system. Conversely, the organization already has an installed ERMS, but management desires to integrate EDMS capabilities. In this scenario, the EDMS and the ERMS both have their own databases, user interface, repositories, and server architecture. The two systems are then integrated, either by the EDMS or ERMS vendor, or by a third-party systems integrator. Where dual repositories are operated by both systems, *nonrecords* (documents that have not and may never be declared as records) continue to be managed by the EDMS, while declared documents are managed exclusively in the ERMS repository. Tightly integrated solutions generally share the same database resource, but each system continues to utilize its own search and retrieval tools. In some cases, however, the search tools in one system may be configured to search the content managed by the other system.

- **Option 2: Integrate ERMS Capabilities into an Existing EDMS Solution** – In this scenario, retention / life cycle management functionality is integrated into an existing EDMS having its own user interface and repository / server architecture, but the documents themselves continue to reside and be preserved in their native application (the software environment in which they were originally created). In this scenario, the records engine provides tools to manage the enterprise file plan, retention schedule, and disposition processing. The records engine identifies and categorizes the records so that retention rules may be applied to them. ERMS metadata is sent to a metadata server that tracks the retention and other life cycle management aspects of the record, and then accomplishes subsequent disposition / retention actions in the native applications. Under this approach, each server supporting each application requires integration, but redundant records storage and backup / recovery operations are minimized.

- **Option 3: Acquire a Fully Integrated EDMS / ERMS** – In this scenario, the organization acquires a full-featured EDMS solution with the required ERMS functionality already built in. In this approach, the EDMS / ERMS user interface is pre-integrated, as is the repository and server architecture. This approach provides the organization with full retention / life cycle management capabilities in a single application. Typically, a single vendor or vendor partnership supports systems having these pre-integrated capabilities.

In general, EDMS / ERMS integration is moving towards a shared repository approach, while the traditional differences between the two product groups is slowly but surely breaking down. The market is moving towards this approach as the preferred means of bringing RIM capabilities to unstructured content.[14] Regardless, wherever professional RIM is practiced, records managers need to work with IT specialists to determine which of these approaches should be adopted in order to successfully assimilate EDMS / ERMS solutions.

Common Metadata for Solution Integration

As previously noted, integration of EDMS / ERMS is achieved when both solutions share common metadata as well as features and functions. Metadata is data describing context, content, and structure of documents and records and their management throughout their life cycle. Metadata is, literally, data about data. Metadata is the common language that information architecture components use to interoperate for functional integration. Metadata is a summary of the form and content of a document or record and provides essential context and meaning of that content. Metadata is essential to sharing data across computer applications in order for integration to occur. It is essential to the management, accessibility, and security of electronic documents and records.

The TR48 integration model synthesizes the various national and international sources on EDMS / ERMS metadata and presents various sets of metadata elements relevant to solution integration. Some of these metadata elements include:

- Document classification / category / code
- Document unique identifier
- Author / creator / originator / contributors

- Office of origin / origination organization
- Document distribution / addressee(s)
- Coverage / scope
- Audience
- Date created / received / acquired
- Date edited / modified
- Date available / date closed
- Date published / issued
- Date saved / filed / declared a record
- Document type / title / subject / key words
- Document description / abstract
- Document format / media type / application
- Retention period / disposition instructions / retention event trigger
- Date authorized for disposal
- Date disposal effectuated[15]

Declared Records and ERMS Management

Prior to deployment, records managers, IT specialists, and business users should work together to devise rules and guidelines specifying the criteria for records declaration and identifying what content is authorized or eligible for management by the ERMS. The premise for such rules is that not just anything can or should be stored in the ERMS repository. Rather, the content of the ERMS should be restricted to records of official character that must be retained as per the organization's retention schedule. For example, ERMS content is limited to the following:

- Records required to be retained by law, regulation, or as per the organization's records retention schedule.
- Records of official character or operational importance that are reflective of the organization's official policy or position.
- Fixed content records that have reached a static state; that is, they have been finalized for issuance or publication as reflective of the organization's official policy or position on a matter.
- Conversely, dynamic content, such as drafts or other work-in-process documents are specifically ineligible for management by the ERMS, as are work papers, unless they are of material value as supporting documentation to official records.
- Other records created by certain designated systems and applications.

Such rules and guidelines governing *records declaration* and ERMS content should be customized for each ERMS installation, prior to its deployment.

Sample Solutions

The following examples illustrate the incorporation of RIM / retention functionality into various document technology solutions:

- **Fixed-content archival solutions** – These solutions are designed to provide ERMS storage and management for *fixed-content* (that is, the information content is complete and finalized and not expected to change) records and their associated metadata so that they remain unalterable and authentic, in accordance with predefined retention rules. When information objects reach an immutable state, they are declared as records and transmitted from their native application (e.g., MS Word™, Excel™, PowerPoint™) into a dedicated repository by means of an application programming interface (API). At the time of import, the software creates a unique digital fingerprint, reflecting the content and metadata for each record, as well as its address in the repository. The records are then stored as binary large objects (BLOBs) within the storage array. A mirror copy is also stored for security protection. The software permits each record object or piece of archived data to be assigned its own retention period, as specified by the retention rules. The record objects will remain in an immutable state (i.e., nonrewritable and nonerasable) until the longest retention period associated with them expires, at which time the software effects their destruction by utilizing digital shredding routines to overwrite the stored information multiple times, thereby effecting its complete and irretrievable deletion.

- **Database archiving solutions** – These solutions are designed to provide capabilities for archiving database records. In the past, retention capabilities for database records tended to be very rudimentary. They consisted of retaining annual backup tapes for periods of time specified in the retention schedule, or sometimes indefinitely, in cases where older data was migrated to tape to improve system performance. In these approaches, the software encapsulates selected portions of structured database records so that they can be stored more effectively, on a wide variety of media types—tape, optical, RAID arrays. The software provides the ability to define data from many different tables in the database and retain them under retention rules.

- **Web components of enterprise content management** – This approach is designed to enable organizations to manage the life cycle of all types of Web content. The RIM functionality integrated into the solution enables organizations to capture and archive Web content as records, and manage content retention periods across storage platforms. Content under retention control can be routed to the most cost-effective storage media for backup protection as well as retention compliance.[17]

The DoD 5015.2 Standard

In 1997, the U.S. government issued the first standard prescribing functionality requirements for electronic records in RIM software applications. The standard is DoD 5015.2-STD, *Design Criteria for Electronic Records Management Software Applications*. The applications are referred to as RMAs in the standard, which was revised most recently in 2002.[18] DoD 5015.2-STD is the first standard to establish detailed technical requirements for software that manages records in electronic form. With the issuance of this standard, a technical measurement tool for software products designed to manage records under a formal RIM program is now available. DoD 5015.2 has been endorsed by the U.S. National Archives and Records Administration (NARA), which contributed to its development, and is regarded as a de jure federal standard.

The standard differentiates between *records management* and *document management* software. A RIM software application is defined as software used by an organization to manage its records. An RMA's primary functions are defined by the standard as categorizing and locating records and identifying those due for disposition as provided by an organization's retention schedules. RMA software also stores, retrieves, and disposes of the electronic records stored in its repository. **Document management software**, on the other hand, is defined as a software application used for managing documents that allows users to store, retrieve, and share them with security and version control. DoD 5015.2 prescribes combined design criteria relevant to both classes of software, if the products are intended to provide for the management of electronic records as required by DoD and NARA regulations. Moreover, many observers believe that the 2002 standard blurs the distinction between RMA and EDMS software products. Many of the updated requirements are related to traditional document management capabilities such as folderless filing, publication dates, versioning, document templates, richer metadata tagging, and workflow automation.[19]

The Standard's Applicability

According to some observers, DoD 5015.2 has, or soon will, become the de facto standard for acquisition of RIM software by the state and local governments and by the private sector as well, throughout the U.S. For buyers of RIM software products, the standard assures that products bearing the DoD certification have met certain minimum functional requirements. A RIM software vendor is unlikely to thrive in an increasingly competitive marketplace without having achieved certification for one or more of its products. Consequently, DoD certification has rapidly become a de facto requirement for RIM software vendors in order to compete for the majority of sales.

The standard defines mandatory functionality for RIM software applications to be used within the DoD and among other agencies of the U.S. government. Each mandatory functional requirement is included because it relates to a U.S. federal regulation and / or NARA policy. These requirements reflect the practices and methodologies for managing electronic records in the federal government. The DoD 5015.2 was developed around the needs of agencies of the U.S. government in order to manage their records in conformance with NARA regulations. Therefore, what relevance does the standard have for private businesses and other nongovernmental organizations that wish to implement RIM software? Julie Gable, a leading ERM solutions analyst, writes: "Few of the standard's underlying assumptions on recordkeeping may hold true for the private sector . . ." For nonfederal organizations, the primary importance of the standard is that it provides a starting point to look for RIM software products. Because certified products have been successfully testing against objective criteria, certification provides a certain assurance of basic functionality. Business corporations routinely use the standard as a baseline method against which products can be evaluated, as well as a convenient benchmark for short-listing RIM software vendors. Some companies will consider the requirements in the standard too broad; others will consider them too restrictive. However, the work the DoD has done in this area of software should benefit the vast majority of businesses. Despite its government origins and imperfect application to corporate recordkeeping, the standard has, overall, been beneficial in upgrading the quality of RIM software products in the U.S.

Compliance Testing

The Joint Interoperability Test Command (JITC)—an agency of the DoD—is responsible for maintaining the standard and for administering the software certification testing program. The JITC's RMA Certification Testing page lists RMAs currently certified as being compliant with the standard. Any vendor of a RIM software product may apply to the JITC for testing and possible certification of a particular product. Certification is granted on a particular software version; any new version must also undergo testing. Certification lasts for two years, after which the vendor must apply for recertification.

The standard is designed to provide an objective test of basic functionality within prescribed conditions, with emphasis on authenticity and reliability of electronic records, particularly those possessing archival value. DoD 5015.2 has both mandatory and optional requirements. Useful features and functions of software, although often extremely important to evaluating the quality of software products, cannot become mandatory requirements if they are not required by any federal law, regulation, or NARA policy. The mandatory requirements in the standard are intended to specify what a product must do, not *how* the product should do it. Nor is the testing designed to measure system performance per se; e.g., how quickly searches execute, how easy the product is to use. All tests are on criteria that can be objectively measured. Finally, the standard is designed to be technology-neutral; it does not specify or favor any particular technology-based approach to accomplishing the mandatory requirements it contains.

The Standard's Content

In the context of product functionality for records retention, the following generalizations may be made. Mandatory functions are listed in Figure 12.1:

- Certified products must have the capability for managing electronic records in some sort of repository, as well as providing a means for managing paper as well as electronic records through records profiles.

- Certified products must have a file plan, derived from the retention schedule, to be built into the system. The standard prescribes mandatory requirements pertaining to file plans and records folders.

DoD 5015.2-STD Mandatory Functions*

- Managing records
- Accommodating dates and date logic
- Implementing standard data
- Maintaining backward compatibility
- Providing accessibility
- Implementing file plans
- Scheduling records
- Declaring and filing records
- Filing e-mail messages
- Storing records

Evaluated in every product certification test.

- Retention and vital RIM
  - Screening records
  - Closing records folders
  - Cutting off records folders
  - Freezing/unfreezing records
  - Transferring records
  - Destroying records
  - Cycling vital records
- Searching and retrieving records
- Monitoring access controls
- Conducting system audits
- Maintaining system management requirements[20]

- The standard is based on the assumption that document creators follow record-keeping practices that dictate when and under what circumstances documents become records.

- A requirement for compliance with the standard is that records with historical / archival value must be transferred to archival facilities and that records should be copied with their associated metadata and their folders.

- Compliant software is required to have the capability to view, copy, print, and if appropriate, process any electronic records stored in the RMA for as long as those records must be retained.

- Certified products must have mechanisms to prevent unauthorized access to records. The 2002 version also includes requirements pertaining to records audits, and additional requirements relating to metadata and e-mail.[21]

Europe's MoReq Specification

The DoD standard is directly applicable to RIM operations of the U.S. government, and it is indirectly relevant to the private sector in this country. Records managers of multinational companies having business operations in Europe often need to apply best practice guidelines for RIM in those locations. In March 2001, the Interchange of Data Between Administrations (IDA), an agency of the European Commission (EC), issued its MoReq Specification: *Model Requirements for the Management of Electronic Records.* The MoReq project was part of a larger EC initiative to provide clear guidelines in managing and controlling the capture, storage, accessibility, and distribution of electronic information. This model is a generic specification for systems designed to manage electronic records. It was developed by Cornwell Affiliates plc., a consultancy based in the United Kingdom. The principal authors were Marc Fresko and Martin Waldron.

The MoReq specification is regarded as the most significant effort ever undertaken to define best practices in electronic RIM in Europe. MoReq has been widely accepted across Europe as an effective tool in developing ERMS specifications. Developed for use in both the public and private sectors, it addresses a wide range of information management requirements and operational needs outside the RIM discipline. MoReq is comprised of 390 requirements and 127 metadata elements. The specification covers:

- Core RIM functions
- Other system functions, including electronic signatures, document management, and workflow
- Detailed metadata elements[22]

MoReq focuses mainly on the functional requirements for the management of electronic records by an ERMS, defined broadly in the specification as a software application for the management of electronic records, and sometimes paper and records on other media. The specification contains an overview of ERMS requirements and guidelines in the following areas:

- Classification schemes
- Controls and security
- Retention and disposal
- Capturing records
- Searching, retrieving, and rendering
- Administrative functions
- Nonfunctional requirements
- Metadata requirements

Unlike the DoD 5015.2 standard, MoReq does not have a program for vendor certification, accompanied by compliance testing of specific software solutions. However, in March 2004, the DLM Forum signaled its intention to enhance MoReq and explore the feasibility of an accreditation system for the specification.[23]

Implementation Issues

Many people labor under the misapprehension that computer software, including ERMS solutions, is magic and that once it has been installed onto servers, all recordkeeping problems will somehow miraculously vanish from the organizational landscape. Nothing could be further from the truth. ERMS technology can seldom deliver immediate results, mostly because organizations do not manage documents and data sources well enough to identify quickly and consistently what should be managed as a record and what should be disposed of. ERMS solutions are indeed a valuable component of enterprise information management, but those who adopt them should be mindful that these initiatives are likely to take a long time and that much work is involved in changing employees' document management practices.

Bringing better management to electronic records means that employees must manage their content properly *before* it is either declared a record and subjected to continuing retention or destroyed. In practice, employees must move towards a consistent way of creating, saving, and tagging their documents. However, in a world where these activities are inherently chaotic, such consistency is difficult to achieve. Steps to achieve it depend on a standard classification / taxonomy, tools, and metadata.[24]

If an organization is not currently practicing electronic RIM, attempting to deploy a comprehensive solution scaled at the enterprise level is an ambitious undertaking. In many environments, the best path to successful ERMS deployment is to proceed with a phased implementation beginning with pilot installations at the workgroup or departmental level. Moreover, most organizations should look for a solution that will be minimally invasive to users and that can integrate with technologies and tools already in place. Most document management systems offer multiple options for user interfaces, including Web browser-based interfaces as well as integration with common desktop tools such as Microsoft Office products and Windows Explorer. These interfaces allow users to continue using tools with which they are already familiar. They can profile documents and check them into the repository, which provides features such as version control, revision history, document security, full-text and fielded searching, and audit trail logging. Document management systems provide repositories that can be organized around taxonomies or document properties that can be defined at either the workgroup or organizational level.[25]

The goal of enterprise electronic RIM is within reach for organizations. If records managers can work cooperatively with IT specialists to successfully assimilate ERMS throughout the enterprise, it will indeed be a major step towards the achievement of a higher level of professional RIM practice.

Notes

1. Doculabs, *The EMC Centera / Documentum Solution* (Chicago: Doculabs, 2004).

2. Robert Williams, *Electronic Records Management Survey: A Call to Action* (Chicago: Cohasset, Inc., 2004), 16; see also William Saffady, *Records and Information Management: A Benchmarking Study of Large U.S. Industrial Companies* (Lenexa, KS: ARMA International, 2002).

3. Connie Moore, Kate Tucker, Susan Wiener, and Stacey Jenkins, *The Role of Electronic Records Management in North American Organizations* (Cambridge, MA: Forrester Consulting, April 2004).

4. Nikki Swartz, "Acquisitions All Around," *The Information Management Journal* 37, no. 1 (January / February 2003): 6.

5. Ibid., 5.

6. ANSI/AIIM/ARMA TR48-2004: *Framework for Integration of Electronic Document Systems and Electronic Records Management Systems* (ANSI/AIIM/ARMA July 4, 2004),

6; see also Timothy Sprehe, "A Framework for EDMS / ERMS Integration," *The Information Management Journal* 38, no. 6 (November / December 2004): 54.

7. ANSI/AIIM/ARMA TR48-2004, 6.

8. Ibid.

9. See, for example, Julie Gable, "The Role of Records Management in Electronic Document Management," in *Proceedings of the 41st Annual Conference, ARMA International, Denver, CO, October 13 – 16, 1996* (Prairie Village, KS: ARMA International, 1996), 116.

10. Ibid., 117.

11. Sprehe, "A Framework for EDMS / ERMS Integration," 54-59.

12. ANSI/AIIM/ARMA TR48-2004, *Framework for Integration of Electronic Document Systems and Electronic Records Management Systems* (Chicago; Silver Spring, MD; Prairie Village, KS: ANSI/AIIM/ARMA, 2004).

13. Ibid., 15-24.

14. Sprehe, "A Framework for EDMS / ERMS Integration," 58-62.

15. ANSI/AIIM/ARMA TR48-2004, iv.

16. Sprehe, "A Framework for EDMS / ERMS Integration," 58-59.

17. Julie Gable, "Innovations in Information Management Technologies," *The Information Management Journal* 38, no. 1 (January / February 2004): 30-31.

18. United States Government, Defense, U.S. Department of, DoD 5015.2-STD: *Design Criteria for Electronic Records Management Software Applications* (Assistant Secretary of Defense for Command, Control, Communications, and Intelligence, 2002).

19. Toby Bell, "ERM and IDM Markets Converge in DoD 5015.2 Standard," *TechRepublic*, 31 July 2003, 1-2.

20. Julie Gable, "Everything You Wanted to Know About DoD 5015.2," *The Information Management Journal* 36, no. 6 (November / December 2002): 32-38, 24-46.

21. MoReq Specification – *Model Requirements for the Management of Electronic Records*, 2001. See also Piers Cain, "MoReq: The Standard of the Future?" *The Information Management Journal* 37, no. 2 (March / April 2003): 27-28; and Martin Waldron, "Adopting Electronic Records Management: European Strategic Initiatives," *The Information Management Journal* 38, no. 4 (July / August 2004): 31.

22. United States Government, DoD 5015.2-STD.

23. Waldron, "Adopting Electronic Records Management," 31, 34.

24. Sarah Kittmer and Alan Pelz-Sharpe, "The Electronic Records Management Challenge," *KMWorld*, October 2004, 14.

25. Richard Medina and Joe Fenner, "Controlling Your Documents," *The Information Management Journal* 38, no. 1 (January / February 2005): 20-22.

Chapter 13

Managing Information Content

Enterprise content management (ECM) is a generic term that refers to the technologies, tools, and methods used to create, capture, process, store, deliver, and preserve information content, particularly unstructured content, across an enterprise. The term was introduced by AIIM International in 2001, but it has since been widely adopted by solution developers and indeed throughout information management circles. For purposes of this chapter, ECM is defined as enterprise-wide efforts to optimize the value of information assets by enhancing the accessibility of all information objects owned by the organization, regardless of type, media format, or storage repository. ECM solutions are designed to provide a set of tools and processes for managing all types of content, from simple documents to interactive real-time video, throughout its life cycle, from creation through updating and distribution to archiving.[1] Although the various solutions under the ECM umbrella vary among organizations, they typically include those solutions directed towards bringing better management to unstructured content, "including document management, records management, Web content management, document imaging, and digital asset management, among other things."[2]

With regard to the business case for ECM, Gartner Inc., a leading information technology research organization, predicts that, without good content management, the average knowledge worker will waste 30 to 40 percent of his or her time on non-value-added content-related tasks.[3] Further, according to the IDC (formerly the International Data Corporation), an organization employing 1,000 knowledge workers wastes $48,000 per week, or nearly $2.5 million per year, due to an inability to locate and retrieve information.[4] Regardless of the validity of these statistics, Web content management, collaborative content, and document management should not have different interfaces. For example, the CIO of a large hospital had a vision of a clinical database where all medical data (patient-specific and general) would be accessible from a single repository and would be instantly available to attending physicians and other clinical staff—at the patients' bedside, the laboratory, or any other location where this information is needed. The CIO found, however, that patient medical records resided in 117 different systems and that consolidating them into a single repository was not feasible. However, using an ECM tool, the hospital was able to consolidate some 80 percent of patient-specific data into a single repository, which effectively accomplished the goal of enhanced patient care through hospital-wide accessibility of patient content.[5]

ECM and RIM

RIM is a key component of ECM. As their major contribution to ECM, electronic records management software (ERMS) systems are used to manage the information content life cycle, which begins with capture and continues until the expiration of the total retention period.[6] Commenting on the role of RIM in ECM, Cliff Sink, president of Tower Software (North America) writes: "The recent consolidation of the ECM marketplace reflects industry's response to the increased need of organizations to properly manage their vital information assets, regardless of format . . . legislative and judicial bodies make no distinction between records, documents, e-mails, and other corporate information formats – and neither should an enterprise. This has led to a renewed focus on RIM in the ECM space, but with an updated definition. The new records management is ECM . . . it's about identifying, managing, and securing any vital business information, now or in the future."[7]

The role of RIM in ECM is heightened due to the changing nature of organizational recordkeeping, as well as the RIM discipline itself. In traditional RIM practice, paper records were managed on a *media-centric* basis. Because paper records are, in essence, a physical commodity, their management was driven largely by need and space: the time period for retaining them was based on need, and the location for storing them was determined by the availability of space. In the traditional RIM model, the life cycle management of paper was based on an observable, physical location of records, controlled by humans. In recent years, however, the RIM discipline has evolved from the media-centric model to a new paradigm—*content-centric* management of records. In the new model, the management of records is based on an invisible, logical location controlled by computers. For records managers, however, the challenges of the new content-centric management are much greater than in the past.[8]

Finally, the role of RIM in ECM should be focused on ensuring that the life cycle of information content is managed under approved retention rules and policies. In the past, much of the development work surrounding ECM solutions was done without considering this key issue. If deployed, these systems will add another deep layer of difficulty to the application of retention rules, particularly in cases where retention functionality must be retrofitted into installed solutions already populated with substantial quantities of unstructured content. Wherever professional RIM is practiced, its practitioners must work in close concert with data owners and computer specialists to ensure that these matters are addressed prior to solution deployment.

ECM—Fad or Long-Term Solution?

ECM is not without its detractors. Indeed, the cynical records specialists might dismiss ECM as just another label or buzzword; a fad perpetrated by vendors and consultants who are attempting to sell products and services around the next big thing. A management fad is an innovative concept or technique that is lavishly touted as the vanguard of progress, only to fade from popularity within a few years. The concept is embraced with the utmost enthusiasm by its early adopters, who are eager to ride the crest of the wave. Finally, after the organization's executives realize that the expected benefits have not been attained, the innovation is relegated, quickly and quietly, to the back burner of minimal usage or is abandoned altogether.[9]

Ample reason to think that ECM will turn out to be just another fad does exist. In the early 1980s, productivity improvement was all the rage. It was followed by downsizing, rightsizing, and other efforts at cost reduction. Then came total quality management (TQM) with its quality circles. In the early to mid-1990s business process reengineering (BPR) and then knowledge management (KM) took the country by storm. Like BPR and KM before it, ECM is likely to be superseded by some other approach to managing information within a few years. Each of these approaches, however, made some noteworthy contributions to the state of the art in enterprise information management. The same may be expected of ECM.

A more substantive criticism of ECM is that its core concept is predicated on some assumptions of dubious merit: (1) that everyone in the organization needs to enjoy ready access to most if not all information content, and (2) that all the content in the organization, regardless of its source or purpose, can and should be managed by a single ECM solution.[10] Both assumptions are either false or unrealistic. As to the first assumption, the need for information sharing among departments is nowhere near as pervasive as ECM solution providers would like users to believe. As for the second assumption, although a single-solution or platform-independent approach to computing has been the holy grail of information technologists for decades, it is simply not practical for most organizations, particularly the larger ones that must rely on application-specific software solutions that run on all manner of operating systems and platforms.

Knowledge Management

Perhaps the best way to introduce the topic of *knowledge management (KM)* is to recite some observations of Peter Drucker, who was generally regarded as the foremost authority on business management in the U.S. Dr. Drucker wrote:

> The productivity of knowledge has already become the key to productivity, competitive strength, and economic achievement. Knowledge has already become the primary industry, the industry that supplies the economy the essential and central resources of production.[11]

Like ECM, KM is often derided as lacking clear definition and boundaries. KM, in this text, is referred to as the management discipline concerned with the systematic, effective management and utilization of an organization's knowledge resources. KM is a general term that describes initiatives designed to use the human knowledge and the recorded information that exists within an organization more efficiently. It emphasizes the value of an organization's intellectual assets—its inventions, customer intelligence, business processes, and other aspects of its knowledge base—for competitive advantage. KM encompasses the creation, storage, arrangement, retrieval, and distribution of the organization's knowledge, to the achievement of significant business objectives and overall business effectiveness.

KM's central purpose is generally agreed to be that of leveraging or converting information assets into knowledge of a strategic quality, which, in turn, generates innovation that enables improved revenue and competitive position in the organization's market.[12] Sometimes described as intellectual capital, organizational knowledge may be more important than physical and financial assets, such as buildings, equipment, and cash, that are listed in corporate balance sheets and annual reports. In a recent report, Gartner Inc. opined that "Intellectual capital—delivered through the leverage of knowledge management and information management—will be the primary way in which businesses measure their value."[13] In an earlier Gartner report, KM was described as a discipline to "promote a collaborative and integrative approach to the creation, capture, organization, and use of an enterprise's information assets [and] includes databases, documents, and most importantly, the uncaptured, tacit experience of individual workers."[14]

To highlight the importance of KM as a management issue, according to the IDC, poorly managed knowledge costs Fortune 500 firms some $12 billion per year due to "substandard performance, intellectual rework, and a lack of available knowledge management resources."[15] According to the Delphi Group (a leading U.S.-based KM consultancy), in many organizations that have adopted the concept, KM has subsumed the many fragmented and disparate niche technologies that have evolved in the information management field over the past two decades. These technologies include relational databases, electronic imaging and workflow, document management, data warehousing and data mining, search and retrieval, object technology, and Internet and related technologies. However, the existence of these technologies is not, by itself, sufficient for an organization to consider that it is fully leveraging its knowledge assets by deploying KM methodologies. The Delphi Group describes KM functionality as consisting of the following:

- The ability to index and catalog nontext resources
- The ability to automatically abstract or summarize content
- The ability to create clusters of conceptual relationships automatically
- The ability to provide advanced relevancy ranking in full-text search and retrieval operations
- The ability to manage voice information as content

- The ability, generally, to provide new and more dynamic means of capturing the interrelationships and usage characteristics of all information objects and resources[16]

Although these capabilities are ascribed to KM, they are really advanced records management. As discussed next, this list points to the lack of definition and boundaries of KM as compared to other approaches to managing organizational information.

KM's Detractors

Some RIM professionals have said that organizations have enough trouble even recognizing knowledge, let alone managing it. Others have stated that KM's underlying premise is inherently flawed—knowledge cannot be managed. Still others have said that another flaw in KM is that its proponents and practitioners often neglect to ask: *what knowledge should we attempt to manage and to what end?* Nearly all critics, however, have decried a lack of definition and clearly established boundaries for the KM discipline. The sharpest critics assert that KM activities are all over the map: building databases, measuring intellectual capital, establishing corporate libraries, building intranets, sharing best practices, installing groupware, leading training programs, leading cultural change, fostering collaboration, [and] creating virtual organizations—all of these are knowledge management."[17] Finally, like ECM, some professionals have dismissively waved away KM as just another management fad. Because KM has already been eclipsed by ECM in some quarters, it may indeed be nearing the end of its life cycle.[18]

KM and RIM

In the minds of many observers, RIM has and should continue to play a key role in the deployment of KM solutions. In many organizations in the U.S, a close relationship exists between KM and RIM as business disciplines. The two fields have a common objective: the improvement of organizational effectiveness through systematic management of information-oriented resources. Records and recordkeeping are valuable knowledge resources. *Recorded information*, whether in human-readable or electronic form, is an important embodiment of an organization's knowledge and intellectual capital. It is the principal manifestation of explicit knowledge, which is externalized in documents and data repositories. RIM concepts and activities complement and promote knowledge management. Drawing on their experience and expertise, records managers can make significant contributions to KM initiatives. A well-implemented RIM program should pave the way for KM, while a successful KM initiative presupposes effective RIM systems and programs.[19]

RIM concerns itself with well-defined and auditable policies while KM works to marginalize organizational habits standing in the way of uninhibited, organization-wide creativity and knowledge exchange.[20] Traditionally, RIM has been concerned with the management of document-based information systems, mostly in paper or other physical forms. Overall, then, RIM is emerging as a core component of KM. It will continue to move from a standalone function to become an integral part of the business infrastructure. Records are corporate knowledge and managing them is a part of managing knowledge.[21] Generally, the role of RIM is to serve as a key player in teams of IT staff members as they evaluate KM solutions and integrate RIM functionality into them.[22]

ECM Technology Components

If ECM includes a wide array of technologies for creating, capturing, delivering, customizing, and managing information content across an enterprise, what specific categories of technology solutions must be deployed in order to make information content management happen? The following list contains solutions that organization executives should consider if they are serious about managing the content of their information assets to high standards of quality on an enterprise-wide scale:

- Document imaging / digitization
- Text retrieval / content search tools
- Electronic document management software
- Workflow automation tools
- Data warehousing / mining software
- Enterprise information portals
- Content classification and taxonomy

Document Imaging / Digitization

Even today, despite having used computers for thirty years or longer, the offices of most organizations remain heavily populated with paper records. As recently as twenty years ago, the only alternative to paper recordkeeping was microfilm. In 1983, however, a new technology was introduced to the world of recordkeeping—electronic document imaging (sometimes referred to as *document digitization* or *scanning*). Today, document imaging and digitization projects are increasingly being deployed as one component of larger ECM initiatives. It is the key technology for converting "legacy" record collections to digital format.

Imaging Benefits
Well-planned and executed document imaging initiatives can offer a number of significant strategic and tactical benefits, which include:

- **Rapid retrieval** – Digitized documents can be effectively indexed for accurate identification and near-instantaneous retrieval, thereby eliminating time-consuming manual searches for needed information. Rapid desktop access to documents and data will speed business transactions and decision-making activities that depend on the timely availability of information.

- **Enterprise accessibility** – Digitized documents and data are available to authorized employees at all times. Physical proximity to filing installations is not required, as it is with paper records. Authorized employees are able to access imaged content from any location. With online access, enterprise-wide content distribution can be significantly improved.

- **Enhanced information sharing** – Imaging initiatives can significantly enhance the sharing of content within and among various departments, particularly in cases where a high level of collaboration is required. Employees can route imaged content via e-mail to coworkers throughout the organization for reference, action, or other purposes.

- **Enhanced record integrity** – Because imaged content is not physically removed from files for reference purposes, continuous availability of information is assured. The problems of misfiled and lost records can be effectively eliminated.

- **Enhanced information security** – Imaging initiatives can offer enhanced protection of valuable information resources. Access to imaged content can be restricted to authorized employees. Security copies of content can be produced by regular computer backup procedures, thereby minimizing corporate vulnerability to business disruptions associated with the loss of mission-critical records. Compared to paper records, security copies of imaged content can be produced much faster and less expensively.

- **Reduced space requirements** – Compared to paper records, imaged content significantly reduces office space requirements. Moreover, future purchases of filing equipment and supplies for paper documents are eliminated.

- **Reduced document duplication** – Digitization initiatives can eliminate the duplication of records among multiple departments. Associated problems of security, space, and file maintenance is correspondingly reduced if not eliminated.[23]

Imaging Media and Applications

Because of the many advantages of digital recordkeeping as compared to paper, any serious initiative in ECM should start with these key questions: *What paper records should be converted to digital format? When? How?* Answers to these key RIM questions are based on a clear understanding of the strengths, limitations, and best applications of the three major media types—paper, microfilm, and digital imaging—illustrated in Figure 13.1.

Best practice in RIM requires records managers to evaluate their organization's recordkeeping systems based on the criteria listed in Figure 13.1 and to develop recommendations for which systems need to be converted to imaging or other digital format, and in what order of priority.

In professional practice, the RIM program should assume the role of championing the assimilation of this technology throughout the organization. An important role of RIM is to analyze paper-based recordkeeping systems to determine the best candidates for conversion to imaging, and to work with content owners and IT specialists on other aspects of system acquisition and deployment. The best candidates for conversion to imaging recordkeeping systems are listed in Figure 13.2.

Strengths,
Limitations, and
Best Applications
of Common
Recordkeeping
Media Types

Figure 13.1

A Comparison of Common Recordkeeping Media Types			
Media Type	**Strengths**	**Weaknesses**	**Best Applications**
Paper records	• High user comfort • Low investment in equipment • Long life expectancy, if properly stored	• Slow access time • Easily lost • Difficult to protect • Cumbersome to handle • Labor-intensive to process • Small volumes of paper	• Low access records • Low value records
Microfilm / Microfiche	• Space efficient • Good file integrity • Efficient copying • Good archival properties • Can speed retrieval • Legally accepted	• Serial search • Hard to update • Not eye-readable • Expensive to convert • Special equipment required	• Medium-high volumes • Low to medium retrieval • Vital records • Stable documents • Long retention
Digital Imaging	• Very rapid retrieval • Space effective • Random access • Can enhance workflow • Easy to update • Simultaneous, network access	• Limited life expectancy • System obsolescence • High cost per image and per user/seat • High conversion cost	• High-value documents • Quick-access documents • Medium-retention documents • High-reference documents

Characteristics of
Systems That
Should Be
Converted to
Imaging

Figure 13.2

Characteristics of Best Candidates for Conversion to Imaging

- High value; more than ordinary departmental files; strategically important to the achievement of key business objectives.
- Used frequently; active files accessed numerous times daily.
- Rapid access required; significant operational benefits (i.e., productivity improvements and better customer services) result from rapid access to requested records.
- Updated frequently during active stage of life cycle.
- Relatively voluminous; accumulate rapidly.
- Difficult to process in paper form; cumbersome and inefficient paper flow process.
- Vital and protected; cannot or should not risk losing them; need to provide protection through offsite backup methodologies.

Paper-based recordkeeping systems that display several or all these characteristics should be considered for conversion to image format. If the business benefits are shown to be demonstrable, these recordkeeping systems should be converted to imaging as soon as resources and priorities allow.

Assimilating Imaging: Strategic Recommendations

In order to take fullest advantage of imaging technology, organizations should consider the following recommendations for implementing imaging capabilities:

- **A standard imaging platform** – Most organizations should standardize on a single imaging product for all their departmental applications. Generally, one vendor should be selected as the sole provider of document imaging software and solutions. The organization should acquire and install that vendor's software for use by departments with demonstrable imaging requirements. The imaging software selected for that purpose must be suitable, adaptable, and scalable for a broad range of records, including administrative documents, project files, personnel files, financial records, and many other types of records.

- **A phased implementation** – To increase the likelihood of successful deployment, a conservative, phased implementation plan is recommended. Imaging should be applied to well-selected applications over a multiyear period, with the intention of having most or all top-priority applications online at the end of that time.

- **Simple applications first** – Self-contained, straightforward applications that require little or no customized programming to interface with external software products are easiest to implement and should be done first.

- **Outsource as necessary** – Departmental imaging operations should be limited to scanning and indexing of documents that are created and received after an imaging application is implemented. Outsourcing is the preferred approach for document conversions that require special components such as multiple high-speed scanning stations that will not be needed once the initial conversion has been completed.[24]

Text Retrieval / Content Search

Text retrieval is defined as a software solution designed to retrieve textual documents based on words, phrases, or concepts contained in the documents. The documents are typically stored in a text database or other document repository. This technology facilitates the location and use of documents based on their *full content*, rather than on conventional file or document identifiers such as title, author, subject, or other descriptive fields typically used in manual indexing operations.[25]

For enterprises that have launched ECM initiatives, text retrieval or document search engines are generally key components of such endeavors. A search engine is one of the first enhancements to be made to most intranets. Search vendors were the first to offer knowledge management products, and search technology is one of the core elements of any enterprise portal. Text retrieval is not a new technology. The first commercially available text retrieval system was the STAIRS system, which was developed by IBM during the early 1970s to manage the enormous quantity of documents resulting from its antitrust case against the U.S. government. However, the advent of this technology marked a milestone in the management of electronic records. For the first time, text retrieval systems offered a solution for content accessibility based on the full content of all documents in a collection. The predecessors to text retrieval—keyword search methods and document abstracting by human indexers—start with the full content of the document and reduce it down to a few key words in a manual indexing process. However, in these types of electronic recordkeeping environments, whether a user can locate a single document in a collection of millions is wholly dependent on the indexer's view of the document—the accuracy of human judgments made by the indexer. Text retrieval systems are designed to overcome these limitations.

Text retrieval software is widely used for content-based document retrieval in large, text-based records collections. These solutions are typically deployed in cases where single or multiple index terms or key words selected by indexing personnel are not sufficient to optimize the use and value of the records. Text retrieval systems search document collections based on user-defined words or phrases, typically joined using Boolean search techniques. These systems utilize various methods to execute searches of full document content: relevancy ranking, concept-based searching, and pattern recognition.

An example will illustrate the need for and benefits of this type of software. Police departments or other law enforcement agencies maintain criminal investigative case files, which are typically indexed by the name of the incident and sometimes by the name of the prime suspect. However, during the course of these investigations, dozens of persons may be interviewed, but the names of these individuals are typically unindexed if they are not considered a prime suspect; they lie buried in the case files. The result is that, as a practical matter, the records collection is irretrievable, except in cases where investigative officers happen to remember both person and case. As any law enforcement officer will attest, efficient access to any and all important details in the investigative cases of the jurisdiction can often make a crucial difference in the successful prosecution of crimes. Text retrieval offers a solution to this type of content management issue.

The goal of the latest generation of search solutions is to provide guides and filters in a world of information glut. Innovations, such as conceptual search, document categorization, and user profiling, are helping to achieve that goal. The latest and most advanced search engines provide some level of personalization. The search engine has some capability to learn the patterns of the search habits of individuals and to present them with the information that most closely matches their needs. Through a process often termed "semantic mediation," the search engine acts as an interpreter to the request based on user syntax (choice of slang or other terminology) and other search behavior patterns.

Full-text retrieval may sound like "retrieval utopia," but at the current level of technology development, the reality is somewhat different. The current state-of-the-art in automatic content indexing still falls far short of what is needed to satisfy complex query statements. Because retrieval occurs by computer analysis of the occurrence and frequency of content-bearing terms, the systems can result in false hits, or an overload of scannable terms, which can sometimes impede retrieval.

Regardless of the degree of technology sophistication, in order for precise retrieval to occur, users must formulate their search queries into the language of the system, as precisely as possible. Even advanced search engines can still benefit by well-developed files classification schemes or enterprise taxonomies. In fact, many search engines are now bundled with ready-made classification systems that automatically index an organization's information assets. Often included as well are ready-to-customize taxonomy systems that further tailor classification to specific business processes.

According to Hadley Reynolds of the Delphi Group, the accuracy of enterprise search can be improved with navigation aids such as classification and taxonomy tools that help workers browse through information before searching. Reynolds states, "It's not so much that classification and taxonomy replaces search but makes it more efficient by providing a filter, a way to see information around a business category."[26] For example, one popular solution is a classification and taxonomy software product that provides functionality designed to simplify and distribute the process of building and maintaining enterprise taxonomies. The tool allows distributed subject-matter experts to collaborate with corporate librarians and other professional specialists to organize information content according to business functions and categories. The product distributes the responsibility of creating directories by assigning creation and modification duties to editors who have technical knowledge of the content and by delegating approval and publishing functions to technical specialists who understand taxonomies.[27] Chapter 9 provides further discussion concerning this key aspect of search solutions.

Although they are no panacea and certainly no substitute for high-quality human indexing, text retrieval systems do provide the best last resort search capabilities for finding that "needle in the haystack" in large collections of text-based records.

Workflow Automation Tools

Most organizations, especially the larger ones, operate various business processes in which large quantities of documents are processed by cadres of administrative personnel. Many of these business processes are characterized by the desk-to-desk routing of documents by various specialists until the transactions have been completed. This type of work activity tends to be labor-intensive and is subject to frequent bottlenecks and other inefficiencies. Workflow software was developed to automate these types of business processes, and it is a key component of many ECM initiatives.

The term *workflow* is generally used to describe a structured business process with predictable results. Simply stated, workflow is the flow of work through an organization. Work is what employees do; flow is how the work moves through the organization. "Flow" can be expressed in a number of ways: sequence of events, routing, timing, number of transactions processed, etc. Workflow tools, then, are software systems that provide for the automation of business processes by providing the capability to define, analyze, and track work processes and transactions, as well as schedule, control, and route electronic documents and other work items around the enterprise.

Workflow applications tend to be targeted at transaction-type work environments where large volumes of paper-based transactions are taking place, particularly in cases where the transactions take longer to complete than is desirable, due to the limitations of manual processing. In workflow environments, each document, or other piece of work, moves through a fully documented process, which is managed and directed by the workflow software. The software is designed to provide proper controls for the handling of transactions on an exception basis, as well as those transactions that may be handled routinely.

For organizations experiencing rapid growth, workflow provides a potential solution to automating business processes that must handle an ever increasing quantity of transactions. In these situations, the organization must either hire more staff to handle the increased workload, or provide the existing staff with new tools to process the work more efficiently. Workflow tools can provide solid returns-on-investment in these situations, as well as better customer service.

Data Warehousing and Data Mining

How well do organizations understand their customer base? More precisely, what computing tools are in place to answer just about any question any decision-maker would want to know from any of the systems and applications currently installed? Suppose that an employee is required to locate and assemble most or all information on file throughout the organization on a specific individual customer, institution, or organization. What would be needed to do this task with any semblance of efficiency and rapidity? *Data warehousing* and *data mining* (the terms are often used interchangeably) solutions provide an answer, as do *enterprise information portals*, discussed later in this chapter.

Consider the case of Wal-Mart, the world's largest retailer. This company's jurisdiction is global, but its customer base is local—every community in which the company operates one of its stores. For years, every byte of data about who buys what at a Wal-Mart store has been fed back to headquarters in Arkansas, where it is stored in a huge and very powerful data warehouse. This information gives the company the ability to predict which products will sell at which stores and at what volume. The company's analysts use sophisticated tools such as 3-D visualization to display the data and make educated guesses about what customers will buy based on geographic location, weather patterns, demographic characteristics of the market, or any one of thousands of other factors.[28]

Although many organizations do not have such sophisticated data analysis requirements, they do need much better integration between disparate parts of their computing environments, with the objective of better understanding and serving their customer-base. Data warehousing or data mining software provides a solution to this problem. These solutions, developed during the 1990s, attempt to optimize an organization's electronic records on an enterprise-wide scale by assembling information from various applications, platforms, and storage devices for presentation management, strategic analysis, and decision-making. As a result, the islands of information maintained in fragmented, unintegrated systems in traditional computing environments are bridged if not eliminated entirely.[29]

Data warehousing as an approach to the enterprise management of computer-based information that arises from the fact that data from disparate operational systems cannot be quickly accessed and analyzed. These systems are optimized for processing daily business transactions rather than for ad hoc analysis. Data warehouses are designed to provide integrated business intelligence from both historical data as well as data from an organization's current business transaction systems. The goal is to create decision support systems that integrate and distill mission-critical data for key decision-makers and standardize business analyses for more meaningful comparisons. As is the case in other areas of business computing, one of the major trends in data warehousing is the transition to Web-based strategies for managing enterprise content.[30]

Data warehouses provide integration between the following four levels of the computing environment:

1. **Source level** – Data managed and accessed by the warehouse can reside in any number of sources in the computing environment—from mainframe and client/server applications to external data sources made available by the Internet.

2. **Data level** – The actual home of the data managed by the data warehouse—typically, a proprietary data warehousing software package or one of the major database management software systems such as Oracle and others.

3. **Application level** – The online analytical processor or applications server, which is the tool(s) that perform the data manipulations required by user queries.

4. **Presentation level** – The tool for viewing the data.

Like other solutions discussed in this chapter, data warehousing / mining software can be quite expensive to deploy. However, in recent years solution pricing has become more favorable. Even the smaller organizations should begin evaluating this technology with a view towards possible deployment at some future time.

Enterprise Information Portals

The term *enterprise information portal (EIP)* is frequently used rather loosely in the IT and business communities. It refers to a simple information management concept but one hitherto elusive in practice: portals are designed to provide a *single point of access* for all information that is meaningful to a business user, regardless of application, repository, or data type. The portal tightly organizes this information for the user, much like a personalized table of contents, so that it may be easily navigated and customized to the user's requirements, all without requiring the user to know what enterprise systems are being accessed, or where.[31]

The Delphi Group defines the enterprise portal as a single point of integrated, personalized, online access; a Web site offering a broad array of resources and services for its users throughout the enterprise such as e-mail, forums, search engines, chat rooms, and other online services.[32] EIPs are designed to provide a single point of access to structured data stored in databases, unstructured information stored in desktop repositories, as well as to mission-critical legacy applications. Some approaches target structured data residing in databases and legacy applications while others focus on unstructured information in desktop and network repositories. All definitions, however, imply a single, browser-based point of entry into all repositories of information assets. For example, corporate executives from an automotive company want to visit a car dealer to evaluate the dealer's performance. Information about that dealer may reside in numerous system applications. To assemble it in order to accomplish the visit may take hours or even days of preparation. However, with a portal to consolidate all that data from its disparate sources, a single, browser-based enterprise system reduces the time to minutes.[33]

The primary function of a portal, then, is to give users access to heterogeneous data sources through a single interface. EIPs provide a jumping off point to content and applications from a variety of internal and external sources, and they consolidate access to information that previously required multiple interfaces. Further, EIPs are being touted as a key access and delivery mechanism for Web services. A research report published by Merrill Lynch captured the essence of the EIP—a window, via the basic Web browser, into all of an organization's information assets and applications.[34]

During the past several years, the deployment of EIP solutions has been one of the top priorities of IT departments everywhere. They combine aspects of the technology solutions of document management, text search and retrieval, data warehouses, and knowledge management. Portal technology has its origins in these and other information technologies. The true roots of portals date back to 1994 when Netscape introduced the first commercial Web browser based on the immensely popular shareware product called *Mosaic.*

The need for application integration continues to be a major issue in most organizations. According to most estimates, only about 20 percent of enterprise information is captured in the production applications managed by IT departments. The remainder is scattered throughout the enterprise—in e-mail folders, personal file folders, Notes databases, Web pages, etc. EIPs are designed to search through this information and present it to users on demand.

Users of enterprise information need to access relevant business information, whether structured or unstructured, alphanumeric or text. The problem is that structured and unstructured data have been managed separately with little or no thought to common access. Knowledge workers today continue to struggle to find information on crowded desktops and to master the complexities of accessing data residing in various applications and platforms throughout the IT infrastructure. In contrast, portals offer a single, personalized point of access to relevant business information no matter where it resides. Not only does the portal offer a way into disparate knowledge repositories, but also it can be used to organize content in appropriate taxonomies to satisfy the needs of internal and external communities of users.

EIP Features

As is the case with most rapidly growing sectors of the business computing marketplace, the EIP space is heavily populated with dozens of vendors and solutions. The most common features and functions are shown in Figure 13.3, together with the content sources that are leveraged by the portal. The latest generation of portals promises features such as instant text and voice messaging, audio- and video-conferencing, shared calendaring and, perhaps most important, dynamic document sharing.[35]

Enterprise
Information
Portals—
Content,
Features, and
Functions

Figure 13.3

Enterprise Information Portals		
Content Sources	**Functions**	**Features**
• Databases	• Data query	• Personalization
• Documents	• Browse	• Workflow
• E-mail	• Search	• Auto-classification
• Internet	• Collaboration	• Notification
• News feeds / syndicated services		• Quality control
• Business intelligence reports		• Version control
		• Security standards
		• Metadata management

Building an EIP

The goal of an EIP is deceptively simple: pull together all the information users need to do their jobs, regardless of where it resides in the organization, and present it to them in a consistent manner through their desktop browser. However, exactly how to accomplish this goal involves some significant technological and organizational challenges. Many options are available—from a relatively modest intranet front-end to a total solution with intelligent text and data mining.

The following requirements should be considered when designing and building any enterprise information portal:

- **Completeness** – Portals should provide seamless access to structured data, unstructured data, and legacy applications in the organization.

- **Proven technologies** – Enterprise portals should be built on proven products, not immature technologies.

- **Plug-and-play** – The portal framework should support adding more components as needed.

No organization should attempt to deploy a portal on an enterprise-wide scale all at once. The first step is to identify a business process that would benefit from being able to launch queries through a single point of access rather than having to rely on multiple query tools to access different systems. Next, the source and nature of the data types must be identified for which better content management is required via the portal. Then, a customized taxonomy must be built. As discussed in Chapter 9, a taxonomy is a hierarchy of subject categories reflecting the information content and the users' needs for all types of queries—from the simple and straightforward to the most complex. Once the taxonomy is in place, all information objects submitted to the portal are automatically classified according to that taxonomy.

Portal technology has begun to provide automated solutions to this problem. An enterprise information portal is Web-based, front-end to internal and external information that is classified according to a customized taxonomy scheme, which sorts the information into useful content categories. To populate the taxonomy, portals provide technology that automatically analyzes and classifies information, looking beyond the metadata and file / field-level descriptors of document content. The result is the best chance of achieving the goal of accurate and timely retrieval of enterprise content, every time and all the time, in response to any properly formulated search query.[36]

Organizations cannot simply buy an off-the-shelf solution for all their content management problems. No single technology solution provides a panacea for all forms of unstructured information content. In the world of information management, few if any "magic wand" solutions are available. Organizations cannot indiscriminately throw any technology, including ECM or any of its components, across the enterprise and expect sudden and miraculous results.

The important question is not *whether* to apply new information technology, but *when* and *how*. Ultimately, the only way any organization can remain competitive is to apply new information related methods, tools, and practices, including ECM solutions, aggressively but intelligently. These realities were underscored in a recent ECM survey conducted by AIIM International. The respondents reported that the biggest challenges in assimilating ECM solutions are not the technology solutions themselves. Rather, planning and managing the organizational and cultural changes represented by these solutions and justifying the required investments were seen as larger issues. Notwithstanding these realities, ECM approaches to enterprise information management have much to offer. Indeed, if such approaches are applied judiciously, the result will be truly revolutionary.[37]

Notes

1. See, for example, Alan Pelz-Sharpe and Chris Harris-Jones, "Enterprise Content Management: Is Anything New?" *KMWorld*, May 2002; and Christine Chudnow, "Enterprise Content Management Makes the Most of What You've Got," *Computer Technology Review*, February 2003, 30.

2. Connie Moore, Kate Tucker, Susan Wiener, and Stacey Jenkins, *The Role of Electronic Records Management in North American Organizations*, Forrester Consulting, April 2004.

3. Chudnow, "Enterprise Content Management Makes the Most of What You've Got," 30.

4. Jennifer Jones, "Looking Inside," *InfoWorld*, 7 January 2002.

5. Judith Lamont, "Adapting ECM to Enterprise Goals," *KMWorld*, March 2004, 16.

6. Chudnow, "Enterprise Content Management Makes the Most of What You've Got," 30.

7. "What's Ahead for ECM," *KMWorld*, March 2004.

8. Robert F. Williams, *Electronic Records Management Survey: A Call to Action* (Chicago: Cohasset, Inc., 2004), 3.

9. Swartz, Nikki, "The Wonder Years of Knowledge Management," *The Information Management Journal* 37, no. 3 (May / June 2003): 54.

10. Pelz-Sharpe and Harris-Jones, "Enterprise Content Management: Is Anything New?"

11. Quoted in: John Naisbitt, *Megatrends: Ten New Directions Transforming Our Lives* (New York: Warner Books, 1982).

12. Michael Pemberton, "KM & RM: Oil & Water?" *The Information Management Journal* 38, no. 3 (May / June 2004): 48.

13. Cynthia Lynchbaugh, "The Writing on the Wall." *The Information Management Journal* 36, no. 2 (March / April 2002): 18.

14. Pemberton, "KM & RM: Oil & Water?", 14.

15. Swartz, "The Wonder Years of Knowledge Management," 55.

16. Delphi Group, "Enterprise Portals Bring Risk / Rewards to the Enterprise," June 25, 2002.

17. Thomas Stewart, "The Case Against Knowledge Management," *Business 2.0.*, February 2002.

18. French Caldwell, "The Future of Knowledge Management," *KMWorld*, October 2004, 1.

19. William Saffady, *Knowledge Management: A Manager's Briefing* (Prairie Village, KS: ARMA International, 1998).

20. Pemberton, "KM & RM: Oil & Water?", 50.

21. Bassam Zarkout, "Next-Generation Records Management," *KMWorld*, June 2002, S7.

22. Lynchbaugh, "The Writing on the Wall," 18.

23. William Saffady, *Electronic Document Imaging: Technology, Applications, Implementation* (Lenexa, KS: ARMA International, 2001).

24. William Saffady, Unpublished manuscript, n.d.

25. Alan Pelz-Sharpe, "The Next Generation of Search," *KMWorld*, January 2002.

26. Cathleen Moore, "Search Gets Organized," *InfoWorld*, 21 June 2004, 17.

27. Ibid.

28. William Holstein, "Data-Crunching Santa: Wal-Mart Knows What You Bought Last Christmas," *U.S. News & World Report*, 21 December 1998.

29. Mark Ferelli, "Why Data Warehousing?" *SMS* (March 1998).

30. Judith Lamont, "Ten Rules for Successful Data Warehousing," *KMWorld*, March 1999; see also Mitchell Seigle, "From Quicksand to Concrete: Laying the Foundation for a Successful Data Warehouse," *SMS* (July 1997).

31. See, for example, Alan Pelz-Sharpe, Chris Harris-Jones, and Angela Ashenden, "The Need for Portals," *KMWorld*, November / December 2001; and Dave Trowbridge, "Welcome to the Profit Portal," *Computer Technology Review*, April 2000.

32. Jerrold Rose, "The Joys of Enterprise Portals," *The Information Management Journal* 37, no. 5 (September / October 2003): 64.

33. Eric Knorr, "The New Enterprise Portal," *InfoWorld*, 12 January 2004, 43.

34. Sara Roberts-Witt, "Making Sense of the Portal Pandemonium," *Knowledge Management*, July 1999.

35. Peter Ruber, "Portals on a Mission," *Knowledge Management*, April 2000.

36. _____, "Framing a Portal Strategy," *Knowledge Management*, May 1999.

37. ARMA International, "AIIM Study Reveals ECM Drivers," *The Information Management Journal*, 29, no. 1 (January / February 2005): 18.

Chapter 14

Digital Records Preservation

Where electronic records are concerned, the long-term or permanent preservation of digital data entails challenges unlike any that have ever been encountered in the worlds of RIM and business computing. For computer-based records, unless special preservation measures are instituted, the *outer limits* of life expectancy can range between ten to twenty years and sometimes even as few as five years or so—a period of time consistent with the average service life of the hardware and software required to read and process the records. Although this time period is adequate for many electronic records, for many others it is not. The only way extended-term data retention requirements can be satisfied is by a series of carefully planned preservation practices which must be implemented by IT departments.

This chapter does not address issues for archival institutions that need to transition their preservation programs from physical to digital capabilities, although much of its content will be useful in that regard. Rather, this chapter is for the benefit of records managers who need to work with IT specialists to give their organization solid capabilities in the preservation of electronic records for extended periods of time, as required by approved retention policies.

The premise of this chapter is that most organizations are now in the embryonic stage of putting into place all that is needed to provide for the long-term retention of data in applications that require it. Apart from performing routine ***data migrations***, most IT departments have no policies or procedures on long-term data retention, nor have they employed any specialized technical expertise in this area. Further, most organizations have no special budget allocated for long-term data retention, nor have they addressed the issue in their long-range strategic plans. This situation was confirmed in a recent survey, which reported that:

- 85 percent of the respondents indicated that their organization does not have a specific budget for migrating their electronic records.

- 53 percent of the respondents indicated that they do not believe their organization's IT staff realizes that migration of data will be required for many types of electronic records in order to comply with established retention policies.
- 70 percent do not have a data migration plan in place.[1]

In most organizations today, efforts to provide for the extended-term retention of archival data have been limited to routine data migrations, performed as the need arose, and unaccompanied by other key preservation practices or a cohesive plan for **digital preservation**. Within the next five years or so, organizations having significant, even modest, requirements to retain computer data for extended periods of time will have to institute more comprehensive and formal data preservation practices.

Edith Allen, the retired records manager at the Battelle Memorial Institute, with characteristic levity, stated, "Our in-house computer staff tells me that they can provide storage for 3 to 5 years with certainty; 7 to 10 years with a 'little bit of luck;' and if storage is required after 10 years, *there are no guarantees.*"[2] In the same vein, Jeff Rothenberg, senior research scientist at the RAND Corporation, offers the tongue-in-cheek observation that "digital documents last forever – or five years, whichever comes first."[3] As with most such utterances, these two resonate because each contain more than a grain of truth to them. Briefly, the situation is as follows:

> If an organization creates a record in electronic format in, say, the year 2006, and this record will need to be digitally processed and read many years later, how, exactly, can this requirement be supported in a technology environment in which the only constant is rapid change?

Digital information is only as permanent as the hardware and software that gives it intelligibility. A significant percentage of organizational information is born digital, lives, and dies digital without ever being made manifest in the form of paper. As technological evolution and innovation over the past ten years has shown, nothing can assure that today's digital information possesses any greater permanence than a 1989 VisiCalc file stored on an eight-inch floppy disk. The fact that a file, record, or image is backed up on archival media is no guarantee of long-term accessibility, let alone permanence.

No one in the world has yet developed an ideal method of permanently preserving electronic records. An ideal solution would be "once-and-done"; that is, preservation routines would not need to be repeated over time, every time data formats or other elements of technology change. The preservation method would have to provide a proven solution to the problems of hardware and software obsolescence and media stability. Unfortunately, no such solution exists today. However, organizations do not have the luxury of doing nothing while they wait for such a solution to appear on the horizon. Electronic records of enduring value are getting older by the day, and they may be threatened with attacks on their integrity / processability or even abandoned by their owners. For these reasons, organizations must have a plan for how to deal with this situation.

Archival Data Storage Requirements

In business computing today, the current trend is that less data is being deleted while archival data is being retained longer. *Archival data*—data subject to extended-term retention requirements—is becoming the fastest growing segment of the total data storage requirements of most organizations, particularly the larger ones. Applications such as voice, text, graphic, images, audio, 3-D graphics, and movies all create high demands for archival preservation. The data in the category of "long-term retention" are being viewed differently than in the past. Historically, when data reached archival status, it had reached the final stage of its life cycle before being deleted. It was almost always assumed that the value of the data decreased as it aged. However, this assumption can no longer be used. An increasing number of archival data applications must be retained indefinitely for various legal, regulatory, and business reasons. As every records manager knows, in some cases, the value and utility of the data actually increases as it ages, even as the access requirements decrease.[4]

As a segment of an organization's total information resources, archival data possesses the following characteristics:

- Requires retention periods measured in years, sometimes decades, or even in perpetuity.
- Requires large-scale storage capacity, scalable to terabytes or even *petabytes.*
- Has low access and reference requirements but relatively high data transfer rate (bandwidth) requirements.
- Consists of mostly unstructured, fixed content.
- Has delayed access time (up to a few minutes) that is generally acceptable.
- Requires a data classification taxonomy to facilitate content-based searches.
- Needs adequate protection using appropriate backup methodologies, although no longer mission-critical due to its inactive status.[5]

Each of these requirements is addressed in this chapter or elsewhere in this book. The following data types are commonly maintained by organizations that frequently require retention in excess of ten years:

- Certain corporate and legal documents and data
- Engineering data
- Books of account and other tax documentation
- Research and development data
- Intellectual property data
- New product development and product history data
- Environmental data
- Certain medical data, particularly concerning long-term health effects
- Regulatory compliance data

Most large organizations, and many smaller ones, will have to address the problem of how to support long-term retention of digital data at some point in the future.

IT departments often have their first encounters with extended-term data retention in their efforts to comply with the provisions of *IRS Revenue Procedure 98-25*, which is, in effect, a regulatory requirement for extended-term retention of tax documentation that is subject to audit scrutiny. This directive is based on the fact that the technology environments in which tax documentation reside may have been upgraded one or even several times before a given tax year is closed. These technology upgrades could compromise the integrity of the records and thus adversely affect the ability of the IRS to audit them. Thus, *98-25* is intended to ensure that electronic tax documentation subject to audit is retained in fully auditable form for the duration of the organization's tax liability.

Compliance with *98-25* is particularly difficult for companies that acquire other businesses and wish to decommission the legacy computer systems of the acquired entities and consolidate them into their own systems. In cases where these legacy systems contain tax documentation, the acquiring entity must ensure that they are in compliance with the requirements of this revenue procedure so that the records retain their integrity and are fully auditable.

ISO 15489 and Digital Preservation

In the technical report that accompanies ISO 15489, the issue of digital preservation is addressed. Section 4.3.9.2 addresses the issue of continuing retention. The report states:

> Preservation strategies for records, especially electronic records, may be selected on the basis of their ability to maintain the accessibility, integrity and authenticity of the records over time, as well as for their cost-effectiveness. Preservation strategies can include copying, conversion and migration of records . . . Other methods may be used to retain electronic records for long periods, as new technologies become available. Strategies for retaining electronic records and associated metadata removed from systems have to be formulated and integrated into all system design processes to ensure that the records and associated metadata will remain accessible and usable for the entire period of their retention.[6]

Media Stability and Technology Obsolescence

The term *media stability* refers to the extent to which a given recordkeeping medium retains its physical and chemical properties, or the period of time during which the medium remains useful for its intended purpose. Or, in more practical terms, media stability refers to the ability of various records media to retain their information content in usable form for the duration of its period of retention.[7]

For magnetic tapes, which remain the predominant storage media for the retention of inactive computer data, stability varies from 10 to 20 years. For optical media, stability varies from 25 to 100 years, depending on the specific media type. Magnetic diskettes, the most fragile of the magnetic media, provide stability for only about five years. By contrast, analog formats (i.e., paper and microfilm) often provide stability for several hundred years, even in cases where preservation practices are less than ideal.

The life expectancy of a particular storage medium for digital data depends on many factors. The main factors that help determine the life expectancy of a storage medium are: (1) the quality of the media resulting from its manufacture; (2) the quality of the recorder used to write to the media; (3) the number of times data resident on the media is accessed during the media life; (3) the care with which the media is handled; (4) and the storage conditions (temperature and humidity).[8]

In the context of the capability to support extended-term retention requirements, media stability is an issue, but not the most important one. Many commentators almost unanimously agree that technological obsolescence represents a far greater threat to the preservation and utility of electronic records than media stability. For all types of hardware and software, service lives of less than five years are the order of the day. Even the most fragile media will likely exceed the continued availability of readers for those media. Thus, efforts to preserve physical media and the information residing on them provide only a short-term, partial solution to the general problem of long-term data retention.

Although computer tapes, disks, and other electronic storage media are constantly being improved with respect to their ability to maintain the stability and integrity of their data for long periods of time, these media cannot be read without the proper hardware and software. The larger issue, then, is ***technology obsolescence***. A strategy for obsolescence protection—the ability to provide access to digital content through successive generations of new hardware and software—is needed. The recommended practices presented next address this requirement.

Digital vs. Paper Preservation

Because of the rapid obsolescence of computer hardware and software, retaining archival data in computer-processable format is often *impractical*, even though it may be desirable to do so. For a given set of archival data, the expense and technical complexity associated with the long-term preservation of electronic records are such that preservation in digital format should be selected only after careful consideration of which particular preservation solution—paper or digital—can best meet the organization's needs. Many preservation requirements can be amply satisfied by relying on analog formats such a paper or microfilm. Microfilm, in particular, is an ideal preservation medium in many fixed-content situations. If preservation in digital form is selected, the benefits should be demonstrable. At a minimum, these benefits should include a high degree of expected usage. Therefore, preservation of data in digital form is recommended only under the following circumstances:

- When the value of the data and the benefits of preservation in digital form have been clearly established. The value of the data should be substantial and the benefits of preservation in digital form should be demonstrable if not compelling.

- When preservation of the data in manipulatable, computer-processable form is required to support significant business requirements; that is, when preservation in fixed content form is not an option.

- When conversion of the data from a dynamic to a static state—from digital to analog format—would severely diminish its value or render it unusable in order to satisfy required (rather than "nice to have") business requirements.

These criteria are intended to set a relatively high standard for selecting the optimum format for long-term preservation, but again, this standard is justified given the fact that going digital necessitates a continuing, even perpetual, commitment. However, in situations where preservation in digital format is the best or indeed the only option, the practices discussed next should be implemented to ensure that the data retains its integrity for as long as the records need to be retained.

Data Preservation Practices

During his tenure as principal storage media analyst at the now defunct National Media Laboratory, Dr. John W. C. Van Bogart made the oft-quoted remark, "Digital archives should be transcribed every 10 to 20 years. To realize lifetimes greater than this, one would be required to archive the recording system and media, archive the system hardware and software, archive the operating system, archive operations manuals, and archive ample spare parts."[9] This wry observation suggests that the "museum approach," in which all components of a computer system are stored and maintained in perpetuity in a museum type environment, is the way to support extended-term digital preservation requirements. Fortunately, this approach is not the preferred one. IT departments can institute a variety of preservation practices to meet the organization's long-term data retention needs. The role of records managers is to communicate these requirements to IT specialists and work with them to ensure that they are fully satisfied.

Storage Media

First, preservation copies of data intended for extended-term retention must be stored on suitable media. The initial step in digital preservation is the selection of appropriate blank (unrecorded) media. Media selection should be based on the ability of the media to provide the greatest stability and resistance to obsolescence. The media should conform to specifications contained in national and international standards. Such standards have been developed for most types of magnetic tapes, 3.5-inch diskettes, and certain optical media, including magneto-optical disks and compact disks. Computer media must also comply fully with specifications established by the manufacturer of the equipment on which the media will be recorded or played. Media selection should be limited to high-quality magnetic or optical media from proven manufacturers. Compared with less expensive, generic products, brand-name magnetic media are manufactured from higher-quality materials and subjected to more rigorous manufacturing and testing processes.[10]

Data Migration

Data migration is the process of periodically converting electronic records to new file formats and/or new storage media to ensure that the records will remain usable for the entire duration of authorized retention.[11] Data migration, which is performed routinely by IT departments, is necessary because the future usability of electronic records may be adversely affected by changes to computer installations and by the limited life spans of magnetic or optical media on which the data reside. The purpose of data migration is to preserve the integrity of the records and to support the ability to retrieve, display, and otherwise use them over time. Data migration may occur when hardware and/or software becomes obsolete, or the practice may be employed to transfer electronic records from one file format to another. Conversion of electronic records to new file formats is intended to preserve the usability of recorded information when computer hardware and/or software components are upgraded or replaced.

Data migration involves a set of organized tasks designed to periodically transfer electronic records from one hardware / software configuration to another, or from one generation of technology to a subsequent generation. During the migration process, the original sequence of the structural and data elements of digital records are rearranged to conform to the newer configuration. The major risk with this digital preservation practice is the risk of altering records during conversion from the source to the target format. For migrations to be executed successfully, individuals performing them must have knowledge of the original application and data formats. This knowledge is more important when the file structure is more complex. With each successive format conversion over time, the possibility of data loss or corruption increases. Thus, migration is at best an imperfect solution as it can lead to the loss of record integrity.

Data migration will typically be required where one or more of the following three conditions apply:

1. The scheduled destruction date for electronic records is greater than five years from the initial installation date or last major upgrade of the computer storage device or software that reads, processes, or maintains the records. For example, if electronic records must be read by a ***magnetic tape*** drive that was installed in 2002, data migration will be required if the records must be retained until 2006 or later. Similarly, if electronic records must be processed by database management software that was upgraded in 2004, data migration will be required if the records must be retained until 2009 or later.

2. The total retention period for the electronic records is greater than ten years from the date the records were created. Consequently, electronic records created in 2004 will require data migration if they must be retained until 2014 or later.

3. The usability of electronic records will be affected by replacement, upgrades, or other changes in computer hardware or software components before the specified retention periods for the records elapses.[12]

Data migration requirements apply only to electronic records that are designated as official copies to satisfy the organization's retention requirements. Data migration is not required for electronic records that are considered duplicate records. Finally, when planning for data migrations, IT departments should adhere to the requirements of the records retention schedule in making decisions as to whether some, none, or all the older ***legacy data*** need to be migrated to the new environment.

Data Migration Plan

IT departments should review data migration requirements and, where indicated, develop a data migration plan for all existing applications that operate on network servers, timeshared computers, and other shared or centralized computing resources. As required practice, IT departments must consider data migration requirements when new applications are planned and implemented. At a minimum, the data migration plan for a given application must:

- Identify the data to be migrated, as well as the data to be excluded from migration, if any.

- Specify anticipated migration intervals, where required, for conversion of electronic records to new file formats, or for copying of electronic records onto new media.

- Specify functional requirements for data migration tools to be developed or acquired, as well as functional requirements for electronic storage media to be used in the migration process.

- Provide a method for testing and verifying that the data migration was performed accurately and reliably without loss or corruption of information from the original electronic records.

- Maintain the original electronic records until accurate, reliable data migration is confirmed.

Data migration plans must be reviewed periodically and revised, if necessary, based on experience or other considerations. At a minimum, data migration plans must be reevaluated whenever computer hardware and/or software components are upgraded or replaced, or whenever recorded information is transferred to new storage media.[13]

Alternatives to Data Migration

Where electronic records are subject to long retention periods, data migration plans will involve a significant future commitment of personnel and technology resources through multiple iterations of file format conversion and/or storage media conversion. Moreover, data migration can be expensive—by some estimates up to 2.5 times the original cost of data creation and capture. Where electronic records are designated for permanent retention, the commitment is perpetual. The practicality of such data migration commitments must be carefully considered.

To reduce data migration burdens, electronic records must be discarded promptly when their retention periods have elapsed. To avoid data migration, electronic records can be printed onto paper for filing and retention where practical and possible. However, certain electronic records cannot be printed without loss of content or functionality. Data migration is unavoidable in such circumstances.

Where the usability of electronic records is affected by upgrading or replacement of computer hardware or software components, data migration can be avoided by keeping the superseded hardware or software components in service for the limited purpose of retrieving older electronic records when needed. This practice should be limited to electronic records that are subject to very occasional retrieval and that will be eligible for destruction within three years, assuming that the superseded hardware or software components can be kept in service for that entire time.[14]

File Formats

Standardization of file formats is a data preservation strategy in which an organization adopts one or more standard formats for recording electronic records on digital media. The particular type of coding scheme employed in creating text, data, or image files can have important implications concerning the ease with which digital records can be read and processed over time on a variety of computing devices. In a preservation context, the most important consideration is that a generic document format be universally useable, standard in technical specifications over time, and sufficiently robust in capabilities to allow accurate, authentic content preservation and document format presentation.

To be universally usable, a document format must be readable without regard to the specific software available on individuals' desktops. For image and textual data, TIFF Group 4, *portable document format (PDF)*, *standard generalized markup language (SGML)*, and *ASCII* are the most common file formats currently in use for purposes of supporting extended-term retention requirements. Some IT specialists think that open, nonproprietary file specifications theoretically give TIFF, SGML, *hypertext markup language (HTML),* and *extensible markup language (XML)* a technical edge for long-term document preservation. However, none of these markup languages are in common use on the desktop computer of most document creators. The following file formats are useful for long-term data preservation.

- **ASCII** – The ASCII format provides the broadest compatibility for text file interchange across platforms and has thus enjoyed wide acceptance in support of long-term data preservation requirements. As a matter of policy, organizations should not record data having lengthy retention requirements onto proprietary formats; that is, onto formats dependent on specific hardware and software.

- **XML** – Many organizations are now considering the potential use of this markup language in digital preservation initiatives, and some are beginning to mandate its use. Several attributes of XML make it attractive for digital preservation applications: (1) The semantic nature of XML tags makes XML suitable for recording metadata. (2) Its extensibility allows organizations to expand their systems to accommodate evolving needs. (3) As an open standard, XML reduces if not eliminates the problem of proprietary software. (4) XML files can be readily interpreted by disparate computer systems because they are basically text files. (5) The human-readability of XML tags permits archival records to be preserved on paper as well as computer media so that they will be automatically readable through optical character recognition.

- **PDF** – A product of Adobe Systems, PDF has become a de facto standard for providing universal access to electronic documents over the Internet. This file format preserves all the fonts, formatting, graphics, and color of any source document, regardless of the application used to create it. In other words, PDF retains the content, look, and feel of the document exactly as it was created, while also ensuring integrity, security, and accessibility. An international group is currently working with Adobe to develop an archival version of the standard—PDF/Archival. The aim is to create a common, nonproprietary standard that will enable preservation of electronic records over multiple technology generations. The U.S. National Archives and Records Administration (NARA) recently announced that PDF is an acceptable file format for the archival preservation of federal records. Although PDF will be the file format of choice in certain preservation situations, issues associated with metadata capture and other technical issues will render it inappropriate in others.[15]

Media Recopying

Media recopying has long been a key data preservation practice. The practice involves recopying the data residing on old media onto to new, industry standard media at regular intervals—sometime prior to the expiration of the media life expectancy. Copying electronic records onto new storage media is intended to preserve the usability of recorded information where the stable life span of a given storage medium is shorter than the retention period for the recorded information or where product modifications or discontinuations render a given storage medium unusable.

As a preservation practice, media recopying may be performed in conjunction with data migration, or as a separate task. The practice applies principally to inactive electronic records that have been transferred from hard drives to removable media, such as magnetic tapes or optical disks, for off-line storage. Electronic records stored on hard drives will presumably be migrated to new equipment when servers or hard drives are replaced. Electronic records stored on hard drives will presumably be backed up on magnetic tapes, which will be replaced at frequent intervals with new backup copies.[16]

If new media are used, periodic recopying can extend the life of recorded information indefinitely, thereby effectively overcoming problems associated with the nonarchival nature of computer media. Copying can also be used to transfer information from deteriorating or obsolete media onto new media. Digitally encoded information can be copied an indefinite number of times without degradation. To minimize the adverse effects of temperature and humidity variations, media copying should be performed in the long-term storage environment itself.

NARA requires federal agencies subject to its regulations to recopy permanent data stored on industry standard magnetic tapes onto tested and verified new tapes before the tapes are ten years old.[17] The American National Standards Institute (ANSI) states, in its standard for the storage of magnetic tapes, that in order to provide additional protection against permanent errors that can render information irretrievable, the contents of computer media should be copied onto new media at regular intervals. No time period is specified, however. To minimize risks associated with defective media, organizations should create two or more storage copies of very important information intended for long-term retention.

Metadata Requirements

Metadata is essential for managing record objects throughout their retention life cycle. Without an adequately defined metadata strategy, digital preservation initiatives cannot be supported. In fact, in the opinion of some commentators, metadata is *the* key practice for managing electronic records over time. Traditionally, the term *metadata* has been widely used to characterize the descriptive information that will support search and retrieval of both paper and electronic information. More recently, the term has been expanded to include additional information that must be acquired and retained in order to manage electronic records effectively over long periods of time, including permanently.[18]

The proper management of metadata is essential for preserving the integrity of records objects for as long as they must remain in a computer-processable format. The metadata must support the authenticity and reliability of the records objects, their structure and context as well their content, for the full duration of their retention life. These terms are defined as follows:

- *Content* includes the words, numbers, sounds, and images made by the record's creator.

- *Structure* refers to the appearance and arrangement of the record's content. It includes the meaning of a record as conveyed by the appearance of its characteristics (i.e., typeface), the location of specific data fields on the document (i.e., a form), and the pointers used to link physical or logical groups of data.

- *Context* includes the background information describing the origin of the record—which organizational unit created the record, which unit has used it, the purpose for which it was used, and how it relates to other records.

- *Fixity* means that the content must be fixed as a discrete object in order to be a preservable record. If a digital record is subject to change without notice, its integrity may be compromised.

- *Authenticity* refers to the fact that a record is what it purports to be and has not been tampered with or otherwise corrupted since its creation—it is proven reliable over time. The record must be genuine and determined to have been managed by specific records custodians through all phases of its life cycle. Authentication of a record is critical in the context of digital preservation because electronic records can only be preserved by copying or reproducing them.

- *Reliability* refers to the ability of a record to stand for the facts it contains—the trustworthiness of the record's content. It must be trustworthy based on its mode (method by which it is communicated over time and space), form (format or media on which it is created or received), state of transmission, and the manner of its preservation.

The above attributes must be captured at the time of creation of electronic records, and any preservation initiatives must consider how they will be addressed.[19]

Arguably, all contextual information that classifies or interprets data may be validly considered as forms of metadata. However, exactly what metadata is required in order to ensure the trustworthiness of the records—their completeness, authenticity, and preservability over time? For every document created on popular software programs such as Microsoft Word or Lotus Notes, a wealth of metadata is retained that does not appear on the screen, including descriptions of the properties of the document (e.g., character, word, and line counts), personal settings, preferences for fonts and styles used in creation, and revision information.[20] The long-term preservation of electronic records in hardware / software independent formats requires that such records be linked to information about their structure, context, and use history. Such metadata must include information about:

- The source of the records
- How, why, and when the records were created, updated, or changed
- The intended purpose or function of the records
- How to open and read the records
- The terms of access of the records
- How the records are related to other software and data used by the creating organization

These metadata must be sufficient to support any changes made to records through various generations of hardware and software, to support the reconstruction of the decision-making process, to provide audit trails throughout a record's life cycle, and to capture internal documentation.

Systems Documentation

The preservation of systems documentation for computer applications having extended-term retention requirements is a key component of digital preservation because, without the requisite documentation, such data cannot be processed and read. The extended-term retention of data requires maintaining up-to-date documentation about all systems in order to understand the purpose and functions of the system, define the contents of the files and records, and specify all technical characteristics necessary for reading and processing the records.

Adequate technical documentation necessary to read and process electronic records over time would include the following:

- The name of the system and the unique identifiers of the owners;
- The hardware, software, and network installation, modification, and maintenance;
- A description of the content and structure of data records;
- A list and description of interconnected systems;
- How the data is entered, accessed, modified, and deleted;
- A data dictionary or the equivalent information associated with a database; management system, including a description of the relationship between data elements in the database;
- Any other technical information needed to read and process the records.[21]

Documentation for data files and databases would generally include records layouts, data element definitions, and code translation tables (codebooks) for coded data. Data element definitions, codes used to represent data values, and interpretations of these codes must match the actual format and codes.

Media Storage and Maintenance

If they are not stored under good environmental conditions, the life expectancy of storage media, and the electronic records residing on them, can be expected to suffer. The basic rule-of-thumb for storage environments is that they be *cool, dry, and free of fluctuations*. The two organizations that have issued the most authoritative pronouncements relating to media storage for purposes of long-term data retention are NARA, which prescribes digital preservation requirements applicable to the federal government, and ANSI, which has issued a standard pertaining to the storage of imaging and magnetic media. The technical guidelines of both these organizations are reviewed below.

ANSI Standard for Media Storage

ANSI/NAPM IT9.23-1996, *American National Standard for Imaging Materials – Polyester Base Magnetic Tape – Storage.*[22] This standard specifies two categories of media storage conditions: medium-term storage, which is suitable for preservation requirements for a minimum of ten years, and extended-term storage, suitable for storage of permanent records. The ANSI standard states that protection against environmental damage is enhanced when magnetic tapes are stored at a low temperature and relative humidity, but very low temperatures can lead to separation of tape lubricants from binder materials. The following guidelines are recommended for medium- and extended-term storage of magnetic tape:

- **Medium-term storage** – The ANSI standard specifies a maximum temperature of 25 degrees Celsius (77 degrees Fahrenheit) for extended time periods, and 32 degrees Celsius (90 degrees Fahrenheit) for short periods of time. The recommended relative humidity specified is 20 to 50 percent. Temperature variations in the storage area must not exceed two degrees Celsius (4 degrees Fahrenheit) over a 24-hour period. Humidity variations must not exceed 10 percent over a 24-hour period. The minimum acceptable storage temperature is 8 degrees Celsius (46 degrees Fahrenheit).

- **Extended-term storage** – The ANSI standard specifies three combinations of temperature and relative humidity:
    1. A maximum temperature of 20 degrees Celsius (70 degrees Fahrenheit) with relative humidity ranging from 20 to 30 percent;
    2. A maximum temperature of 15 degrees Celsius (60 degrees Fahrenheit) with relative humidity ranging from 20 to 40 percent; or
    3. A maximum temperature of 10 degrees Celsius (50 degrees Fahrenheit) with relative humidity ranging from 20 to 50 percent.

- **Fluctuations** – As the storage temperature rises, relatively humidity must be more tightly controlled. Temperature variations in the storage area must not exceed two degrees Celsius (4 degrees Fahrenheit) over a 24-hour period, as noted above. Humidity variations for extended-term storage must not exceed 5 percent over a 24-hour period.

Media Inspection

To facilitate the early detection of tape stress, evaporation of lubricants, or other dangers to recorded information, computer media in long-term storage should be inspected regularly. The ANSI standard recommends inspection of magnetic tapes at five-year intervals, with more frequent *media inspections* if temperature and humidity deviations have occurred. Inspection intervals for other computer media are not defined by national or international standards. Inspection routines should include a visual examination of media and their housings, followed by the retrieval or playback of recorded information. In a large collection of computer media, a portion of the collection can be sampled. If permanent errors are detected in the sampled media, the entire collection must be examined.

NARA's technical guidelines specify that organizations should read a statistical sample of all reels of magnetic tapes containing permanent records to identify any loss of data and to discover and correct the causes of data loss. In tape libraries with 1,800 or fewer reels, a 20 percent sample or a sample size of 50 reels, whichever is larger, should be read. In tape libraries with more than 1,800 reels, a sample of 360 reels should be read. Tapes with ten or more errors should be replaced with new industry standard media and, when possible, lost data should be restored. All other tapes that might have been affected by the same cause (i.e., poor quality tape, high usage, poor environment, improper handling) should be read and corrected as appropriate.

NARA's guidelines also provide that organizations should test magnetic computer tapes no more than six months prior to using them to store electronic records that are scheduled for permanent retention. These tests should verify that the tapes are free of permanent errors and are in compliance with applicable standards promulgated by the National Institute of Standards and Technology or other relevant industry standards.[23]

Media Refreshing / Rewinding

Media refreshing or rewinding is a procedure intended to maximize the life expectancy of data resident on magnetic tapes by unspooling and rewinding the tapes to relieve stresses, or to transcribe and rewrite the data in order to refresh the magnetic signals and prevent or minimize data loss. In order to minimize the likelihood of cinching, magnetic tapes can undergo a slow wind/rewind cycle to obtain a smooth, evenly tensioned pack prior to storage or prior to initial use or removal from storage.

In the past, various authorities have recommended that magnetic tapes in storage be rewound at regular intervals, perhaps annually, to alleviate accumulated stress or to tighten up loose tapes. Such rewinding is described as "exercising" or "retensioning" a tape. At present, however, wide disagreement exists among the several parties having an interest in this matter as to its necessity or desirability, and a definitive recommendation for or against periodic rewinding cannot be provided. Recent research suggests that periodic rewinding of magnetic tapes may not be necessary, particularly for magnetic tape cartridges or cassettes with small diameters.

In its technical guidelines, NARA specifies that organizations should rewind, under controlled tension, all tapes containing permanent records every 3.5 years. However, NARA reportedly has discontinued the practice of periodic rewinding of its magnetic tapes, presumably because it does not consider this procedure required to assure the integrity of archival data.

The ANSI standard is silent on this issue; periodic rewinding is not mentioned in its discussion of tape tensioning. Media manufacturers' recommendations are based on their own test results. Imation, the leading manufacturer of magnetic storage media, recommends against periodic rewinding of quarter-inch magnetic tape cartridges, although it does recommend a full unwinding and rewinding to exercise stored tapes immediately prior to use. Ampex, by contrast, recommends that metal particle tapes in storage be retensioned at five-year intervals to relieve stresses.[24]

Future Preservation Solutions

No ideal solution for digital preservation has yet been invented. However, solutions are under development. Perhaps the most promising of these solutions is *emulation*—the use of a new computer to impersonate an older one. An *emulator* is a software program that runs on a new computer to make it operate like the old computer. Emulation has been in practical use on computer systems for many years. The aim is to preserve the original software environment in which digital data of long-term value were created.

This potential solution to long-term data retention was articulated by Jeff Rothenberg in his seminal essay, *Avoiding Technological Quicksand: Finding a Viable Technical Foundation for Digital Preservation.*[25] The central idea of this preservation strategy (Rothenberg calls it the only "true solution" yet proposed) is to emulate obsolete computer systems on future, unknown systems so that a digital document's original software can be run in the future despite being obsolete. This approach involves developing techniques for the following:

- Specifying emulators that will run on unknown future computers and that capture all the attributes required to recreate the content and look and feel of future digital documents;

- Preserving, in human-readable form, the metadata needed to find, access, and recreate digital documents under the emulation methodology; and

- Encapsulating documents and their attendant metadata, software, and emulator specifications in ways that preserves the integrity of these digital objects.

Although this strategy for digital preservation may be promising, it is in the experimental stage of development. A prototype has, however, been developed, at the IBM Almaden Research Center in California. This organization has developed what is referred to as a "universal, virtual computer" that provides an architecture and language designed to be logical and accessible so that future computer developers will be able to write instructions to emulate it on their machines. In this sense, it may be thought of as a "Digital Rosetta Stone." However, before this or any other emulation solution evolves into a proven archival solution, it will have to be adopted as a standard throughout the computer industry and among archival institutions worldwide. Software developers with new file formats will need to write additional software that can read and display files in the language of the machine. Moreover, descriptions of the universal, virtual computer will need to be widely available for future computer developers throughout the U.S. and the world.[26]

Records managers and IT specialists must work cooperatively together to put into place all that is required to enable the organization to support whatever extended-term data retention requirements it may have. Digital preservation should be a key component of the long-range strategic plans of every organization having these requirements. Development of new policies, procedures, guidelines, allocation of budget resources, and development of technical expertise cannot happen overnight. However, with records managers and IT working together, they will have a greater likelihood of developing the capabilities for digital preservation for their organizations.

Notes

1. Robert F. Williams, *Electronic Records Management Survey: A Call to Action* (Chicago: Cohasset, Inc., 2004), 6; 30-35.

2. Edith Gaylord Allen, "After the Records Inventory and Retention Decisions: Implementation Issues in Electronic Records Management," in *Proceedings of the 46th Annual ARMA International Conference in Montreal, Quebec, September 30 – October 3, 2001* (Prairie Village, KS: ARMA International, 2001), 5.

3. Jeff Rothenberg, "Avoiding Technological Quicksand: Finding a Viable Technical Foundation for Digital Preservation," January 1998, 5. Accessible at www.clir.org/pubs/ abstract/pub77.html. (Accessed January 31, 2006.)

4. Fred Moore, "Long Term Data Preservation," *Storage Inc.* (Q3 1999), 32, 36.

5. Ibid.; see also Fred Moore, "Archival Data Has a New Mission: Critical," *Computer Technology Review*, February 2003, 36-37.

6. International Organization for Standardization, ISO 15489-1 2001: *Information and Documentation – Records Management – Part 1: General* (Geneva, Switzerland: ISO, 2001), 20.

7. See, for example, Karen E. K. Brown, and Franziska Frey, "How Long Will It Last?: Life Expectancy of Information Media," in *Proceedings of the 44th Annual Conference, ARMA International, Cincinnati, OH, October 17 – 20, 1999* (Prairie Village, KS: ARMA International, 1999), 217-224.

8. Charles M. Dollar, "Selecting Storage Media for Long-Term Access to Digital Records," *The Information Management Journal* 33, no. 3 (July 1999): 36-43. See also the data preservation requirements of the U.S. National Archives and Records Administration, accessible at www.archives.gov.

9. John Van Bogart, *Archival Stability of Digital Storage Media* (St. Paul, MN: National Media Laboratory, 1995).

10. Dollar, "Selecting Storage Media." See also the data preservation requirements of the U.S. National Archives and Records Administration, accessible at www.archives.gov.

11. William Saffady, Unpublished manuscript, n.d.

12. Ibid.

13. Ibid.

14. Ibid.

15. See John Phillips, "Should PDF Be Used for Archiving Electronic Records?" *The Information Management Journal* 35, no. 1 (January 2001): 60-62; "Will PDF Prevent a Digital Dark Age?" *The Information Management Journal* 37, no. 3 (May / June 2003): 13.

16. Saffady, Unpublished manuscript, n.d.

17. NARA data preservation requirements, accessible at www.archives.gov.

18. See, for example, Michael Day, "Extending Metadata for Digital Preservation." Available at: http://www.ariadne.ac.uk/issue9/metadata/, 1-5; and Jason Baron, "Recordkeeping in the 21st Century," *The Information Management Journal* 33, no. 3 (July 1999): 10. See also Sue McKemmish and Dagmar Parer, "Towards Frameworks for Standardizing Recordkeeping Metadata," *Archives and Manuscripts* 26, no. 1 (1998).

19. Charles Arp and Joseph Dickman, "Information Preservation: Changing Roles," *The Information Management Journal* 36, no. 6 (November / December 2002): 55; see also Greg S. Hunter, "The Digital Future: A Look Ahead," *The Information Management Journal* 36, no. 1 (January / February): 71.

20. Baron, "Recordkeeping in the 21st Century," 10.

21. Arp and Dickman, "Information Preservation: Changing Roles," 58-59.

22. American National Standards Institute, ANSI/NAPM IT9.23-1996. *American National Standard for Imaging Materials – Polyester Base Magnetic Tape – Storage* (Washington, DC: ANSI, 1996).

23. ANSI Standard and NARA data preservation requirements.

24. Ibid.

25. Jeff Rothenberg, *Avoiding Technological Quicksand.*

26. "A Digital Archiving Standard," *The Information Management Journal* 36, no. 6 (November / December 2002): 14.

Glossary

The following terms are considered essential to the purpose of furthering an understanding of professional RIM. For a more complete explanation of specific terms in the context of their relevance to RIM practice, consult the individual chapters.

A

access. (1) The act of gaining usage of a record; (2) permission and means to use a record.

access time. A measure of the interval of time between the time documents are requested by a user and the time the information is delivered to the user. Also termed *timely retrieval.*

accessibility. The ease with which records or information can be obtained by those requesting it.

active record. A record needed to perform current operations or ongoing business matters. It is consulted frequently, and it must be conveniently available for immediate reference, either manually or via a computer system.

admissibility. A legal term that refers to the conditions under which evidence, including records and information, may be introduced into legal proceedings. To be admissible as evidence, a record must satisfy two basic requirements: (1) Its content must be relevant to the issue at hand; and (2) its authenticity must be firmly established.

adverse inference. A finding by a court during litigation that information contained in documents or other evidence was inappropriately destroyed by a party and is unfavorable to that party, even though the full content of the records or evidence was never reviewed by the court. The adverse inference sanction is a judicially imposed penalty whereby the jury is instructed that it is at liberty to infer that the defendant destroyed potentially relevant evidence because it feared that the evidence would be unfavorable or incriminating.

American standard code for information interchange (ASCII). A widely utilized coding scheme that specifies bit patterns for computer-processable information. The most popular coding method provides 128 possible character combinations and is used by personal computers for converting letters, numbers, punctuation, and control codes into digital form. Once defined, ASCII characters can be recognized and understood by other computers and communication devices.

application. A collection of one or more related software programs that enables a user to enter, store, view, modify, or extract information from files or databases. The term is commonly used in place of "program" or "software." More broadly, the term is used to describe a separate and discrete business process and accompanying records that are processed and managed in a computing environment.

archival data. Information typically stored on secondary, off-line media and is not directly accessible to users of a computer system, but it is nevertheless required for retention.

archives. (1) Records created or received and accumulated by an organization in the course of conduct of affairs and preserved because of their historical or continuing value. (2) The building or part of a building where archival materials are located. (3) The agency or program responsible for selecting, acquiring, preserving, or making available archival materials.

archiving, data. The transfer of data from online processing environments to near-line or off-line storage systems for purposes of providing for its ongoing retention on storage media suitable for that purpose. The process of archiving typically involves the transfer of inactive records and information from primary to secondary media repositories and may take place automatically at scheduled intervals or periodically as determined by system administrators or data owners / users.

attachment. A record or file associated with another record for the purpose of transfer and storage in a computer system or application. In common usage, the term refers to a file associated with an e-mail for transfer and storage as a single message unit.

attribute. A characteristic or property of a record that sets it apart from other records.

audits, records. Periodic inspections conducted to determine whether recordkeeping operations are in compliance with RIM policies and procedures, particularly those pertaining to records retention.

authenticity, of a record. Efforts to establish that a record is what it purports to be and has not been tampered with or otherwise corrupted since its creation; that is, its reliability can be demonstrated through the various phases of its life cycle.

B

backup, data. The process of making a copy, at regular, scheduled intervals, of data residing on primary, online storage devices. The data is copied (backed up) onto secondary media for purposes of off-line, off-site security storage. The primary purpose of data backup is to provide the capability of recovering critical data when online processing is interrupted or when a data loss of any kind occurs.

benchmarking. The process of identifying and imitating business practices or processes deemed to be optimum for a given application or set of requirements.

bit. The abbreviation for binary digit; the smallest unit of information recognized by a computer, represented by a single zero or one. Used as a unit of measurement of the storage capacity of computer devices.

C

categorization, automatic. A software program that facilitates the categorization of electronic records within their proper categories in a classification system or taxonomy. The software is designed to identify and extract patterns and concepts in unstructured content residing on hard disks, servers, intranet sites, portals, and Web sites. The taxonomy engine residing on servers performs the categorization process and usually populates a database of metadata to support subsequent retrieval and maintenance operations.

classification. The act of analyzing a document or record to determine its subject content and then selecting the proper subject category under which the record will be filed.

classification system. A method of organizing records and information in accordance with a logical scheme of primary and subordinate subjects or topical categories, arranged in hierarchical fashion from the most general to the most specific. See also *taxonomy*.

confidential record. Any business record containing sensitive information. Such records are typically subject to special rules and policies concerning their access, use, and disclosure.

content management. See *Enterprise Content Management*.

cookies. Blocks of text characters placed by a Web server onto the Internet browsers of desktop computers when users transmit Web pages or images. Their main purpose is to enable an application to work better by preserving a history of the Web pages a user had visited previously. However, the use of cookies constitutes a privacy issue because these files permit users' Internet activities to be tracked and monitored, including those that may be considered personal in nature.

cost-avoidance. A management concept whereby funding for a proposed system or project is justified based on the supposition that immediate acceptance will be less costly than a future alternative.

cost-benefit analysis. An approach to cost justification in which the costs associated with a particular investment in a record-keeping system or other RIM initiative are compared to the quantitative or nonquantitative benefits to be derived from that investment. Generally, such investments are deemed cost-justified if a positive return on investment is derived prior to the time the system must be replaced.

D

data. A general term used to denote computer-based records or information. Data provide the content for records and information.

data criticality assessment. In information protection, assessments to determine the consequences of loss of computer data and the protection strategy most appropriate to mitigate these risks. These assessments typically employ a three-tier criticality rating scale—high, medium, and low—which is analogous to the vital, important, and useful ratings typically assigned to vital paper records.

data mining. Optimizing an organization's electronic records on an enterprise-wide scale by assembling information from various applications, platforms, and storage devices for presentation management, strategic analysis, and decision-making.

data protection. A term closely related to *privacy* and generally refers to the European Union (EU) *Directive on Data Protection*, the main purpose of which is to harmonize the privacy laws of the EU member states. Issued in 1998, the directive applies to the collection, transmission, and processing of personal data, which is defined as any information relating to an identified or identifiable natural person residing within a member state of the EU. The directive has served as a model for privacy legislation throughout the world.

data warehouse. A database designed to support decision-making in an organization. Data from the production databases are copied to the data warehouse so that queries and analyses can be performed without disturbing the content or integrity of data in the native applications.

database. A collection of related data stored on a computer system that can be manipulated or extracted for use with various applications but managed independently of them. A set of data elements, consisting of at least one file or group of related files, usually stored in one location and made available to several users. See also *structured data*.

declaration, records. The act of designating documents as *official records* and thus eligible for retention management in an electronic RIM system. Typically, these determinations are reserved for static or fixed-content records of official character or operational importance as reflective of the organization's official policy or position on a matter. These records also may be required to be retained by law, regulation, or as per the organization's retention schedule. Conversely, dynamic content, such as drafts or other work-in-process documents, are generally ineligible for such declaration.

delete, deletion. The removal from ordinary use of data that existed on a computer as live data. Deleted data may remain on storage media in whole or in part until it has been overwritten or wiped. Even then, directory listings, pointers, or metadata relating to the deleted data may remain on the computer. "Soft deletions" are data marked as deleted and thus not generally available to the user but not yet physically removed or expunged. Soft-deleted data can generally be restored with complete fidelity.

departmental retention schedule. A retention schedule prepared for a specific department or other organizational unit. The schedule lists records series maintained by that unit.

digital. Any data or recorded information that exists as binary code (zeros and ones).

digital preservation. Any measures employed to assure the integrity of computer data that must be retained for lengthy periods of time. These measures are necessary because the computer technology used to create, process, and read the data may become obsolete prior to the expiration of the retention period.

digital signature / electronic signature (e-signature). An electronic version of a person's signature that appears in an electronic record. When managed in accordance with national and international standards, the application used to create and transmit the digital signature will provide a means of verifying the identity of the person such that business transactions may be consummated in a lawful and secure manner.

digitize. The process of converting records, documents, or information in paper and other formats to binary representations that may be processed by a computer.

disaster recovery. Any measures instituted to plan for and/or recover from an event that significantly interrupts normal business operations.

discovery. The investigative phase of litigation or other legal proceedings when the parties are required to produce records and information that is or may be relevant to the case.

disposition. The final retention action carried out on a record. This action generally is to destroy the record or transfer it to archival storage for permanent retention.

document. A single item of recorded information, such as a letter, memorandum, report or form, consisting of one or more pages.

document management software. A software application used for managing documents that allows users to store, retrieve, and share them with security and version control.

DoD 5015.2. A technical standard entitled *Design Criteria for Electronic Records Management Software Applications*. Issued by the U.S. Department of Defense in 1997 (and subsequently revised), the standard prescribes functionality requirements for the management of electronic records in RIM software applications.

E

electronic commerce (e-commerce). The execution of business transactions utilizing electronic records in lieu of paper documents. When managed in accordance with national and international standards, computer applications executing the transactions will provide a means of supporting the integrity of the records in a manner that is lawful and agreeable to the various parties.

electronic document management software (EDMS). A type of software that provides for the management of electronic documents, in a variety of forms and formats, contained in an IT system, using computer equipment and software to manage, control, locate, and retrieve information in the system. EDMS systems are designed to capture, route, and organize electronic documents in workgroups and on an enterprise-wide scale. Many of these systems also provide document collaboration, distribution, revision / version control, secure access, and other features.

electronic mail (e-mail). In common usage, an electronic means for communicating information, generally in the form of text messages, through systems that can send, receive, process, and store such messages and their attachments, until they are accessed and disposed of by their recipients or by administrators of the messaging system.

electronic messaging. A general term referring to various forms of communication in electronic form; e.g., e-mail, instant messaging, VoIP, and others.

electronic records. Records that consist of machine-readable, as opposed to human-readable, information. Information recorded in a form that requires a computer or other digital device to process it and that otherwise satisfies the definition of a record.

electronic records management (ERM). A general term referring to any initiatives to manage electronic records in accordance with accepted RIM principles and practices.

electronic records management software (ERMS). Software designed to manage physical and electronic records in accordance with RIM principles. As their core objective, ERMS systems provide a method for managing the life cycle of electronic records from the point at which work-in-process documents are declared as records until their final disposition, under approved retention rules and policies.

electronic records retention. The act of retaining computer-based records in digital format for specified, predetermined periods of time, commensurate with their value, with subsequent disposal or permanent preservation as a matter of organizational policy.

electronic records series. A separate, discrete body of computer data (text files, data files, or image files) maintained within a computer system or application and is logically related, serves a common purpose or function, and requires a separate retention period to provide for its disposition as a matter of organizational policy.

electronic vaulting (e-vaulting). The movement of data over private or public communications lines from a local (primary) computer storage device to a remote (secondary) storage device for the purpose of restoring the data in the event the primary copy is lost or otherwise unavailable.

emulation. The use of a new computer to impersonate an older one.

emulator. A software program that runs on a new computer to make it operate like the old computer.

encryption. A mathematical process performed by special computer software for scrambling plain text and other digital information in such a way that it can only be rendered intelligible by a person with the ability to decrypt the content.

enterprise content management (ECM). A general term that refers to the technologies, tools, and methods used to create, capture, process, store, deliver, and preserve information content, particularly unstructured content, across an enterprise. ECM solutions provide a set of tools and processes for managing all types of content, throughout its life cycle, from creation through updating and distribution to archiving. The solutions are designed to optimize the value of information assets by enhancing the accessibility of all information objects owned by the organization, regardless of type, media format, or storage repository.

enterprise information portal (EIP). See *portal, enterprise information.*

extensible markup language (XML). A set of open (nonproprietary) standards for tagging information so that it can be transmitted via Internet protocols and readily interpreted by disparate computer systems.

F

field. A data element within a record contained in a data file.

file. A general term that denotes a collection of related records that is stored and used together. In most cases, the term is modified by one or more adjectives that indicate the characteristics or type of information the file contains, the applications it serves, or its relationship to other records.

filing. The process of organizing information in accordance with a scheme or system to facilitate its future access and use.

fixed content. Term referring to documents, records, and information in other forms that have attained a static state; that is, the content has been finalized, and no future changes or revisions are anticipated.

floppy disks. Small, platter-shaped, magnetic recording media comprised of flexible substrates, typically used as removable media in personal computer systems. Also termed *diskettes.*

format, file / data. The internal structure of a file, based on the particular coding scheme that has been utilized, which defines the way it is stored and used. Many files may only be viewed or printed using their originating or native application or by an application designed to work with compatible formats. In a digital preservation context, the particular type of coding scheme employed in creating text, data, or image files can have important implications concerning the ease with which digital records can be read and processed over time on a variety of computing devices.

functional retention schedule. A retention schedule on which records series are categorized by the business functions to which they pertain.

functional taxonomy. A taxonomy organized by the major and subordinate business functions or processes of the enterprise.

G

gigabyte (GB). Approximately 1,000 megabytes of computer data.

good faith / bad faith. A legal term referring to the conduct of business affairs in a manner such that adherence to the law—in letter and spirit—can be demonstrated. The obverse, bad faith, refers to conduct that may be viewed with suspicion as to motive and intent. In records retention, conduct involving records disposal actions motivated to suppress or conceal unfavorable evidence may be construed as bad faith, thereby exposing those who committed such acts to legal penalties or criminal prosecution.

H

hard disk. A type of magnetic disk comprised of a rigid aluminum substrate on which information is recorded. Hard disks are the storage media of choice in high-performance computing applications. The disks are usually fixed in their drives, but removable disk systems are also available.

hypertext markup language (HTML). The markup language used for documents on the World Wide Web; the formatting tool that enables text files to be linked and viewed by Web browsers.

I

imaging, electronic. The technology or process that records documents as digitized images on computer storage media for subsequent retrieval and use.

inactive record. A record no longer needed for current business operations and is not consulted frequently, but it is still required for retention for legal, operational, or historical reasons.

information. Data that has been given value through analysis, interpretation, or compilation in a meaningful form.

information life cycle. The life span of a record from its creation or receipt to its final disposition or retention as a historical record.

information life cycle management (ILM). The policies, processes, practices, and tools used to align the business value of information with the most appropriate and cost-effective storage media and other computer resources from the time it is conceived and created through its final disposition. From a RIM perspective, the information life cycle should be governed by retention rules and policies.

information security. Any measures instituted to prevent the unauthorized use or disclosure of confidential, proprietary, or otherwise sensitive business records and information.

information technology (IT). Any tool, device, or process based on technology applied to an information handling function or to any part of the information life cycle. In certain organizations, the name of the department responsible for the management of the computing infrastructure.

instant messaging (IM). A form of electronic communication that provides instant correspondence between two or more users who are all online simultaneously. IM technology allows users to communicate in real time between computers without a record of the conversation. The messages can be captured in record form and retained on an IM server only if special software is installed on the organization's computer networks.

integrity, record. A record that is complete and unaltered. To assure that the integrity of a record will not be compromised, RIM policies and procedures should specify what additions or annotations may be made to a record after it is created, under what circumstances additions or annotations may be authorized, and who is authorized to make them. Any authorized annotation, addition, or deletion to a record should be explicitly indicated and traceable.

Internet. The worldwide collection of computers that provides public access to send, store, and receive electronic information over public networks using the TCP/IP protocol.

intranet. A private Internet network established within an organization behind a firewall for use, depending on access rights, by employees, business partners, customers, or other authorized parties.

ISO 15489. The world's first global standard for records management. It was issued by the International Organization for standardization in 2001 and has been influential in enhancing the global legitimacy of the RIM discipline.

K – L

keyword. A word or phrase taken from the title or text of a document that characterizes its content and facilitating its access and retrieval.

knowledge management (KM). A general term describing initiatives designed to make more efficient use of the human knowledge as well as the recorded information that exists within an organization. Knowledge management emphasizes the value of an organization's intellectual assets—its inventions, customer intelligence, business processes, and other aspects of its knowledge base—for competitive advantage.

legacy system / data. A computer application that has been replaced by newer / newest technology. The term *legacy data* refers to the records remaining in the old system after its replacement.

legal evidence. Oral testimony of witnesses or facts or opinions imputed from physical objects, such as records, that are submitted for introduction into legal proceedings. When thus submitted, the litigants or the court itself may call into question the authenticity of the items.

legal hold. An order typically issued by an organization's legal counsel that prohibits destruction of specified records because such records are or may be relevant to litigation or government investigation, even if disposal is otherwise permitted by the records retention schedules. A failure to adequately preserve such records can lead to charges of spoliation or destruction of evidence which can, in turn, lead to judicially imposed sanctions or criminal prosecution for obstruction of justice.

legal retention research. The process of discovery of all statutes, regulations, consent decrees, and other legally imposed requirements to retain records with which an organization is obliged to comply.

life expectancy. The projected longevity, in years, of various records media, when exposed to specified storage conditions.

limitation of assessment. A type of tax law specifying the period during which revenue authorities are empowered to conduct audits to assess the amount of taxes owed. Although an organization's tax liability may exceed this time period, it is often considered to be the minimum period of retention for tax documentation.

M

magnetic media. A variety of magnetically coated materials on which computer data are recorded and stored; e.g., hard disks, floppy disks, magnetic tapes, etc.

magnetic tape. A thin ribbon or strip of plastic film coated with a magnetic material on which electronic records are recorded; the medium of choice for data backups and other off-line digital storage requirements.

media, record. The various types of storage materials on which organizational information is recorded such as paper, microfilm, photographs, magnetic disks and tapes, and optical disks.

media inspection. Any efforts to determine the integrity of stored electronic records to assure that they remain uncorrupted and are fully usable throughout their prescribed period of retention. Such inspections typically involve a visual examination of media and their housings, as well as the retrieval or playback of recorded information to identify data errors or other problems.

media recopying. The process of periodically copying or recopying electronic records onto new storage media prior to the expiration of the life expectancy of the existing media, for the purpose of ensuring the integrity of the data in conformance with retention requirements.

media stability. The extent to which a given recordkeeping medium retains its physical and chemical properties, or the period of time during which the medium remains useful for its intended purpose. The ability of various records media to retain their information content in usable form for the duration of its period of retention

megabyte (MB). A measure of computer storage capacity equivalent to approximately one million bytes.

metadata. Data that describes other data by providing context for digital content. An integral component of an electronic record, metadata describes how, when, and by whom the record was collected, created, accessed or modified, how it is formatted, transferred, and other attributes.

migration, data. The process of periodically converting electronic records to new file formats and / or new storage media to ensure that the records will remain usable for the entire duration of authorized retention. Conversion of electronic records to new file formats is intended to preserve the usability of recorded information when computer hardware and / or software components are upgraded or replaced. The purpose is to preserve the integrity of the records and to support the ability to retrieve, display, and use them over time. Data migration may occur when hardware and/or software become obsolete, or the practice may be employed to transfer electronic records from one file format to another.

mirroring, disk. A data backup technique in which data recorded on disk drives is copied onto identical media for ease of restoration in the event of system interruption or failure.

MoReq Specification. *Model Requirements for the Management of Electronic Records*; a generic specification for systems designed to manage electronic records issued in 2001 by an agency of the European Commission. The specification is regarded as the most significant European statement issued to date concerning the management of electronic records.

N – O

native application / format. The original application and format used to create an electronic record.

near-line storage. The storage of data on secondary media (rather than online disk drives) that can be accessed by system users without human intervention. In recent years, storage of data on optical platters housed in jukeboxes has been a common methodology for near-line storage.

nonrecords. Information-bearing objects that are excluded from the scope and authority of an organization's RIM program. They are not required to be retained and do not appear on a records retention schedule.

obstruction of justice. A deliberate act designed to interfere with a government investigation or other legal proceeding.

office of record. A department or other organizational entity designated responsible for satisfying the retention requirements of the *record* or *official* copy of a particular record in an organization.

official record. (1) Significant, vital, or important record of continuing value to be protected, managed, and retained according to established retention schedules, Often, but not necessarily an original. (2) Recorded information in any form or medium which is generated or received by an organization and retained as evidence of business decisions and transactions. To attain the status of an official record, a document or other information object must attain this key attribute of evidentiary value. (3) In law, an official record has the legally recognized and legally enforceable quality of establishing some fact.

off-line storage. Storage of electronic records on media located outside the computer system where the primary data are retained. Off-line storage generally occurs on removable media, for purposes of archival retention or data backup.

online backup. The use of high-performance disk drives, as opposed to off-line media, to accomplish data protection objectives. The primary purpose of this method of data backup is to enhance the speed of recovery over what off-line methodologies can provide. Forms of online backup include data mirroring, snapshots, and replication.

online storage. Storage of computer data on media residing in drives housed directly within a computer system, thereby permitting rapid access and continuous processing; data resident on a primary storage device.

open-file backup. Software programs designed to prevent the loss of open-file data; that is, files that remain open and in-use during scheduled backups. When traditional data backup methodologies are employed, these open files may be skipped and remain unprotected. These backup systems are designed to capture open-file data without interrupting applications or continuous system operations.

organizational taxonomy. A standard records arrangement. Enterprise classification and taxonomy systems are based on the concept of organizing and retrieving information whereby documents and records are organized and indexed in a hierarchical structure of major and subordinate categories, from the most general to the most specific—arranged by department and subdepartment.

original record. A primary or first generation record from which copies can be made.

outsourcing. The act or process of subcontracting to vendor service providers those operational functions that are not related to an organization's core business or primary mission.

P – R

permanent record. A record that has been designated for retention for the life of the organization because of its enduring value for business, legal, or historical purposes. As provided by the organization's retention schedule, such records are not authorized for disposal.

petabyte (PB). One thousand terabytes of computer data. This extremely large measure of computer data is often used to refer to the quantity of computer data on a nationwide or global basis.

platform. A general term used to refer to the type of operating systems and other major features of the hardware and software used in a given computing environment.

portable document format (PDF). A proprietary software product of Adobe Systems that is a de facto standard for providing universal access to electronic documents via the Internet. The format preserves all the fonts, formatting, graphics, and color of any source document, regardless of the application used to create it.

portal, enterprise information. Software that is designed to provide a single, browser-based point of access to an organization's information assets, regardless of application, repository, or data type. A portal is a collection of links, content, and services designed to guide users to information they are likely to use. Some approaches target *structured data* residing in databases and legacy applications while others focus on *unstructured information* in desktop and network repositories.

precise retrieval. The ability of a recordkeeping system to consistently deliver to its users exactly the information they request—no more and no less—in response to any properly formulated search query statement. Precise retrieval is the most important measure of recordkeeping system performance.

privacy. The rights of individuals to decide for themselves when, how, and to what extent information about them is collected, used, and disclosed. In an organizational content, privacy encompasses how personal information about employees, customers, or citizens is collected, used, and disseminated, in both paper-based and electronic formats.

purge. Any effort to remove and effect the destruction of expired records or information from a recordkeeping system, usually according to a records retention schedule. When performed under RIM controls, this process occurs systematically, and is sometimes effectuated or otherwise facilitated by special software.

purge days, records. Dedicated workdays when employees are required to review records under their custody and control, and effect their proper disposal or other disposition as authorized by the organization's retention schedules. Such days are sometimes referred to as *records retention days* or by other terms.

record. Recorded information, regardless of physical medium or format, created, received, and maintained as evidence by an organization or person in pursuance of legal obligations or in the transaction of business. Recorded information produced or received in the initiation, conduct, or completion of an institutional or individual activity that comprises content, context, and structure sufficient to provide evidence of that activity, regardless of form or medium.

record copy. The official copy of a record, sometimes the original, that is designated to satisfy an organization's retention requirements.

recorded information. Any and all information created, received, maintained, or used by an organization.

recordkeeping. Any organized or systematic efforts to keep, maintain, and retain organizational records.

recordkeeping system. A manual or automated system in which organizational records are collected, organized, and maintained in a manner that facilitates their retrieval, use, preservation, and disposition.

records inventory. A listing and description of records maintained by an organization and generally used for retention schedule development and other RIM purposes. A fact-finding survey used to determine the types, locations, quantities, equipment, and other aspects of an organization's record-keeping operations.

records and information management (RIM). The systematic control of all records from their creation, or receipt, through their processing, distribution, organization, storage, and retrieval to their ultimate disposition. It consists of the leadership, administration, coordination, and other work required to ensure that adequate records are created to document business functions and meet administrative, legal, and other operational needs; that recordkeeping requirements are analyzed and included when information systems are first developed; that professionally sanctioned techniques are applied throughout the life cycle of records; that records are retained and disposed of based on analysis of their functions and value; and that records of continuing value are preserved and accessible. RIM endeavors to optimize the value of business information by managing it so that it is accurate, timely, complete, cost-effective, accessible, and fully usable for any and all legal and business purposes.

RIM software. Software designed to index, track, and monitor the location and retention status of physical records (i.e., paper and microfilm) throughout its life cycle, and to facilitate its proper disposition under retention rules and policies.

records manager. The individual within an organization who is responsible for systematically managing the recorded information generated and received by the organization. The person responsible for managing an organization's RIM program in accordance with professionally accepted principles and practices.

records retention. A program established and maintained to provide retention periods for records in an organization. Organizational records are retained for specified periods of time, commensurate with their value and in accordance with approved policies and procedures.

records series. A group of similar or related records, kept together as a unit, because they serve a common purpose or function. In retention scheduling, separate, discrete types or categories of records to which individual retention periods are assigned.

recovery, data. The process of restoring computer data from a corrupted source—whether that source has experienced a software malfunction or has suffered a severe physical trauma—by locating files on the disk drives and recreating the file structure so that normal operations can be resumed.

recycling, tapes. The process whereby magnetic tapes are overwritten with new data, generally in conjunction with data backup operations.

reference activity. The frequency with which a given records series is consulted by users for business or other purposes.

regulatory compliance. In RIM, the state of adherence to all government-mandated retention and other recordkeeping requirements with which an organization is obliged to comply.

repository. A storage system designated for electronic records and their associated metadata.

retention-capable. A recordkeeping system designed for retention rules and policies compliance.

retention compliant. A recordkeeping system or environment that can demonstrate full compliance with the organization's records retention schedule, policies, and procedures.

retention functionality. A software program that facilitates compliance with retention rules and policies. Generally, the software must be capable of recognizing inactive or expired data effecting its proper disposition, either by purging the data or moving it to another application or repository for ongoing retention.

retention period. The period of time specified in an organization's retention schedule during which the specified records must be retained as a matter of policy.

retention schedule. A listing of the records series maintained by all or part of an organization, together with retention periods prescribing how long each series must be kept as a matter of policy. May include retention in active office areas, inactive storage areas, and when and if such series may be destroyed or formally transferred to another entity such as an archives for historical preservation.

retrieval. The act or process of obtaining desired information from a recordkeeping system.

S

search query. A statement formulated by a person seeking information from a recordkeeping system defining the information or records sought. To be effective, search queries must be formulated in a manner consistent with the rules of the system and with sufficient specificity and precision such that the system can deliver the requested records accurately.

security, information. Any measures instituted by an organization to prevent the unauthorized use or disclosure of its confidential, proprietary, or otherwise sensitive records and information.

spam. Unsolicited and unwanted e-mail or other electronic messages.

spoliation. The intentional or unintentional destruction or disappearance of documents or other forms of evidence that an organization or its employees knew or should have known to be relevant to ongoing or anticipated legal proceedings. Courts differ in their interpretation of the level of intent required before sanctions for destruction of legal evidence may be warranted.

stability, media. The extent to which a given storage medium retains physical characteristics and chemical properties such that its information content can be expected to remain in usable condition over time.

standard generalized markup language (SGML). A language specification issued by the International Organization for Standardization in 1986 as ISO 8879. The standard provides a means of defining the structure, information content, and presentation format of electronic documents.

statute of limitation. A law specifying the period of time during which a lawsuit or other legal action may be initiated. Statutes of limitation are of high but indirect importance to decisions to retain records that may be relevant to the subject matter covered by the statute, because they indicate the length of time the records may possess legal value and thus may be needed in the resolution of disputes concerning matters to which they relate.

storage area network (SAN). A type of dedicated storage network in which servers and storage devices are connected to permit the centralized management of data regardless of platforms or media. This storage architecture has particular significance for data protection because it simplifies the process of creating mirror data images at remote locations, thus ensuring that remote, up-to-date copies of databases are available in case of interruption at the primary location. In SAN storage environments, if one site is disabled, the entire organization is not affected by the event.

structured data. Data that resides in fixed fields (rows and columns) within a record or file in a database.

T – W

tax hold. An order typically issued by an organization's tax manager that certain tax documentation may not be destroyed, even if such destruction is permitted by the retention schedule, because the records are or may be needed to support a tax audit or the audit period for those records has been extended.

taxonomy. The science of classification according to a predetermined system. The word *taxonomy* comes from the Greek words "taxis," meaning arrangement or division and "nomos" meaning law. In RIM, taxonomies classify information into logical categories that allow users to readily browse through content. See also *classification system*.

technology obsolescence. In digital preservation, the life expectancy of hardware, software, and other components of an electronic recordkeeping system, as related to the retention requirements of the system content. In cases where system obsolescence occurs prior to the expiration of the retention period of the records, special measures must be instituted to ensure the preservation of the records in usable form.

terabyte (TB). Approximately 1,000 GB or one trillion bytes of computer data.

text file. A computer file containing character-coded data and other symbols commonly contained in documents typically created by word processing programs, electronic messaging programs, or other computer software.

text retrieval. A software solution designed to retrieve text-based documents based on words, phrases, or concepts contained in documents typically stored in a text database or other document repository.

timely retrieval. A measure of the interval of time between the time documents are requested by a user and the time the information is delivered to the user. Also termed *access time*.

unstructured data. Data that does not reside in fixed fields of a database; e.g., word processing documents, e-mail, and other non-database records.

virus. A computer program that can insert a copy of itself into another program, thereby resulting in its corruption.

vital record. A record that is indispensable to a mission-critical business operation. A record identified as essential for the continuation of an organization during or following a disaster. Such records are required to recreate the organization's legal and financial status and to support the rights and obligations of employees, customers, shareholders, and citizens. Also known as *mission-critical records.*

voice over Internet protocol (VoIP). A communication technology used for integrating voice mail into an organization's larger messaging environment and computing infrastructure. The technology represents the convergence between voice and data communication systems in which e-mail, voice mail, instant messaging, and other communications systems are integrated. The RIM significance of this technology is that digitized voice mail messages will require management as organizational records under retention and other business rules and policies.

workflow. The automation of structured business processes by the use of special software that provides the capability to define, analyze, and track work processes and transactions, as well as schedule, control, and route electronic documents and other work items in collaborative workgroup environments or throughout the enterprise. In workflow environments, each document, transaction item, or other piece of work moves through a fully documented process that is managed by the software.

Select Bibliography
Classified by Subject Matter

The following list contains the primary sources used in preparing this book. Entries have been selected to provide useful reference sources for anyone interested in the topics listed.

The World Wide Web and all that it comprises, including its content, is highly dynamic and fast disappearing. Nevertheless, where a Web source is used, the URL has generally been provided for the source. However, the life expectancy of these sources may be shorter than that of this book.

Records Management – General

ARMA International. "Companies Will Spend More on RIM in 2004." *The Information Management Journal* 38, no. 1 (January / February 2004).

ARMA International. "FAQs for Corporate Executives and Decision-Makers." Downloaded from www.arma.org. Lenexa, KS: ARMA International, n.d.

Benedon, William. *Records Management.* New York: Prentice Hall, 1969.

Brumm, Eugenia. *Managing Records for ISO 9000 Compliance.* Milwaukee, WI: ASQC Press, 1995.

Cisco, Susan, and Karen Strong. "The Value Added Information Chain." *The Information Management Journal* 33, no. 1 (January 1999).

Dearstyne, Bruce. "Records Management of the Future: Anticipate, Adapt, and Succeed." *The Information Management Journal* 33, no. 10 (October 1999).

_____. "The Information-Proficient Organization: Mastering and Using Information for Strategic Advantage." *Records and Information Management Report* 18/7 (September 2000).

_____. *Effective Approaches for Managing Electronic Records and Archives.* Lanham, MD: Scarecrow Press, 2002.

_____. "Tragedies, Controversies, and Opportunities: Redefining RIM's Role in a Turbulent Time." *The Information Management Journal* 37, no. 2 (March / April 2003).

_____. "Strategic Information Management: Continuing Need, Continuing Opportunities." *The Information Management Journal* 38, no. 2 (March / April 2004).

Kreger, Larry. "Paper and the Information Age." *The Information Management Journal* 33, no. 10 (October 1999).

Lamont, Judith, Lynette Downing, Richard Medina, and Cheryl McKinnon. "Discussion Roundtable: Records Management." *KMWorld*, April 2004.

Launchbaugh, Cynthia. "The Writing on the Wall." *The Information Management Journal* 36, no. 2 (March / April 2002).

_____. "E-Records Management: A Sad State of Affairs or Golden Opportunity?" *The Information Management Journal* 38, no. 3 (May / June 2004).

Miller, Bruce. "Implementing Electronic Recordkeeping." *ProfessioNotes.* Institute of Certified Records Managers (Winter 2004).

Moore, Andy. "Pressure Mounts, But RM Immune to Huge Growth." *KMWorld*, October 2003.

Moore, Connie, Kate Tucker, Susan Wiener, and Stacey Jenkins. *The Role of Electronic Records Management in North American Organizations.* Cambridge, MA: Forrester Consulting, 2004.

Osterman, Michael. "Records Management Requirements in the Enterprise." In *Proceedings of the 48th Annual Conference, ARMA International, Boston, MA, October 19–22, 2003.* Lenexa, KS: ARMA International, 2003.

Pelz-Sharpe, Alan. "Records Management Redux: The Nudge Towards Compliance." *KMWorld*, September 2003.

Robek, Mary, Gerald Brown, and David Stephens. *Information and Records Management*, 4th ed. New York: Glencoe / McGraw-Hill, 1995.

Saffady, William. *Managing Electronic Records*, 3rd ed. Lenexa, KS: ARMA International, 2002.

_____. *Records and Information Management: A Benchmarking Study of Large U.S. Industrial Companies.* Lenexa, KS: ARMA International, 2002.

_____. *Records and Information Management: Fundamentals of Professional Practice.* Lenexa, KS: ARMA International, 2004.

U.S. General Accounting Office. *Information Management: Challenges in Managing and Preserving Electronic Records.* Report No. GAO-02-586. Washington, DC: GAO, June 2002.

_____. *Study of Exemplary Practices in Electronic Records Management.* Washington, DC: GAO, May 1, 2003. Available at www.gao.gov.

Williams, Robert F. *Electronic Records Management Survey: A Call to Action.* Chicago: Cohasset, Inc., 2004. Available from www.cohasset.com.

Content Management

AIIM International. "Enterprise Content Management (ECM) Definitions." Available at www.aiim.org.

ARMA International. "AIIM Study Reveals ECM Drivers." *The Information Management Journal* 39, no. 1 (January / February 2005).

_____. "Google Brings Search to the Desktop." *The Information Management Journal* 39, no. 1 (January / February 2005).

Blair, Barclay. "An Enterprise Content Management Primer." *The Information Management Journal* 39, no. 6 (September / October 2005).

Caldwell, French. "The Future of Knowledge Management." *KMWorld*, October 2004.

Chudnow, Christine. "Key Themes for Document Technologies." *SMS* 6, Issue 4 (2001).

_____. "Enterprise Content Management Makes the Most of What You've Got." *Computer Technology Review* 22, no. 2 (February 2003).

Delphi Group. "Enterprise Portals Bring Risk / Rewards to the Enterprise." Boston: Delphi Group, June 25, 2002.

Duffy, Jan. "Knowledge Management: What Every Information Manager Should Know." *The Information Management Journal* 34, no. 7 (July 2000).

"Enterprise Content Management: Roundtable Discussion." *KMWorld*, February 2004.

Frappaolo, Carl, and Stacie Capshaw. "Knowledge Management Software: Capturing the Essence of Know-how and Knowledge." *The Information Management Journal* 33, no. 7 (July 1999).

Gincel, Richard. "Focusing Enterprise Search." *InfoWorld* 18 October 2004.

Harney, John. "Convergence in Content Management." *KMWorld*, July / August 2004.

Heck, Mike. "Content Control on Demand." *InfoWorld*, 25 October 2004.

_____. "Index Engines Innovates Search." *InfoWorld*, 24 March 2005.

Jones, Jennifer. "Looking Inside." *InfoWorld*, 7 January 2002.

Knorr, Eric. "The New Enterprise Portal." *InfoWorld*, 12 January 2004.

Lamont, Judith. "Adapting ECM to Enterprise Goals." *KMWorld*, March 2004.

Mescan, Suzanne. "Why Content Management Should be Part of Every Organization's Global Strategy." *The Information Management Journal* 38, no. 4 (July / August 2004).

Moore, Andy. "The Universe of Search." *KMWorld*, July / August 2004.

Moore, Cathleen. "Search Gets Organized." *InfoWorld*, 21 June 2004.

_____. "Search Eyes Enterprise Desktops." *InfoWorld*, 13 December 2004.

Pelz-Sharpe, Alan, Chris Harris-Jones, and Angela Ashenden. "The Need for Portals." *KMWorld*, November / December 2001.

Pelz-Sharpe, Alan. "The Next Generation of Search." *KMWorld*, January 2002.

Pelz-Sharpe, Alan, and Chris Harris-Jones. "Enterprise Content Management: Is Anything New?" *KMWorld*, May 2002.

Pemberton, Michael. "KM & RM: Oil & Water?" *The Information Management Journal* 38, no. 3 (May / June 2004).

Roberts-Witt, Sara. "Making Sense of the Portal Pandemonium." *Knowledge Management* (July 1999).

Rose, Jerrold. "The Joys of Enterprise Portals." *The Information Management Journal* 37, no. 5 (September / October 2003).

Ruber, Peter. "Framing a Portal Strategy." *Knowledge Management* (May 1999.)

_____. "Portals on a Mission." *Knowledge Management* (April 2000).

Saffady, William. *Knowledge Management: A Manager's Briefing.* Prairie Village, KS: ARMA International, 1998.

_____. *Electronic Document Imaging: Technology, Applications, Implementation.* Lenexa, KS: ARMA International, 2001.

Stewart, Thomas. "The Case Against Knowledge Management." *Business 2.0*, February 2002.

Swartz, Nikki. "The Wonder Years of Knowledge Management." *The Information Management Journal* 37, no. 3 (May / June 2003).

"Through the Looking Glass: A Progress Report on the Enterprise Portal." *Knowledge Management* (February 2001).

Trowbridge, Dave. "Welcome to the Profit Portal." *Computer Technology Review* 20, no. 4 (April 2000).

Watson, James, and Joe Fenner. "Understanding Portals." *The Information Management Journal* 34, no. 7 (July 2000).

"What's Ahead for ECM." *KMWorld*, March 2004.

Woods, Eric. "The Next Generation Search Market." *KMWorld*, November / December 2002.

————. "Knowledge Management 2002-2003: The End of the Beginning." *KMWorld*, January 2003.

Yakel, Elizabeth. "Knowledge Management: The Archivist's and Records Manager's Perspective." *The Information Management Journal* 33, no. 7 (July 2000).

Zimmerman, Kim Ann. "Document Management Targets the Enterprise and Beyond." *KMWorld*, September 2002.

Digital Preservation

Allen, Edith Gaylord. "After the Records Inventory and Retention Decisions: Implementation Issues in Electronic Records Management." In *Proceedings of the 46th Annual Conference, ARMA International, Montreal, Quebec, Canada, September 30–October 3, 2001.* Prairie Village, KS: ARMA International, 2001.

American National Standards Institute. ANSI/NAPM IT9.23-1996, *American National Standard for Imaging Materials – Polyester Base Magnetic Tape – Storage.* Washington, DC: ANSI, 1996.

ARMA International. "A Digital Archiving Standard." *The Information Management Journal* 36, no. 6 (November / December 2002).

————. "Will PDF Prevent a Digital Dark Age?" *The Information Management Journal* 37, no. 3 (May / June 2003).

Arp, Charles, and Joseph Dickman. "Information Preservation: Changing Roles." *The Information Management Journal* 36, 6 (November / December 2002).

Brown, Karen E. K., and Frey, Franziska. "How Long Will It Last?: Life Expectancy of Information Media." In *Proceedings of the 44th Annual Conference, ARMA International, Cincinnati, OH, October 17–20, 1999.* Prairie Village, KS: ARMA International, 1999.

Commission on Preservation and Access and Research Libraries Group. *Preserving Digital Information: Report of the Task Force on Archiving of Digital Information.* Washington, DC: Commission on Preservation and Access and Research Libraries Group, 1996.

Day, Michael. "Extending Metadata for Digital Preservation." Available at www.ariadne.ac.uk/issue9/metadata/ (accessed February 4, 2006).

De Witt, Donald, ed. *Going Digital: Strategies for Access, Preservation, and Conversion of Collections to a Digital Format.* Binghamton, NY: The Haworth Press Inc., 1998.

Dollar, Charles M. "Selecting Storage Media for Long-Term Access to Digital Records." *The Information Management Journal* 33, no. 7 (July 1999).

_____. *Authentic Electronic Records: Strategies for Long-term Access.* Chicago: Cohasset Associates, Inc., 1999.

Duranti, Luciana, and Marc Fresko. "Preserving Electronic Records: Research Findings and Practical Approaches." In *Proceedings of the 48th Annual Conference, ARMA International, Boston, MA, October 19–22, 2003.* Lenexa, KS: ARMA International, 2003.

Ghetu, Magia. "Two Professions, One Goal." *The Information Management Journal* 38, no. 3 (May / June 2004).

Hunter, Gregory S. *Preserving Digital Information: A How-To-Do-It Manual.* New York: Neal-Schuman Publishers, 2000.

_____. "The Digital Future: A Look Ahead." *The Information Management Journal* 36, no. 1 (January / February 2002).

Kenney, Anne, and Nancy McGovern. "Preservation Risk Management for Web Resources." *The Information Management Journal* 36, no. 5 (September / October 2002).

McKemmish, Sue, and Dagmar Parer. "Towards Frameworks for Standardizing Recordkeeping Metadata." *Archives and Manuscripts* 26, no. 1 (1998).

Moore, Fred. "Long-Term Data Preservation." *Storage Inc.,* (Quarter 3 1999).

_____. "Archival Data Has a New Mission: Critical." *Computer Technology Review* 23, no. 2 (February 2003).

Phillips, John T. "Should PDF be Used for Archiving Electronic Records?" *The Information Management Journal* 35, no. 1 (January 2001).

_____. "The Challenge of Web Site Records Preservation." *The Information Management Journal* 35, no. 1 (January / February 2003).

Rothenberg, Jeff. "Ensuring the Longevity of Digital Documents." *Scientific American,* January 1995.

_____. *Avoiding Technological Quicksand: Finding a Viable Technical Foundation for Digital Preservation.* A Report to the Council on Library & Information Resources (CLIR). January 1999. Available from www.clir.org/pubs/abstract/pub77.html (accessed February 4, 2006).

_____. "Preservation of the Times." *The Information Management Journal* 36, no. 3 (March / April 2002).

United Kingdom National Archives. Digital Preservation. Available from www.pro.gov.uk/about/preservation/digital/default.htm (accessed February 4, 2006).

U.S. National Aeronautics and Space Administration. *Reference Model for an Open Archival System – CCSDA 650.0-R-1.* Washington, DC: NASA, 1999.

Van Bogart, John. *Archival Stability of Digital Storage Media.* St. Paul, MN: National Media Laboratory, 1995.

_____. *Magnetic Tape Storage and Handling: A Guide for Libraries and Archives.* St. Paul, MN: National Media Laboratory, 1995.

_____. *1996 Media Stability Studies.* St. Paul, MN: National Media Laboratory, 1996.

Document Classification / Taxonomy

Bruno, Denise, and Heather Richmond. "The Truth About Taxonomies." *The Information Management Journal* 37, no. 2 (March / April 2003).

Delphi Group. Information Intelligence: Intelligent Classification and the Enterprise Taxonomy Practice. BPM2005 Market Milestone Report. A Delphi Group White Paper, 2005. Available from www.delphigroup.com (accessed February 4, 2006).

Feldman, Susan. "The High Cost of Not Finding Information." *KMWorld*, March 2004.

_____. "Why Categorize?" *KMWorld*, October 2004.

Graef, Jean. "Managing Taxonomies Strategically." *Montague Institute Review* (March 2001).

Lamont, Judith. "Dynamic Taxonomies: Keeping Up With Changing Content." *KMWorld*, May 2003.

Lubbes, Kirk. "Automatic Categorization: How It Works, Related Issues, and Impacts on Records Management." *The Information Management Journal* 35, no. 10 (October 2001).

_____. "So You Want to Implement Automatic Categorization." *The Information Management Journal* 37, no. 2 (March / April 2003).

Meyers, J. "Automatic Categorization, Taxonomies, and the World of Information: Can't Live With Them, Can't Live Without Them." *E-DOC Magazine*, November / December 2002.

Moore, Cathleen. "Bringing Structure to Data." *InfoWorld*, 20 September 2004.

Schewe, Donald. "Classifying Electronic Documents: A New Paradigm." *The Information Management Journal* 36, no. 2 (March / April 2002).

Venkata, Ramana. "The Importance of Hierarchy Building in Managing Unstructured Data." *KMWorld*, March 2002.

Woods, Eric. "The Corporate Taxonomy: Creating a New Order." *KMWorld*, July / August 2004.

Electronic Records Retention / Information Life Cycle Management

Achenbach, Joel. "The Too-Much-Information Age." *Washington Post*, 12 March 1999.

Chudnow, Christine. "No Such Thing as Delete: Information Life Cycle Management." *SMS* 8, Issue 5 (2004).

_____. "Active Archiving." *Computer Technology Review* 22, no. 2 (February 2002).

EMC. "Making the Case for Information Lifecycle Management." Available at www.emc.com/ilm.

Fisch, Michael. "Top 10 Things You Should Know About Information Life Cycle Management." *Explorer*. Wellesley, MA: The Clipper Group, May 11, 2004.

Geis, Jim. "The ILM Socialization Experiment." *SMS* 9, Issue 1 (2005).

General Counsel Roundtable. *Attributes of an Effective Document Retention Program.* Washington, DC: Corporate Executive Board, January 2001.

Moore, Fred. "Digital Data's Future: You Ain't Seen Nothin' Yet." *Computer Technology Review* 20, no. 10 (October 2000).

_____. "Data Growth Outruns Ability to Manage It." *Computer Technology Review* 22, no. 2 (February 2002).

_____. "Sizes of Rich Media Files Are Changing the Rules." *Computer Technology Review* 22, no. 10 (October 2002).

_____. "Cradle to Grave Storage Management Now a Reality." *Computer Technology Review* 23, no. 1 (January 2003).

_____. "Archival Data Has a New Mission: Critical." *Computer Technology Review* 23, no. 2 (February 2003).

Rhodes, Glenn. "How to Achieve Significant Savings Through Tiered Storage Implementation." *SMS* 8, Issue 2 (2003).

Saffady, William. *The Document Life Cycle: A White Paper*, 1996.

_____. *Records and Information Management: A Benchmarking Study of Large U.S. Industrial Companies.* Lenexa, KS: ARMA International, 2002.

Shaath, Kamel. "The Present and Future of Policy-based Storage Management." *SMS* 7, Issue 5 (2002).

Simpson, David. "Cut Your Storage Management Costs." *Datamation*, November 1996.

Skupsky, Donald. *Legal Requirements for Information Technology Systems.* Greenwood Village, CO: Information Requirements Clearinghouse, 1997.

Stephens, David, and Roderick Wallace. *Electronic Records Retention: New Strategies for Data Life Cycle Management.* Lenexa, KS: ARMA International, 2003.

Straub, Joe. "The Digital Tsunami: A Perspective on Data Storage." *The Information Management Journal* 38, no. 1 (January / February 2004).

Vellante, David. "In Search of Storage ROI: Part 3 – The TCO Trap." *SMS* 7, Issue 4 (2002).

Wang, Paul. "Understanding Online Archiving." *SMS* 5, Issue 11 (2000).

Whiting, Rick. "Tower of Power: IT Managers Brace for the Inevitable: Petabyte-Size Databases." *InformationWeek*, 11 February 2002.

E-mail / Electronic Messaging

ARMA International. "Instant Messaging Goes Corporate." *The Information Management Journal* 37, no. 4 (July / August 2003).

_____. "IM the Focus of Investigations." *The Information Management Journal* 38, no. 1 (January / February 2004).

_____. "President Bush Signs Law to Can Spam." *The Information Management Journal* 38, no. 1 (January / February 2004).

_____. "Worldwide War on Spam Continues." *The Information Management Journal* 38, no. 2 (March / April 2004).

_____. "Interoperability – At Least for Business." *The Information Management Journal* 38, no. 5 (September / October 2004).

_____. "Companies Must Manage IM, Study Says." *The Information Management Journal* 39, no. 1 (January / February 2005).

Arnette, Greg. "Killer App: New E-mail Requirements are Driving Significant Technology Purchases." *Storage Inc.* (Quarter 4 2002).

Boutin, Paul. "Can E-Mail Be Saved?" *InfoWorld*, 19 April 2004.

Carlisle, Diane. "Managing E-mail Overload." *The Information Management Journal* 38, no. 2 (March / April 2004).

Cavanaugh, Christina. *Managing Your E-Mail: Thinking Outside the Box.* New York: John Wiley & Sons, 2003.

Chudnow, Christine. "Business Dilemma: Email Retention Policy." *Computer Technology Review* 23, no. 1 (January 2003).

Cisco, Susan, and Bob Guz. "Managing Electronic Messages: Policies and Technologies." In *Proceedings of the 48th Annual Conference, ARMA International, Boston, MA, October 19–22, 2003.* Lenexa, KS: ARMA International, 2003.

Claburn, Thomas. "Policies Lag E-Mail's Popularity." *InformationWeek,* 12 July 2004.

Cunningham, Patrick. "IM: Invaluable New Business Tool or Records Management Nightmare?" *The Information Management Journal* 37, no. 6 (November / December 2003).

Duhon, Bryant. "Email Chaos." *E-DOC Magazine,* November / December 2001.

Erlanger, Leon. "The 411 on VoIP." *InfoWorld,* 7 June 2004.

_____. "Calling All VoIP Apps." *InfoWorld,* 16 August 2004.

Flynn, Nancy, and Randolph Kahn. *E-Mail Rules: A Business Guide to Managing Policies, Security, and Legal Issues for E-Mail and Digital Communications.* New York: American Management Association, 2003.

Franklin, Curtis, Brian Chee, and Mike Heck. "Getting Serious About Enterprise IM." *InfoWorld,* 23 February 2004.

Harney, John. "Managing the Message." *KMWorld,* April 2003.

Levitt, Mark, and Robert Mahowald. "E-mail Retention Trends and Challenges." *KMWorld,* January 2003.

Moerdler, Mark. "Managing Organizational E-mail." *KMWorld,* March 2005.

Mojica, Peter. "Simply Speaking: Messaging as a Corporate Record." *KMWorld,* March 2005.

Montaña, John. *Legal Obstacles to E-Mail Message Destruction.* Pittsburgh, PA: ARMA International Educational Foundation, 2003.

_____. "Email, Voice Mail, and Instant Messaging: A Legal Perspective." *The Information Management Journal* 38, no. 1 (January / February 2004).

National Association of Securities Dealers. "Notice to Members 03-33." Baltimore, MD: NASD, July 2003.

Osterman, Michael. "Records Management Requirements in the Enterprise." In *Proceedings of the 48th Annual Conference, ARMA International, Boston, MA, October 19–22, 2003.* Lenexa, KS: ARMA International, 2003.

Porter, Alan. "A Ten-Step Strategy for Defending Your Company's E-Mail System." *Disaster Recovery Journal* (Winter 2004).

Rhinehart, Craig. "E-mail Management: Key to Business Processes." *KMWorld,* March 2005.

Rosenfelt, Michael. "Never a Good Time to be Without E-Mail." *Disaster Recovery Journal* (Spring 2004).

Schwartz, Ephraim. "Rethinking Message Storage." *InfoWorld*, 14 June 2004.

Sink, Cliff. "E-Mail Management: How to Succeed Step-by-Step." *KMWorld*, March 2004.

Symons, George. "Take Control of E-mail: Protect the Surging Tide." *SMS* 8, Issue 4 (2003).

Tolson, Bill. "Controlling the Flood: A Look at E-mail Storage and Management Challenges." *Computer Technology Review* 22, no. 9 (September 2002).

Varchaver, Nicholas. "The Perils of E-mail." *Fortune*, 17 February 2003.

Worthen, Ben. "Message Therapy." *CIO*, 15 January 2005.

Worthy, Susan. "The Case for E-mail Archiving." *KMWorld*, March 2005.

Information Access, Privacy, and Security

ARMA International. "Survey Assesses the State of Information Security Worldwide." *The Information Management Journal* 38, no. 1 (January / February 2004).

_____. "California Passes Online Privacy Bill." *The Information Management Journal* 38, no. 5 (September / October 2004).

_____. "U.S., Canadian Firms Have Different Views of Privacy." *The Information Management Journal* 38, no. 5 (September / October 2004).

_____. "Businesses Improve Cyber Security." *The Information Management Journal* 38, no. 6 (November / December 2004).

Baker, Stephen, et al. "Europe's Privacy Cops: The EU Wants Others to Protect Electronic Data as It Does." *Business Week*, 2 November 1998.

Budden, Michael. "Safeguarding Trade Secrets." *Security Management* (March 1997).

Clayton, Gary. "Safeguarding the World's New Currency." *The Information Management Journal* 36, no. 3 (May / June 2002).

Cunningham, Patrick. "Are Cookies Hazardous to Your Privacy?" *The Information Management Journal* 36, no. 3 (May / June 2002).

Duff, Wendy, Wally Smieliauskas, and Holly Yoos. "Protecting Privacy." *The Information Management Journal* 35, no. 4 (April 2001).

Electronic Privacy Information Center and Privacy International. *Privacy and Human Rights 2000: An International Survey of Privacy Laws and Developments.* Available at www.privacy.org/pi/survey/phr2000/ (accessed February 11, 2006).

Fjetland, Michael. "Global Commerce and the Privacy Clash." *The Information Management Journal* 36, no. 1 (January / February 2002).

Groves, Shanna. "Protecting Your Identity." *The Information Management Journal* 36, no. 3 (May / June 2002).

_____. The Unlikely Heroes of Cyber Security." *The Information Management Journal* 37, no. 3 (May / June 2003).

Haller, Susan. "Privacy: What Every Manager Should Know." *The Information Management Journal* 36, no. 3 (May / June 2002).

Hoffman, M. "ISO 17799: A Standard for Information Security Management." London, Ontario, Canada: The Info-Tech Research Group, 2003.

Holmes, Allan. "Riding the California Privacy Wave." *CIO*, 15 January 2005.

Hulme, George. "Future Security." *InformationWeek*, 25 November 2002.

Lemieux, Victoria. "Two Approaches to Managing Information Risks." *The Information Management Journal* 38, no. 5 (September / October 2004).

_____. *Managing Risks for Records and Information*. Lenexa, KS: ARMA International, 2004.

McAdams, Arthur. "Security and Risk Management: A Fundamental Business Issue." *The Information Management Journal* 38, no. 4 (July / August 2004).

Patton, Susannah. "Privacy Is Your Business." *CIO*, 1 June 2004.

Pemberton, Michael. "Chief Privacy Officer: Your Next Career Move?" *The Information Management Journal* 36, no. 3 (May / June 2002).

Phillips, John. "Privacy vs. Cybersecurity." *The Information Management Journal* 36, no. 3 (May / June 2002).

Reynolds, John. "European Union Privacy Directive Enters Into Force." *Messaging Magazine*, January / February 1999.

Roberts, Paul. "The Shaky State of Security." *InfoWorld*, 26 July 2004.

Robinson, Stephen, and Linda Volonino. *Principles and Practices of Information Security*. Upper Saddle River, NJ: Pearson Prentice Hall, 2004.

Schulz, Greg, and David O'Leary. "Securing Storage Networks." *Disaster Recovery Journal* (Spring 2004).

Stephens, David O. "Document Security and International Records Management." *Records Management Quarterly* (October 1997).

_____. "Data Protection in Europe." *Records Management Quarterly* (October 1998).

Swartz, Nikki. "The Lock Down on Data Has Begun." *The Information Management Journal* 37, no. 5 (September / October 2003).

_____. "The Electronic Records Conundrum." *The Information Management Journal* 38, no. 1 (January / February 2004).

_____. "Offshoring Privacy." *The Information Management Journal* 38, no. 5 (September / October 2004).

_____. "The World Moves Toward Freedom of Information." *The Information Management Journal* 38, no. 6 (November / December 2004).

Ungerman, Mark. "Sign Up For a Corporate Information Security Policy." *SMS* 9, Issue 1 (2004).

Worlton, Amy. "Overview of the EU Privacy Directive." Wiley Rein & Fielding LLP, 2002. Available at www.wrf.com (accessed February 6, 2006.)

Yager, Tom. "Security Lockdown." *InfoWorld*, 14 July 2003.

Information Protection / Disaster Recovery

ARMA International. "Survey Reveals Disaster Recovery Expectations and Reality." *The Information Management Journal* 37, no. 6 (November / December 2003).

Aronson, Steve. "The Crucial Role of Vital Records in Business Continuity / Disaster Recovery." *SMS* 8, Issue 1 (2003).

Blair, Jeanne. "Re-centralizing Backup Management." *SMS* 7, Issue 4 (2002).

Buffington, Jason. "New Acronyms for Disaster Recovery." *SMS* 8, Issue 3 (2003).

Chudnow, Christine. "Issues in Online Backup." *SMS* 8, Issue 2 (2003).

Croy, Michael. "The Business Value of Data." *Disaster Recovery Journal* (Summer 2004).

Ferelli, Mark. "What Has the IT Industry Really Learned from 9/11?" *SMS* 7, Issue 4 (2002).

Ganong, Ray. "The Emergence of E-Vaulting." *The Information Management Journal* 37, no. 1 (January / February 2003).

Groves, Shanna. "Records Under Fire." *The Information Management Journal* 36, no. 6 (November / December 2002).

Hague, David R. "How NFPA 232 Can Help You Protect Your Records." *NFPA Journal* (March / April 2002).

Hannestad, Stephen E. "Trial by Fire: Protecting Federal Records." *NFPA Journal* (March / April 2002).

Harless, Eric. "Dissecting Disaster Recovery Solutions." *SMS* 8, Issue 3 (2003).

Jones, Virginia. "Protecting Records: What the Standards Tell Us." *The Information Management Journal* 37, no. 2 (March / April 2003).

"Learning from Disaster: Vital Records in Turbulent Times." *inFocus*, December 2001.

Levine, Ron. "Rapid Database Recovery." *SMS* 8, Issue 3 (2003).

Moore, Fred. "Backup is Important, Recovery is Everything." *Computer Technology Review* 22, no. 3 (March 2002).

National Fire Protection Association. *NFPA 75 – Standard for the Protection of Electronic Computer / Data Processing Equipment.* Quincy, MA: NFPA, 1999 edition.

_____. *NFPA 232 – Standard for the Protection of Records.* Quincy, MA: NFPA, 2000 edition.

Nelson, April. "Open File Solution." *SMS* 7, Issue 4 (2002).

O'Leary, Ted. "Paper Amid the Rubble." *E-DOC Magazine*, November / December 2001.

Reinert, Jim. "Data Recovery Completes Disaster Recovery." *Disaster Recovery Journal* (Spring 2004).

Stephens, David. "Protecting Records in the Face of Chaos, Calamity, and Cataclysm." *The Information Management Journal* 37, no. 1 (January / February 2003).

International Records Management

Barata, Kimberly, and Piers Cain. "Records Management Toolkits from Across the Pond." *The Information Management Journal* 37, no. 4 (July / August 2003).

eEurope Action Plan, 2002. Available at http://europa.eu.int/information_ society/eeurope/2002/action_plan/index_en.htm (accessed February 11, 2006).

International Organization for Standardization. ISO 15489-1:2001. *International Standard: Information and Documentation – Records Management – Part 1 – General.* Geneva, Switzerland: ISO, 2001. Available from www.iso.ch/ iso/en/prods-services/ISOstore/store.html.

National Archives of Australia. DIRKS Methodology. Available from www.naa.gov.au/recordkeeping/dirks/summary.html (accessed February 8, 2005).

Public Record Office Victoria. *Management of Electronic Records – PROS 99/007.* Australia: Public Record Office of Victoria, April 2000.

_____. Victorian Electronic Records Strategy (VERS). Victoria, Australia. Available at www.prov.vic.gov.au/vers (accessed February 8, 2006).

Sletten, Laurie. "Lessons from Down Under: Records Management in Australia." *The Information Management Journal* 33, no. 1 (January 1999).

Standards Australia. *Australian Standard 4390: Records Management.* Sydney, New South Wales, Australia, February 1996.

Stephens, David. "Towards a Global Theory of Records Management." *Records Management Quarterly* (October 1992).

_____. *Information Management for Multinational Corporations: A Manager's Briefing.* Lenexa, KS: ARMA International, 1999.

Waldron, Martin. "Adopting Electronic Records Management: European Strategic Initiatives." *The Information Management Journal* 38, no. 4 (July / August 2004).

Records Management – Legal Aspects

Allman, Thomas. "Fostering a Compliance Culture: The Role of *The Sedona Guidelines.*" *The Information Management Journal* 39, no. 2 (March / April 2005).

Cogar, Rae, and Frank Moore, "The Sarbanes-Oxley Act: How Does It Affect Records Managers and Records Management Programs?" In *Proceedings of the 47th Annual Conference, ARMA International, New Orleans, LA, September 29–October 1, 2002.* Prairie Village, KS: ARMA International, 2002.

Colledge, Gillian, and Michael Cliff. "The Implications of the Sarbanes-Oxley Act: It's Time to Take Records Management Seriously." *KMWorld,* September 2003.

Dietel, J. Edwin. "Recordkeeping Integrity: Assessing Records' Content After Enron." *The Information Management Journal* 27, no. 3 (May / June 2003).

Juhnke, Deborah. "Electronic Discovery in 2010." *The Information Management Journal* 37, no. 6 (November / December 2003).

Leahy, Patrick J. "Preserving the Paper (and Electronic) Trail." *The Information Management Journal* 37, no. 1 (January / February 2003).

Marlin, Steve. "Gaining Strength from Sarbox." *InformationWeek,* 21 March 2005.

Marobella, Julie Rahal. "The World Is Watching." *The Information Management Journal* 39, no. 2 (March / April 2005).

Montaña, John. "Sarbanes-Oxley One Year Later." *The Information Management Journal* 37, no. 4 (July / August 2003).

_____. "The End of the Ostrich Defense." *The Information Management Journal* 39, no. 1 (January / February 2005).

Moore, Cathleen, and Ephraim Schwartz. "Sorting Through SarbOx." *InfoWorld,* 14July 2003.

Moore, Frank, and Nikki Swartz. "Keeping an Eye on Sarbanes-Oxley." *The Information Management Journal* 37, no. 6 (November / December 2003).

Pelz-Sharpe, Alan. "Records Management Redux: The Nudge Towards Compliance," *KMWorld*, September 2003

Rahal, Julie. "What Role Will Content Technologies Play in This Era of Regulatory Compliance?" *KMWorld*, June 2004.

Sarbanes-Oxley Act. Public Law 107-2004. 116 Stat. 745 (2002).

Sedona Conference. *Sedona Guidelines: The Best Practice Guidelines & Commentary for Managing Information & Records in the Electronic Age.* Sedona, AZ: The Sedona Conference, 2004. Available at www.thesedonaconference.org (accessed February 11, 2006).

Swartz, Nikki. "What Every Business Needs to Know About HIPAA." *The Information Management Journal* 37, no. 2 (March / April 2003).

Tillman, Bob. "Who's Afraid of Sarbanes-Oxley?" *The Information Management Journal* 37, no. 6 (November / December 2003).

United Nations Commission on International Trade Law. UNCITRAL *Model Law on Electronic Commerce with Guide to Enactment,* 1996. Available at www.uncitral.org (accessed February 11, 2006.).

_____. *Draft Guide to Enactment of the UNCITRAL Model Law on Electronic Signatures.* May 17, 2001. Available at www.uncitral.org (accessed February 11, 2006).

Records Management Program Development

AIIM/Cohasset. *Realizing the Need and Putting the Key Components in Place to Getting It Right in Records Management,* White Paper, 2002. Available from www.cohasset.com.

ARMA International. *ARMA e-Assessment for RIM Programs.* Developed by ARMA International and NetDiligence® Online. Available from www.arma.org/bookstore.

_____. "Companies Will Spend More on RIM in 2004." *The Information Management Journal* 38, no. 1 (January / February 2004).

Crockett, Margaret, and Janet Foster. "Using ISO 15489 as an Audit Tool." *The Information Management Journal* 38, no. 4 (July / August 2004).

International Organization for Standardization. ISO 15489-1:2001. *International Standard: Information and Documentation – Records Management: Part 1 – General.* Geneva, Switzerland: ISO, 2001. Available from www.iso.ch/iso/en/prods-services/ISOstore/store.html.

_____. ISO 15489-1:2001. *International Standard: Information and Documentation – Records Management: Part 2 – Technical Report.* Geneva, Switzerland: ISO, 2001. Available from www.iso.ch/iso/en/prods-services/ISOstore/store.html.

McLean, Bob. "The ISO 15489 Imperative." *The Information Management Journal* 36, no. 6 (November / December 2002).

Meagher, Robert. "The IM Building Blocks." *The Information Management Journal* 36, no. 1 (January / February 2002).

Moore, Connie, Kate Tucker, Susan Wiener, and Stacey Jenkins. *The Role of Electronic Records Management in North American Organizations.* Cambridge, MA: Forrester Consulting, 2004.

Robek, Mary F., Gerald F. Brown, and David O. Stephens. *Information and Records Management,* 4th ed. New York: Glencoe/McGraw-Hill, 1995.

Saffady, William. "The Value of Records Management." *InfoPro,* December1999.

_____. *Cost Analysis Concepts and Methods for Records Management Projects.* Prairie Village, KS: ARMA International, 1998.

Sellen, Abigail, and Richard Harper. *The Myth of the Paperless Office.* Cambridge, MA: MIT Press, 2002.

Stephens, David O. "The World's First International Standard for Records Management." *The Information Management Journal* 35, no. 7 (July 2001).

Records Retention – General

Dietel, Edwin. "Improving Corporate Performance Through Records Audits." *The Information Management Journal* 34, no. 4 (April 2000).

_____. *Designing an Effective Records Retention Compliance Program.* Vol. 3, Corporate Compliance Series. Egan, MN: West Group, 1993.

General Counsel Roundtable. *Attributes of an Effective Document Retention Program.* Washington, DC: Corporate Executive Board, 2001.

Kahn, Randolph. "Records Management & Compliance: Making the Connection." *The Information Management Journal* 38, no. 3 (May / June 2004).

Lee, Jim. "Reduce the Cost of Compliance: Database Archiving and Information Lifecycle Management. *SMS* 8, Issue 5 (2003).

Saffady, William. *The Document Life Cycle: A White Paper,* 1996.

_____. *Records and Information Management: A Benchmarking Study of Large U.S. Industrial Companies.* Lenexa, KS: ARMA International, 2002.

Skupsky, Donald. *Records Retention Procedures.* Greenwood Village, CO: Information Requirements Clearinghouse, 1994.

Stephens, David. "Making Records Retention Decisions: Practical and Theoretical Considerations." *Records Management Quarterly* (January 1988).

Williams, Robert. *Electronic Records Management Survey: A Call to Action.* Chicago: Cohasset, Inc., 2004. Available from www.cohasset.com.

Records Retention – Legal Aspects

Allman, Thomas. "Fostering a Compliance Culture: The Role of *The Sedona Guidelines.*" *The Information Management Journal* 39, no. 2 (March / April 2005).

ARMA International Educational Foundation. "Legal Holds and Spoliation: Identifying a Checklist of Considerations that Trigger the Duty to Preserve." Lenexa, KS: ARMA International. Available from www.arma.org/bookstore.

Austin, Robert. "Ten-thousand Reasons for Records Management." *Records Management Quarterly* (July 1985).

Carlucci v. Piper Aircraft Corp., 102 F.R.D. 472 (S.D. Florida, 1984).

Cogar, Rae. "Case Law on Records Management." *Digital Discovery and e-Evidence* 2, no. 4 (April 2002). Silver Spring, MD: Pike & Fisher, Inc.

Egan, Christopher. "Arthur Andersen's Evidence Destruction Policy: Why Current Spoliation Policies Do Not Adequately Protect Investors." *Texas Tech Law Review* 34 (2002).

Fedders, John, and Lauryn H. Guttenplan, "Document and Destruction: Practical, Legal and Ethical Considerations," *The Notre Dame Lawyer* 56, no. 1 (October 1980).

Federal Sentencing Guidelines. U.S.S.G. Section 8B2.1 (Revised as of November 1, 2004).

Heller Ehrman LLP. "Retaining Business Records: Directives and Implications of the Sarbanes-Oxley Act of 2002 and Lessons of the Arthur Andersen Criminal Prosecution of Destruction of Its Enron Audit Documents." Heller Ehrman White & McAuliffe LLP, August 2002.

In re Prudential Ins. Co. of Amer. Sales Practices Litig., 962 F.Supp.450,497 (D.N.J. 1997).

Isaza, John. "Know When to Hold 'Em, When to Destroy 'Em." *The Information Management Journal* 39, no. 2 (March / April 2005).

LeBoeuf, Lamb, Greene & MacRae, LLP. "Effect of Sarbanes-Oxley on Document Retention Policies." May 30, 2003. Available from www.llgm.com.

Lewy v. Remington Arms Co., Inc., 836 F.2d 1104 (8th Circuit, 1988).

Prudential Ins. Co. of America Sales Litig., 169 F.R.D. (D.N.J., 1997)

Rambus Inc. v. Infineon Technologies. 220 F.R.D. 264, 282 (E.D. Va, 2004).

Scheindlin, Shira, and Kanchana Wangkeo. "Electronic Discovery in the Twenty-First Century." 11 Mich. Telecomm. *Tech. L. Rev.* 71 (2004). Available from http://mttlr.org/voleleven/scheindlin.pdf.

Sedona Conference. *Sedona Guidelines: The Best Practice Guidelines & Commentary for Managing Information & Records in the Electronic Age.* Sedona, AZ: The Sedona Conference, 2004. Available at www.thesedonaconference.org (accessed February 11, 2006).

Skupsky, Donald. *Recordkeeping Requirements.* Greenwood Village, CO: Information Requirements Clearinghouse, 1994.

————. *Records Retention Procedures.* Greenwood Village, CO: Information Requirements Clearinghouse, 1994.

————. *Records and Information Management: The Court Cases.* Greenwood Village, CO: Information Requirements Clearinghouse, 1994.

Stephens, David. "Lies, Corruption, and Document Destruction." *The Information Management Journal* 36, no. 5 (September / October 2002).

Stevenson v. Union Pacific. 354 F.3d739 (8th Cir. 2004).

U.S. Security and Exchange Commission. *Final Rule: Retention of Records Relevant to Audits and Reviews,* Release No. 33-8180; 34-47241. Modified January 27, 2003. Available from www.sec.gov/rules/final/33-8180.htm (accessed February 11, 2006).

U.S. v. Arthur Andersen, LLP. 374 F.3d281 (5th Cir. 2004).

"Zubulake IV." *Zubulake v. UBS Warburg,* LLC. 220 F.R.D. 212, 217 (S.D.N.Y.2003)

"Zubulake V." *Zubulake v. UBS Warburg,* LLC. No. 02 Civ. 1243 (SAS), 2004 WL 1620866, 12 (S.D.N.Y. July 20, 2004).

Software Solutions for Electronic Records Management

ANSI/AIIM/ARMA TR48-2004: *Framework for Integration of Electronic Document Systems and Electronic Records Management Systems,* July 2004. Available from www.arma.org/bookstore.

Bell, Toby. "ERM and IDM Markets Converge in DoD 5015.2 Standard." *TechRepublic,* 31 July 2003.

Cain, Piers. "MoReq: The Standard of the Future?" *The Information Management Journal* 37, no. 2 (March / April 2003).

Doculabs. *The EMC Centera / Documentum Solution.* Chicago: Doculabs, 2004.

Gable, Julie. "The Role of Records Management in Electronic Document Management." In *Proceedings of the 41st Annual Conference, ARMA International, Denver, CO, October 13–16, 1996.* Prairie Village, KS: ARMA International, 1996.

_____. "Software for Managing Electronic Records: Comparative Analysis." In *Proceedings of the 44th Annual Conference, ARMA International, Cincinnati, OH, October 17–20, 1999.* Prairie Village, KS: ARMA International, 1999.

_____. "Everything You Wanted to Know About DoD 5015.2." *The Information Management Journal* 36, no. 6 (November / December 2002).

_____. "Innovations in Information Management Technologies." *The Information Management Journal* 38, no. 1 (January / February 2004).

International Organization for Standardization. ISO 15836:2003, *Dublin Core Metadata Element Set.* Geneva, Switzerland: ISO, 2003. Available from www.niso.org/standards (accessed February 11, 2006).

Kittmer, Sarah, and Alan Pelz-Sharpe. "The Electronic Records Management Challenge." *KMWorld*, October 2004.

Lamont, Judith, Lynette Downing, Richard Medina, and Cheryl McKinnon. "Discussion Roundtable: Records Management." *KMWorld*, April 2004.

Medina, Richard, and Joe Fenner. "Controlling Your Documents." *The Information Management Journal* 39, no. 1 (January / February 2005).

MoReq Specification – *Model Requirements for the Management of Electronic Records.* 2001. Available from www.inform-consult.com/services_moreq.asp; www.cornwell.co.uk/moreq (accessed February 11, 2006).

Open Document Management API. Version 2.0, September 19, 1997. Available at www.infonuovo.com/odma/downloads/odma20.htm (accessed February 11, 2006).

Phillips, John. "Comparing Leading RIM and e-RIM Software." In *Proceedings of the 48th Annual Conference, ARMA International, Boston, MA, October 19–22, 2003.* Lenexa, KS: ARMA International, 2003.

Sprehe, Timothy. "A Framework for EDMS / ERMS Integration." *The Information Management Journal* 39, no. 6 (November / December 2005).

Strong, Karen V. "Integrating EDMS Functions and RM Principles." *Information Management Journal* 33, no. 7 (July 1999).

U.S. Department of Defense. DoD 5015.2-STD: *Design Criteria for Electronic Records Management Software Applications.* Washington, DC: Assistant Secretary of Defense for Command, Control, Communications, and Intelligence, 2002. Available at http://jitc.fhu.disa.mil/recmgt/ (accessed February 11, 2006).

Index

A

access, 179; access time, 10, 148, 149
accessibility, 10
accuracy ratio, 148
active stage (reference), 60
activity ratio, 148
administrative staff function, RIM, 21
admissibility, 86; admissibility into evidence, 86
adverse inference, 110
AIIM International, 215, 203, 230
alphanumeric coding schemes, 156
Andersen case: the last word, the, 119
ANSI standard for media storage, 245
application(s), 30, 43, 64; analysis, 170
application programming interface (API), 203, 207
archival: data, 235, 237; function, RIM, 22; preservation, 242
archives, 126
ARMA International, 29, 185, 203
Arthur Andersen, LLP, 7, 39, 95, 115
ASCII, 241
assimilating imaging: strategic recommendations, 223
attachments, 125, 129
attributes, 9
audit / policy compliance function, RIM, 22
audit records, retention of, 107
audits, retention, 79
Australian National Standard for Records Management (AS 4390), 9
authenticity, 99, 196, 243
automatic categorization, 157; software solutions for, 157

B

backup(s): data, 168; data, retention of, 174; Delta, 165; differential, 165; full, 164; incremental, 165; media, 128, 174; methodology, twelve-tape, 166; online, 168, 169; open-file, 168; tapes, 166
bad faith, 107
Basel II, 99
business impact analysis, 170
business recordkeeping and the law, 83

C

California privacy laws, 184
Canada's new privacy law, 184
Carlucci vs. Piper Aircraft, 114
category selection, 153
classification, 28, 134, 151, 201, 225; schemes, hierarchical content, 154; taxonomy, 235
Cohasset electronic records management study, 2, 3, 54
compact disks (CDs), 173, 238
compliance, with EU's privacy rules, 183; documentation, 78; testing, 209
confidential records, 192
content, 243; content-based searches, 235; content-centric, 216
context, 243
contrasting capabilities, paper vs. electronic records, 9
cookies, 181
cost-avoidance, 58
cost-benefit considerations, 57

D

data, 5; archiving, 164; backup(s), 164, 168; life cycle, electronic records retention, managing the, 53; losses, routine, 163; message, 88; migration(s), 233, 238; alternatives to, 240; mining, 226; plan, 240; preservation practices, 238

data protection, 164; data protection methodologies, traditional, 164

data recovery speed, 167

data storage: *mis*management, 56; key trends in, 55

data warehousing and data mining, 226

database archiving solutions, 207

declared records, eligible for ERMS management, 206

degree(s) of criticality, 164, 169, 170; assessments, 171

delete / destroy stage (reference), 60

Delta backup, 165

departmental retention schedules, 40

designing and implementing recordkeeping systems (DIRKS), National Archives of Australia, the, 13

desktop: backup, user requirements for, 172; environment, 171; records, 30; records protection, 171; retention, principles for, 63; RIM at the, 8; and records retention, 62

destruction, 33; effecting under retention rules, 202

differential backup, 165

digital, 8, 234; imaging, 222; preservation and ISO 15489, 236; preservation, 234, 243; preservation methodologies, 164; record, preserving the, 233; recordkeeping, 10, 17, 19; signatures, 90; signatures and electronic commerce, 86

digital vs. paper preservation, 237

digitized, 135

disaster: recovery plan(s), 163, 175; recovery planning, 174; protection information from, 161

discovery, 110; retention obligations in, 113; retention obligations prior to, 115

disk mirroring, 168

diskettes, 238

disposition, 11, 30, 206

document(s), 17, 27; abstracting, 224; classification schemes, 26; digitization, 220; imaging / digitization, 220; life cycle, 201; management software, 208

DoD 5015.2-STD, *Design Criteria for Electronic Records Management Software Applications*, 9, 207; mandatory functions, 210; standard's applicability, the, 208; standard's content, the, 209

E

ECM: and RIM, 216; technology components, 220

EDMS solutions, 199; EDMS solutions, retention functionality in, 201

eEurope, 14

effective governance structure, an, 73

EIP, building an, 228; features, 228

electronic commerce, (e-commerce), 13, 87; electronic commerce and digital signatures, 86

electronic document management system (EDMS), 195, 198, 199, 201-205

electronic imaging, 17

electronic media, 50

electronic messages, 127; messaging systems, 8

electronic recordkeeping systems, 101

electronic records (e-records), 5, 88, 105; explosive growth in, 55; explosive growth of, 5; electronic records, regulatory requirements pertaining to, 105

electronic RIM, software solutions for, 195

electronic records management, 2, 59

electronic records management software (ERMS), 64, 65, 195, 202, 203, 216

electronic records retention, 53, 65; current status of, 54; managing the data life cycle, 53

electronic records series, 25

electronic RIM, categories, of, 197; status of, 3; issues, 196

Electronic Signatures in Global and National Commerce Act, 91

e-mail, 125, 134; retention, 131; retention policy, 132; usage patterns, 128

emulation, 247; emulator, 247

Enron, 8, 95, 115

enterprise classification and taxonomy, 149

enterprise content management, 207

enterprise electronic RIM, 212

enterprise information portal(s) (EIPs), 227

enterprise taxonomy, the, 152

E-Sign Act, 91

Europe's MoReq Specification, 210

EU's data protection directive, 182

e-vaulting, 167; e-vaulting and online backup, 167

evidence spoliation, 112
executive sponsorship, sustained, committed, 18
extended-term storage, 245
extensible markup language (XML), 241

F

facilities management function, RIM, 23
Ferris Research, 8
field, 42
file, 65; format(s), 241, 242
filing, 10
fireproof vaults, 175
fire-resistive filing cabinets, 175
five recordkeeping environments, retention implementation in, 80
fixed-content, 207; fixed-content archival solutions, 207
fixity, 243
floppy disks, 173
fluctuations, 246
format, 20
Forrester report, 2, 3, 27, 196
full backup, 164
full-text retrieval, 224; searches, 131; software, 26
functional equivalence approach, 87
functional retention schedules, 40
future, strategic plan for the, 19; future, preservation solutions, 247

G–H

General Motors Corporation vs. Volkswagen Group, 187
good faith, 43, 71
governance structure, 20
Gramm-Leach-Bliley, 99
growing role of information in organizational success, the, 6
Health Insurance Portability and Accountability Act (HIPAA), 98
hypertext markup language (HTML), 241

I

imaging and applications, 221; benefits, 220; standard platform, a, 223
implementation issues, 211
inactive records, 12
inadequate funding, 4
inadequate management recognition, 4
incremental backup, 165
information, 1; access, privacy, and security, 179
information life cycle, 28, 149; managing the, records retention, 33
information life cycle management (ILM), 53, 58, 197
information protection, status of, 162
information security, 161, 186; legal aspects of, 188
information technology (IT), 2; function, RIM, 22; issues, 129; issues and Sarbanes-Oxley, 98; IT-managed system applications, 64; strategic partnership with, 27
instant messaging (IM), 5, 133
integrity, 96, 101, 196; usability, and reliability, 100
internal controls, 97; new mandate for the, 96
international RIM, 13
Internet, 6, 18, 180, 218, 227, 241
interoperability issues, IM, 134
intranet-based schedules, policies, and guidelines, 74
investment options, define, 23
ISO 15489-1:2001, *International Standard: Information and Documentation – Records Management – Part 1: General,* 9, 13; and digital preservation, 236; and records retention, 37; program development in compliance with, 29
ISO 9000 standards for quality records, 8
ISO global information security standard, 189; ISO 17799, 189

J–L

judicially imposed sanctions, 110
key legal principles, summary of, 119
key RIM actions, 190
key stakeholders, governance structure of, 20
keyword search, 224
knowledge management (KM), 2, 22, 217; detractors, 219; and RIM, 219
knowledge worker(s), 142, 215
law and records retention, the, 103
laws and regulations cited in schedules, 44
legacy data, 239
legal / regulatory function, RIM, 21
legal: evidence, 86; issues, 127; retention research responsibilities, 43; risks, IM, 134
legally proven, 84
legally valid retention periods, 48
Lewy vs. Remington Arms, 112
life cycle, 50, 235; management, 131; of information assets, managing the, 34; records, 1

life expectancy, 11, 233, 242, 245
limitation on assessment, 105
litigation holds, 118
litigation risks, increasing, 7
litigation and records, 111

M

magnetic media, 173, 236, 238; recovery of, 173
magnetic storage, 28
magnetic tape(s), 165, 173, 238, 242
magneto-optical disks, 238
management challenges, 126
managing: information content, 215; messages as records, 131; recorded information: the new challenges, 7; the message, 125
media, 20, 206; backup, 128; independent schedules (retention), 43; inspection(s), 246; optical, 238; recopying, 242; refreshing / rewinding, 246; removable, 242; media stability, 234; stability and technology obsolescence, 236; storage, 149, 164, 238; storage and maintenance, 245
media-centric, 216
media-neutral, 91
media-specific schedules (retention), 43
medium-term storage, 245
megabyte, 56
messaging technology solutions, 136
META Group, 55
metadata, 28, 200; requirements, 243
microfilm, 198, 237; microfilm / microfiche, 222
mission-critical records, 10, 28
Model Requirements for the Management of Electronic Records, 9, 210
multilevel protection, 169
multimedia schedules (retention), 42

N–O

National Fire Protection Association, 161
near-line: retention, 50; storage, 58
new recordkeeping technologies, 84
new regulatory compliance mandates, 7
new regulatory initiatives, 92
new standards, 8
new technologies, 5
noncompliance, penalties for, 79
nonrecords, 204
office of record, 42; designation, 42
off-line: retention, 50; storage, 125, 164, 242
offsite: protection, 175
online: backup, 168, 169; and e-vaulting, 167; retention, 50; storage, 28

open document management application programming interface (ODMA API), 203
open-file backups, 168
optical: disks, 242; media, 236, 238; storage, 28
organizational placement, optimum, 21
organizational retention programs, status of, 34
outsourcing, 25; outsourcing options, 26

P–Q

paper, 198; paper records, 222
paper preservation vs. digital, 237
Penn, Shoen & Berland study, 2, 3, 4
permanent records, 73
petabytes, 235
platform, 39
poor accessibility: causes and consequences, 141
portable document format (PDF), 241
positive trends, 5
precise retrieval, 146
preservation solutions, future, 247
privacy, 179; and the Internet, 180; in the United States, 182; requirements, guidelines for RIM compliance, 186; laws in California, 184; international aspects of, 181
professional discipline in transition, a, 12
protection priorities, 169
Prudential Insurance Co. of America, 114
purge days, 63, 72; strategies, 127
query analysis, 148

R

Rambus vs. Infineon Technologies, 113
rapidly growing problem, a, 235
reasonable retention goals, 71
record(s), 12; authenticity of, 99; declaration, 206; inventory, 40; life cycle, 1
recordable DVDs, 173
recorded information, 2, 219, 239, 246
recordkeeping, 1; media, 85; system performance, improving, 141; systems, 10, 20, 29; technologies, new, 84
records and information management (RIM), defined, 1
records management, 207
records manager(s), 2, 17, 79, 206, 248
records purge days, 74
records retention and ISO 15489, 37
records retention, 3, 26, 106; benefits of, 34; the business case for, 36; common mistakes in, 37; and desktop, the, 62; government's role in, the, 103; and the law, 103; and litigation, 108; managing the information life cycle, 33; program, 33;

records retention schedule, 33; sample, showing U.S. federal, state, and international citations, 47
records series, 35, 40; descriptions, 41
records storage media, 12
recovery, 167; point objective, 171; procedures, 173; time objective, 170
reference: activity, 60; analysis, 148; archival stage, 60; stage, 60; time, 148
regulatory compliance, 18
regulatory initiatives, new, 92
reliability, 101, 243; integrity and usability, 100
removable media, 242
repository, 61
required skill sets, 24
requisite funding and staffing, 23
requisite technology solutions, deployment of, 28
retention, 11; audits, 79; compliance audits, 79; e-mail, 131; functionality, 65; goals, reasonable, 71; implementation in five record-keeping environments, 80; implementation, auditing, and compliance, 71; implementation, individual responsibilities for, 74; laws and regulations, compliance with, 104; near-line, 50; off-line, 50; online, 50; training, 72
retention-capable, 24, 30
retention period(s), 35, 174, 202, 206; average distribution of, 49; expression and justification of, 50; legally valid, 48; where litigation is likely, 111
retention policy(ies), 18, 201; e-mail, 132
retention program, 78
retention requirements, relevant citations for, 43
retention rules, effecting destruction under, 202
retention schedule(s), 18, 30, 38, 131; content, type, and format of, 39; departmental, 40; development, 38; functional, 40; management approval of, 50; multimedia (retention), 42; records media specified in, 42
retrieval, 1; precise, 146; timely, 147
return-on-investment, 171
RIM: and ECM, 216; desired state of, 12; and e-mail, 8; implications, 185; international, 13; and KM, 219; legally discretionary, 84; proactive agenda for, 29; role, 164; status of, 2
RIM software, 17, 28, 191, 197, 198, 208; retention functionality in, 199
risk avoidance, 36

S

Saffady benchmarking study, 2-4, 17, 21, 38, 41, 42, 44, 54, 72, 77
Sarbanes-Oxley Act, 84, 95, 105, 107, 196; and IT issues, 98; removes ambiguities in the law, 117
scanning, 220
schedule preparation: database for, 39; responsibility for, 38
search queries, 143, 229
security, 185; risks, IM, 134
September 11, 2001, lessons of, 174
seven-year myth, the, 105
single pathway, 199
software, RIM, 14, 17
solution(s): convergence, 202; integration, common metadata for, 205; integration, options for, 204; sample, 206
spam, 128, 130, 134
spoliation, 110
standard categories, 153
standard generalized markup language (SGML), 241
status and trends, introduction, 1
statutes of limitation, 106
Stevenson vs. Union Pacific, 112
storage, 125; area networks, 169; extended-term, 245; magnetic, 28; management, 55; media, 12, 149, 164, 238; medium-term, 245; near-line, 58; Storage Networking Industry Association, 58; off-line, 164, 242; online, 28; optical, 28
strategic plan, 19
structure, 243
structured data, 27
success keys to (retention), 72
successful programs, building, 17
support function to a major operational business unit, RIM, 22
system performance: evaluation, 145; levels of, 146; other measures of, 148; performance, qualitative analysis of, 148
systems documentation, 244
systems with no taxonomy, 150

T

taxonomy, 29, 150, 225, 229
technology obsolescence, 237; and media stability, 236
technology solutions, deployment of requisite, 28
terabyte, 56, 58
terrorism, 175
text files, 27

text retrieval, 223; content search, 223; software, 224
timely retrieval, 147
TR48 integration model, the, 203
traditional data protection methodologies, 164
turnaround ratio, 148
twelve-tape backup methodology, 166

U–Z

U.S. E-Sign Law, 91
U.S. federal retention requirements, summary of, 45; California, summary of, 46
U.S. Safe Harbor Agreement, 183
U.S. vs. Arthur Andersen, LLP, 115
U.S. vs. Taber, 113
UN Model Law on Electronic Commerce, 9, 87; Electronic Signatures, 9, 90
Uniform Electronic Transactions Act (UETA), 92

Uniform Trade Secrets Act, 189
United Nations Commission on International Trade Law (UNCITRAL), 9, 87, 90
United States, privacy in the, 182
unstructured content, 151
usability, 101; usability, reliability, and integrity, 100
Victorian Electronic Records Strategy (VERS), Australia, 13
viewing time, 148
virus, 172
vital paper records, 18; protection, 175; records, 10
voice messaging, 135
voice over Internet protocol (VOIP), 5, 135
workflow, 225; workflow automation tools, 225
World Wide Web, 265
Zubulake vs. UBS Warburg, 114

About The Author

David O. Stephens, CRM, FAI, CMC, is Director of the Records Management Consulting Division at Zasio Enterprises, Inc., a leading records management software and consulting firm based in Boise, Idaho. In this capacity, he directs records and information consulting studies and projects for clients in government and industry throughout the United States and in other countries.

Mr. Stephens is an internationally recognized author, speaker, and consultant. He is co-author of the Fourth Edition of *Information and Records Management*, Glencoe/McGraw-Hill, 1995. As a consultant since 1979, he has developed comprehensive records management programs for over 300 organizations in all types of businesses and at all levels of government.

Mr. Stephens served as President and CEO of ARMA International in 1989–1990, and he was inducted into the Company of Fellows of that organization in 1992. Mr. Stephens is a Certified Records Manager and a Certified Management Consultant. He earned a master's degree in public administration from North Carolina State University.

About ARMA International

ARMA International is the leading professional organization for persons in the expanding field of records and information management.

As of January 2010, ARMA International has about 11,000 members in the United States, Canada, and more than 20 other countries around the world. Within the United States, Canada, Japan, Jamaica, Trinidad and the European region, ARMA International has 122 local chapters that provide networking and leadership opportunities through monthly meetings and special seminars.

The mission of ARMA International is to educate, advocate, and provide resources that enable professionals to manage information as a critical element of organizational operations and governance.

The ARMA International headquarters office is located in Overland Park, Kansas, in the Kansas City metropolitan area. Office hours are 8:30 A.M. to 5:00 P.M., Central Time, Monday through Friday.

ARMA International
11880 College Blvd., Suite 450
Overland Park, Kansas 66210
+1 913.341.3808
Fax: +1 913.341.3742
headquarters@armaintl.org
www.arma.org